THE
LANAHAN
READINGS
IN
STATE & LOCAL
GOVERNMENT

Diversity · Innovation · Rejuvenation

Second Edition

THE LANAHAN READINGS IN STATE & LOCAL GOVERNMENT

Diversity · Innovation · Rejuvenation

Second Edition

edited by
John R. Baker
WITTENBERG UNIVERSITY

LANAHAN PUBLISHERS, INC.   *Baltimore*

The text of this book was composed in Bembo
with display type set in
Garamond and Bernhard Modern Roman.
Composition by Bytheway Publishing Services
Manufacturing by Victor Graphics, Inc.

ISBN-10:   1-930398-12-3
ISBN-13:   978-1-930398-12-2

LANAHAN PUBLISHERS, INC.
324 Hawthorne Road, Baltimore, MD 21210
1-866-345-1949 (toll free)
WWW.LANAHANPUBLISHERS.COM

1 2 3 4 5 6 7 8 9 0

CONTENTS

PREFACE

WITH THIS SECOND EDITION OF *The Lanahan Readings in State and Local Government,* I am excited to continue my collaboration with Don Fusting and LANAHAN PUBLISHERS, INC. The world has changed dramatically since the publication of the first edition, and state and local governments have become more central to our lives than ever before in recent times. Yet, the original thematic framework not only remains fresh as a conceptual lens through which to view state and local government, recent events have also served to strengthen the framework's efficacy and unifying characteristics. As noted in the original edition, there is a solid rationale for this reader, and it remains for this new edition, largely because so many professors have successfully incorporated it into their courses over the years. Several of the leading textbooks on state and local government are built around one or more of three predominant themes: first, the diversity of state and local governments, second, the innovation in government often originating at the state and local level, and third, the resurgence, or rejuvenation, of state and local governments in the American federal system. This second edition, just like the first, is designed to complement these basic textbooks by illustrating each of these (and other) themes throughout the collection. For example, the diversity in the way states attempt to regulate campaign finance is nicely captured by Craig B. Holman's article, "The Nuts and Bolts of Public Financing of State Candidate Campaigns." The article by Jim Chrisinger and Babak Armajani about Iowa's experiment with "charter agencies" and Don Hamilton's "The Oregon Voting Revolution" discussing the only state-wide vote-by-mail system in the country both illustrate innovations originating in the states. And rejuvenation is clearly prominent in "The Miracle of Jury Reform in New York," by James P. Levine and Steven Zeidman which discusses the efforts made in that state to combat the problems of shrinking jury pools. The focus on major themes has been a hallmark of this reader from the beginning, and this second edition continues that focus with new and updated material, thus allowing instructors and students to more easily dovetail their textual materials with these illustrative readings — thirty-three in all.

Several other important features from the first edition are continued in this edition to help students grasp and understand the institutional structure and political dynamics of state and local government. First, Part One serves as a primer on how we go about studying this field. It orients students by offering explanations of the themes outlined above, as well as by providing some historical context *via* an overview of the classic commentaries on state and local politics. All of this material has been updated in light of recent events and scholarship.

A second feature is the introduction to each of the parts of the reader all of which have been updated. Here I again try to give some historical and/or political context to the topics at hand and to the selections in each part. In addition, there is a list of questions for review and discussion at the end of each part's introduction. These are intended to help students focus on certain key points as they read the selections. The questions also provide excellent points of departure for classroom discussion.

Third, the reader integrates state and local government articles within each part rather than separating them. This helps foster a sense of the important interconnectedness of the states with their local subunits — a fact that reflects the actual relationship between state and local governments.

Finally, a fourth feature results from a goal of providing readings on various types of analyses of state and local politics and government. In this new edition, there is a good mix of analytical, historical, empirical, biographical, and journalistic pieces — and more than most of us would need to supplement the course. But, unlike other readers, this second edition continues to make use of a few more carefully selected empirical analyses of state and local politics. The reason for this is basic: the state and local government course is among the central courses in the political science curriculum. Hence, some of the readings should represent mainstream political science as we study and develop our field. So, I have included a few such articles. And, several of them allow professors and students to do some in-class modeling. To be helpful to students in this regard, this edition continues the inclusion, in Part One, of a section on how state and local government and politics are studied, including a brief methodological primer. Nothing is more satisfying to me as a professor than to have students working to understand a statistical table or graph, and then all of a sudden, see the light bulb go on as they realize that they no longer have to skip the tables when they read the articles. The purpose of this primer on method is to help them more critically evaluate and understand the findings of empirical research included in this reader. Having mastered this, students will be equipped to read and challenge the popular press.

Aside from significant updates, this edition differs from the first in two other ways. First, material on small town government and politics is no longer relegated to a separate part as structured in the first edition, rather, it is integrated more carefully into other parts of this edition. Second, the part on "Issues, Innovations, and Controversies in State and Local Policy-Making" has been omitted to make room for additional articles on other aspects of state and local government. The reason for this second change is that in the period since the publication of the first edition, an explosion in the availability of numerous sources of information about policies at the state and local level has occurred, primarily with the emergence of excellent websites on policies. This has made accessing information about state and local policies much easier compared to just a few years ago. So, rather than include a sample of different policies in a separate part of the reader, I decided to let professors and students choose for themselves what state and local policies they would like to explore. Certainly, it is my hope and belief that the framework of "diversity, innovation, and rejuvenation" presented in this reader will provide a solid baseline for understanding whatever additional research and reading students want to pursue. My experience with my own students has shown this to be true.

As always, I am grateful to Don Fusting at LANAHAN for continuing to believe in my ideas and encouraging me over the years. I have especially appreciated the consistent positive feedback from the many students in my state and local government classes over the years. I once again dedicate this reader to them.

John R. Baker

PART ONE

STATE AND LOCAL

GOVERNMENT AND POLITICS:

AN INTRODUCTION

It is a very exciting time to be studying state and local government and politics. In the years since the first edition of this text was published, dramatic events have occurred to underscore the essential role that state and local governments play in our federal system. The terrorist attacks on the World Trade Center in 2001, the devastation of our Gulf Coast by hurricanes Katrina and Rita in 2005, and the shootings at Virginia Tech University in 2007 horrifically combined to remind all of us how very critical the jobs of first responders, that is, local government employees, are to public safety. It has become cliché, yet accurate, to think about our collective governing perspective in terms of pre- and post-9/11 frames of reference. How to protect the public from terrorists, natural disasters, and other dangers such as pandemics is often debated most vividly at the national level, but the significant responsibilities state and local governments have in this regard punctuate their increasingly vital role in the new politics of homeland security.

Although less dangerous, but no less dramatic in terms of effects, events in the political arena in the last few years have served to highlight this book's themes. The presidential election of 2000 and its Supreme

Court-determined outcome accentuated (albeit in a negative fashion) the great diversity of election procedures and ballot methods utilized across the states. It also was a poignant lesson in judicial federalism as Florida's Supreme Court decision was overturned by the U.S. Supreme Court. The fallout from that election debacle culminated in the passage of the 2001 Help America Vote Act (HAVA) and a dizzying array of efforts by states and counties across the country to update their election machinery. Additional, though fewer problems during the 2004, 2006, and 2008 election cycles continued to produce concerns about the administration of elections, one of the most important functions state and local governments perform.

The closeness of the 2000 election also produced what has become one of the most often-articulated, but fundamentally inaccurate, descriptions of diversity across the states: the mythic Red State, Blue State division. As a shorthand way of understanding American state politics, this distinction has some limited utility, but the slight ideological cleavages that exist in the American electorate are not large enough to really give much empirical meaning to the implied chasm and culture war that exist between the so-called Red and Blue states when these terms are used. In their careful examination of survey data, Morris Fiorina, Samuel Adams, and Jeremy Pope have essentially shown that political elites and party candidates have become more polarized in recent years, but that the American electorate has not. Consequently, when presented with polarized candidates as options, voters pull the electoral levers for each party in roughly equal proportions making it seem like we have become more polarized, and that there is this huge Red/Blue divide across the states.[1]

As the war on terrorism ratcheted up with the invasions of Afghanistan and Iraq, federal funds for domestic programs were squeezed significantly. This fact, combined with continuing partisan gridlock in Washington, D.C. during the administration of George W. Bush resulted in an incredible flurry of policy innovation at the state and local government level. Laws dealing with illegal immigration, embryonic stem-cell research, minimum wage, same-sex marriage, and climate change, for example, have been enacted in numerous states and localities in recent years.[2] Indeed, it could be argued that the first several years of the 21st century have seen a trend in which some of the most pressing domestic issues have been addressed most successfully by subnational governments.

In sum, the initial years of the new century have brought about several significant changes and trends in the American federal system as a whole and in the various regions, states, and localities across the country. What is clear is that these changes continue to highlight the importance of three unifying themes—diversity, innovation, and rejuvenation—around which this book is organized. These changes have come on the heels of a dramatic couple of decades during which a major shifting of power between national and subnational governments occurred. Of particular significance in this regard was the trend, begun in the Reagan years (1981–1989), and continued under President Clinton (1993–2001), toward devolution, that is, the shifting of policy and power from the national government to state and local governments. The landmark 1996 federal welfare reform legislation which ended the federal cash entitlement program for impoverished citizens and replaced it with a program whereby states receive grants from the federal government to determine their own benefit and eligibility rules for welfare recipients still stands as a major symbol of the "newest federalism" with several governors acting as catalysts for change in this particular policy arena. While most scholars and observers would quickly point out the inherent contradictions in what has come to be called the "Devolution Revolution,"[3] most would also agree that states and the "creatures of states," that is, local governments, became more politically significant and powerful than ever before, except perhaps during the founding period. Buttressed by several key Supreme Court decisions which enhanced state and local authority such as *Gregory v. Ashcroft* (1991) which upheld Missouri's mandatory retirement law for judges, *U.S. v. Lopez* (1995) which greatly limited the federal Gun-Free School Zones Act, *Seminole Tribe of Florida v. Florida* (1996) which provided states greater immunity from suits by individuals in federal courts, and *Printz v. U.S.* (1997) which struck down Congress' attempt to force state and local law-enforcement personnel to conduct background checks on prospective handgun purchasers, a new balance of power in the federal system had emerged at the dawn of the 21st century. In short, the states experienced a resurgence, or rejuvenation, in the federal system.[4]

For the most part, the above-discussed trend has continued in more recent years, although some recalibration in the balance of power has occurred. For example, the passage of HAVA noted above, and the 2002 No Child Left Behind Act signaled greater federal roles in the standardization of elections and the politics of education. The federal government also imposed the standardization of state drivers' licenses with the passage of the REAL ID Act in 2005.[5] In addition, the Supreme Court more recently has pulled back somewhat from its state-centered decisions of the late 1990s, exemplified perhaps most clearly in a trio of cases which weakened state sovereign immunity.[6] Yet, in spite of these recent centralizing factors, some of which have been linked to the new terrorism threat, it can be argued that a significant consensus has emerged around a new paradigm characterized by a much more decentralized federal system. This paradigm places state and local governments in a more prominent position of political authority compared to other eras in American politics. Indicative of this increased prominence is the fact that in 2001 a new journal, *State Politics & Policy Quarterly,* dedicated specifically to the study of state politics and government, was founded by scholars in the field resulting in an explosion of new research and knowledge.

As we progress further into the new century, however, it is important to understand just how far state and local governments have come in recent decades. It was not too long ago that states were considered the weakest links in the federal system. Thus, in this part we will also take a look at some classic commentaries on state and local government. In doing so, the goal will be to compare broadly the past state of the states with the current situation as a way of understanding the newly-found strength of state and local governments. With such change taking place in the federal system, it is an exciting time for you to be studying state and local government and politics.

The articles in this book offer a wide look at the field. Some of them will take you more or less deeply into the ways by which political scientists approach this field. Some understanding of their methodology, therefore, will help. For that reason, the last part of this Introduction offers a methodological primer for reading and understanding certain articles that follow. But first, we begin with a description of the three themes of diversity, innovation, and rejuvenation.

The Diversity of State and Local Governments

One of the most enduring legacies of American constitutional democracy is the preservation of, and respect for, diversity among state and local governments. Cultural and ideological differences among the states have contributed to some of the most fascinating, as well as unfortunate, periods of American political history. The manifestations of this diversity can be seen today in the institutions and processes of state and local governments. Differences in the powers of governors, electoral systems, competition among the political parties, and the way in which judges are selected are a few examples. Moreover, what state and local governments do, that is, the policies they favor, adopt, implement, and enforce, also reflects diversity. Abortion, education, economic development, environmental protection, and correctional policies provide good illustrations of policy differences across the states.

Clearly there has been and still is diversity, but there are similarities among the states and localities as well. In fact, the states are not as diverse today as they have been historically. There has been a "nationalization" of the states[7] which has tended to diminish cultural and regional differences. An important key to understanding state and local politics, therefore, is the ability to identify the similarities, while at the same time noticing the diversities in the American federal system. One goal of this book is to help you do that.

The Innovation of State and Local Government

Another enduring legacy of American federalism is the incredible innovation originating from state and local governments. Referred to as "laboratories of democracy" by former Supreme Court Justice Louis Brandeis,[8] state and local governments have always been at the forefront of experimentation with new ways to address society's political, social, and economic challenges. In recent years, many innovative policies have been tried at the state and local level. Some were clear successes; some were not warmly embraced by an entire state or local constituency. Some remain quite controversial. Examples range from Oregon's Death With Dignity Act, which at the time made that state the only one where assisted suicide is legal, to Ohio's spearheading efforts to redevelop old industrial wasteland *via* innovative "brown site" legislation, to Massachusetts' 2006 law aimed at providing universal health insurance for its citizens. A brief synopsis of these three policies helps to highlight the inherent advantages, as well the risks, that states experience when they seek to push the envelope by undertaking new policy initiatives.

Regarding Oregon's legalization of assisted suicide, in the first year of the law's application (1998), the state reported that ". . . 15 terminally ill people in the state ended their lives with lethal medication."[9] In the wake of the 1997 ballot initiative decision by the Oregon voters to allow assisted suicide, the debate has sharpened over the legal and moral issues the law raises. Initially, the federal government threatened to prosecute doctors who participated in the program, but eventually backed off allowing the law to take effect. However, in 2001 then U.S. Attorney General John Ashcroft issued an Interpretive Ruling under the federal Controlled Substances Act that argued the lethal drugs used under Oregon's law were not for "legitimate medical purposes." This resulted in a lawsuit eventually decided by the Supreme Court in favor of the state of Oregon's continued use of the lethal drugs for assisted suicide.[10] Twenty other states have considered laws, either in the legislature or by initiative, legalizing the practice, with Michigan being the most recent state to reject it in the form of a ballot proposition.[11] But, in 2008, voters in the State of Washington approved a ballot provision legalizing physician-assisted suicide.

In 1994 the Ohio state legislature passed and Governor Voinovich signed Senate Bill 221 which created a program called the Voluntary Action Program whereby old contaminated industrial and manufacturing "brown sites" could be investigated and cleaned up without direct oversight from the Ohio Environmental Protection Agency (EPA), thereby reducing red tape and delay. By following set standards of cleanup, depending on the proposed re-use, private citizens can work with certified professionals, laboratories, and local governments to expedite the revitalization of these old brown sites. Since the program took effect in 1996, numerous old sites have been cleaned and new jobs have been created in urban areas that heretofore had been severely blighted and deteriorated. Several states have followed Ohio's lead.

Roughly 46 million Americans do not have health insurance,[12] and several million others are underinsured. Congress has basically not acted to address this problem, except for the passage of the Medicare Prescription Drug Act of 2003 which helps senior citizens with the costs of their prescription drugs. With no other action from Congress, several states have recently begun to innovate in this area, with Massachusetts going the farthest in 2006 by requiring all citizens to have health insurance or pay fines if they do not. Indigent citizens are subsidized, some citizens are exempted from coverage, and the state has the authority to negotiate low rates with private insurance companies. Still, though, with the exemptions written into the law roughly 20 percent of the state's uninsured adult population remains without coverage illustrating the serious challenges all states face in this area of health care policy.[13]

An often utilized method for innovative policy change at the state and local level is the direct democracy mechanism of the initiative petition. Oregon's assisted suicide statute, for example, was adopted via the initiative process. Through this procedure citizens vote directly on proposed laws in an election, as opposed to having the state or local legislature set policy. Currently, 24 states and the District of Columbia, plus hundreds of local governments allow the initiative process to be used by their citizens.[14] There are considerable arguments in favor of and against this process, but only state and local governments have this mechanism. There is no provision in the U.S. Constitution for a national referendum or initiative procedure. In short, another aspect of innovation in the states is the advent and adoption of three forms of direct democracy—initiative, referendum, and recall—which have provided an avenue for citizens to bypass traditional legislative processes. Many of the more innovative and provocative state and local policies have been adopted in this way, including the institution of state legislative term limits in over 20 states and the more recent controversial same-sex marriage bans in several states. Clearly, an important reason that states continue to play their role as "laboratories of democracy" is the existence of direct democracy mechanisms which provide additional decision-making options beyond a legislative body for setting policy.

At the local level, diversity and innovation are alive and well as substate jurisdictions wrestle with their particular concerns. A sampling would include the interesting effort by the city of Lancaster, California, to combat sprawl with its "distance surcharge" tagged onto services that have to be provided outside its urban core, the introduction of a city-run municipal valet parking system in downtown Decatur, Georgia, and the imposition of smoking bans in numerous cities across the country including one in Bangor, Maine, that bans smoking in automobiles that are carrying children.[15]

At both the state and local levels, technology has often played a key role in promoting policy diversity and innovation. For instance, the November, 1997, mayoral election in Houston, Texas, saw the creation of a candidate Web page used and shared by all the mayoral candidates as a way of making more information available to voters. These days, candidate websites are the primary sources of information for voters and contributors.

Another innovative policy is that many counties and cities provide interactive mapping software, known as GIS, on their websites for citizens to use to learn about property transfers and ownership, property tax assessments, and answers to numerous other geographic-based questions about their communities. Additionally, the process of paying state and local taxes via the internet, known as "e-filing," has become commonplace, and it was pioneered at the state level with the federal government following suit once it was shown to be successful around the country.

Since 1986, the Ford Foundation, in cooperation with Harvard University, has been sponsoring the Innovations in American Government Awards to recognize the most innovative public-sector policies and programs at the subnational level. Some of the recipients in recent years include Broward County, Florida's "Urban Academies Program" designed to recruit and retain aspiring teachers for poor and minority schools, Hampton, Virginia's "Youth Civic Engagement" initiative that provides young people a place and voice at the decision-making table for that community, and Iowa's "Charter Agencies" initiative which seeks to promote bureaucratic innovation and creativity in exchange for exemptions from many state rules and regulations.[16] A discussion of these charter agencies is contained in article 26.

Innovation is such an important function state and local governments perform that scholars and researchers have long been interested in the fact that some states tend to be more innovative than others, and have been leaders in certain policy areas. In a path-breaking article written forty years ago at the beginning of the era of state resurgence, Jack Walker asked two basic questions about this phenomenon of state innovation: First, what factors seem to contribute to a state becoming a leader in innovative policy making?; and second, how quickly do innovative policies spread across the states, and are there regional patterns to this process of "innovation diffusion"?[17] His findings indicated that more urbanized, resource-rich states, tended to be more innovative, that regional state leaders existed, and that the average time for diffusion to occur had dropped by more than half over the time-frame examined.[18] Since then, due to technological advances in communications, the diffusion of innovation among state and local governments has accelerated over the years, contributing to their historic role as "the outriders who test the limitations and restrictiveness of our accepted doctrines."[19] To understand this innovation is to understand more clearly the important role of state and local governments in American politics.

The Rejuvenation of State and Local Government

Some 35 years ago, political scientist Ira Sharkansky wrote of the incredibly poor reputation the states had developed among scholars and observers of American politics.[20] The states at that time were being described as the weak link in American federalism, and they were maligned by individuals at both ends of the political spectrum. Sharkansky noted that not since John Calhoun's nineteenth-century theories of nullification and secession had the states been defended as the strong links in American constitutional democracy. According to Calhoun, the states' governments were created by, and received their powers from, the sovereign people in each respective state. The states, relying on the sovereignty of their people, had entered into a compact to establish a national government. Given this, if a state did not wish to accede to an action taken by the national government, it could exercise its negative right of interposition and declare the action null and void. Further, Calhoun argued that if interposition was ineffective at curbing the national government's action, interposing states were guaranteed the right to secede from the Union.[21] In practice, of course, Calhoun's theory resulted in a devastating civil war.

Sharkansky went on to point out that prior to Calhoun's writings it had been nearly seventy years since the states were viewed as the bulwarks of democracy. At the founding, James Madison described the importance of the states in the following manner:

> [B]eyond doubt . . . the first and most natural attachment of the people will be to the governments of their respective states. Into the administration of these a greater number of individuals will expect to rise. From the gift of these a greater number of offices and emoluments will flow. By the superintending care of these, all the more domestic and personal interest of the people will be regulated and provided for. With the affairs of these, the people will be more familiarly and minutely conversant.[22]

At the time Sharkansky was writing, the popular sentiment among lay people and academicians was summed up best by Terry Sanford, a former governor and U.S. Senator from North Carolina, in his book *Storm Over the States*. He began this book in the following way:

> The states are indecisive.
> The states are antiquated.
> The states are timid and ineffective.
> The states are not willing to face their problems.
> The states are not interested in the cities.
> The states are not responsive.[23]

He went on to say that "[t]hese half-dozen charges are true about all of the states some of the time and some of the states all of the time."[24] Indeed, evidence from survey research suggested that the general public shared this antipathy toward the states. As reported by M. Kent Jennings and Harmon Zeigler, a national random sample of adults was asked how closely they followed different levels of government and politics. The states came in last behind national, local, and international affairs, respectively.[25]

Although Sharkansky and Sanford both attempted to defend the states from this negative view, it continued to be prominent throughout the 1970s. However, years later, as we plough into the 21st century, there is a new storm over the states; not a black-cloud thunderstorm like the one Sanford described, but a gathered storm of enthusiasm and optimism. As mentioned earlier, the last three decades saw tremendous changes in the American federal system. As the Reagan-led philosophy of New Federalism began to take effect in practice, and was essentially continued relatively unabated under the Clinton administration, the states responded with a resurgence of innovation and activity in a variety of policy areas. They had already responded with various reforms and structural changes in their governmental institutions and processes. Even though there has been a perceptible increase in federal control during the Bush years, the states are still now thought to have become more decisive, less antiquated, less timid, more willing to face their problems, more interested in the cities, and more responsive.[26]

What Carl E. Van Horn has called the "quiet revolution,"[27] however, did not take place overnight. Yet, in the last thirty-five years the states have made steady strides in making their three branches of government more effective and responsive. In policy areas such as education and environmental protection, the states are more innovative and flexible. And, despite some instances of fiscal stress, the states have been relatively successful in raising the revenue needed to pay for this renewed activism, but whether they can continue to do so is a perennial question. For example, the economic crisis that emerged in the late fall of 2008 placed extreme pressures on state and local government revenue systems. While some observers are careful to point out the ironies, complexities, and struggles that confront the states in this new era of resurgence,[28] the upshot is that state government capacity has been strengthened in the last three decades, allowing the states to respond better to the challenges they face.[29]

A similar, although quieter revolution has occurred at the local level as well. Counties, once called the "dark continent of American politics,"[30] have improved their governing capacity considerably, and although cities have had perhaps the most difficult time in responding to the problems facing them, they still have managed to be innovative in their efforts to deliver services. In short, both state and local governments are in a better position to respond to citizen's demands than they have ever been. Understanding this is crucial to understanding the American federal system today.

Classic Commentaries on State and Local Government

What kind of background do we have for studying contemporary politics and government of the states and localities? Let's consider briefly some of the past views and characteristics of the subnational governments. This will put their recent rejuvenation into perspective. We begin with a consideration of the founders' view of the role of the states in the new Republic, specifically James Madison's ideas. He was one of the writers, along with Alexander Hamilton and John Jay, of *The Federalist,* a series of newspaper editorials published between 1787 and 1789 in support of the new constitution. This period between the Constitutional Convention and the Constitution's ratification was a tense time for the emerging republic. The opponents to the ratification—the anti-federalists as they came to be called—objected to what they saw in the new document as unwarranted intrusion into state authority and the establishment of an uncontrollable superior level of government. Madison, in *The Federalist,* No. 46, sought to remind his adversaries that they had forgotten that the ultimate authority rested with the people, not with any one level of government in the proposed federal system. He went on to respond to those who argued that the state and national governments would be rivals in the new system, by arguing that instead of being rivals, the state and national governments would be largely independent of each other, with their own spheres of jurisdiction. He pointed out that people will be more naturally attached to their state governments, and that the policies and legislation considered by the new national Congress would be informed and considered in light of state and local interests in many cases. Moreover, Madison suggested that if the national government attempted to supersede state power in a patently offensive manner, the states would almost assuredly resist. In his words:

> . . . ambitious encroachments of the federal government, on the authority of the State governments, would not excite the opposition of a single State, or of a few states only. They would be signals of general alarm. Every government would espouse the common cause. A correspondence would be opened. Plans of resistance would be concerted. One spirit would animate and conduct the whole. The same combinations, in short, would result from an apprehension of the federal, as was produced by the dread of a foreign, yoke; and unless the projected innovations should be voluntarily renounced, the same appeal to a trial of force would be made in the one case as was made in the other.[31]

In the closing summary to the editorial, Madison argued that the powers which were being placed in the federal government were the minimum necessary to carry out the purposes of the new Constitution, and that the alarms being sounded by the opponents to the new government were to "be ascribed to the chimerical fears of the authors of them."[32] In Part Two, as we consider the contemporary role of the states in American federalism, a burning question will be whether the early arguments of the anti-federalists were indeed chimerical, or prophetic.

One of the most enduring and astute analyses of American local government has been that of the young French scholar Alexis de Tocqueville who, along with his companion, Gustave de Beaumont, arrived in America in the spring of 1831 with the intention of examining American democracy firsthand. The result was his classic account of the American democratic tradition, *Democracy in America*. In one section of this massive work, Tocqueville focuses on the unique local government institution found in New England—the township. It is usually referred to as a New England town, to distinguish it from mid-western townships which have lost considerable authority over the years. Tocqueville was fascinated with the New England town's brand of democracy. It was, and still is, the closest we have come in America to the ideal of direct Athenian democracy. There, the main governing mechanism is the "town meeting" whereby everyone in the town is eligible to attend a meeting and vote on the pressing issues facing the community. This town meeting concept has been used in recent years by many politicians and media organizations to gauge public opinion on current issues. In its classic configuration, it is still being used today in several New England towns, such as Chelmsford, Massachusetts. In an analysis of the current government of Chelmsford, one citizen had this to say:

> Another interesting phenomenon of my town's government is the issue of debate. Any concept or public [issue] within the town is subject to opinion by anyone in the town during weekly town meetings. For example, if I wanted to put an addition onto my house, not only would I have to obtain a permit and permission from the town's board [of Selectmen], but I would have to get permission granted by fellow neighbors. To my knowledge, I don't know if this is the case in other small town communities, but I have been told that it is a rarity in local government.[33]

For Tocqueville, the idea of township government helped foster what he referred to as the spirit of democracy in America. In his discussion of state and local government, he emphasizes the importance of local government, in this case the township, by stating "[i]t is not without intention that I begin this subject [of state and local government] with the township. The village, or township is the only association which is so perfectly natural that, wherever a number of men are collected, it seems to constitute itself."[34] As you consider the articles about modern local governments in this book, you might want to keep Tocqueville's assessment in mind and ask if they have become more or less important in fostering the democratic spirit in America.

While they do have certain powers of their own, counties are essentially local administrative units of state government. They exist in forty-eight states,[35] and traditionally handle most governmental matters in rural areas, while urban counties typically render "city-like" services to unincorporated areas surrounding major cities. Although counties, particularly rural ones, have experienced a significant degree of professionalization in the last forty years, they are still often criticized as the most backward and unprofessional level of government in America, and are often the targets of reform. Writing at the turn of the century, H.S. Gilbertson referred to counties as "the Dark Continent of American politics"[36] because of their political backwardness. As a member of the Progressive reform movement dedicated to cleaning up corruption and stopping party boss rule at the local level in the early part of the 20th century, Gilbertson applauds the reformers' efforts aimed at county government. In his classic article, "The Discovery of the County Problem," he notes that the problems of the counties were not as visible to citizens until the problems of the cities were exposed, and he presents a litany of defects in the structure of county government including lack of leadership, and the existence of the long ballot for choosing officials. He goes on to extol the virtues of the reform proposals that were being adopted in the counties of Oregon, including the institution of a county administrative manager who was supposed to be trained in the skills of managing local governments.[37] Counties have improved their images and capacity greatly in the last hundred years, yet they still seem to languish in limbo as intermediate levels of government between the states and cities.

"The South may not be the nation's number one political problem, as some northerners assert, but politics is the South's number one problem."[38] So begins V.O.Key's famous exposition, *Southern Politics*. He was right. The unique historical circumstances surrounding southern politics have presented that region of the country with problems that have not been duplicated elsewhere. From the vestiges of slavery and Jim Crow, one-party domination, and civil rights, to the emerging problems of unrestricted Sun-belt growth, the politics of the South has always been a fascinating subject for political scientists to explore. In his book, Key presents in considerable detail, the nature of politics in the South, and reminds us of the roots of the problems still facing southerners as they grapple with the tenets of democracy in that region. In a significant effort to reevaluate the politics of the South, particularly with regard to civil rights, Frederick Wirt has detailed how and why many southerners believe "we ain't what we was."[39] With the rise of Atlanta as the corporate center for the worldwide cable news network CNN, and later, the focal point during the 1996 Olympics, the image of the South has certainly been modified. Yet, the issue of negative race relations continues to haunt its politics and culture epitomized by the gory incident in the summer of

1998 when a black man in Jasper, Texas was dragged to death behind a truck driven by white men who prosecutors argued were plotting to organize a white supremacist group.[40] More recently, the devastation left behind in 2005 by Hurricane Katrina in New Orleans' 9th Ward, a predominantly low-income, black neighborhood, brought scathing charges of racism against the city, and portrayed the painful effects of years of discrimination and neglect in that community.[41] In short, the unique historical aspects of the South compared to other regions clearly underscore the significance of the theme of diversity that is used throughout this text.

Studying State and Local Government and Politics

How do we "know" political reality? This question gets to the heart of how politics and government are studied. In short, by what method can we seek to understand state and local government and politics? In order to make good sense of the articles in this book, you will need to spend some time wrestling with this question. In this section, the aim is to explain the primary method used by scholars to study and understand state and local government. Some helpful suggestions will be made for how to read some of the articles, particularly those that include statistical information, to make comparisons and generate conclusions. To begin, it is useful to keep in mind the theme of diversity, and that we are trying to make sense of the governments and politics of fifty states and over 80,000 local governments. This is a difficult task, to be sure. However, as noted above, states and localities across the country share certain common characteristics, in spite of their diversity. In light of this, scholars and researchers who study state and local government tend to use the comparative method of inquiry which emphasizes "comparing political institutions and behaviors from state to state and community to community in order to identify and explain similarities or differences."[42] As noted scholar Thomas Dye argues, "comparative analysis helps us answer the question *why.*"[43]

In their study of state and local government, scholars essentially are seeking to be able to achieve three goals: 1) understanding, 2) analysis, and 3) critical evaluation. Understanding is considered the basic goal of political scientists, and essentially refers to the ability to describe what is observed about state and local government. Examples would be describing the roles of citizens in different states and locales, and describing the different political structures, institutions, and processes across the states. Analysis refers to the ability to utilize political science tools, concepts, theories, and data to explain what is observed. The heart of analysis is an effort to answer the "Why?" question. A first tool in this regard is the application of statistical techniques to data in order to produce generalizations about state and local government and politics. Some of the articles in this book involve the uses of this particular tool of analysis, and by way of advice, it is often best to remember not to skip the tables, charts, and graphs when reading these articles if you want to get a deeper understanding of their findings. Often, the more interesting information can be found in the tables, rather than in the author's narrative. In particular, you will want to be on the lookout in these articles for points at which the authors use what are called measures of central tendency, or statistics that help determine general patterns in data. A common example in this regard is the "average" or "mean" value. We use this term all the time in everyday conversation, but we need to understand its specific usage in political science research. When an average value is determined, it helps us say something in general about the phenomenon we are studying. It helps us determine patterns that lead to our ability to answer the *why* question.

Second, in addition to statistics that help us determine general patterns, it is also important to understand the degree to which individual cases—states and localities—deviate from the average case. Statistics that help us with this question are called measures of dispersion. A most common measure in this regard is the range. For example, researchers have determined that on average we tend to have competitive two-party systems in the states. However, the degree of inter-party competition varies within a range of One-party Democratic to One-party Republican.[44] Put another way, some states do not have much competition between the two parties, and it is helpful to know which ones if we are to understand state and local politics.

Measures of association are a third type of statistical indicator that political scientists use in an effort to analyze and evaluate state and local politics. These measures tell us how closely two or more factors, or variables, are correlated with each another. While correlation is not the same as causation, knowing, for example, that the presence of a strong civic culture is associated with good government performance in a state gives us greater insight into understanding variations we might observe in the performance of state governments. Political scientists often hypothesize that certain variables are correlated, and then test these hypotheses using statistical measures of association. An even more sophisticated, but widely used statistical method to examine the relationship between several variables at once, is regression. This technique allows researchers to see how different variables are related while controlling for the possible effects of other variables.

You will want to be on the lookout for these sorts of measures in some of the articles that follow as they will significantly improve your ability to "know" about state and local government and politics.

Finally, a higher order skill that is developed through the use of the comparative approach to state and local government is the ability to make critical evaluations of the strengths and weaknesses of different governmental structures, institutions, and processes. Through the melding of understanding (description) and analysis, you will enhance your capacity to make reasoned judgments about the differences and relative merits of the political systems across the states. An important goal of this book is to help you develop the ability to critically evaluate state and local government and politics.

Notes

1. Morris P. Fiorina, Samuel J. Abrams, and Jeremy C. Pope. *Culture War?: The Myth of a Polarized America,* 2nd Edition. (New York: Pearson/Longman Publishers, 2006).

2. John Dinan, "U.S. State Capitols Take on Policymaking," *Federations.* 5 (October/November, 2006): 27–29.

3. See Sanford F. Schramm and Carol S. Weissert, "The State of American Federalism, 1996–1997," *Publius: The Journal of Federalism* 27 (Spring, 1997): 1–32.

4. David M. Hedge. *Governance and the Changing American States.* (Boulder, Colorado: Westview Press, 1998), p. 5.

5. John Dinan and Dale Krane, "The State of American Federalism, 2005," *Publius: The Journal of Federalism.* 36 (Spring, 2006): 333–343.

6. For a discussion of these cases and their effects, see Ibid, pp. 356–358.

7. See Kathleen A. Kemp, "Nationalization of the American States," *American Politics Quarterly* 6 (April, 1978): 237–247.

8. Quoted in David Osborne, *Laboratories of Democracy.* (Cambridge, MA: Harvard Business School, 1988).

9. Sam Howe Verhovek, "Oregon Reporting 15 Deaths in Year Under Suicide Law," *The New York Times,* (February 18, 1999): A1.

10. *Gonzales v. Oregon* 126 S. Ct. 904 (2006).

11. Verhovek, p. A17.

12. Alan Greenblatt, "Gimme Coverage," *Governing.com,* June, 2007. *http://www. governingmagazine.com/articles/6insure.htm* (Retrieved July 24, 2007).

13. Ibid, p. 3.

14. Elisabeth R. Gerber, Arthur Lupia, Mathew D. McCubbins, and D. Roderick Kiewiet, *Stealing the Initiative: How State Government Responds to Direct Democracy,* (Upper Saddle River, NJ: Prentice Hall, 2001).

15. Pam Belluck, "Maine City Bans Smoking in Cars Carrying Children," *The New York Times,* (January 19, 2007): A14.

16. Ash Institute for Democratic Governance and Innovation, Harvard University John F. Kennedy School of Government, "Innovations in American Government Award." *http://www.innovationsaward.harvard.edu/Awards_Cycle.cfm.* (Retrieved September 5, 2007).

17. Jack L. Walker, "The Diffusion of Innovation Among the American States," *American Political Science Review* 63 (September, 1969): 880–899.

18. Ibid, pp. 886–898.

19. Quoted in Terry Sanford, *Storm Over the States,* (New York: McGraw-Hill Book Company, 1967), p. 4.

20. Ira Sharkansky, *The Maligned States,* (New York: McGraw-Hill Book Company, 1972).

21. Alan Pendleton Grimes, *American Political Thought,* (New York: Henry Holt and Company, 1955), p. 275.

22. Quoted in Sharkansky, p. 2.

23. Sanford, p. 1.

24. Ibid, p. 1.

25. M. Kent Jennings and Harmon Zeilger, "The Salience of American State Politics," *American Political Science Review.* 64 (June, 1970): 523–535.

26. See for example, Ann O'M. Bowman and Richard C. Kearney, *The Resurgence of the States,* (Englewood Cliffs, NJ: Prentice-Hall, 1986); John J. Harrigan, *Politics and Policy in States and Communities,* 6th ed., (New York: AddisonWesley Longman, Inc., 1998); David M. Hedge, *Governance and the Changing American States,* (Boulder, CO: Westview Press, 1998); and Carl E. Van Horn, Editor, *The State of the States,* 4th ed., (Washington, D.C.: Congressional Quarterly Press, 2006).

27. Van Horn, p. 2.

28. See for example, Hedge, pp. 6–11 and Van Horn, pp. 1–13.

29. See Ann O'M. Bowman and Richard C. Kearney, *State and Local Government,* 3rd ed., (Boston, MA: Houghton Mifflin Company, 1996).

30. H.S. Gilbertson, *The County: The "Dark Continent" of American Politics,* (New York: National Short Ballot Organization, 1917).

31. James Madison, "The Federalist No. 46," in Garry Wills, ed., *The Federalist Papers by Alexander Hamilton, James Madison and John Jay,* (New York: Bantam Books, 1982, pp. 237–243).

32. Madison, quoted in Wills, p. 243.

33. Jon Morris, "Early Governmental Backgrounds: A Look at Chelmsford, Massachusetts." Unpublished Paper, Wittenberg University, Springfield, Ohio, 1999.

34. Alexis de Tocqueville, "American Townships and the Spirit of Democracy," from *Democracy in America.* (New York: Alfred A. Knopf, Inc., 1973).

35. Only Connecticut and Rhode Island do not have counties.

36. Gilbertson, 1917.

37.   H.S. Gilbertson, "The Discovery of the County Problem," *American Review of Reviews.* (November, 1912).

38.   V.O. Key, *Southern Politics.* (New York: Alfred A. Knopf, 1949), p. 3.

39.   Frederick M. Wirt, *"We Ain't What We Was": Civil Rights in the New South.* (Durham, NC: Duke University Press, 1997).

40.   Rick Lyman, "Man Guilty of Murder in Texas Dragging Death," *The New York Times.* (February 24, 1999): A1.

41.   Russell McCulley, "Healing Katrina's Racial Wounds," *Time.com,* April 27, 2007. *http://www.time.com/time/nation/article/0,8599,1656660,00.html.* (Retrieved September 5, 2007).

42.   Quoted in Thomas R. Dye, *Politics in States and Communities, 10th* ed., (Englewood Cliffs, NJ: Prentice-Hall, Inc., 2000, p. 2).

43.   Ibid, p. 2, emphasis in original.

44.   See Frank Feigert, "Postwar Changes in State Party Competition," *Publius: The Journal of Federalism.* (Winter, 1985): 99–112.

PART TWO

STATE AND LOCAL
GOVERNMENTS IN THE
FEDERAL SYSTEM

Perhaps the most fundamental constitutional question concerns the relationship between the states and the federal government. Woodrow Wilson called it "the cardinal question of our constitutional system," and argued that it is never really resolved "by one generation, because it is a question of growth, and every new successive stage of our political and economic development gives it a new aspect, makes it a new question."[1] Those words certainly ring true if we examine the efforts by the Reagan, Bush, and Clinton administrations of the 1980s and 1990s to alter the structure of American federalism from that of previous decades, as well as the more recent developments of the first decade of the new century. In this Part we consider the theoretical underpinnings of American federalism, as well as the dramatic changes that have taken place in our federal system. In doing so, we will ask the "cardinal constitutional question."

In the Introduction, we considered part of the founders' theory of federalism in reference to James Madison's *Federalist,* No. 46. There, Madison attempted to convince the opponents to the new constitution that state and national governments would not be rivals under the new system. In a letter he wrote to Edmund Randolf just prior to the convention, he asked ". . . whether any middle ground can be taken, which will at once support a due supremacy of the national authority, and leave in force the local authorities so far as they can be subordinately useful."[2] The decision at the convention to propose a compromise between "federal" and "national" forms of government resulted in what Madison called a "compound republic."[3] However, his apparent defense of the new system in *The Federalist* has been debated by scholars and observers ever since. Some have viewed his arguments as merely providing a thin veneer of disguise over his true support for a radically centralized form of government. Others have praised his passionate voice in support of federalism. Our first article is an exploration of this timeless debate in which Francis Greene argues that "charges of disingenuousness" against Madison are off base. Madison, Greene contends, was simply ambivalent about the future relationship between the states and the federal government, and that he preferred to see the Constitution in operation before considering reform. His principal normative allegiance was to limited government, and as Greene points out, Madison attempted to remind the readers of *The Federalist* that this was an unprecedented Constitution without positive role models paving its way. Thus, only time and practice would tell us if changes were needed. These points have been referenced by those who argue Madison was barely covering his inherent desire to see a stronger federal government, but Greene notes that these arguments were aimed just as squarely at the Anti-federalists who wanted to see the federal government stripped of some of its proposed power. Madison simply preferred to wait and see.

Against this theoretical backdrop of *The Federalist*, it is important to note that the development of American federalism tends to support the views of the Anti-federalists who feared the national government would have a tendency to increase its power as the Constitution began to be put into practice. The nineteenth century and Civil War put an end to the notion that the states would be the primary arbiters of disputes over the distribution of governmental power, and most of the twentieth century witnessed a tremendous growth of federal power emanating largely from the doctrine of implied powers derived from the Constitution's elastic clause.[4] As pointed out in the Introduction, however, the recent resurgence of the states has resulted in the pendulum of power swinging away from the federal government. President Reagan's "New Federalism" characterized by an increased emphasis on the use of block grants and intergovernmental regulatory reform began a significant period of change in the federal system that reached a zenith in the 1990s. During that decade, all three branches of the federal government contributed to the evolution of a more state-centered, or as some would prefer to describe it, a more balanced federal system. Led by a narrow conservative majority, the Supreme Court rendered decisions that upheld the right of a state to determine the qualifications for office of its constitutional officers,[5] struck at the heart of Congress's power to regulate interstate commerce,[6] weakened the Justice Department's efforts to implement the federal Voting Rights Act,[7] protected states from being sued in federal court by citizens of other states,[8] and struck down federal requirements that state and local officials conduct background checks on prospective gun purchasers.[9] Justice Antonin Scalia, who wrote the majority opinion in the latter case, included phrasing in the opinion that harkened back to pre-Civil War theories about federalism when he argued that "the Constitution established a system of 'dual sovereignty.'"[10] These words seemed to echo the words of former Chief Justice Roger Taney in the case of *Abelman v. Booth* (1858) when he argued that "the powers of the General Government, and of the State, although both exist and are exercised within the same territorial limits, are yet separate and distinct sovereignties, acting separately and independently of each other, within their respective spheres."[11] While in the strictest sense Dual Federalism is not an accurate description of the modern relationship between the states and national government, it is clear that the states have become significantly more prominent in the system in the last 20 years.

In the midst of all this Supreme Court action, the other two branches also made decisions that devolved policy responsibility back to the states with the most dramatic example being the Welfare Reform Act of 1996 which replaced the old AFDC program with the new Temporary Assistance for Needy Families (TANF) program giving states greater flexibility to design their own welfare programs with the use of federal block grants. In another key decision, the Clinton administration issued new regulations making it easier for states to obtain federal approval to attempt innovative approaches to health care under the Medicaid Section 1115 waivers program.[12]

Another dramatic example of the new philosophy of state power was the passage of the Unfunded Mandates Reform Act (UMRA) of 1995, a plank of the 1994 Republican *Contract With America* designed to reduce the financial pressures on the states of various federal requirements and mandates. The issue of unfunded mandates had become increasingly controversial, and the UMRA was hailed as a major symbolic victory by many observers. As finally passed, it allows members of Congress, by raising a point of order on the floor, to stop a proposed mandate that has a net cost to states and localities of $50 million or more. A majority of members can override the point of order, but by allowing the possibility of debating the mandate, the chances increase that it might be rescinded, funded, or reduced in terms of its net costs.[13]

In more recent years, the pendulum of power in the federal system has swung back a bit toward the national government, particularly in the wake of the 9/11 terrorist attack and the incredible centralization of power under the rubric of homeland security. And as mentioned previously in the Introduction, federal laws in the area of education and election administration have brought about a greater federal role in these areas, while the Supreme Court has backed away somewhat from the more clearly state-centered decisions of the 1990s. Yet, the devolution of political power in the American federal system is still a dominant paradigm. Indeed, the early indications from the Obama administration are that states will play a broader role. In particular, the term "progressive federalism" has been coined to describe the role that innovative governors and attorneys general will be relied upon to play with regard to policy changes.[14]

Intergovernmental relations are not always contentious and competitive, and it should be noted that whenever possible cooperation between levels of government, between states, and between local governments is quite often the goal of political and administrative leaders. John Mountjoy's article examines the expanded use of interstate compacts. As can be seen cooperation is often the goal, but is fraught with its own challenges.

Finally, in an examination of two of the constitutional clauses that help circumscribe interstate relations—the Full Faith and Credit and the Interstate Compact clauses—Joseph Zimmerman provides examples of how these clauses are currently affecting American federalism. Subsumed in this discussion is a consideration of how the controversial issue of gay marriage is affected by these clauses.

Notes

1.   Woodrow Wilson, *Constitutional Government in the United States,* (New York: Columbia University Press, 1908), p. 173.
2.   Quoted in Martha Derthick, "American Federalism: Madison's Middle Ground in the 1980s," *Public Administration Review,* (January/February, 1987), p. 66.
3.   James Madison, "The Federalist, No. 39," in Garry Wills, *The Federalist Papers of Alexander Hamilton, James Madison, and John Jay,* (New York: Bantam Books, 1982), p. 193.
4.   Derthick, 1987, p. 67.
5.   *Gregory v. Ashcroft,* 11 S. Ct. 2395 (1991).
6.   *U.S. v. Lopez,* 63 USLW 4343 (1995).
7.   *Miller v. Johnson,* 63 USLW 4726 (1995).
8.   *Seminole Tribe of Florida v. Florida,* 116 S. Ct. 1114 (1996).
9.   *Printz v. U.S.* 117 S. Ct. 2365 (1997).
10.   117 S. Ct. 2365 (1997).
11.   62 U.S. 506 (1858).
12.   Saundra K. Schneider, "Medicaid Section 1115 Waivers: Shifting Health Care Reform to the States," *Publius: The Journal of Federalism,* 27 (Spring, 1997): 99.
13.   Paul L. Posner, "Unfunded Mandates Reform Act," *Publius: The Journal of Federalism,* 27 (Spring, 1997): 53.
14.   John Schwartz, "From New Administration, Signals of Broader Role for States," *The New York Times,* (Jan. 30, 2009): A13.

Questions for Review and Discussion

2.1   What three charges of disingenuousness does Francis Greene say have been leveled against Madison? Which side of this debate do you think has the more plausible case? Why?

2.2   How is intergovernmental cooperation fraught with pitfalls? Who benefits from it? How do the Full Faith and Credit and Interstate Compact clauses affect interstate relations?

1 Madison's View of Federalism in *The Federalist*

FRANCIS R. GREENE

OVER THE LAST GENERATION or so, scholars have debated James Madison's treatment of federalism in *The Federalist*. Some have read his essays as confirming the work's sobriquet as the "bible of American federalism"; others have read them in light of Thomas Jefferson's comment that "in some parts it is discoverable that the author means only to say what may be best said in defence of opinions in which he did not concur." According to this latter view, Madison's rhetoric was that of a radical centralizer seeking either to mask his antipathy to federal government or to downplay the degree to which the new government deviated from confederal principles.

This debate has remained fairly polarized, the two sides often talking past each other. There is reason to think, however, that neither side has gotten Madison's position exactly right. On the one hand, it is difficult to accept the contention that his "numbers of *The Federalist* did not defend a system that he privately regarded as severely flawed." Shortly after the Constitutional Convention, he expressed grave concerns about the states' residual autonomy, and there is little evidence to suggest that he changed his mind in the ensuing few months. On the other hand, equally implausible is a view of Madison as, in essence, Alexander Hamilton's alter ego.

Such a view has contributed to exaggerations of Madison's disingenuous-ness in *The Federalist.*

Although Madison was certainly capable of calculated silence and ambiguity, there are three instances in which Madison's rhetoric has been falsely alleged to obscure more deeply considered views: that, especially in Number 39, his talk of residual state sovereignty concealed a conviction that the Constitution was a plan for a unitary state; that, especially in Numbers 45 and 46, his concern about the states' centrifugal tendencies was gratuitous because he expected those "dangerous centrifugal tenden-cies to diminish in the future"; and that, in general, while writing all of his *Federalist* essays, he hoped the new government would succeed in obtaining even more power for the purpose of keeping the states in check.

While plausible — as well as possessing distinguished adherents — these claims are mistaken. Madison in fact saw the Constitution as a plan for a supreme but limited government. In addition, he was far less certain than Hamilton about how the new government would fare in practice. Various scenarios were possible, none of which can be said to have been "expected." Like his New York colleague, of course, he had deep theoretical reservations about the Constitution; unlike him, he appears to have been willing to reserve ultimate judgment about its merits until after it had actually been tested. Before then, no useful purpose was served by serious contemplation of constitutional reform.

Federalist 39

Although Madison refers to the states' sovereign powers in other essays, it is in Number 39 that he most systemically sets forth his view (as opposed to evaluation) of the new system's structure. The essay was designed to answer the Anti-Federalist criticism that the Constitution was a plan for consolidated government, an innovation that exceeded the bounds of the Convention's commission and threatened America's repub-lican institutions. The constellation of powers granted the federal govern-ment was on indication of the plan's consolidationist character; another was the Constitution's failure to pass what might be called the "identity" test: For whom or what is power exercised? Over whom or what?

> There are but two modes by which men are connected in society, the one which operates on individuals, this always has been, and ought still to be called, *national government*; the other which binds States and governments together . . . this last has heretofore been denominated a *league or confederacy*.[1]

Because various aspects of the Constitution largely applied to individuals rather than states, it was regarded as a consolidation.

In response, Madison examined five different aspects of the proposed government, concluding that it was neither exclusively federal nor exclusively national but "a composition of both." Insofar as it "operated" on individuals rather than on states, it was more or less exclusively national. Otherwise, it was, as in the ratification process, either wholly federal or— as in the electoral and amendment processes, respectively, neither "wholly *national* nor wholly *federal.*" Ratification was federal because, though the Constitution would receive popular rather than legislative ratification, it was *state* citizenries rather than one single national citizenry which would decide. By the same reasoning, elections were of a mixed character because individuals and states were both represented in the Congress and involved in the selection of the president. Because amending the Constitution was by states, it was federal, but because unanimity was not required, "it loses again the *federal,* and partakes of the *national* character."

Madison's discussion of the extent of federal power has elicited the most controversy. Consolidations, he argued, concentrate in a single national legislature an "indefinite supremacy over all persons and things, so far as they are objects of lawful government," a supremacy giving complete superiority over "all local authorities," which "may be controlled, directed, or abolished by it at pleasure." In "communities united for particular purposes," in contrast, supremacy is "vested partly in the general and partly in the municipal legislatures." These "local or municipal authorities form distinct and independent portions of the supremacy, no more subject, within their respective spheres, to the general authority, than the general authority is subject to them, within its own sphere." Because its authority "extends to certain enumerated objects only, and leaves to the several States a residuary and inviolable sovereignty over all other objects," the new government was federal.

One of the few passages in Number 39 that John C. Calhoun did not find "contradictious," the analysis has elicited the opposite reaction from Garry Wills. This and other references to state sovereignty, he has argued, were mainly designed to assuage Anti-Federalist fears. Although the states were "potential" sovereigns—a status they would re-assume if ever required to ratify another constitution in the future—they were no more than this. The Constitution was a plan for unitary government, the creation of a sovereign people delegating its necessarily indivisible authority to the federal government exclusively.

Wills points to the U.S. Supreme Court, which has the last word in the state-federal conflicts, as well as to all the passages where Madison (and Hamilton) indicates that sovereignty is and ought to be indivisible. the "greatest proof," however, is Madison's effort to get the Constitutional Convention to accept a federal veto on state legislation. Although thwarted, these efforts conclusively show that he had no intention of creating anything but a unitary state. "In the Convention, as well as in his pre-Convention writings, Madison persistently located the weakness of the Confederation in the sovereignty of the states. he can hardly have written *The Federalist* to maintain that condition."[2]

That Madison sought the veto, however, does not prove that he regarded the Constitution as unitary; after all, just because he wanted a unitary system does not mean he got one. If he did believe he had obtained a unitary system, why after the Convention does he say that the "system involves the evil of *imperia in imperio*"? Wills is curiously silent, moreover, about the passage in which Madison appears to endorse the Federalists' famous innovation in sovereignty theory, the passage where, in the words of Jack Greene, it is claimed that "the basic powers of sovereignty could be divided without dividing sovereignty itself." Said Madison:

> The Foederal and State Governments are in fact but different agents and trustees of the people, instituted with different powers, and designated for different purposes. . . . [U]ltimate authority, wherever the derivative may be found, resides in the people alone.

Wills assumes that for Madison to have conceded some autonomy to the states, he would have had to violate traditional sovereignty theory. But by conceiving the sovereign people as capable of delegating its powers to two different sets of subordinate governments, no such violation occurs.

Number 39's Disclaimers

Wills' case is also weakened by the disclaimers dotting Number 39 which, when properly understood, support the conclusion that Madison regarded the Constitution as establishing a supreme but limited federal government. The analysis in Number 39 was designed to answer the specific charge that, in Madison's paraphrase, instead of preserving "the *federal* form, which regards the union as a *confederacy* of sovereign States," the Constitutional Convention had "framed a *national* government, which regards the union as a *consolidation* of the States." At the outset, however, Madison states his intention to ascertain the "real character" of the Constitution without "enquiring into the accuracy of the distinction [between national and federal] on which the objection [to the Constitution] is founded." He implies, thus, that the analysis in Number 39 was an exercise. For the sake of argument, he was using definitions favored by the Anti-Federalists to analyze the Constitution, but those definitions were not ones that he actually subscribed to—or at least not fully. While hinting five different times at objections, however, he never spelled out what they were.

Martin Diamond is the only scholar to have ventured a guess as to the disclaimers' significance. His answer was that they were echoes of Hamilton's rhetorical challenges to the Anti-Federalists' definitions in Number 9:

> By not plainly accepting his opponents' understanding of the terms federal and national, Madison is able to retain for *The Federalist* any rhetorical advantage gained by Hamilton in Number 9. . . . [But] by the end of the paper, and in other papers, Madison drops even the demurrer, and in effect accepts that, strictly speaking, federalism is what his opponents understand it to be.[3]

Although plausible, this is clearly not the whole story. For one thing, while the demurrers do stop halfway through the newspaper version, this was probably due to the haste in which the essay was originally written. In the first edition of the collected papers, two more were added, including one to the essay's concluding sentence: "The proposed Constitution therefore *even when tested by the rules laid down by its antagonists* is in strictness neither a national constitution; but a composition of both" (emphasis added). Moreover, plausible bases for the disclaimers can in fact be found, suggesting that they were not meant merely to echo Hamilton's rhetoric in Number 9.

The Government's Foundation

Disclaimers are found at both the beginning and the end of Number 39. They also accompany two specific discussions: the government's "foundation" and "operation," respectively. A closer look suggests that they point to what Madison was later to refer to as the Constitution's two "characteristic peculiarities": the ratification procedure establishing the Constitution's supremacy over the state constitutions and the distribution of powers leaving the states exclusive jurisdiction in some legislative areas.

Madison's discussion of the ratification process may have been inspired by Anti-Federalist Luther Martin, who testified before the Maryland legislature that the Constitution was

in its very *introduction* declared to be a compact between the *people* of
the United States as *individuals,* and it is to be *ratified* by the *people* at
large in their capacity *as individuals;* all which . . . would be quite right
and proper, if there were *no State governments,* if *all the people* of this
continent were in a *state of nature,* and we were forming one *national*
government *for them as individuals.*[4]

Madison's response was that the people were not ratifying the Constitution
"at large," as "individuals composing one entire nation," but rather as
individuals "composing the distinct and independent States to which
they respectively belong." In ratifying the Constitution, each state was
"considered as a sovereign body, independent of all others, and only to
be bound by its own voluntary act"; ratification, therefore, was "a federal
and not a national act, *as these terms are understood by the objectors*" (emphasis
added).

How else could they be understood? The answer is found most
clearly articulated at the Constitutional Convention where "the true
difference between a *league* or *treaty,* and a *Constitution*" is said to depend
on whether ratification is by state citizenries or by state legislatures, not
state citizenries or a single national citizenry (as in Number 39). The
Convention's work, Madison argued, ought to be ratified by the people
because, in so doing, they would be endowing it with the status of what
elsewhere he calls a "political Constitution." Although differing little "in
point of *moral obligation,* a treaty and a constitution differed "in point of
political operation" in two respects. First, while a law in violation of a treaty
might still be regarded as law, albeit "unwise or perfidious" law, a law
in violation of a constitution "would be considered by the Judges as null
and void." Second, while a treaty violation "frees the other parties from
their engagements," in and of themselves, unconstitutional acts do not.

In Number 43, Madison reiterates that "mere" legislative ratification
"can pretend to no higher validity than a league or treaty between the
parties." He then alludes to a passage in Number 22 where, distinguishing
between legislative and popular ratification, Hamilton argues that the latter
establishes a foundation "deeper than in the mere sanction of delegated
authority." Here then is an alternative logic to that found in Number
39. Do they conflict? George Carey, for one, thinks not. While initially
describing Number 39's analysis as "misleading," hypothesizing that Madison was seeking to portray the Constitution as less national than he actually
believed it to be, he ultimately declares the conflict to be more apparent
than real. In Number 39, "Publius—somewhat obliquely, to be sure—
does not hold to the position he has outlined in Federalist 22" because

in both passages the Constitution is said to rest upon the authority of the people. But why is popular ratification said to be federal in one paper and—in so many words—national in another?

This apparent conflict is resolved once Madison's disclaimer is taken into account. In Anti-Federalist analysis, the choice presented was either ratification by the people at large or by a process that involved the states (i.e., by the state legislatures). Not encompassed, as Madison pointed out, was a third possibility: ratification by the people of each state. He calls this a federal act because it appeared to be the only choice available to him, given how the "terms are understood by the objectors." Understood differently—and in his view correctly—as they are in Numbers 22 and 43, ratification by the people of each state was a national act.

Years later, with reasoning essentially identical to that of the Convention and *Federalist* 22 and 43, Madison singled out the ratification process as one of the Constitution's two "characteristic peculiarities":

> Being thus derived from the same source as the Constitution of the States, it has within each State the same authority as the Constitution of the State; and is as much a Constitution, in the strict sense of the term, within its prescribed sphere, as the Constitutions of the States are within their respective spheres; but with this obvious and essential difference, that, being among the States in their highest sovereign capacity, and constituting . . . one people for certain purposes, it cannot be altered or annulled at the will of the States individually, as the Constitution of a state may be at its individual will.[5]

Ratification by state citizenries gave the Constitution its "political" status; it was not a treaty and, for this reason, it was "within its prescribed sphere" superior to state laws and constitutions as well as unchangeable by any individual state alone."Within its prescribed sphere," however, implies a sphere of authority outside federal jurisdiction. It is precisely this sphere to which Madison refers in Number 39 and which Wills denies should be taken seriously at this stage of Madison's career. However, the disclaimers accompanying the discussion of the government's "operation" suggest otherwise.

The Government's Operation and Extent

According to Hamilton in Number 9, the Anti-Federalists considered the "essential characteristic" of confederacy to be "the restriction of its authority to the members in their collective capacities, without reaching to the individuals of whom they are composed." In recognition of its importance perhaps, Madison hints not once but twice of unstated objections when discussing the Constitution's "operation." Thus, he begins by declaring that the difference between a federal and a national government.

> is supposed by the adversaries of the plan of the convention to consist in this, that in the former, the powers operate on the political bodies composing the confederacy, in their political capacities: In the latter, on the individual citizens, composing the nation, in their individual capacities.

He ends by concluding that, excepting "trials of controversies to which the States may be parties," the "operation of the Government on the people in their individual capacities, in its ordinary and most essential proceedings, will *in the sense of its opponents* on the whole designate it in this relation a *national* Government" (first emphasis added).

Again, what other sense was there? Here, the answer is found in the discussion immediately following where it is argued that federal jurisdiction over individuals did not necessarily imply that the government's powers were unlimited. Implied, moreover, is the belief that consideration of any constitution solely by reference to its operation will always be misleading; while attention to its operation might rule out the possibility that a constitution had a confederal form, without attention to the extent of its powers, no definite conclusion could be drawn about whether it was a consolidation. Like the plan under consideration, it might be a limited constitution, a plan for what Madison later refers to as a "compound" rather than a "simple" republic. By adding disclaimers to his discussion of the government's operation, therefore, he drew attention to what he regarded as an illegitimate Anti-Federalist inference: that—to clarify part of his original paraphrase of the Anti-Federalists' objection— a "*national* government [in operation, necessarily] . . . regards the union as a consolidation [in extent] of the States."

By distinguishing between the operation of government and its extent, Madison drew attention to the ambiguity of the concept of "national government." It would not be the last time he would do this; writing years later about the Constitutional Convention, he made essentially the same point:

> Will you pardon me for pointing out an error of fact into which you have fallen, as others have done, by supposing that the term *national* applied to the contemplated Government, in the early stage of the Convention . . . was equivalent to *unlimited* or consolidated. The term

was used, not in contradistinction to a limited, but to a *federal* Government.[6]

[T]he term "National" . . . was not meant to express the *extent* of power, but the *mode* of *its operation*, which was to be not like the power of the old Confederation operating on *States*; but like that of ordinary Governments operating on individuals.[7]

Then, as in Number 39, he attempted to make clear that at the core of the Constitution was what he later described as its second distinctive peculiarity, the "division of the supreme powers of Government between the States in their united capacity and the States in their individual capacities."[8]

Madison's Outlook on the Future

Madison's disclaimers, therefore, more than merely echo Hamilton's rhetoric in Number 9. They point, on the contrary, to a conviction that the Constitution established a supreme but limited federal government. But did Madison hope the government would remain limited? Did he expect it to? Some scholars have argued in the negative on both counts. Diamond, for example, contended that despite rhetoric aimed at convincing the Anti-Federalists that the states had little to fear in the contest between the state and federal governments, "the careful reader will find such 'strings' attached to the mollifying assurances as make clear that *The Federalist* has actually a different expectation or hope regarding the contest."[9] Beyond what had already been included in the Constitution, in fact, "a very substantial increase in the scope and power of the central government would be regarded by *The Federalist* as proper."[10]

If Hamilton had written the work alone, these contentions would be unquestionable. Shortly after the Convention, he was already expressing both hope and cautious confidence that the federal government might secure greater power for itself. It all depended on how the new government were administered: if badly, state-federal disputes would ultimately cause "a dissolution of the Union"; if well—a strong possibility with George Washington as president—then the "confidence and affection of the people" would be "conciliated," and the federal government would be able

to acquire more consistency than the proposed constitution seems to promise for so great a Country. It may then triumph altogether over the state governments and reduce them to an intire [sic] subordination, dividing the larger states into smaller districts. The *organs* of the general government may also acquire additional strength.[11]

In *The Federalist*, Hamilton repeated the substance of this argument in Numbers 17 and 27. While it was a natural for people to feel greatest attachment to the government nearest them, superior federal administration would win over that attachment, presumably securing thereby—this is left unstated—support for the states' "intire subordination."

Hamilton, however, was not the sole author of *The Federalist*, and Madison's view was not identical to that of his New York colleague. There is little question that Madison shared Hamilton's ultimate hope that state encroachments on other states, on the federal government, and, perhaps most especially, on minorities, which had been endemic to the Articles of Confederation, would cease under the new Constitution. It is difficult to find, however, in either *The Federalist* or any other public or private source, Madison giving explicit support for an actual increase in federal power beyond what the Constitution had already granted. His alleged support for such an increase is, in fact, only an inference: that as a leading nationalist at the Convention, and a disappointed nationalist afterwards, he must have covertly hoped for an increase in federal power when writing his *Federalist* essays. Although plausible, the inference is nonetheless questionable.

To begin with, it must be recognized that Madison does not appear to have left the Convention dissatisfied with how the Constitution divided positive power. As is well known, his chief regret was the unwillingness of the Convention to give the new government an all-purpose power to veto state legislation. But no constellation of positive powers could check state encroachments as effectively as such a veto. Piecemeal checks—the Constitution's provisions against "paper [money] emissions, and violations of contracts," for example—were unlikely to be effective, because "injustice may be effected by such an infinitude of legislative expedients, that where the disposition exists, it can only be controuled by some provision which reaches all cases whatsoever." Even a grant of plenary power was no substitute for the veto. For, as he said repeatedly before the Convention, "however ample the federal powers may be made . . . , on paper, they will be easily and continually baffled by the Legislative sovereignties of the States." To the extent, therefore, that he may have been thinking about amending the Constitution while writing his *Federalist* essays, it would have been the veto about which he was thinking.

In light of his failure to get the federal veto, however, it seems unlikely that Madison would have regarded its future procurement as a very realistic possibility. It is probably for this reason that no mention of such a possibility is found in his private writings of the time. The available evidence does suggest that while Hamilton was dreaming of radical reform, Madison was (albeit partly—but only partly—out of necessity) rather consciously reserving final judgment on the Constitution's practical merits.

Writing from New York in late October 1787, Madison noted that "[n]othing is more common here . . . than to see companies of intelligent people" sharply disagreeing over the Constitution's merits:

> What is the proper conclusion from all this? That unanimity is not to be expected in any great political question: that the danger is probably exaggerated on each side, when an opposite danger is conceived on the other side—that if any Constitution is to be established by deliberation & choice, it must be examined with many allowances, and must be compared not with the theory, which each individual may frame in his own mind, but with the system which it is meant to take the place of, and with any other which there might be a probability of obtaining.[12]

This letter anticipates some of the themes—and much of the tone—of Numbers 37 and 38 of *The Federalist*: the difficulty of achieving consensus, the tendency of discussion to degenerate, and finally the necessity of judging the Constitution, not in comparison to the standard set by theory, but to the alternatives, real (the Articles of Confederation) or imagined (a constitution drafted at a second convention). Despite preliminary reservations, therefore, "many allowances" ought to be made and the new government at least be given a try.

More than once in *The Federalist*, Madison reminded his readers that the Convention was without positive models to guide it. All it could do, therefore, was "to avoid the errors suggested by the past experience of other countries, as well as of our own." The lack of precedents, however, made guessing how the new system would work in practice particularly risky. What defects it actually possessed, therefore, would only be determined "as future experience may unfold them." However, because defects would "not be ascertained until an actual trial shall have pointed them out," final judgments and concrete proposals for reform were precipitate. Contrary to the impression left by *The Federalist*, this plea for tolerance was directed not only at Anti-Federalists but also at nationalists who thought the new government possessed "too much of the weakness & instability of the Governments of the particular States," who thought, in other words, it too republican. Madison was out of sympathy with these critics as well, critics who, like Hamilton, may have already been devising plans for reform.

Besides illuminating why Madison did not actively hope for additional federal power, this wait-and-see attitude also suggests why he did not expect future federal predomination. He did not know what the future would bring, and to suggest that he expected any particular outcome is to imbue him with more certainty than he actually possessed. It is possible, of course, that Madison's uncertainty was really a pose, one he could afford to adopt because he did expect the federal government to prevail—with or without the veto—in future conflicts with the states. But on the face of it, such a conclusion runs up against convincing evidence to the contrary.

In his first letter to Jefferson after the Convention, for example, Madison expressed precisely the opposite view, that there was a greater "danger of encroachments" from the states than the federal government. Without the federal veto, the new government did not possess an effective check on the actions of the "local authorities" who in the future would be "stimulated by ambition" to "sacrifice the aggregate interest, and even authority, to the local views of their Constituents." The Convention's alternative to the veto—the Supreme Court— would not be an adequate substitute, because its decisions would in all likelihood be ignored by the states. For Madison, therefore, the necessity of "a recurrence to force" was a real possibility which, he reminded his friend, "the new Constitution [was] meant to exclude as far as possible."

Three months later, Madison stated in *Federalist* 45 that "the more I revolve the subject the more fully I am persuaded that the balance is much more likely to be disturbed by the preponderancy" of the states than of the federal government. Many of the arguments found in the letter to Jefferson are deployed in Numbers 45 and 46 to demonstrate this point. Moreover, without mentioning the Supreme Court specifically, Madison makes clear that he continued to regard "a recurrence to force" as a real possibility:

> If an act of a particular State, though unfriendly to the national government, be generally popular in that State, and should not too grossly violate the oaths of the State officers, it is executed immediately and of course, by means on the spot, and depending on the State alone. The opposition of the Foederal Government, or the interposition of Foederal officers, would but inflame the zeal of all parties on the side of the State, and the evil could not be prevented or repaired, if at all, without the employment of means which must always be resorted to with reluctance and difficulty.

The reiteration in *The Federalist* of concerns which he had expressed privately constitutes very powerful evidence of the genuineness of those concerns. In light of this, what evidence is there that he expected the federal government to dominate?

Proponents of the "expectation" thesis point to Madison's reiteration of Hamilton's "superior administration" argument in Number 46. Like Hamilton earlier, he argues that a citizenry's first inclination is loyalty to the government closest to it:

> If therefore, as has been elsewhere remarked, the people should in future become more partial to the foederal than to the State governments, the change can only result, from such manifest and irresistible proofs of a better administration, as will overcome all their antecedent propensities. And in that case, the people ought not surely to be precluded from giving most of their confidence where they may discover it to be most due.

Given that Madison believed the federal government would be better administered than the state governments, this passage indicates—in so many words—that he expected the federal government to prevail in conflict with the states. From this perspective, the concerns he expressed in the rest of Numbers 45 and 46 were largely designed to soothe Anti-Federalist fears and conceal his real view of the matter.

Of course, sometime between late October 1787 and late January 1788, Madison may indeed have been won over by the "superior administration" argument. The mere reiteration of the argument, however, cannot be considered decisive proof. Unlike his anxiety about state predominance, his belief in the benefits of superior federal administration cannot be independently confirmed. No such belief may be found expressed in his private writings of the time. For all we know, therefore, he may have repeated the argument merely out of deference to Hamilton. Without fully endorsing it, he simply may have wished—out of respect, perhaps, or polite collegiality—to acknowledge it as a possibility.

Casting additional doubt, moreover, is the fact that Madison did not merely reiterate the argument. He added an important qualification, signaling that, however plausible it might be, he had not been completely won over by it. Echoing his position at the Convention—and perhaps in veiled criticism of Hamilton—he declared that "it is only within a certain sphere, that the foederal power can, in the nature of things, be advantageously administered." No matter how well the federal government were administered, in other words, there would always be a reservoir of popular attachment to the state governments, establishing a limit, thereby, to how far federal power could ever be extended.

There is no way of knowing what Madison really thought of Hamilton's argument. Without more evidence, the most that can be said is that he regarded his colleague's scenario as no less a possibility than his own pessimistic conjecture that periodic "recurrences to force" could be expected in the future. He was, in other words, no more certain about the outcome of future federal-state conflicts than he was about whether—and in what respect—the Constitution would require correction.

Conclusion

At least since Irving Brant's biography of Madison, many scholars have considered Madison to be a nationalist in the Hamiltonian mold. Recently, new studies have persuasively challenged that view, pointing out important differences in the two men's outlooks as far back as the Continental Congress. Far from being a "nationalist by instinct," Madison was a republican, driven by his frustration with the Articles of Confederation to strengthen the federal government, but only in a manner consistent with his core principles.[13]

The analysis here corroborates this view of Madison as only a moderate nationalist, a supporter of energetic national government within a republican—and federal—framework. In his conviction, for example, that ratification by citizenries most clearly established the Constitution's supremacy, all three of these values are reflected. Likewise, his belief that the new government's authority extended "to certain enumerated objects only" reaffirms both his long-standing commitment to "chartered limitations of authority"[14] and his position in Number 10 that political representation—a hallmark of republican government—was strengthened by the new system's divided character.

It is true that his "almost Marshallian view of implied powers"[15] in Number 44 might seem to undercut his apparent dedication to constitutionalism. It seems likely, however, that it was his discussion of implied powers that he was referring to years later when he suggested [in a letter to Jefferson] that *The Federalist* "did not foresee all the misconstructions which have occurred." It is also true that his enduring belief in the utility of a federal veto might seem to call into question his commitment either to divided government or to reserving final judgment about the Constitution's practical merits until after it had begun to operate. As has been suggested, however, Madison understood the veto not as an instrument for the states' complete subordination, but merely as a safeguard against state malfeasance. There is nothing inconsistent, moreover, about holding that the Constitution was not a plan anyone would come up with "in his closet or in his imagination" while at the same time being willing to let experience determine whether, and in what respect, revision of that plan was justified.

Notes

1. Farmer, "Essays," *The Complete Anti-Federalist*, 5:29.
2. Garry Wills, *Explaining America: The Federalist* (Garden City, N.Y.: Doubleday, 1981), p. 167.
3. Martin Diamond, "*The Federalist's* View of Federalism," in *Essays in Federalism*, ed. George C. S. Benson (Claremont, Calif.: Institute for Studies in Federalism, 1961), p. 34.
4. Luther, Martin, "The Genuine Information Delivered to the Legislature of the State of Maryland Relative to the Proceedings of the General Convention Lately Held at Philadelphia," *The Complete Anti-Federalist*, 2:45.
5. Madison to Edward Everett, August 1830, *Letters and Other Writings of James Madison* (Philadelphia: J. B. Lippincott, 1867), 4:96.
6. Madison to Andrew Stevenson, 25 March 1826; Farrand, *The Records of the Federal Convention of 1787*, 3:473.
7. Madison to Thomas Cooper, 26 December 1826; Ibid., 3:474–475.
8. Madison to Edward Everett, August 1830, *Letters and Other Writings of James Madison*, 4:95.
9. Op. cit., Michael Diamond, "*The Federalist's* View of Federalism," p. 50.
10. Op. cit., Michael Diamond, "*The Federalist's* View of Federalism," p. 54.
11. Alexander Hamilton, *The Papers of Alexander Hamilton*, eds. Harold C. Syrett and Jacob E. Cooke (New York: Columbia University Press, 1961–1979), 4:276–277.
12. Madison to Archibald Stuart, 30 October 1787, ibid., 10:232.
13. Lance Banning, "James Madison and the Nationalists, 1780–1783," *William & Mary Quarterly* 40 (April 1983): pp. 254–255.
14. Ibid., pp. 235–239, and Lance Banning, "The Hamiltonian Madison: A Reconsideration," *Virginia Magazine of History and Biography* 92 (January 1984): p. 12.
15. Jean Yarbrough, "Madison and Modern Federalism," in *How Federal is the Constitution?*, eds. Robert A. Goldwin and William A. Schambra (Washington, D.C.: American Enterprise Institute, 1987), p. 90.

2 National Center for Interstate Compacts

JOHN J. MOUNTJOY

DESPITE THEIR LEGAL AND STRUCTURAL DIFFERENCES, states share many common problems in a world in which economic and political issues are often discussed in global terms. These complex problems arise in many contexts, including homeland security, environmental concerns, an aging infrastructure, pioneering technology and an ever-evolving citizenry.

As we become more integrated socially, culturally and economically, the volume of these issues will only increase and interstate compacts may well prove to be an apt mechanism for developing state-based solutions to supra-state problems.[1]

The last two decades have seen a resurgence in the development of new interstate compacts and the revision of existing, though outdated compacts. As a tool reserved exclusively for the states, interstate compacts can provide states the means to address state problems with state solutions, avoiding federal intervention and preemption.

More than 200 interstate compacts are currently in effect between and among the several states, each housed independently within a member-state agency most closely associated with the policy identity of the compact. While it seems every sector of state government has an established membership and support association, e.g. state budget officers, emergency managers, transportation officials, legislators, etc., the interstate compact community has gone largely unnoticed and underserved.

To that end, The Council of State Governments' (CSG) new National Center for Interstate Compacts combines policy research with best practices, and functions as a membership association, serving the unique needs of compact administrators, compact commissions and the state agencies in which interstate compacts reside. The center promotes the use of interstate compacts as an ideal tool to meet the demand for cooperative state action, to develop and enforce stringent standards, and to provide an adaptive structure for states that can evolve to meet new and changing demands over time.

A distinctly American invention, interstate compacts promote multistate problem solving in the face of complex public policy and federal intervention.

Interstate Compacts: Brief History

Interstate compacts are powerful, durable, and adaptive tools for promoting and ensuring cooperative action among the states and avoiding federal intervention and preemption. They are also among the oldest mechanisms available for states to work together as their use predates the founding of the nation. Unlike federally imposed mandates interstate compacts provide state-developed solutions to complex public policy problems.

Interstate compacts are contracts between states that carry the force and effect of statutory law and that allow states to perform a certain action, observe a certain standard or to cooperate in a critical policy area. Generally speaking, interstate compacts:

Establish a formal, legal relationship among states to address common problems or promote a common agenda.

Create independent, multistate governmental authorities (e.g., commissions) that can address issues more effectively than a state agency acting independently, or when no state has the authority to act unilaterally.

Establish uniform guidelines, standards, or procedures for agencies in the compact's member states.

Create economies of scale to reduce administrative costs.

Respond to national priorities in consultation or in partnership with the federal government.

Retain state sovereignty in matters traditionally reserved for the states.

Settle interstate disputes.[2]

Prior to the 1920s, interstate compacts were typically bi-state agreements, addressing boundary disputes and territorial claims. In fact, only 36 interstate compacts were formed between 1783 and 1920. But in the last 75 years, more than 150 compacts have been created, most since the end of World War II. They apply to a range of subject areas from conservation and resource management to civil defense, education, emergency management, energy, law enforcement, probation and parole, transportation, and taxes.[3]

While the theory and purpose behind interstate compacts has changed little over the last 228 years, modern compacts differ greatly, tackling broader public policy issues and forging state partnerships for problem solving and cooperation. What also differs is the way in which compacts are structured. Unlike federal actions that generally impose unilateral and rigid mandates, compacts afford states the opportunity to develop dynamic, self-regulatory systems, of which the member states can maintain control through a coordinated legislative and administrative process. Compacts also enable the states to develop adaptive structures that can evolve to meet new and increased challenges that naturally arise over time. In short, through the compact device, states acting jointly can not only control the solution to a problem but can also shape the future response as the problems to be addressed change.

Modern compacts are a reinvigoration of our federalist system in which states may only be able to preserve their sovereign authority over interstate problems to the extent that they share their sovereignty and work together cooperatively through interstate compacts.[4]

Interstate Compact Survey: Findings

In February 2004, CSG conducted a 50-state survey of interstate compacts. This in-depth survey sought detailed information on compact administrators' interstate compact experiences, the experiences of their state in regards to compacts and their assessment of current needs in the compact field. With a 51 percent response rate ($p = 444$, $s = 226$), the surveys results are sound and when combined with CSG's observations and compact experience, reinforce the specific needs for a National Center and help outline the specific duties and role such a center would play in assisting states to better understand and utilize the interstate compact device.

Summary survey findings include:

78 percent said they could use additional resources and assistance in their compact work;

73 percent of respondents stated that they wanted more networking opportunities with their compact colleagues;

71 percent of respondents said they needed legal assistance in interpreting compact requirements;

65 percent of respondents stated that they desired common tools for use in the compact process;

61 percent of survey respondents said they needed a national information clearinghouse on compacts;

61 percent said they wanted more ways to build coalitions and partnerships to promote compacts;

53 percent said they encountered obstacles to enforcement and compliance within their compact;

52 percent said they needed assistance monitoring and evaluating the impacts of federal activities on compacts;

52 percent said they wanted non-technical explanations of compact requirements;

47 percent said they needed support in determining the costs associated with their compact;

46 percent of respondents stated that they thought the need existed to make changes to their compact;

42 percent of survey respondents claimed they had encountered difficulties in educating legislators and other state officials about compacts;

40 percent stated they had encountered obstacles in the drafting of compact language;

35 percent said they had difficulty in determining their funding needs and potential revenue sources; and

31 percent thought the need existed for the development of new compacts.

National Center for Interstate Compacts: Mission

The National Center for Interstate Compacts is designed to be an information clearinghouse, a provider of training and technical assistance, and a primary facilitator in assisting states in the review, revision and creation of new interstate compacts as solutions to multi-state problems or alternatives to federal preemption. The National Center is research-based and member-driven with significant services provided to and participation sought from the interstate compact community. The National Center combines policy research with best practices and functions as a membership association, serving the needs of compact administrators, compact commissions and the state agencies in which interstate compacts reside.

The goals of the National Center for Interstate Compacts are:

Education and Information: educate stakeholder groups, compact staffs, state and local officials on the background, history, legality, structure, mechanics and use of interstate compacts and promote their use to solve multi-state and cross-jurisdictional problems.

Technical Assistance and Training: provide technical assistance to states in determining the need for new interstate compacts, and to examine and, where appropriate, revise existing interstate agreements.

Legal Support and Assistance: to provide legal interpretations of compact law, requirements, rules and the effects of other laws or impending state/federal action; to provide general legal assistance with compact issues.

Administration and Resources: assist states in streamlining administrative structures and procedures, promote the use of technology in compact activities, assist states in gaining federal support for their compact efforts, and create standards for compact operations and rules and regulation development and publishing.

National Center for Interstate Compacts: Services

The Council of State Governments is uniquely positioned to offer a full-range of services to states that are in need of not only information and expertise, but also guidance and technical assistance in dealing with interstate compacts and other interstate agreements. Throughout its 70-year history, CSG has been at the forefront of promoting multi-state problem solving and advocating the role of the states in determining their respective futures. CSG has played an integral role in the development of numerous interstate compacts, tracking the progress of over 200 active interstate compacts, researching innovative problem solving solutions for the states and bringing the states together to build consensus on national issues.

Most recently, CSG has been involved in the development and implementation of the Interstate Compact for Adult Offender Supervision, the Interstate Compact for Juveniles and the Interstate Compact for the Placement of Children. CSG also houses the Emergency Management Assistance Compact through its affiliate, the National Emergency Management Association, as well as the new Interstate Commission for Adult Offender Supervision.

The National Center for Interstate Compacts offers a range of services to states, compact administrators and compact commissions. Based on CSG's extensive interstate compact experience, coupled with the results of the national survey, the national center's services and activities are tailored for information gathering and dissemination, technical and legal assistance, training, and compact revision and creation. Specific services and activities of the National Center include:

Information Sharing: comprehensive and consistent source of reference and advisory information on compact issues with an online library/repository containing the language, bylaws, rules and assorted documents for every compact currently in existence as well as a variety of general interstate cooperation materials.

Federal and State Activity Updates: updates on compact activities from around the country, including the impacts of federal and state activities on current compacts, compact law and administration.

Education and Outreach: educational outreach on a state, regional and national basis for compact administrators and their staffs, other state officials and stakeholder groups, and other levels of government; where applicable, encourage membership in regional and national compacts.

Technical Assistance: technical assistance, both remote and onsite, to states, compact commissions and other identified parties as related to compact reviews and evaluations, compact implementation, compact amendment and revision and drafting new compacts as policy responses to emerging trends and/or federal intervention.

Legal Assistance: legal (and where applicable non-technical) interpretations of compact law, requirements, rules and the effects of other laws and impending state or federal action; general legal assistance with compact issues, including dispute resolution to states, when requested, in interstate compact conflicts, mediation/arbitration between states, administrators, or between the states and federal government; assist states in defining legal authority in compact matters and resolving reciprocity issues.

Training: training curriculum for compact administrators, their staffs and key stakeholder groups, i.e. judges on compact issues; conduct an annual training institute; convene an annual compact technology conference to share information and practices relative to the administration of compacts and the implementation of technology tools.

Standardization: assist states to streamline and standardize the compact administration process, i.e. forms, timelines, procedures, etc.; assist states in defining budgetary needs for compact operations and in gaining federal support for compact efforts and activities; develop interstate compact standards relating to compact structure and language, rules and regulations, commission administrative authority, and compliance and enforcement.

National Center for Interstate Compacts: Future

While the National Center is actively involved with revisions to the Interstate Compact for Juveniles and the Interstate Compact on the Placement of Children, several other prospects for assistance to states on interstate issues currently exist. With federalism use and states scrambling to tackle a range of issues, such as prescription drug pricing, and anti-terror cooperation, the opportunity exists for the National Center to not only help states revise existing agreements, but also craft new contracts of cooperation to address emerging issues that belong under state control. Emerging areas ripe for interstate cooperation include:

CRIMINAL JUSTICE INFORMATION SHARING

While several intrastate information sharing systems have been developed and/or are under development, the fundamental question of true interstate national criminal justice information sharing has yet to be answered. While efforts such as the Global Justice Information Sharing Initiative, sponsored by the U.S. Department of Justice, seeks to establish standards and mutual understanding of the information sharing process, no true interstate mechanism whether on a regional or national level currently exists to allow multi-jurisdictional access to criminal justice information. An interstate compact could be a useful tool in helping facilitate state standards and establishing the framework for interstate cooperation in this area.

EMERGENCY MEDICAL ASSISTANCE

Prior to the 9/11 terror attacks, states had made great headway in adopting interstate agreements such as the Emergency Management Assistance Compact to cope quickly with natural and other disasters. Since 9/11 and the 2001 anthrax attack, states have realized the need for more than just the sharing of equipment and resources for physical clean-up, they see the dramatic need for interstate cooperation for medical assistance. Currently states have no mechanism in place to facilitate nonfederal interstate emergency medical assistance in the event of an NBC attack. While several governors are examining mutual aide agreements, regional compacts and perhaps an overarching national interstate compact would help states be better prepared for this eventuality by sharing personnel, lab capacity and medical expertise.

ELDER GUARDIANSHIP

A July 2004 GAO report, *Guardianships: Collaboration Needed to Protect Incapacitated Elderly People (GAO-04-655),* indicated that an emerging area of concern for states is the need to protect incapacitated elderly adults. The report highlighted specific breakdowns in collaboration between states and federal programs that jeopardized the safety of seniors, specifically in the areas of state court operation, accountability and consistency, state jurisdictional fluctuations, a lack of systematic information sharing between and among varying agencies and levels of government and a lack of adequate tracking of elder guardianship statistics. These problems, similar to issues already encountered in the juvenile justice and adult corrections fields, may be effectively addressed via an interstate compact.

BIOTERRORISM PREPAREDNESS

Regional cooperation for bioterrorism preparedness is on the minds of many state officials. Health care surge capacity, multistate training and prearranged payment provisions, chain-of-command issues and identified roles for key players are critical to an effective response. While other agreements may tackle broader cooperation issues, specific agreements might be crafted to promote independent regional responses based on that region's unique need.

While the National Center for Interstate Compacts seeks to directly assist states with the revision and creation of interstate compacts in addition to a range of training, education and technical assistance services, limitations will exist. The creation of new interstate agreements must be a state motivated solution with state officials and stakeholder experts supporting and driving the compact process. As the integral players to crafting state solutions, states must ultimately be in a position to support the enactment and implementation of the mechanism.

In large part, the National Center and its capacities for assisting states are reactive, but reactive to the trends of public policy in that interstate compacts are an ideal and often the only effective response for addressing the current and emerging cooperative policy needs of our states.

Notes

1. Michael L. Buenger, Richard L. Masters, "The Interstate Compact for Adult Offender Supervision: Using Old Tools to Solve New Problems," *The Roger Williams University Law Review, 1,* 9 (Fall 2003).
2. Michael H. McCabe, *Interstate Compacts: Background and History,* (The Council of State Governments, 1997).
3. William K. Voit, *Interstate Compacts and Agencies, 1998,* (The Council of State Governments, 2000).
4. Michael L. Buenger.

3 Trends in Interstate Relations

JOSEPH F. ZIMMERMAN

THE DRAFTERS OF THE U.S. CONSTITUTION included in the fundamental document five most important clauses—full faith and credit, interstate commerce, interstate compacts, privileges and immunities, and rendition—governing relations between sister states.

Full Faith and Credit

This clause (Art. IV, §1) stipulates: "Full Faith and Credit shall be given in each State to the public acts, records, and judicial proceedings of every other State." Congress by general law is authorized to "prescribe the manner in which such acts, records, and proceedings shall be proved, and the effect thereof." This authority was exercised in 1790, 1804, 1980, 1994, 1996 and 1999. The 1996 clarification was prompted by the Hawaiian Supreme Court's 1993 decision in *Baehr v. Miike* (852 P.2d 44 at 57-72) holding that the statutory denial of a marriage license to same sex couples violated equal protection provision and equal rights amendment to the state constitution and remanding the case for a trial. On December 3, 1996, trial judge Kevin S.C. Chang ruled same sex couples had the constitutional right to marry. Implementation of the decision was delayed until the state legislature had an opportunity to act. Voters on November 3, 1998, reversed the decision of the Supreme Court by ratifying a legislatively proposed constitutional amendment (Art. I, §23) granting the legislature "the power to reserve marriage to opposite sex couples."

Congress responded to the Hawaiian Supreme Court's decision by enacting the Defense of Marriage Act of 1996 (110 Stat. 2419, 1. U.S.C. §1) defining a marriage as "a legal union between one man and one woman as husband and wife" and the term "spouse" as "a person of the opposite sex who is husband or a wife" and authorizing states to deny "full faith and credit to a marriage certificate of two persons of the same sex." Currently, 39 states have enacted a state defense of marriage act, and Maryland, New Hampshire, Wisconsin and Wyoming have statutes or court decisions banning same sex marriages. Missouri voters on August 3, 2004, and Louisiana voters on September 18, 2004, ratified a proposed defense of marriage constitutional amendment. Georgia, Kentucky, Mississippi, Oklahoma and Utah also voted on the question of prohibiting same sex marriages on November 2, 2004.

The controversy over same sex marriages was re-ignited on November 18, 2003, by the 4 to 3 decision of the Massachusetts Supreme Judicial Court in *Goodridge v. Department of Health* (440 Mass. 309, 798 N.E.2d 941) holding unconstitutional a statute denying "the protections, benefits, and obligations conferred by civil marriage to two individuals of the same sex who wish to marry." The decision immediately raised the question whether same sex nonresidents could marry in the Commonwealth. The answer is found in a 1913 Massachusetts statute disqualifying individuals from marrying if they are ineligible to marry in their home state.[1]

The Massachusetts Senate requested an advisory opinion from the Court whether a civil union statute would comply with the court's decision. The answer rendered on February 4, 2004, was no (440 Mass. 1201, 802 N.E.2d 565), but indicated the General Court (state legislature) had the option of not calling a same sex civil union a marriage if the term was dropped for heterosexual marriages. . . .

A number of courts in sister states have commenced to receive petitions for dissolutions from persons united in a civil union in Vermont since July 2000. To be eligible for dissolution of a civil union in Vermont, one party must be a resident of the state for one year. Courts in other states have to wrestle with the question whether they have authority to dissolve a union. In 2002, a Connecticut judge dismissed a petition for a dissolution on the ground the state does not recognized a civil union, but in 2003, a Sioux City, Iowa, judge granted a dissolution petition.

On March 24, 2004, Essex County [Massachusetts] Probate and Family Court judge John Cronin granted a petition for dissolution of a Vermont civil union, the first such dissolution in Massachusetts.

Interstate Compacts

The U.S. Constitution (Art. I, §10) authorizes a state to enter into a compact with one or more sister states with the consent of Congress. The U.S. Supreme Court in 1893 (148 U.S. 503 at 520) opined the consent requirement applies only to political compacts encroaching upon the powers of the national government. A compact may be bilateral, multilateral, sectional or national in membership, and may be classified as advisory, facility, flood control and water apportionment, federal-state, promotional, service provision, and regulatory. There are 26 functional types of compacts administered by a commission or by regular departments and agencies of party states.[2]

Recent developments include congressional consent (116 Stat. 2981) for an amendment to the New Hampshire-Vermont Interstate School Compact authorizing incurring debts to finance capital projects when approved by a majority vote at an annual or special district meeting of voters conducted by a secret ballot. The newly drafted Interstate Compact for Juveniles was enacted first by the North Dakota Legislative Assembly on March 13, 2003, and its lead has been followed by 20 additional state legislatures in 2003 and 2004. Arkansas is dissatisfied with the Interstate Compact on the Placement of Children because each of the 50 member states have individual laws pertaining to participation in the compact, thereby causing bureaucratic delays. The American Public Human Services Association established a task force to review the compact and the American Bar Association's Center on Children and the Law is also reviewing possible compact amendments.

The Registered Nurses (RNs) and Licensed Practical or Vocational Nurses (LPN/VNs) Interstate Compact dates to 1998, when Utah Gov. Michael O. Leavitt signed Senate Bill 149 adopting the compact subsequently enacted by 20 additional state legislatures. The National Council of State Boards of Nursing (NCBN) on August 16, 2002, approved an Advanced Practice Registered Nurses (APRNs) Interstate Compact. The Utah Legislature on March 15, 2004, became the first state to enact this compact.

The business of insurance was regulated by state legislatures until 1944 when the U.S. Supreme Court (322 U.S. 533) opined the business was interstate commerce. Congress overturned this decision by enacting the McCarran–Ferguson Act of 1945 (59 Stat. 33, 15 U.S.C. §1011) devolving to states authority to regulate the insurance industry. Continuation of nonharmonious state regulation of the industry encouraged firms to lobby Congress to preempt specific areas of state regulatory authority. The Gramm-Leach-Bliley Financial Reorganization Act of 1999 (113 Stat. 1353, 15 U.S.C. §6751) preempted 13 specific areas of state regulation of insurance and threatened to establish a federal system of licensing insurance agents if 26 states did not establish a uniform licensing system by November 12, 2002. This threat was averted when 35 states were certified as having such a system on September 10, 2002. Recognizing the danger of preemption, the National Association of State Insurance Commissioners drafted the Interstate Insurance Product Regulation Compact creating a commission with regulatory authority and the Utah Legislature in 2003 enacted the compact and its lead has been followed by eight other state legislatures.

The U.S. Supreme Court on May 19, 2003, settled an original jurisdiction dispute—*Kansas v. Nebraska* and *Colorado* (538 U.S. 720, 123 S.Ct. 1898)—involving the Republican River Interstate Compact and failure of Nebraska to deliver water to Kansas by issuing a decree approving the final settlement stipulation executed by the parties and filed with the special master on December 16, 2002. It provides "all claims, counterclaims, and cross-claims for which leave to file was or could have been sought . . . prior to December 15, 2002, are hereby dismissed with prejudice . . ." Kansas had anticipated Nebraska might have to pay up to $100 million in damages.

Other developments relating to the interstate compact device include continuing pressure for restoration of the Northeast Dairy Compact that became inactive on October 1, 2002, when Congress refused to extend its consent for the compact. U.S. Sen. Charles Schumer of New York in 2003 proposed an expansion of the original compact to include Delaware, Maryland, New Jersey, New York, Pennsylvania and West Virginia. A number of certified public accountants (CPA) are advocating a CPA interstate licensing compact and the Section on Administrative Law of the American Bar Association in 2003 established a committee to draft an administrative procedure for interstate compact commissions. Currently, commissions rely upon a 1981 model administrative procedures act drafted by the National Conference of Commissioners on Uniform State Laws (NCCUSL) or the federal administrative procedure act. Both have disadvantages for interstate compact commissions.

In a related development, 13 state legislatures have enacted the *Uniform*

Interstate Enforcement of Domestic Violence Protection Orders Act drafted by the NCCUSL. In 2004, South Carolina added the U.S. Postal Service electronic postmark to the *Uniform Electronic Transactions Act* as an alternative to certified or registered mail. Forty-six states, the District of Columbia, and the U.S. Virgin Islands have enacted the uniform act.

Interstate Administrative Agreements

State legislatures have delegated broad discretionary authority to department heads to enter into administrative agreements with their counterparts in sister states. Numerous such agreements, formal written and verbal, are in effect, but it is impossible to determine the precise number.

The 39 states operating lotteries became aware that the larger the jackpot, the larger the ticket sales. In consequence, 27 states, the District of Columbia, and U.S. Virgin Islands by administrative agreement are members of the Multi-State Powerball Lottery, 11 states participate in the Mega Millions Lottery, seven states operate the Big Games Lottery, three states are members of the Tri-State Megabucks Lottery, and three states are participants in Lotto South. Recent developments include the 2003 decision by the Texas Lottery commissioner to become a member of the Mega Millions Lottery, the 2004 decisions of Maine and Tennessee to join the Powerball Lottery, and in 2003, the newly established Tennessee Lottery Board termination of negotiations with the Georgia Lottery Corporation to form a joint operation because of fears lawsuits would reduce the amount of money available for scholarships.

Attorneys general continue to form cooperative administrative partnerships to conduct investigations and file lawsuits against companies. Their greatest success in terms of a settlement was the recovery of $246 billion in Medicaid costs from five tobacco companies. The settlement does not require manufacturers of other brands, often sold at a major discount, to contribute to the escrow account in each state. In consquence, 35 states by 2004 established directories of brands approved for sale.

Other recent developments include legal actions in May 2004 by the attorneys general of Connecticut, New Jersey and New York and the Pennsylvania Secretary of Environmental Protection against Pennsylvania-based Allegheny Energy, Inc., for emitting air pollution causing smog, acid rain, and respiratory problems in Pennsylvania and the other suing states. The action was initiated in response to a decision by the U.S. Environmental Protection Agency to change its clean air enforcement policy in late 2003 and terminate 50 investigations. Joint actions by attorneys general in 2004 also resulted in Medco agreeing to pay $29.3 million to settle complaints by 20 states the company violated consumer protection and mail fraud statutes by switching patients to more expensive drugs and a group of rare stamp dealers agreeing to create a $680,000 restitution fund to settle a lawsuit brought by California, Maryland and New York charging them with a 20-year conspiracy to rig stamp auctions.

New Hampshire, Vermont and Rhode Island in 2004 formed the New England Compact Assessment Program to establish a common system for measuring student achievement and saving money. The U.S. Department of Health and Human Services in 2004 approved plans by five states—Alaska, Michigan, Nevada, New Hampshire and Vermont—to pool their purchasing powers in order to obtain larger discount on prescription drugs for their Medicaid recipients. Illinois, Indiana, Maine, New Hampshire and Virginia have joined the E-Zpass consortia, an electronic toll network for motor vehicles extending from the Canadian border to the mid Atlantic States and the Midwest. And Arizona and New Mexico signed the first interstate homeland security agreement.

The Pacific Northwest Economic Region (PNER), a statutory public–private organization, was created by the state legislatures of Alaska, Idaho, Montana, Oregon and Washington, provincial legislatures of Alberta and British Columbia, and the legislature of the Yukon Territory. In 2001, PNER organized the Partnership for Regional Infrastructure Security to develop and coordinate action to protect all types of infrastructure.

One interstate administrative agreement—Multistate Anti-Terrorism information Exchange (MATRIX)—appears to be dissolving. Utah on March 25, 2004, became the eighth state to drop out of the agreement. Florida, Michigan, Ohio and Pennsylvania remain members. MATRIX promoters were convinced the computer-driven program would integrate data and information from various sources including criminal records, driver's licenses, vehicle registrations, etc. Concerns over privacy were expressed by the American Civil Liberties Union, Electronic Privacy Information Center, and Electronic Frontier Foundation.

The Excise Tax Problem

Each state is free to determine the amount of excise and sales taxes (if any) to be levied on various products. The wide variation in excise taxes on alcoholic beverages and tobacco products results in buttlegging and bootlegging which often involve organized crime. Recent sharp excise tax increases for cigarettes in a number of states offered new incentives for buttleggers and are responsible for the dramatic increase in the number of domestic and foreign online sellers of cigarettes which are required by law to report sales to state tax officials, but who seldom do so and cite the Internet Nondiscrimination Act of 2001 (115 Stat. 703, 47 U.S.C. §151). Cigarette sales and excise tax revenues in Delaware and New Hampshire also increased dramatically as nonresidents make purchases in these states to avoid high excise taxes in their home states.

Congress enacted the Jenkins Act of 1949 (63 Stat. 844, 15 U.S.C. §375) prohibiting use of the postal service to evade excise tax payments, but a violation is only a misdemeanor. U.S. attorneys prefer to prosecute violators under the Mail Fraud Act of 1909 (35 Stat. 1088, 18 U.S.C. §1341) as a violation is a felony. In 2004, the U.S. Bureau of Immigration and Customs Enforcement arrested 10 persons and charged them with trafficking in a multi-billion dollar black market in counterfeit major brands of tobacco products made in Asia.

Summary and Conclusions

Court legalization of same sex marriages in Massachusetts and same sex civil unions in Vermont will continue to result in controversies in states lacking a defense of marriage act relative to enacting such an act. It will also raise questions whether courts in sister states possess authority to dissolve a Massachusetts same sex marriage or a Vermont same sex civil union.

Interstate cooperation generally continues to be excellent as additional states enact interstate compacts and enter into interstate administrative agreements on a wide variety of subjects. Compacts and enactment of harmonious regulatory laws have been promoted as a means to discourage Congress from exercising its powers of preemption removing regulatory authority completely or partially in specified fields from states. Nevertheless, disparate state regulatory statutes, increasing globalization of the domestic economy, international trade treaties, lobbying by interest groups, and technological developments will result in Congress enacting preemption statutes in addition to the 499 enacted since 1789.

Notes

1. *Massachusetts Laws of 1913, chap. 360, §2, and Massachusetts General Laws,* chap. 207, §11.

2. Joseph F. Zimmerman, *Interstate Cooperation: Compacts and Administrative Agreements,* (Westport, CT: Praeger Publishers, 2002) and Ann O'M. Bowman, "Trends and Issues in Interstate Cooperation," *The Book of the States, 2004* (Lexington, KY: The Council of State Governments, 2004), 34–40.

PART THREE

THE LEGAL AND CULTURAL

ENVIRONMENT OF STATE

AND LOCAL POLITICS

The diversity of state and local politics results significantly from their various legal and cultural environments. In this part, we consider how those differing environments help to circumscribe and define politics in different areas of the country.

The basic legal framework for states is set forth in their constitutions. And, just like the federal constitution they contain numerous phrases and clauses that are subject to interpretation. Therefore, the question of how to interpret state constitutions is a crucial one. In our initial article, Alan Tarr articulates several significant differences between the federal and state constitutions that he believes underscore the way state documents should be interpreted. Perhaps the most basic distinction he discusses is the idea that while the federal document is usually considered a framework containing grants of power, state constitutions traditionally have been viewed primarily as sets of limitations on the states. This is due to the historical legal premise that states are assumed to possess "plenary" or absolute power. Given this notion of absolute power, state constitutional authors have taken great pains to write fairly detailed restrictions and limitations into state constitutions so as to rein in state actions in all kinds of policy areas. The implications of this for state constitutional interpretation are fascinating, and Tarr's discussion illuminates the nuances of this process.

In our second article, Dorothy Beasley discusses the importance of developing state constitutional law that fosters the principle of "an adequate and independent state ground" with regard to individual rights. She argues that the U.S. Supreme Court should welcome the development of this principle because it would significantly reduce the federal courts' workload. Discussing Georgia's experience, Beasley outlines possible approaches to state constitutional interpretation, and in the process, concludes that state Bills of Rights are alive and well.

A municipality's fundamental legal document is its charter, and the essential point to keep in mind with regard to the legal authority of cities is that they essentially are "creatures of the state legislature" in that they only have powers that are granted by the state. This fundamental point was made by Judge John Dillon in 1868 who stated very emphatically that:

> The true view is this: Municipal corporations owe their origins to, and derive their powers and rights wholly from the legislature. . . . They are, so to phrase it, the mere *tenants at will* of the legislature.[1]

For the most part, the manner in which states grant power to municipalities is through chartering provisions in three types of charters: 1) general act charters, 2) special act charters, and 3) home rule. General act charters are broadly construed grants of authority which classify municipalities according to their size. Laws are then drawn up and applied to cities by classes. Special act charters are the most restrictive types and essentially allow the state legislature to control particular cities through state legislation. Home rule charters are used to grant the most leeway to cities in determining their governmental structure and providing municipal services. Over 40 states allow for some type of home rule charter. An essential step in becoming a "home rule city" is the drafting of a home rule charter which lays out the general governmental framework and the procedures and powers of the local government. States with the home rule option have laws that govern the writing and amending of these charters. In the next article Lawrence Keller discusses the role that municipal charters play in the constitution of local government by carefully considering the nature of municipalities, their origins, and their roles.

To a great extent, the legal framework for each state emerges from its political culture. Indeed, the cultural environment of a state sets the boundary for what citizens believe state and local governments should do, and how politics should be conducted. A clear indication of the diversity of state and local governments can be seen in their political cultures. In his landmark study, Daniel Elazar argued that there are essentially three state political cultures—the moralistic, the individualistic, and the traditionalistic—although more recently several scholars have noted the possible breakdown of the traditionalistic political culture and a blending of the three cultures.[2]

According to Elazar, the three cultures differ in terms of the role of government and who should participate in politics. In the moralistic political culture, politics is the duty of every citizen and the public interest is the paramount concern. The individualistic political culture emphasizes the market transactions of politics, and personal aggrandizement and interests are viewed as the legitimate concerns of politicians. Finally, in the traditionalistic political culture, politics is seen as a paternalistic endeavor coupled with an elitist conception of power. This culture values hierarchical social relationships and protects the status quo via the political process. An inherent continuum of political participation in this typology ranges from very high in the moralistic culture to very low in the traditionalistic culture. In his essay, Elazar discusses the characteristics and origins of each political culture.

While Elazar's initial formulations remain theoretically intriguing, considerable continuing controversy exists as to their empirical validity. In light of this, several scholars have attempted to provide alternative formulations and measures of political culture in the American states, and in their article on this topic, Tom Rice and Alexander Sumberg build on the work of Robert Putnam and his conception of "civic culture" in Italy.[3] Civic culture is a multi-dimensional concept involving a set of core characteristics related to political engagement, political equality, feelings of solidarity, trust, and tolerance, and the existence of social structures that promote cooperation. Tom Rice and Alexander Sumberg attempt to measure the variation across the states in the strength of civic culture, and then ask whether strong civic culture improves government performance in the states. You may want to consider the degree to which Elazar's typology correlates with the civic culture ranking created by Rice and Sumberg.

Our final article is another example of continuing efforts to test the empirical validity of Elazar's formulations. David Miller, David Barker, and Christopher Carman propose a method for what they refer to as "mapping the genome of American political subcultures," and their pilot study results lend some additional support to Elazar's arguments, but they also suggest a need for continued research and refinement of the concept of state political culture.

Notes

1. *City of Clinton v. Cedar Rapids and Missouri Railroad Company,* 24 Iowa 455 (1868), at 461, quoted in Deil S. Wright, *Understanding Intergovernmental Relations,* 3rd ed., (Pacific Grove, CA: Brooks/Cole Publishing Co., 1988, p. 310).

2. On this point, see John J. Harrigan, *Politics and Policy in States and Communities,* 6th ed., (New York: Addison Wesley Longman, Inc., 1998), pp. 7–11; and John R. Baker, "Exploring the 'Missing Link': Political Culture as an Explanation of the Occupational Status and Diversity of State Legislatures in Thirty States," *Western Political Quarterly* (September, 1990): 597–611.

3. Robert Putnam, *Making Democracy Work,* (Princeton, NJ: Princeton University Press, 1993).

Questions for Review and Discussion

3.1   What are the key distinctions Alan Tarr makes between state and federal constitutions? What does he say about the implications of these distinctions for state constitutional interpretation?

3.2   What reasons does Dorothy Beasley give for the newly developed interest in state constitutional law? What three approaches to its development does she mention? In your opinion, is the emerging greater interest in state constitutions and Bills of Rights advantageous to the federal system? Why or why not?

3.3   What are the purposes of municipal charters, and how does Lawrence Keller conjoin the development of municipalities with that of their charters? What are his conclusions?

3.4   What are the origins of the three political cultures posited by Daniel Elazar? Does what you know about the politics in your state conform to the arguments he makes? What forces may have contributed to a blending of these three cultures over time? Have any forces worked to keep the cultures distinct?

3.5   How do Tom Rice and Alexander Sumberg measure "civic culture" and government performance? Do you think their measure of political culture has more validity compared to Elazar's typology? Are they correlated? How does the study by Miller, Barker, and Carman add to our understanding of state political culture?

4   State Constitutional Interpretation

G. ALAN TARR

THE INTERPRETATION OF STATE CONSTITUTIONS, like the interpretation of the federal Constitution, should be rooted in the text and original understanding of the document. This similarity in approach does not mean that interpretations of a state constitution should mirror those of the federal Constitution. Fidelity to a text requires an understanding of the nature of the text being interpreted. One approaches a poem differently than a statute, and state constitutions are not simply miniature versions of the United States Constitution. Rather, they differ from their federal counterpart in crucial respects that affect how a jurist, public official, or citizen should interpret them. This article details some of the important differences between state constitutions and their federal counterpart. It also highlights some of the implications of these differences, especially as applied to state constitutional interpretation with regard to text and original understanding. The article ends with a few illustrative examples.

State constitutions are distinctive in their origins. The United States Constitution is a product of the late eighteenth century and is infused with the political thought of that era. The majority of current state constitutions, in contrast, were adopted in the late nineteenth century, and nine were adopted after 1960.[1] State constitutions thus have very different sets of founders, and those founders confronted different sets of problems when drafting their respective constitutions. Moreover, the prevailing understanding of political life and the problems of republican government were different in the late nineteenth century than in the late eighteenth century and different again in the mid-twentieth century. In interpreting state constitutions, it is a mistake to assume that state constitutions reflect the same political theory found in the federal Constitution.

State constitutions are likewise distinctive in their legal premises. The federal Constitution is understood as a grant of power, and the government it creates is limited to those powers granted to it.[2] In contrast, state governments have historically been understood as possessing plenary legislative power.[3] In view of this, state constitutions operate primarily as documents of limitation, placing limits on state governments rather than granting powers to them. Because state legislative power exists in the absence of constitutional limitations and because state courts have characteristically interpreted such limitations narrowly, many state constitution-makers have found it necessary to elaborate in considerable detail the restrictions that they sought to impose on state legislatures.[4] This in turn helps to explain why many state constitutions are very lengthy documents with at least nine state constitutions containing more than 45,000 words.[5] Thus, state constitutions offer textualists a lot of text to interpret.

Another distinctive aspect of state constitutional design deserves mention. The federal Constitution grants powers and imposes limitations on power. In contrast, state constitutions impose duties on state governments. Education is an example of these constitutional duties. The Michigan Constitution instructs the state government that "[r]eligion, morality and knowledge being necessary to good government and the happiness of mankind, schools and means of education shall forever be encouraged."[6] Other state constitutions are more straightforward. The New Jersey Constitution mandates that "[t]he Legislature shall provide for the support of a thorough and efficient system for free public schools."[7] The Texas Constitution states that "it shall be the duty of the legislature of the state to establish and make suitable provision for the support and maintenance of an efficient system of public free schools."[8] The duties assigned to state governments are not limited to education. For example, the government of Illinois is required to "provide and maintain a healthful environment for the benefit of this and future generations";[9] the government of Alaska to "provide for the promotion and protection of public health";[10] and the government of Idaho "to pass all necessary laws to provide for the protection of livestock against the introduction or spread of various diseases."[11] These duties and the alleged failure of state governments to meet their responsibilities can be a basis for litigation quite different from those found under the federal Constitution.

State constitutions are also distinctive in their history. The federal Constitution was adopted 215 years ago, and has been amended only twenty-seven times since then.[12] In contrast, states change their constitutions regularly, amending them frequently, even replacing them periodically. Only nineteen states retain their original constitutions, and most states have had three or more.[13] The majority of current state constitutions have averaged more than one constitutional amendment for every year they have been in operation.[14]

This propensity for change complicates the task of state constitutional interpretation in at least three respects. First, current constitutional provisions must be interpreted in light of their similarity to or divergence from earlier constitutional provisions of the state, and they must interpret the language of constitutional amendments in light of the changes they introduced to the unamended constitution. Second, given the level of amendment, state constitutional interpreters must reconcile provisions adopted at various points in time that, at least potentially, reflect different political perspectives. Third, insofar as states often borrow ideas and provisions from sister states, state constitutional interpreters must be aware of the origins of a state's provision and how the similar language was interpreted in the originating state.

Faithful interpretation in light of the text and original understanding of state constitutions plays out in ways that from a political perspective are neither consistently liberal nor consistently conservative. Some examples from the civl-liberties area may serve to make the point. One can begin with the issue of public school finance. In *San Antonio Independent School District v. Rodriguez*, the U.S. Supreme Court ruled that even though Texas's reliance on local property taxes to finance public schools led to substantial inter-district differences in per-pupil funding, this did not violate the Equal Protection Clause of the Fourteenth Amendment.[15] This ruling, while dispositive for federal Constitutional law, is altogether irrelevant for state constitutional interpretation. The pertinent state constitutional language is very different from the federal Equal Protection Clause, as illustrated in the education provisions quoted earlier.[16] Moreover, the state language was adopted by a different set of founders and typically at a different point in time than was the Equal Protection Clause.[17] Do state constitutions permit or prohibit the inter-district disparities that result from reliance on local property taxes? The answer may vary from state to state. What is clear, however, is that *Rodriguez* offers little guidance for states attempting to answer that question.

A second instructive issue is voucher plans for school choice, which may enable students to use their state-provided vouchers to attend parochial schools. The U.S. Supreme Court in *Zelman v. Simmons-Harris* ruled that voucher programs did not violate the federal Establishment Clause.[18] However, the text and generating history of state provisions dealing with religion are far different. Most states do have a functional analogue of the Establishment Clause, though frequently it is more detailed than the federal provision. Mississippi's, for example, states that "no preference shall be given by law to any religious sect or mode of worship; but the free enjoyment of all religious sentiments and the different modes of worship shall be held sacred."[19] However, most state constitutions also include provisions adopted during the latter half of the nineteenth century dealing specifically with state aid to religious schools. California's Article IX, section 8 is typical: "No public money shall ever be appropriated for the support of any sectarian or denominational school."[20] Michigan's Article VIII, section 2 makes clear the stringency of the prohibition being introduced:

> No public monies or property shall be appropriated or paid or any public credit utilized, by the legislature or any other political subdivision or agency of the state directly or indirectly to aid or maintain any private, denominational or other nonpublic, pre-elementary, elementary, or secondary school. No payment, credit, tax benefit, exemption or deductions, tuition voucher, subsidy, grant or loan of public monies or property shall be provided, directly or indirectly, to support the attendance of any student.[21]

Were I a judge in Michigan, I would find it impossible to uphold a voucher plan in light of this language. Were I a citizen of Michigan, I would be campaigning for a constitutional amendment to permit vouchers.

Another issue of particular interest under the Michigan Constitution is freedom of speech. Michigan's Article I, section 5 reads: "Every person may freely speak, write, express and publish his views on all subjects, being responsible for the abuse of such right; and no law shall be enacted to restrain or abridge the liberty of speech or of the press."[22] The language of the last clause resembles that of the First Amendment, but a state constitutional interpreter cannot treat the language of the earlier clauses as mere surplusage.

Three aspects of these earlier clauses are particularly interesting. First, the Michigan provision includes not merely a ban on interferences with freedom of speech but also a positive right to "freely speak."[23] Some states have interpreted this positive right as broader than that guaranteed by the First Amendment, encompassing a right in some circumstances to speak on private property open to the public.[24] Second, the Michigan provision protects a person's right to "express . . . his views."[25] The addition of "express" to the Michigan Constitution occurred in 1908 and carried over to the present constitution.[26] The inclusion of "express" expanded the protection provided by the 1835 constitution, which had already protected the rights to "speak, write . . . and publish."[27] Those interpreting the Michigan Constitution must therefore view this addition as protecting something beyond what was protected by the 1835 language, though exactly what this right of free expression encompasses is not obvious on its face. Third, the Michigan Constitution protects speech "on all subjects."[28] The United States Supreme Court has tended to distinguish the level of protection for speech depending on its character, with the greatest protection accorded to political speech.[29] The language of the Michigan Constitution, however, seems to point in a different direction, requiring the same protection for speech "on all subjects."[30] Thus the precedents of the U.S. Supreme Court may not provide much assistance in interpreting the distinctive language of the Michigan Constitution.

Likewise of interest under the Michigan Constitution is the right to bear arms. The Second Amendment to the U.S. Constitution reads: "A well regulated Militia being necessary to the security of a free State, the right of the people to keep and bear Arms, shall not be infringed."[31] Advocates and opponents of restrictions on the private possession of firearms have offered starkly divergent interpretations of the amendment, with gun-control advocates claiming that it protects only a collective right to bear arms and then only while in service in the militia.[32] Whatever the strengths or weaknesses of this "collective right" interpretation of the Second Amendment, it has no place in the interpretation of the Michigan Constitution. Article I, section 6 of the Michigan Constitution states: "Every person has the right to keep and bear arms for the defense of himself and the state."[33] It thus makes clear that the Michigan Constitution protects an individual, not a collective right, to bear arms and that the right extends to personal self-defense as well as to defense of the state.

A final area of interest involves the constitutional protection against unreasonable search and seizure. Most state provisions are identical or virtually identical in language to the federal Fourth Amendment, prohibiting "unreasonable searches and seizures."[34] This textual similarity, however, does not require—and need not lead to—state courts reaching the same results as the U.S. Supreme Court has reached in Fourth Amendment cases. Take, for example, the question of whether police can constitutionally search without a warrant bags of trash that have been deposited on the curb for collection. In *California v. Greenwood*, the U.S. Supreme Court concluded that the Fourth Amendment did not require police to obtain a search warrant to search the trash.[35] One year later, confronting the same set of facts and interpreting a state constitutional provision virtually identical to the Fourth Amendment, the New Jersey Supreme Court in *State v. Hempele* reached the opposite conclusion.[36] I do not know whether or not the New Jersey Supreme Court's interpretation of the New Jersey Constitution was correct. However, I do know that it was perfectly legitimate for the New Jersey justices to disagree with the Supreme Court, even though the text of the federal and state constitutions was the same. The legitimacy of the New Jersey Supreme Court's disagreement stems from two factors. First, the New Jersey justices were interpreting a different document, and a different generating history might justify a divergent interpretation of identical language. Second, even if the meaning of the state and federal constitutional provisions is the same, the New Jersey Supreme Court can still legitimately disagree with the U.S. Supreme Court's interpretation. With regard to the interpretation of the federal Constitution, disagreement with the Supreme Court does not absolve state courts of their obligation to adhere to authoritative Supreme Court precedents. But with regard to the interpretation of the state constitution, the state supreme court is the authoritative interpreter, and it is obliged to give the best interpretation of the constitutional language, even if that interpretation diverges from the U.S. Supreme Court's interpretation of identical language.[37] With regard to the interpretation of the state constitution, the rulings of the Supreme Court may be persuasive, but they are no more authoritative than the rulings of other state supreme courts interpreting their own constitutions.

The previous examples were limited to civil liberties, but what I have said applies to the interpretation of other state constitutional provisions as well. State understandings of the separation of powers and of the definition of executive, legislative, and judicial powers may also be distinctive.[38] For the state constitutional interpreter, the situation is simultaneously daunting and invigorating. Easy reliance on doctrines and precedents emanating from the nation's capitol is out; close analysis of state sources is in. Yet, if one is committed to a vibrant American federalism, this is as it should be. Each state is a distinct polity, with its own fundamental law, and it is appropriate in a federal system that those constitutions receive the same close attention and careful study as is given to the federal Constitution.

Notes

1. This figure is computed from data in 35 BOOK OF THE STATES 10 (2003).
2. *See* Marbury v. Madison, 5 U.S. (L. Cranch) 137, 176 (1803) ("The powers of the legislature are defined, and limited: and that those limits may not be mistaken, or forgotten, the constitution is written."); McCullough v. Maryland, 17 U.S. (L. Wheat) 316 (1819) ("This government is acknowledged by all to be one of enumerated powers.").
3. *See e.g.*, Hodel v. Va. Surface Mineral & Reclamation Ass'n, Inc., 452 U.S. 264, 287 (1981) (Rehnquist, J., concurring) (noting that "the reserved police powers of the states . . . are plenary").
4. G. ALAN TARR, UNDERSTANDING STATE CONSTITUTIONS 10–17 (1998).
5. *Id.* at 10.
6. MICH. CONST. art VIII, §1.
7. N.J. CONST. art. VII, §14.
8. TEX. CONST. art VII, §1.
9. ILL. CONST. art XI, §1.
10. ALASKA CONST. art. VII, §4.
11. IDAHO CONST. art. XV, §1.
12. TARR, *supra* note 4, at 23.
13. *Id.*
14. *Id.* at 24.
15. 411 U.S. 1, 40 (1973).
16. *See supra* text accompanying notes 6–8.
17. *See generally* TARR, *supra* note 4, at 58–172.
18. 536 U.S. 639, 644 (2002).
19. MISS. CONST. art. III, §18.
20. CAL. CONST. art. IX, §8.
21. MICH. CONST. art. VIII, §2.
22. *Id.* at art. I, §5.
23. *Id.*
24. *See e.g.*, Robins v. Pruneyard Shopping Ctr., 592 P2d 341) (Cal. 1979); State v. Schmid. 423 A.2d 615 (N.J., 1980); Alderwood Assoc. v. Wash. Envtl. Council, 635 P.2d 108 (Wash. 1981).
25. MICH. CONST. art. I, §5.
26. MICH. CONST. of 1908, art. II, §4.
27. MICH. CONST. of 1835, art. I, §7.
28. MICH. CONST. art I, §5.
29. *See* Buckley v. Valeo, 424 U.S. 1, 14 ("The First Amendment affords the broadest protection to such political expression in order 'to assure [the] unfettered interchange of ideas for the bringing about of political and social changes desired by the people.'" (quoting Roth v. United States, 354 U.S. 476, 484 (1957))).
30. MICH. CONST. art I, §5.
31. U.S. CONST. amend. II.
32. A recent attempt to elaborate an intermediate position is DAVID C. WILLIAMS, THE MYTHIC MEANING OF THE SECOND AMENDMENT (2003).
33. MICH. CONST. art I, §5.
34. U.S. CONST. amend. IV.
35. 486 U.S. 35, 37 (1988).

36. State v. Hempele, 576 A. 2d 793 (N.J. 1990) (holding that N.J. CONST. art I, §7 requires law enforcement to have a warrant based on probable cause to search a defendant's garbage bags, as defendants had a reasonable expectation of privacy in their garbage).

37. Minnesota v. National Tea Co., 309 U.S. 551, 557 (1940) ("It is fundamental that state courts be left free and unfettered by us in interpreting their state constitutions.").

38. *See* G. Alan Tarr, *Interpreting the Separation of Powers in State Constitutions*, 59 N.Y.U. ANN. SUR. AM. L. 329 (2003) ("[T]he political systems created by [state constitutions] are distinct from each other and the Federal Constitution.").

5 State Bills of Rights: Dead or Alive?

DOROTHY T. BEASLEY

A NEW INTEREST has developed recently in state constitutional law, particularly in the area of individual rights. There are three primary reasons for the development of this interest. One is the conviction that federal protections, adopted so long ago, are not adequate for the needs of today's citizens, who live in a more complex society in which government is a pervasive force. Another reason is the renewed interest in federalism, as demonstrated by the political popularity of the concept of "returning" power to the states. This reversal of the trend toward centralizing governmental activity, authority, and might has not gone unnoticed in Georgia.

A third reason is the widespread modernization of state constitutions within the last [several] years. The cumbersome old constitutions, with multitudinous amendments, seemed more like legislation that supported outmoded structures of state government than repositories of fundamental principles. Georgia recently has undergone state constitutional revision for the tenth time in its 250-year history. Whether successful or not, constitutional revision has the salutary effect of thrusting to the fore the public debate on state constitutions and, consequently, on state bills of rights.

How has the judiciary responded? There are three principal approaches to the development of state constitutional law, all of which rely to some extent on the federal Constitution.

The first is an interstitial or supplemental use of state constitutions. Under this approach, the federal Constitution is examined first and the state constitution is used only if federal constitutional protections are inadequate. This approach posits that litigants need not invoke the state constitution if the federal Constitution protects their rights.

Critics of this approach argue that it is reactionary or instrumentalist. Its main flaw is the effect that vicissitudes in interpretation of the federal Constitution would have on protection of civil liberties and rights. When the U.S. Supreme Court is expansive in protecting individual rights, state constitutions will lie dormant; when the courts act conservatively, state constitutions will be resurrected and relied on to assert broader rights. This approach does not allow steady, cohesive development of state constitutional law.

The second approach reverses the order of attention to the two constitutions. The state constitution is examined first, and, if it provides the protections sought, no further examination is called for. Disposition of the question by application of the state constitution may end the matter at an earlier stage. Independently construed, the state constitution may give broader or narrower protections compared to the federal Constitution. Regardless of the outcome, the state constitution should be construed and applied separately, so that people know what it stands for.

Under the third approach, both constitutions are addressed and analyzed, with the recognition that they may have different meanings and therefore produce different results. This approach recognizes the state courts' obligation under our federal system to construe and apply the two constitutions, which guard the rights of citizens. While state courts are not the final authority in the meaning of the federal guarantees, they are bound to address the subject, give their reasoned understanding to the federal Constitution, and contribute to the commonality of meaning that evolves through courts' thoughtfully plumbing its depths. This approach is the most difficult from the standpoint of judicial time and energy, and in these days of chronic appellate overload it is not likely to be favored.

Reasons to Develop State Constitutional Law

An Adequate and Independent State Ground

The development of state constitutional law is in no way an affront to the highest court of the land or an effort to deprive it of jurisdiction.

Rather, this development complies with the principle of federalism. In addition, the responsible discharge of a state court's duty mandates measurement of the activities of a state's officials, employees, and citizens against the standard they themselves have set up in their organic law.

One of the most important doctrines to help catalyze this development is the principle of an "adequate and independent state ground." The need to develop this federal jurisdictional principle, however, did not arise for many years after the Bill of Rights was added to the U.S. Constitution because the federal Bill of Rights was held not to apply to the states. Consequently, when a state prisoner complained of a constitutional violation such as cruel and unusual punishment, it was presumed that he based his objection on a right protected by the state constitution.

The federal Bill of Rights was not applied to the states until 1897 in the landmark case of *Chicago, Burlington & c. R'd. v. Chicago*, in which the Supreme Court held that the due process clause of the Fourteenth Amendment applies to a state's taking of private property. Then began the long and continuing battle between those who believe that the Fourteenth Amendment incorporated the entire Bill of Rights and applied it to the states, those who believe that the Fourteenth Amendment incorporated only selected provisions, which must be identified by judicial interpretation in concrete cases and controversies, and those who believe that the Bill of Rights does not apply to the states at all. In 1947, the Supreme Court in a 5-4 decision refused to take the doctrinal position that the entire federal Bill of Rights is binding on the states.

The complications introduced by the need to determine whether the federal Bill of Rights applies in a given situation only exacerbate the complexity inherent in our federal structure. But the answers to these difficult questions of the meaning and applicability of the federal Bill of Rights provide the relief sought.

Judicial review of legislative acts or official actions challenged on state constitutional grounds is a job peculiarly for the state courts. The test that the Supreme Court applies to determine whether it has jurisdiction of a question goes to the heart of the issue. If the issue is whether the action violated the state constitution, the state appellate court's decision is final. If the only issue is whether the action violated the federal Constitution, the Supreme Court is the final arbiter. If the two issues are involved in the same case, the Court has no authority to construe the state provision if it provides adequate protection independent of the federal Constitution. The doctrine of an "adequate and independent state ground" expresses this accommodation of federalism, which delineates the responsibilities of both sets of courts in our dual system of government. Justice

Robert Jackson articulated the doctrine in its present language: "This court . . . will not review judgements of state courts that rest on adequate and independent state grounds."

In the intervening years, the Court has abided by the doctrine, but has often had difficulty discerning the basis for the state court's decision, a determination which is the threshold for the Supreme Court's exercise of jurisdiction. For example, the Court remanded *Ohio* v. *Gallagher* [1976] so that the Supreme Court of Ohio could specify whether its opinion rested on the federal or state constitution.

Whenever the Court cannot determine whether the state court's decision rests on federal or state constitutional grounds, the Court must decide the federal question that played at least a part in the state court's ruling. Not only must the state court's ruling depend wholly on state law, but the court also must state this finding expressly in its opinion.

Of course, the state ground must also be adequate. As the court indicated in *South Dakota* v. *Neville* [1983], the state court cannot simply assume that the state provision is automatically violated whenever the federal provision is violated. The court must give a reasoned analysis of the state provision that serves as the "adequate" ground.

The Supreme Court should welcome the state practice of deciding constitutional issues on state constitutional grounds. The presence of an adequate and independent state ground obviates the necessity for federal review and, thus, eliminates the complicated task of deciding issues that could be adjudicated by the state supreme courts. Better application of state constitutional law would ease the federal case-load burden and serve judicial expediency.

The case of *Oregon* v. *Kennedy* [1980] illustrates the doctrine's urgency and jurisprudential importance. During Kennedy's state trial for theft, the prosecution asked a question that prompted the trial court to grant a mistrial. [The prosecutor asked a witness if he had ever done business with the Kennedys, and when the witness replied that he had not, the prosecutor asked, "Is that because he is a crook?"] Kennedy was retried, and the trial court rejected his double jeopardy claim after finding that it was not the intention of the prosecutor to cause a mistrial. The Oregon Court of Appeals disagreed and concluded that retrial was barred because the prosecutor's conduct amounted to "overreaching." Bypassing the Supreme Court of Oregon, the case went to the United States Supreme Court, which reversed because of the Oregon Court of Appeals' "overly expansive view of the application of the Double Jeopardy Clause following a mistrial resulting from the defendant's own motion . . . "

Kennedy first contended that the Oregon court's decision was based on an adequate and independent state ground. If the state ground were unclear, he argued that the case should be remanded to the state court for clarification, as the Court had done in *Delaware* v. *Prouse* [1979] and *California* v. *Krivda* [1972]. Reluctantly, the Supreme Court rejected the connection and examined federal constitutional law. Because the court of appeals had rested its decision solely on federal law, the Supreme Court declined to delay the case further by remanding the grounds question. Addressing the merits, the Court decided that the Oregon Court of Appeals had misjudged the breadth of the federal double jeopardy clause. By remanding the case for further proceedings, the court continued the inconclusiveness of Kennedy's conviction for a theft that had occurred two years earlier. The Oregon Supreme Court ultimately affirmed the court of appeals and held that retrial was not double jeopardy under the Oregon constitution.

Because the intermediate state appellate court had based its decision on the federal Constitution, the case proceeded from the state trial court to the second state trial court, to the state court of appeals, to the U.S. Supreme Court (bypassing the state supreme court), back to the state court of appeals, and, finally, to the state supreme court. The delay, expense, extended lack of finality, and involvement of the chronically overburdened Supreme Court all could have been avoided if the state court had followed a fundamental principle of federalism. These considerations are a convincing argument in favor of an initial application of state constitutional law.

Indeed, the Court has implored state courts to keep it out of their business. The Court requires only "a clear and express statement that a decision rests on adequate and independent state grounds" to assume the finality of a state court's decision.

State appellate courts cause an administrative nightmare when they blur or ignore the federal-state dichotomy. They can correct this problem by construing their own state constitutions. They have neglected this role in the past, frequently because counsel's failure to invoke the state constitution has precluded this basis for review. All who believe in the principle of federalism should not only heed but also welcome the U.S. Supreme Court's pleas to seek separate meanings in state constitutions.

Why State Courts Should Favor an Independent and Adequate Ground

From the standpoint of the state judge, the easiest and quickest road to travel when individual rights are at issue is to defer to the federal Constitution and its interpretation as announced by the Supreme Court.

But when the state constitution guarantees a similar or additional right, the state judge has both an opportunity and a duty to construe the state constitution—even when concluding that both constitutions have the same meaning in a particular context.

Above all, the judge's oath of office requires interpretation of the state constitution. The judge does not swear allegiance to the federal Constitution first and to the state constitution only when there are peculiarly state matters at issue, such as zoning, eminent domain, or jurisdiction. Nor does the judge swear allegiance to the state constitution on the condition that the state bill of rights is to be construed in connection with comparable provisions in the federal Bill of Rights. Each stands on its own merits and requires independent adherence.

Second, Georgia's constitution provides that: "Legislative acts in violation of this Constitution or the Constitution of the United States are void, and the judiciary shall so declare them." Note that the provision addresses the commands of the state constitution first. The government, including the judicial branch, has a duty to protect the structure of state government, a structure that must be maintained if the system is to survive. Abdicating a governmental function weakens this structure.

Third, courts must interpret the state constitution if they are to adhere to the principle that cases should be decided on the narrowest possible grounds. When judges establish broader legal rules than are necessary to resolve a case, they risk troublesome application of these precedents to unforeseen circumstances.

Fourth, only state courts can construe the state constitution authoritatively. The federal courts do not share this capacity or function, although the state courts share with the federal courts the function of construing the federal Constitution. Thus, state court failures to construe their state constitution result in a jurisprudential vacuum.

This loss of useful precedent should not be taken lightly. The state constitutions principally define the relationship between the people and their immediate government. Thomas Jefferson recognized the great importance of the state constitution when he wrote that "everyone should be free to appeal to its text."

State courts should welcome this challenge. State bills of rights can protect our liberties more effectively than the federal Bill of Rights for several reasons. Rules enunciated by the U.S. Supreme Court have national significance and applicability. Such repercussions favor a "least common denominator" attitude. In contrast, state courts construing state constitutions make law for fewer people over a smaller area. Unlike the Supreme Court, they need not assess the impact of their decisions on federal–state relations. Nor must state courts construing state constitutions decide whether the Fourteenth Amendment enforces the right in question against the states.

Since their decisions are not so far-reaching in effect, state courts can be more imaginative, more creative, and more experimental. When hindsight counsels that a state pronouncement was unwise, changes are made more easily, either judicially by another case or legislatively by statute or constitutional amendment.

Each state has developed its own constitutions and amendments under different circumstances in different times and by different people and methods. If courts either assume that the meaning of a state constitutional provision is the same as its federal counterpart or ignore the state constitution, we lose the richness of these 50 individual histories. Furthermore, such short cuts may be gravely wrong. For example, the founders' reasons for adopting the cruel and unusual punishment clause of the Eighth Amendment in 1789 were undoubtedly different from the reasons why Georgia first inserted this provision in its 1861 constitution, when it seceded and joined the Confederacy to protect the institution of slavery. Because state and local authorities are close to the people and have daily contact with their lives, they are more likely to accept and apply state-level decisions than pronouncements from Washington. Moreover, state sanctions for compelling adherence are nearer at hand than pronouncements of the U.S. Supreme Court.

Addressing state constitutions demands the scholarship and wisdom of state supreme court justices on the contemporary meaning of fundamental rights in our diverse society. Even if the inquiry must proceed beyond the state constitution and embrace the federal Constitution, examination of state constitutions gives the Supreme Court the benefit of state judicial thinking. As a result, the federal rule that binds courts throughout the country will be more broadly based and more deeply considered. Just as Supreme Court decisions on federal law may guide state courts in ascertaining the meaning of state constitutions, so may state court decisions assist the Supreme Court.

In addition, state court decisions construing state constitutions are an important indication of popular sentiment because democracy is more directly instituted on the state level. Although representatives of the people adopted the U.S. Constitution, the people themselves adopted the state constitutions. As a consequence, the U.S. Supreme Court can profit from state analyses of state constitutional guarantees in construing the corresponding federal provisions.

Protection of individual rights through the state court system is effective also because the innovation and application of a state constitution provides speedier and less costly redress to the person claiming the violation of a fundamental right. The substantial time and resources required to pursue a case to the U.S. Supreme Court are not available to everyone. Because the Court hears relatively few cases each year, it is unable to decide many cases in which the federal Constitution is at issue. Many more litigants have an appeal of right or at least a greater chance of obtaining certiorari from the state supreme court.

Moreover, focusing on the state constitution develops state law into a more cohesive and fuller body of precedent. State courts construe law made by legislatures, boards, state administrative agencies, local governments, and prior judicial decisions in thousands of decisions each day. Why then ignore the state constitution, the highest state level of documentary authority? For example, Georgia state law requires that criminal defendants who demand a speedy trial be tried within two terms in which a jury is available. When a defendant who made such a demand later contends that his right to a speedy trial has been violated, why should the state courts neglect the state constitution's speedy trial provision and apply only the federal guarantee as construed by the U.S. Supreme Court?

If state appellate courts do not study, analyze, and apply the state guarantee consistently, how are state trial judges to know the standards that their state constitution requires? Each state's appellate judiciary must promulgate statewide constitutional guidelines defining concepts such as a "speedy trial" to provide the proper development of this crucial area of the state's law. A Wisconsin case, decided over a century ago, eloquently championed the duty of state courts to examine state constitutional issues: "The people [of Wisconsin] then made this constitution, and adopted it as their primary law. The people of other states made for themselves, respectively, constitutions which are construed by their own appropriate functionaries. Let them construe theirs—let us construe and stand by ours" [*Attorney General ex rel. Bashford v. Barstow*, 4 Wis. 567 (1855)].

Approaches to Constitutional Construction

How should state courts' development of state constitutional law proceed? Commentators have suggested several methods of decisionmaking that courts may use in construing and applying a state constitutional provision.

The first approach utilizes arguments drawn from the history of the provision and of each state. This approach, as well as the textual and structural approaches, are "originalist" arguments based on preexisting sources. The historical method focuses on legislation, history, the social and political settings in which the clause originated, state traditions, and the place of the clause in the state's constitution, and case law over the years. Legislative history includes the proceedings of the constitutional commission or other body that adopted or revised the constitution or amendments.

Application of the second approach, the "textual," requires the reader to examine the words used in the constitutional provision and to compare the provision's language and origins with those of analogous provisions in other constitutions. However, a textual difference does not always denote a difference in meaning, nor does textual sameness always import an identical meaning. In addition, the state provision's language may be more explicit. In interpreting state constitutional provisions, courts should consider not only the meaning of the corresponding federal provision but also the meaning of similar provisions in sister states' constitutions.

The "structural" method is the most difficult to apply because it addresses the interrelationships of governmental entities within the state and local framework. For example, a structural analysis of the constitutionality of government activity could consider whether the decisionmaker is elected or appointed, whether the level of the decision is state or local, and whether the agency acting is a board, commission, executive, or quasi-judicial entity.

The "prudential" method, like the "doctrinal" and "ethical" methods discussed below, is "nonoriginalist" because it does not depend on premises that were previously part of the constitution. A judge applying this method asks two questions: Should the court get involved, and to what degree should the court be a policymaker? The first question addresses problems such as standing, mootness political questions, and advisory opinions. The second question assesses the pragmatic impact of the decision and its costs and benefits as public policy. The court must consider the nature of the subject matter, the nature of the interest affected and whether uniformity or diversity is appropriate.

The "doctrinal" method often involves the creation of court-made formula. Unfortunately, this approach lends itself too readily to application of inapposing catchwords to a given set of circumstances. A court using doctrinal analysis categorizes new questions according to previously developed theories. The danger to that facile compartmentalization may prematurely end the inquiry. Terms such as "stop and frisk" are not part of the constitution, but are merely explanatory labels. Courts may be tempted to sort cases into convenient categories that discourage thorough analysis.

Courts employ the "ethical" approach when they desire a certain result because it appeals to their sense of values or reflects the attitudes or ideals of society. The result may have only a tenuous link to a constitutional provision. The right to privacy, enunciated long ago by the Georgia Supreme Court, is an example [*Pavesich* v. *New England Life Insurance Co.*, 122 Ga. 190, 50 S.E. 41 (1905)]. Courts used this method in developing the law of substantive due process with respect to economic rights. If the court goes too far, however, and mistakes the values of society, the state constitution is easier to amend than the federal Constitution.

Central to the use of the "declaratory" method is a determination of whether the right claimed is "fundamental" in character and thus reserved to a citizen. This decision requires an examination of the treatment of the right at common law and perhaps an extrapolation or refinement of the right to fit today's societal background. Early decisions of the Georgia Supreme Court used this approach. In one antebellum case, the court posited that individuals have certain inalienable rights, that state constitutions declare these rights but do not create them, and that other unnamed rights also exist. The opening paragraph of Georgia's original constitution in 1777 expresses this natural law concept by deriving the authority to adopt a constitution from natural law. This method contemplates the evolutionary development of law from the customs and traditions of the people. This approach reflects a "fundamentalist" rather than an existentialist attitude.

In recognizing the existence of rights which are not explicitly defined, the Georgia Supreme Court in 1846 stated that the rights in the first ten amendments were "virtually adopted" by the people, in their acts of ratification, to guide and control the state legislatures as well as the Congress. This statement illustrates a "fundamental law" theory, not an incorporationist theory. The essential difference is that the state courts are free to decide what rights are fundamental at any given time and circumstances in Georgia law and society, whether or not the Constitution enunciates such rights. If the right existed at common law, the Constitution's silence about it does not foreclose the right's "fundamental" and therefore protectible character. The court examines the principle itself, not merely the constitutional provision which may or may not house it: " . . . principles which lie lower than the Constitution itself . . . principles of right, found in the mind of all enlightened and good men — of universal application, and unchanging as the source from whence they come, the bosom of the Deity." Although the "declaratory" method may seem antiquated, it should not be overlooked. Georgia's constitution still contains a deep depository.

Whatever method is used in argument and analysis, we must not lose sight of an important contextual perspective: the federal Constitution is a grant of power from the people to the federal government, whereas the state constitutions define limits on state and local governmental power over the people. Thus, a different purpose prompts the recitations of rights and liberties. Constitutions such as Georgia's therefore make clear that the individual rights enumerated are not exclusive: the Georgia constitution specifically states that, "The enumeration of rights herein contained as part of this Constitution shall not be construed to deny to the people any inherent rights which they may have hitherto enjoyed." The meaning of "hitherto" suggests interesting questions for debate: (1) How far back in history do we "hither" go? And to what sources? The Magna Carta? English common law? (2) Does "hitherto" embrace rights which may have been omitted from this constitution but were mentioned in earlier ones?

State courts should consider another factor when construing state constitutional provisions: whether the litigant challenges a legislative act or an isolated activity of a governmental agent. Striking down a law that reflects the will of the people as expressed by their elected representatives is a far more serious undertaking than invalidating a particular search and seizure by a police officer. Invalidating a legislative act brings into play the separate roles of two theoretically equal branches of government.

In sum, one must interpret a state's constitution in light of that state's distinctive characteristics—its land, its industry, its people, its history. For these elements are the kaleidoscopic sources of the state's constitution and the liberties that distinguish the people who adopted the constitution from the federal government and from the other states.

6 Municipal Charters

LAWRENCE F. KELLER

THE MUNICIPAL CHARTER IS A neglected area of study. Few understand its purposes, and many approach it in a highly legalistic fashion. The lack of understanding is a result of several factors, many of which have to do with how public administration and politics are studied in this country The field of public administration in the United States focuses largely on public management in the context of the national bureaucracy. Urban political dynamics tend to be analyzed as a contest among partisan actors who can overwhelm existing structures and formal processes as they pursue personal reward with scant regard for a broader public interest. Furthermore, a growing number of urban observers focus on community projects and public participation and underestimate the importance of structures and processes, finding in the broad participation of citizens the true meaning of urban politics. Finally, attorneys are trained clinically and thus approach municipal law from a black-letter perspective. They generally do not think in terms of the spirit of municipal laws as an expression of the nature of a given community.

A better understanding of municipal charters can perhaps be reached by reconsidering the nature of municipalities more deeply A municipality is an empowered government directly controlled by its citizens. Citizens not only create municipalities but can also terminate them. No other government is so completely susceptible to the collective wishes of its citizens. Most Americans live in a municipality, and since it is governed according to its charter, charters are of major significance for the quality of public life for most Americans.

This article develops a relatively complete perspective on municipalities that highlights the crucial role of charters in the political life of this country After a brief sketch of the historical origins of the municipality as a form of government, a concept of the municipality as an empowered polity that maximizes the ability of citizens to participate in public life is developed. From this perspective, the municipal charter can be seen as the blueprint for effective participation and just governance.

Roman Origins of the Municipality

Rome developed several political innovations that are the historical cornerstone of modern society and its governance. . . .

Roman leaders realized that local policies could vary without having that affect their ultimate control over the empire. They conceived of the city as a separate legal entity, called a municipality, and granted it the authority to direct its own local affairs. The word *municipal* refers to the internal affairs of a governmental entity. Thus Rome controlled the external affairs of the empire, and cities were able to direct affairs within their own boundaries. These Roman municipalities were the origin of the municipal corporation in American law.

The Making of Modern America

From approximately 1880 to 1920, population growth in American municipalities exploded. The United States metamorphosed from an agrarian nation to a country dominated by large cities. New York City, formed during this time by the merger of the largest and third largest American cities, grew by a million people each decade from 1880 to 1920. Cleveland, Ohio, went from a city of 50,000 in 1880 to a metropolis of 720,000 by 1920. Spurred by industrial development based on abundant natural resources, this population growth was centered almost entirely in the northeastern and midwestern sections of the country. By 1920, the United States was the major industrial power of the world, with several cities of over a million people.

Rapid urbanization and industrialization created problems beyond the capacity of the political system. Reformers of every stripe and persuasion arose, offering solutions to burgeoning problems. Some of these reformers focused on governance of the rapidly growing cities. The initial response to the political dynamics of growth had been government by a patronage machine controlled by a political party. This system often placed considerable public power in the hands of nonpublic officials (typically the county chair of the dominant party). Although the political machine helped to integrate immigrants into American life, this style of one-party rule rarely afforded solutions to urban problems, which helped create an opening for state officials to interfere with municipal politics.

This involvement from state officials was typically partisan in motivation. State legislative control over agencies and policies at the local level meant that a political party in control of the state government could use power to direct patronage and other policies at the municipal level. This prompted reformers to propose controls on the ability of state government to intervene in municipal affairs. They fought for "home rule," the ability of a city to develop its own government without interference from state government.

Some states implemented home rule by statute. Others secured home rule for their municipalities by amending their constitution. Ohio, for example, added Article XVIII to the state constitution in 1912. The article secured home rule in the broadest terms: "Municipalities shall have authority to exercise all powers of local self-government and to adopt and enforce within their limits such local police, sanitary and other similar regulations, as are not in conflict with general laws." In addition, the article granted all municipalities the ability to design their own government: "Any municipality may frame and adopt or amend a charter for its government and may . . . exercise thereunder all powers of local self-government." This broad grant of home rule in municipal government, and similar provisions in many other states, elevated the importance of the charter. It became in essence a constitution—the governing document, specifying how the municipality was to be constituted as a political community.

Charters and the Law

Local government in the United States is a creature of state government. Even though most states permit some form of home rule, its extent depends upon the nature and interpretation of state law. The courts view constitutional and nonconstitutional entities quite differently and often permit exercises of authority by a constitutional entity (federal government, state government) if such measures are not expressly prohibited by the constitution. In contrast, for a nonconstitutional entity (such as a city under a home rule system) courts may prohibit a particular exercise of authority unless it is explicitly granted. This restriction emphasizes the importance of a well-crafted charter. A well-designed city charter is of great help in dealing with court interpretation by providing clear and explicit language for critical governance functions.

The municipality is a corporation. As such, it must have a charter that clearly declares objectives, grants authority, and establishes processes for obtaining corporate objectives. This underscores the legal fact that a charter is not a constitution and needs more specificity to ensure its adherence to constitutional requirements. The breadth and reach of a charter depends not only upon its content but also on the legal context of state law, as we have noted. If a state has enacted a constitutionally based, encompassing system of home rule, as Ohio did with Article XVIII of its constitution, a charter can take on many characteristics of a constitution.

The expansion of rights and liberties under the national constitution has limited certain of the powers of the municipality. For example, the city of Cincinnati passed an ordinance declaring particular sections of the city to be drug zones, and it gave police the authority to examine people entering such zones or exclude them from doing so. The court struck down this exercise of the municipal police power as a violation of the federally guaranteed right of travel as well as a violation of the limits of home rule authority under the Ohio constitution.

The most important limitation on the municipality is the state law on municipal home rule. A court response to home rule authority depends first upon whether the provision of municipal home rule is constitutional or statutory. Also, court interpretation depends upon how broad the grant of home rule is. Finally, as home rule is now a century old, case law itself may be a source of limitation on municipal authority. The Model City Charter developed by the National Civic League is of great help in dealing with these limitations because it calls attention to critical issues in framing a valid charter and offers careful language to achieve general municipal objectives.

Though a charter faces legal limitations that differentiate it from a constitution, its political function is to constitute the municipality, and as such a charter is directly related to the quality of public life in the municipality The political function is thus supremely important and demands careful conceptual analysis, as it can easily be lost in a misplaced concern with legal restriction or in approaching the charter from a technical orientation.

The Constitutive Function of the Municipal Charter Constitution

Creation of the modern nation state led to the rise of the modern city. Feudalism was eroded by the rise of cities, where citizens were free of feudal restrictions. In fact, running away to a city was a primary method of obtaining freedom from feudal obligations. In many European nations, the monarchy arose by aligning itself politically with the increasingly important cities. Thus the homes of many monarchs were transferred from remote castles selected for protection to capital cities, which often became the dominant city for the nation (London, Paris, and Berlin are just the obvious examples). The city became the abode of free men whose freedoms were typically embedded in a royal charter granted by the monarch.

Initially, charters were for the most part fairly general—such as the Magna Carta, extracted from a reluctant King John. Eventually they became more specific and encompassed such things as a grant of freedom from commercial liability to those promoting economic development. These commercial charters are the basis for the modern corporation. However, the most significant charters for the quality of public life were, and remain, municipal charters. A municipal charter granted to the city almost complete domestic control over public life. For all but foreign affairs, it was the basis for organizing public life for the city This remains the function of the municipal charter; consequently it performs the critical political office of constituting the municipality.

The municipal charter details the authority of the city, the structure of the government, and the processes by which the government exercises authority. State law often defines the authority of the city. However, in many cases, a city may assume all (or only part) of the authority granted by state law. A city may determine that some functions are to be performed by state agencies. For example, a city may decide to have the county or similar unit of state government plan for the municipality.

Some state laws may require a city to declare explicitly its intention to exercise specific authority. Conversely, state laws may permit a city to opt out of some authority by stating in its charter the intention to do so. An example of the latter is the ability to exempt the city from state civil service provisions. In all cases, the charter must be clear on the intent. This is not just a matter of legal nicety; it demands careful and clear writing of key provisions. Again, a model charter can be of crucial support by offering examples of provisions—and, just as importantly, the reasons for such provision. A major strength of the Model City Charter is the commentary describing the nature of the provision and the major options around important functions.

The governing structure of a municipality is obviously important. Another critical function of the Model City Charter is that it states certain preferences on structure. Government is not an organization separate from the community; it is the means by which a political community makes decisions. Conceptually, this is the meaning of the term republic, how public things (res means "thing" in Latin) are to be handled. Private things are left to individuals and such other institutions as the family and religious organizations. Government handles public things, the structure and processes the community has established for that purpose.

Though many conceptions of republic exist, all emphasize the accountability of government to the people. People in this sense are not just voters, or even the current generation of citizens. *People* refers to past, present, and future citizens to which the current government must be accountable. The inclusion of "to us and our posterity" in a municipal charter is not just a rhetorical flourish but recognition that accountability is cross-generational. Accountability includes concern for the future effects of policy as well as sensitivity to the traditions of the past.

Community decisions must be produced by institutions that are established through politically legitimate means—that is, the institution must be part of the formal fabric of the community. It must be based on the constitution, either specifically embodied in it or created by the processes of government established by it. Americans are uniquely a political people; our identity is not an ethnic one. An American is a person who accepts and acts out specific political values, the values that constitute the American polity. Our revolution was a political event, based on a belief that public policy and administrative implementation must reflect constitutional values. Failure to follow the values invalidates actions of government and, in fact, legitimates opposition.

Public authority, the ability to act in the name of the polity, is allocated to offices within a duly constituted institution. Participation is best conceptualized as holding office. From this perspective, a republic is democratic if public offices are open to all qualified citizens. Politically, public schools facilitate expansion of the pool of qualified citizens by teaching both the nature of government and a duty to participate. Perhaps the clearest example of participation by holding office is the jury system. No citizen may be declared a criminal by the community without the unanimous concurrence of fellow citizens. Legally, the failure to establish a jury selection process that faithfully represents the community invalidates any conviction.

Writing a Charter

Many of the historic cities that were republics or democracies traced their civic roots to a lawgiver. Solon and Hammurabi are perhaps the best known. Americans trace their roots to a founding, involving a convention of lawgivers. Conceptually, home rule empowers citizens to create a government. To discharge this power effectively, citizens need well-crafted processes and resources. This is particularly the case when home rule provisions allow a citizen-led mechanism to create a charter. In Ohio, for example, a charter commission develops a charter. The commission is a fifteen-member body elected at large in the municipality. It must write a proposed charter and submit it to the voters by the next election. They cannot discharge their duty effectively unless they are given sufficient resources.

The resources are not just financial. A charter commission requires educated members acting professionally with informed and responsive staff. Providing such staff could be a function of the public urban university. Faculty in such an institution could assist citizens in discharging their public duties by holding them to constitutional norms. Armed with a civic education, most citizens would act professionally, seeking what is best for their community.

A final ingredient in creating an effective and just charter is an agenda. The Model City Charter has performed this role well in all the charter and charter review commissions with which I have worked. The commentary in the model charter helps educate citizens on the choices they must make. It also makes clear that the preferred form of government has many advantages and thus any deviation from it requires demonstrable support. This has helped create a more aware form of council-mayor government in many cases, as citizens realize the consequences of an elected (rather than appointed) chief executive. The decision about the nature and selection of the chief executive is for the citizens to make, but they should know the consequences of how the chief executive is selected.

In sum, implementing operational home rule requires citizens to be able to design and implement effective and just governance. This requires civic knowledge, constitutional and professional norms, prudent political judgment, professional staff, and a model charter as an agenda. Such civic institutions as public schools and public urban universities are an important part of this mix.

Conclusion: Back to the Empowered Municipality

A charter is a critical public document. It organizes the government closest to the citizen and the one over which they have the most control. A home rule charter gives citizens an unparalleled opportunity for realizing a just and effective corporate political reality at the local level.

This realization is difficult in modern America; the post–World War II era of highway construction and suburb development created a metropolitan America that was quite different from the urban landscape that preceded it. As a result, states must now cope with sprawl, which is often driven by small independent municipalities that use home rule for the benefit of local politicians, parties, developers, and real estate interests. Though such private use of public authority is not new, its effects are more widespread than previously. Hopefully, the response to such problems will not negate the benefits of home rule and local control. States must approach the problem of urban sprawl with an understanding of the benefits of home rule, the centrality of urban life in American politics, and discrimination among types of municipality. This is not easy, but how well it is done may well determine the quality of public life in America.

7   Marketplace and Commonwealth, and the Three Political Cultures

DANIEL J. ELAZAR

. . . THE UNITED STATES as a whole shares a general political culture. This American political culture is rooted in two contrasting conceptions of American political order, both of which can be traced back to the earliest settlement of the country. In the first, the political order is conceived as a marketplace in which the primary public relationships are products of bargaining among individuals and groups acting out of self-interest. In the second, the political order is conceived to be a commonwealth—a state in which the whole people have an undivided interest— in which the citizens cooperate in an effort to create and maintain the best government in order to implement certain shared moral principles. These two conceptions have exercised an influence on government and politics throughout American history, sometimes in conflict and sometimes by complementing one another.

The national political culture is itself a synthesis of three major political subcultures which jointly inhabit the country, existing side by side or even overlapping one another. All three are of nationwide proportions, having spread, in the course of time, from coast to coast. At the same time each subculture is strongly tied to specific sections of the country, reflecting the currents of migration that have carried people of different origins and backgrounds across the continent in more or less orderly patterns.

Considering the central characteristics that govern each and their respective centers of emphasis, the three political cultures may be called individualistic (I), moralistic (M), and traditionalistic (T). Each of the three reflects its own particular synthesis of the marketplace and commonwealth.

The Individualistic Political Culture

The *individualistic political culture* emphasizes the conception of the democratic order as a marketplace. In its view, a government is instituted for strictly utilitarian reasons, to handle those functions demanded by the people it is created to serve. A government need not have any direct concern with questions of the "good society" except insofar as it may be used to advance some common conception of the good society formulated outside the political arena just as it serves other functions. Since the individualistic political culture emphasizes the centrality of private concerns, it places a premium on limiting community intervention— whether governmental or nongovernmental—into private activities to the minimum necessary to keep the marketplace in proper working order. In general, government action is to be restricted to those areas, primarily in the economic realm, which encourage private initiative and widespread access to the marketplace.

The character of political participation in systems dominated by the individualistic political culture reflects this outlook. The individualistic political culture holds politics to be just another means by which individuals may improve themselves socially and economically. In this sense politics is a "business" like any other that competes for talent and offers rewards to those who take it up as a career. Those individuals who choose political careers may rise by providing the governmental services demanded of them and, in return, may expect to be adequately compensated for their efforts. Interpretations of officeholders' obligations under this arrangement vary among political systems and even among individuals within a single political system. Where the norms are high, such people are expected to provide high quality government services for the general public in the best possible manner in return for the status and economic rewards considered their due. Some who choose political careers clearly commit themselves to such norms; others believe that an officeholder's primary responsibility is to serve himself and those who have supported him directly, favoring them even at the expense of others. In some political systems, this view is accepted by the public as well as the politicians.

Political life within an individualistic political culture is based on a system of mutual obligations rooted in personal relationships. While in a simple society those relationships can be direct ones, societies with I political cultures in the United States are usually too complex to maintain face-to-face ties. So the system of mutual obligations is harnessed through political parties which serve as "business corporations" dedicated to providing the organization necessary to maintain it. Party regularity is indispensable in the I political culture because it is the means for coordinating individual enterprise in the political arena and is the one way of preventing individualism in politics from running wild. In such a system, an individual can succeed politically, not by dealing with issues in some exceptional way or by accepting some concept of good government and then striving to implement it, but by maintaining his place in the system of mutual obligations. He can do this by operating according to the norms of his particular party, to the exclusion of other political considerations. Such a political culture encourages the maintenance of a party system that is competitive, but not overly so, in the pursuit of office. Its politicians are interested in the office as a means of controlling the distribution of the favors or rewards of government rather than as a means of exercising governmental power for programmatic ends.

Since the I political culture eschews ideological concerns in its "business-like" conception of politics, both politicians and citizens look upon political activity as a specialized one, essentially the province of professionals, of minimum and passing concern to laymen, and no place for amateurs to play an active role. Furthermore, there is a strong tendency among the public to believe that politics is a dirty—if necessary—business, better left to those who are willing to soil themselves by engaging in it. In practice, then, where the individualistic political culture is dominant, there is likely to be an easy attitude toward the limits of the professionals' perquisites. Since a fair amount of corruption is expected in the normal course of things, there is relatively little popular excitement when any is found unless it is of an extraordinary character. It is as if the public is willing to pay a surcharge for services rendered and only rebels when it feels the surcharge has become too heavy.

Public officials, committed to "giving the public what it wants," are normally not willing to initiate new programs or open up new areas of government activity on their own recognizance. They will do so when they perceive an overwhelming public demand for them to act, but only then. In a sense, their willingness to expand the functions of government is based on an extension of the *quid pro quo* "favor" system which serves as the central core of their political relationships, with new services the reward they give the public for placing them in office.

The I political culture is ambivalent about the place of bureaucracy in the political order. In one sense, the bureaucratic method of operation flies in the face of the favor system that is central to the I political process. At the same time, the virtues of organizational efficiency appear substantial to those seeking to master the market. In the end, bureaucratic organization is introduced within the framework of the favor system; large segments of the bureaucracy may be insulated from it through the merit system but the entire organization is pulled into the political environment at crucial points through political appointment at the upper echelons and, very frequently, the bending of the merit system to meet political demands.

The Moralistic Political Culture

To the extent that American society is built on the principles of "commerce" in the broadest sense of the term and that the marketplace provides the model for public relationships in this country, all Americans share some of the attitudes that are of first importance in the I political culture. At the same time, substantial segments of the American people operate politically within the framework of two political cultures whose theoretical structures and operational consequences depart significantly from the I pattern at crucial points.

The *moralistic political culture* emphasizes the commonwealth conception as the basis for democratic government. Politics, to the M political culture, is considered one of the great activities of man in his search for the good society—a struggle for power, it is true, but also an effort to exercise power for the betterment of the commonwealth. Consequently, in the moralistic political culture, both the general public and the politicians conceive of politics as a public activity centered on some notion of the public good and properly devoted to the advancement of the public interest. Good government, then, is measured by the degree to which it promotes the public good and in terms of the honesty, selflessness, and commitment to the public welfare of those who govern.

In the moralistic political culture, individualism is tempered by a general commitment to utilizing communal—preferably nongovernmental, but governmental if necessary—power to intervene into the sphere of "private" activities when it is considered necessary to do so for the public good or the well-being of the community. Accordingly, issues have an important place in the M style of politics, functioning to set the tone for political concern. Government is considered a positive instrument with a responsibility to promote the general welfare, though definitions of what its positive role should be may vary considerably from era to era.

Since the moralistic political culture rests on the fundamental conception that politics exists primarily as a means for coming to grips with the issues and public concerns of civil society, it also embraces the notion that politics is ideally a matter of concern for every citizen, not just those who are professionally committed to political careers. Indeed, it is the duty of every citizen to participate in the political affairs of his commonwealth.

Consequently, there is a general insistence that government service is public service, which places moral obligations upon those who participate in government that are more demanding than the moral obligations of the marketplace. There is an equally general rejection of the notion that the field of politics is a legitimate realm for private economic enrichment. Since the concept of serving the community is the core of the political relationship, politicians are expected to adhere to it even at the expense of individual loyalties and political friendships. Consequently, party regularity is not of prime importance. The political party is considered a useful political device but is not valued for its own sake. Regular party ties can be abandoned with relative impunity for third parties, special local parties, or nonpartisan systems if such changes are believed helpful in gaining larger political goals. Men can even shift from party to party without sanctions if the change is justified by political belief. In the M political culture, rejection of firm party ties is not to be viewed as a rejection of politics as such. On the contrary, because politics is considered potentially good and healthy within the context of that culture, it is possible to have highly political nonpartisan systems. Certainly nonpartisanship is not instituted to eliminate politics but to improve it by widening access to public office for those unwilling or unable to gain office through the regular party structure.

In practice, where the moralistic political culture is dominant today, there is considerably more amateur participation in politics. There is also much less of what Americans consider corruption in government and less tolerance of those actions which are considered corrupt, so politics does not have the taint it so often bears in the I environment.

By virtue of its fundamental outlook, the M political culture creates a greater commitment to active government intervention into the economic and social life of the community. At the same time, the strong commitment to communitarianism characteristic of that political culture tends to channel the interest in government intervention into highly localistic paths so that a willingness to encourage local government intervention to set public standards does not necessarily reflect a concomitant willingness to allow outside governments equal opportunity to intervene. Not infrequently, public officials will themselves seek to initiate new government activities in an effort to come to grips with problems as yet unperceived by a majority of the citizenry.

The M political culture's major difficulty in adjusting bureaucracy to the political order is tied to the potential conflict between communitarian principles and the necessity for large-scale organization to increase bureaucratic efficiency, a problem that could affect the attitudes of M-culture states toward federal activity of certain kinds. Otherwise, the notion of a politically neutral administrative system creates no problem within the M value system and even offers many advantages. Where merit systems are instituted, they tend to be rigidly maintained.

The Traditionalistic Political Culture

The *traditionalistic political culture* is rooted in an ambivalent attitude toward the marketplace coupled with a paternalistic and elitist conception of the commonwealth. It reflects an older, precommercial attitude that accepts a substantially hierarchical society as part of the ordered nature of things, authorizing and expecting those at the top of the social structure to take a special and dominant role in government. Like its moralistic counterpart, the traditionalistic political culture accepts government as an actor with a positive role in the community, but it tries to limit that role to securing the continued maintenance of the existing social order. To do so, it functions to confine real political power to a relatively small and self-perpetuating group drawn from an established elite who often inherit their "right" to govern through family ties or social position. Accordingly, social and family ties are paramount in a traditionalistic political culture, even more than personal ties are important in the individualistic where, after all is said and done, a person's first responsibility is to himself. At the same time, those who do not have a definite role to play in politics are not expected to be even minimally active as citizens. In many cases, they are not even expected to vote. Like the I political culture, those active in politics are expected to benefit personally from their activity though not necessarily through direct pecuniary gain.

Political parties are of minimal importance in the T political cultures, since they encourage a degree of openness that goes against the fundamental grain of an elite-oriented political order. Their major utility is to recruit people to fill the formal offices of government not desired by the established powerholders. Political competition in a traditionalistic political culture is usually conducted through factional alignments, an extension of the personal politics characteristic of the system; hence political systems within the culture tend to have loose one-party systems if they have political parties at all.

Practically speaking, traditionalistic political culture is found only in a society that retains some of the organic characteristics of the preindustrial social order. "Good government" in that political culture involves the maintenance and encouragement of traditional patterns and, if necessary, their adjustment to changing conditions with the least possible upset. Where the traditionalistic political culture is dominant in the United States today, political leaders play conservative and custodial rather than initiatory roles unless pressed strongly from the outside.

Whereas the I and M political cultures may or may not encourage the development of bureaucratic systems of organization on the grounds of "rationality" and "efficiency" in government, depending on their particular situations, traditionalistic political cultures tend to be instinctively antibureaucratic because bureaucracy by its very nature interferes with the fine web of informal interpersonal relationships that lie at the root of the political system and which have been developed by following traditional patterns over the years. Where bureaucracy is introduced, it is generally confined to ministerial functions under the aegis of the established powerholders.

The "Geology" of Political Culture

The three political subcultures arose out of very real sociocultural differences found among the peoples who came to America over the years, differences that date back to the very beginnings of settlement in this country and even to the Old World. Because the various ethnic and religious groups that came to these shores tended to congregate in the same settlements and because, as they or their descendants moved westward, they continued to settle together, the political patterns they bore with them are today distributed geographically. Indeed, it is the geographic distribution of political cultures as modified by local conditions that has laid the foundations for American sectionalism. Sectional concentrations of distinctive cultural groups have helped create the social interests that tie contiguous states to each other even in the face of marked differences in the standard measures of similarity. The southern states have a common character that unites them despite the great material differences between, say, Virginia and Mississippi or Florida and Arkansas. Similarly, New England embraces both Maine and Massachusetts, Connecticut and Vermont in a distinctive way. These sectional concentrations can be traced for every part of the country, and their effects can be noted in the character of the economic interests shared by the states in each section.

The overall pattern of political cultures is not easily portrayed. Not only must the element of geography be considered, but also a kind of human or cultural "geology" that adds another dimension to the problem. In the course of time, different currents of migration have passed over the American landscape in response to the various frontiers of national development (see below). Those currents, in themselves relatively clear-cut, have left residues of population in various places to become the equivalent of geological strata. As these populations settled in the same location, sometimes side by side, sometimes overlapping, and frequently on top of one another, they created hardened cultural mixtures that must be sorted out for analytical purposes, city by city and county by county from the Atlantic to the Pacific.

Quite clearly, the various sequences of migration in each locale have determined the particular layering of the cultural geology of each state. Even as the strata were being deposited over generations and centuries, externally generated events, such as depressions, wars, and internal cultural conflicts, caused upheavals that altered the relative positions of the various groups in the community. Beyond that, the passage of time and the impact of new events have eroded some cultural patterns, intensified others, and modified still others, to make each local situation even more complex. The simple mapping of such patterns has yet to be done for more than a handful of states and communities, and while the gross data which can be used to outline the grand patterns as a whole are available in various forms, they have been only partially correlated. However, utilizing the available data, it is possible to sketch with reasonable clarity the nationwide geography of political culture [Figure 1].

Political Culture and the Continuing Frontier

The geography of political culture is directly related to the continuing American frontier. Since the first settlement on these shores, American society has been a frontier society, geared to the progressive extension of man's control over the natural environment and the utilization of the social and economic benefits gained from widening that control, i.e.,

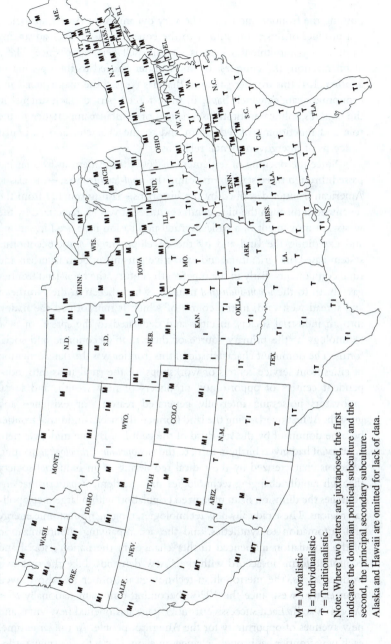

FIGURE 1   The Distribution of Political Cultures within the States

M = Moralistic
I = Individualistic
T = Traditionalistic

Note: Where two letters are juxtaposed, the first indicates the dominant political subculture and the second, the principal secondary subculture. Alaska and Hawaii are omitted for lack of data.

pushing the frontier line back. The very dynamism of American society is a product of this commitment to the conquest of the ever-advancing frontier, a commitment which is virtually self-generating since, like a chain reaction, the conquest of one frontier has led to the opening of another. It is this frontier situation that has created the major social and economic changes which have, in turn, forced periodic adjustments in the nation's political institutions, changes of particular importance to the role and functioning of federalism and to the character and particular concerns of intergovernmental relations.

Since the opening of settlement in 1607, the American frontier has passed through three stages: First came the *rural-land* frontier—the classic American frontier described by the historians—lasting roughly from the seventeenth through the nineteenth centuries. It was characterized by the westward movement of a basically rural population interested in settling and exploiting the land and by the development of a socioeconomic system based on agricultural and extractive pursuits in both its urban and rural components. Early in the nineteenth century, the rural-land frontier gave birth to the *urban-industrial* frontier, which began in the Northeast and spread westward, in the course of which it transformed the nation into an industrial society in cities and dedicated to the spread of new technology as the primary source of the nation's economic and social forms. The dominant characteristic of this frontier was the transformation of cities from service centers or workshops for the rural areas into independent centers of opportunity, producers of new wealth, and social innovators possessing internally generated reasons for existence and growth. At first overlapping the land frontier, the urban-industrial frontier became dominant by the last third of the century. By the mid-twentieth century, it had given birth, in turn, to the *metropolitan-technological* frontier, which is characterized by the radical reordering of an industrial society through rapidly changing technologies and a settlement pattern that encourages the diffusion of an urbanized population within large metropolitan regions. These radically new technologies, ranging from atomic energy and automation to synthetics, and the accompanying suburbanization of the population influenced further changes in the nation's social and economic forms in accord with their new demands. Like the first two frontier stages, the metropolitan-technological frontier has also moved from east to west since the 1920s, becoming dominant nationally after World War II. Each successive frontier stage has opened new vistas and new avenues of opportunity for the American people. At the same time, each new frontier has brought changes in economic activities, new settlement patterns, different human requirements, political changes, and its own social problems that grow out of the collision of old patterns and new demands as much as they are generated by the new demands themselves.

The basic patterns of political culture were set during the period of the rural-land frontier by three great currents of American migration that began on the East Coast and moved westward after the colonial period. Each current moved in the persons of the westward migrants, from east to west along more or less fixed paths, following lines of least resistance which generally led them due west from the immediately previous area of settlement.

Across the northern part of the United States thrusting westward and slightly southwestward is an area settled initially by the Puritans of New England and their Yankee descendants. The Puritans came to these shores intending to establish the best possible earthly version of the holy commonwealth. Their religious outlook was imbued with a high level of political concern, in the spirit of the ancient Israelites whose ideal commonwealth they wished to reproduce. From the first, they established a moralistic political culture.

After five generations of pioneering in New England, where they established several versions of their commonwealth in the several New England states, the Puritans had developed a set of deeply rooted cultural patterns. Then, moving westward into New York State, the Yankees began their great cross-country migration. Across New York, northern Pennsylvania, and the upper third of Ohio, the Yankee current moved into the states of the upper Great Lakes and Mississippi Valley. There they established a greater New England in Michigan, Wisconsin, Minnesota, and Iowa, and they attempted to do the same in settling northern Illinois. Beginning in the mid-nineteenth century, they were joined by Scandinavians and other northern Europeans who, stemming from a related tradition (particularly in its religious orientation), reinforced the basic patterns of Yankee political culture, sealing them into the political systems of those states. Pressing westward, Yankees settled Oregon, then Washington, and were the first "Anglos" to settle California. As Mormons, they settled Utah; then as abolitionists they settled Kansas. They became the leaders of the permanent settlements in Colorado and Montana and even moved into northern Arizona. In all these states, they were joined or followed by the same Scandinavian–northern European group and in each they established the M political culture to the extent of their influence. Within those states and the smaller ones colonized from them, the moralistic political culture flourishes today.

Groups of quite different ethnic and religious backgrounds, primarily from England and the interior Germanic states, settled the middle parts of the nation, beginning with the Middle Atlantic states of New York, New Jersey, Pennsylvania, Delaware, and Maryland. The majority of these highly diverse groups, which together established the basic patterns of American pluralism, were united by one common bond in particular — the search for individual opportunity in the New World. Unlike the Puritans who sought communal as well as individualistic goals in their migrations, the pursuit of private ends predominated among the settlers of the middle states. Though efforts were made to establish morally purposeful communities, particularly in Pennsylvania, the very purpose of those communities was to develop pluralistic societies dedicated to individual freedom to pursue private goals, to the point of making religion a private matter, an unheard-of step at the time. The political culture of the middle states reflected this distinctive emphasis on private pursuits from the first and, by the end of the colonial period, a whole system of politics designed to accommodate itself to such a culture had been developed with distinctive state-by-state variations, modified by moralistic traits only in Pennsylvania and by traditionalistic ones in Maryland and Delaware.

These groups also moved westward across Pennsylvania into the central parts of Ohio, Indiana, and Illinois, then on into Missouri. There, reinforced by immigrants from western Europe and the lower Germanic states who shared the same attitudes, they developed extensions of their pluralistic patterns. Since those states were also settled by representatives of the other two political cultures, giving no single culture clear predominance, pluralism became the only viable alternative. So the individualistic political culture became dominant at the state level in the course of time while the other two retained pockets of influence in the northern and southern sections of each state.

After crossing the Mississippi, this middle current jumped across the continent to northern California with the gold rush (an activity highly attractive to I types). Its groups subsequently helped to populate the territory in between. The areas of Nebraska and South Dakota bordering the Missouri River attracted settlers from Illinois and Missouri; the Union Pacific populated central Nebraska and Wyoming; and Nevada was settled from the California gold fields. Today there is a band of states (or sections of states) across the belt of the country in which the individualistic political culture is dominant.

The people who settled the southern tier of states were seeking individual opportunity in ways similar to those of their brethren to the immediate north. But, while the latter sought their opportunities in commercial pursuits, either in business or in a commercially oriented

agriculture, those who settled the South sought opportunity in a planta-
tion-centered agricultural system based on slavery and essentially anticom-
mercial in orientation. This system, as an extension of the landed gentry
agrarianism of the Old World, provide a natural environment for the
development of an American-style traditionalistic political culture in
which the new landed gentry progressively assumed ever greater roles in
the political process at the expense of the small landholders, while a major
segment of the population, the slaves, were totally excluded from any
political role whatsoever. Elitism within this culture reached its apogee
in Virginia and South Carolina; in North Carolina and Georgia a measure
of equalitarianism was introduced by the arrival of significant numbers
of migrants from the M and I cultures, respectively.

This peculiarly southern agrarian system and its traditionalistic
political culture were carried westward by the southern current. Virginia's
people dominated in the settlement of Kentucky; North Carolina's influence was heavy in Tennessee; and settlers from all four states covered the
southern parts of Ohio and Illinois as well as most of Indiana and Missouri.
Georgians, with a mixture of other settlers, moved westward into Alabama
and Mississippi. Louisiana presented a unique situation in that it contained
a concentration of non-Anglo Saxons rare in the South, but its French
settlers shared the same political culture as the other southerners, regardless
of their other cultural differences. Ultimately, the southern political culture
was spread through Texas, where it was diluted on the state's western
fringes by type I European immigrants, and Oklahoma; into southern
Kansas, where it clashed directly with the Yankee political culture; then
across New Mexico to settle better than half of Arizona and overlap the
Yankee current in southern and central California.

The only major departures from the east-west pattern of cultural
diffusion during the settlement of the land frontier came when the emi-
grants encountered the country's great mountain systems. The mountains
served to diffuse cultural patterns because they were barriers to easy east-
west movement. Thus, in the east, the Appalachian chain deflected the
moralistic-type Scotch-Irish southward from Pennsylvania where they
were isolated in the southern mountains. There they developed traditionalistic patterns of culture over a moralistic base, and created special cultural
pockets dominated by syntheses of the T and M cultures in the mountain
areas of Virginia, the Carolinas, Georgia, and even Alabama.

In the west, the Rocky Mountains served to block the neat westward
flow of the cultural currents and divert people from all three into their
valleys from north to south in search of fortunes in mining and specialized
agricultural pursuits. There the more individualistic types from all three

subcultures diffused from Montana to Arizona, creating cultural pockets in all the mountain states of the West that in some cases—Wyoming, for example—altered the normal regional patterns of political culture.

The development of the urban-industrial frontier coincided with the arrival of other immigrant groups which concentrated in the burgeoning cities of the industrializing states. These groups, primarily from Ireland, Italy, eastern Europe, and the Balkans, also moved from east to west but settled in urban pockets adding new cultural strata to communities scattered throughout the country. Most of these settlers, though bound at first by traditional ties, soon adopted more individualistic attitudes and goals which brought them into the I political culture. Since most of them settled in cities, their cultural impact was less universal in scope but more concentrated in force. In some states (such as Massachusetts) they disrupted established cultural patterns to create new ones, in others (such as New York) they simply reinforced the existing I-dominant pluralism, and in still others (such as Illinois) they served to tip the balance between competing cultural groups.

8 Civic Culture and Government Performance in the American States

TOM W. RICE

ALEXANDER F. SUMBERG

THE INTERPLAY BETWEEN culture and politics has received significant scholarly attention in the last few decades. Of particular interest has been the apparent causal link between civic culture and democracy. Gabriel A. Almond and Sidney Verba were among the first individuals to investigate this relationship, concluding that successful democracy depends on a civic culture.[1] . . .

Recently, Robert D. Putnam examined civic culture and democracy in Italy.[2] He contends that the degree to which Italy's newly empowered regional democratic governments have responded to the needs of their citizens is closely tied to the civic culture of the regions. Where people are generally civic, governments are more efficient and effective, meeting many citizens' needs in a timely and professional manner. Where the prevailing culture is less civic, however, governments are less responsive and politics takes on patron-client characteristics. Putnam further contends that most regions in Italy have retained essentially the same civic culture for centuries and that civic culture enhances the economic development of the regions.

If correct, Putnam's findings are of substantial importance. Not only are the various civic cultures in Italy incredibly tenacious and instrumental in fostering development, they also greatly influence government perfor-mance. This last point warrants special emphasis. Most studies have ex-plored whether democracies are more likely to emerge in a civic culture. For Putnam, democracy is a given; all of Italy's regional governments are democratic. His concern is with the caliber of democratic government. He finds that civic regions have more effective governments.

The purpose of our article is to initiate the process of applying Putnam's methods to the United States. Like the regions of Italy, all of the states are democracies; therefore, we will be investigating the extent to which the performance of these democratic governments differs across the civic cultures in the states. To begin, we need to devise an indicator of the civic culture of the states.

Elements of a Civic Culture

Scholars have long argued about what makes a culture civic. Al-though this debate is far from settled, there does appear to be a widespread agreement on a set of core characteristics. Putnam organizes these into four categories: (1) civic engagement; (2) political equality; (3) solidarity, trust, and tolerance; and (4) social structures of cooperation.

CIVIC ENGAGEMENT   In a civic culture, citizens participate in public affairs and promote the public good. To be sure, self-interest can motivate much of their behavior, but citizens are conscious of the needs of their broader community, and they often act to meet these needs. For many civic citizens, self-interest and civic virtue are deeply intertwined and difficult to separate.

POLITICAL EQUALITY   Citizens in a civic culture view each other as political equals, with the same rights and obligations. The relations be-tween individuals in the public realm—and most private realms—are horizontal and cooperative, not vertical and authoritative.

SOLIDARITY, TRUST, AND TOLERANCE   Citizens feel a strong sense of fellowship in a civic culture. This manifests itself in a readiness to trust and help others, and to tolerate a wide range of ideas and lifestyles.

SOCIAL STRUCTURES OF COOPERATION   A civic culture is home to a dense, interlocking web of social organizations. Citizens are joiners, belonging to a rich array of groups, from professional societies to neighborhood-watch associations, and from recreation volleyball teams to church social clubs. Through these affiliations, people experience firsthand the benefits of being civic.

With this list of civic characteristics in mind, our task turns to devising measures of these properties for the American states. To guide us, we rely on the types of aggregate-level indicators that Putnam used to specify the civic cultures of Italy's regions. Ideally, we would supplement these measures with survey data on individuals' civic attitudes, but such data are scarce. The principal nationwide social science studies, such as the National Election Studies and the General Social Surveys, report their results by Census Bureau regions, not by states. Moreover, they employ cluster sampling, which means that the opinions of smaller states often come from only one or two locations. State data are available in the 1968 Comparative State Elections Project, but that study sampled opinions in only thirteen states. Finally, it might be possible to piece together some state survey data from various polls conducted by private firms, but it is highly unlikely that comparable questions have been asked across all the states. Unfortunately, then, we must rely on aggregate indicators to assess the civicness of the states.

The Civic Cultures of the American States

This research employs three measures to gauge the first component of civic culture—civic engagement. Following Putnam's lead, we use newspaper circulation in the states as one indicator of citizens' concern for public matters. People who read newspapers should be more interested in their communities and should be better equipped to participate constructively in community affairs. As a second measure of civic engagement, we use the number of books per capita in the public libraries in each state. It seems to us that libraries, in their function as education and civic centers, are exactly the type of institutions that should be supported by citizens who are serious about civic engagement. Our third measure is the number of community improvement and philanthropic groups per capita in each state. We reason that citizens involved in groups like these are probably committed to promoting the public good.

Four measures are used to assess the extent to which individuals in the states conceive of each other as equals. The first two have to do with gender in the workplace. For each state, we secured the percentage of public school teachers who are men and the percentage of state legislators who are women. Societies that are committed to equality should be more willing to accept men in occupations traditionally held by women, such as public school teachers, and should be more willing to accept women in occupations traditionally held by men, such as state legislators. The next measure of political equality is the number of civil rights groups per capita among the nonwhite population. Citizens devoted to equality should be more likely to encourage the formation of groups committed to civil rights, and they should be more likely to participate in these groups. A gauge of income distribution is our last measure of equality. It seems to us that citizens in a society dedicated to equal rights would endeavor to reduce disparities in personal incomes.

The third component of a civic culture—solidarity, trust, and tolerance—is assessed with three indicators. The first is the crime rate in each state; clearly, there should be less crime in societies where citizens respect one another. The second measure is the number of lawyers per capita. We reasoned that the need for lawyers should be less in a society where people feel a kinship with one another and trust one another, and where they are tolerant of the differences between individuals. Last, we used the default rate on Perkins student loans as a gauge of the respect and trust among citizens.

Our measure of the social structures of cooperation is a per capita composite index of twenty-six different types of nonprofit organizations. Putnam contends that any association of individuals, whether it is a bird-watching club or a church congregation, can "contribute to the effectiveness and stability of democratic government." Given this, we decided to include a wide variety of organizations in our measure.

These measures of the four components of civic culture are less than ideal. Like Putnam, we are forced by the available data to rely on indicators that are the products of many forces, not just civic culture. For example, newspaper readership may be as much a function of education as it is civic engagement. In order to mitigate the influence of these other factors, we combine our indicators into a single index, thereby maximizing the likelihood of measuring civicness. As added protection, we control for other potential influences, such as education, in the forthcoming regression analyses. Finally, it is important to stress that many of the other influences, like education, may be in part a product of civicness; it is not hard to imagine that a civic society will place more value on education.

To create an inclusive civic culture index for the states from our myriad indicators, we first transformed the values for all of the indicators into z-scores. Next, we ordered the z-scores for each of the indicators so that the low scores (negative values) signified the less civic states and the high scores (positive values) signified the more civic states. It the civicness of the United States can be measured along a single dimension and if our indicators are reliable proxy measures for civicness, then the indicators should be positively correlated with each other.

The data in Table 1 show that all but one of the correlations are positive (the negative correlation is between female legislators and the crime rate), indicating that we have a trustworthy set of measures. The next step in developing our index consisted of calculating the mean z-scores for each component, using only those indicators intended to measure that component. For example, the mean scores for civic engagement were figured by averaging the z-scores for the three indicators of engagement: newspaper circulation, books per capita in public libraries, and community improvement and philanthropic groups per capita.

Within each component, we decided to weigh each of the indicators equally because we could see no compelling theoretical or methodological reason for giving some indicators more influence than others. The correlations between the composite z-scores for the four components are quite high, ranging from .60 to .76. For the final step in creating our comprehensive index of the civicness of the states, we simply calculated the mean of the composite z-scores for the four components. The components were weighted equally because they are all, according to Putnam, integral parts of a civic culture. The comprehensive index is presented in column 1 of Table 2, with the states arranged from most civic to least civic. According to the index, Vermont is the most civic state, followed by Massachusetts. At the other end of the scale, Mississippi and Louisiana are the least civic states.

The Correlates of Civic Culture

Even a quick scan of the civic culture index reveals that many of the most civic states are in a northern tier running from New England to the Northwest, and that most of the least civic states are in the South. This pattern raises questions about the degree to which the index is a product of other factors, such as education or wealth. To test for these and other possibilities, we correlated the index with six common demographic variables: education, income, population, age, region, and the urban nature of the states. The results indicate that our civicness index is not closely linked to any of the demographic measures. The relationship with population is the strongest, but even here the correlation is only a modest .33. Moreover, when all of the factors are entered as independent variables in a multiple regression model where the civic index is the dependent

TABLE 1 Correlation Matrix of the Civic Culture Indicators

| | Components of a Civic Culture | | | | | | | | | | |
| Specific indicators | Engagement | | | Equality | | | | Solidarity, trust, and tolerance | | | Cooperation |
	News[a]	Library[b]	Comm[c]	Malteach[d]	Feleg[e]	Civil[f]	Income[g]	Crime[h]	Lawyer[i]	Loans[j]	Groups[k]
News[a]	1.00										
Library[b]	.36	1.00									
Comm[c]	.49	.71	1.00								
Malteach[d]	.37	.56	.51	1.00							
Feleg[e]	.13	.44	.33	.52	1.00						
Civil[f]	.36	.50	.47	.73	.39	1.00					
Income[g]	.29	.33	.45	.41	.44	.62	1.00				
Crime[h]	.20	.46	.29	.27	-.06	.40	.17	1.00			
Lawyer[i]	.39	.36	.52	.47	.38	.27	.07	.31	1.00		
Loans[j]	.29	.40	.44	.56	.42	.68	.68	.24	.20	1.00	
Groups[k]	.33	.61	.54	.63	.47	.56	.35	.38	.35	.39	1.00

[a]Newspaper circulation per capita; [b]Library books per capita in public libraries; [c]Community improvement and philanthropy/voluntarism groups per capita; [d]Percentage of public school teachers who are men; [e]Percentage of state legislators who are women; [f]Civil rights groups per capita of nonwhites; [g]Income inequality; [h]Crime rate; [i]Lawyers per capita; [j]Default rate on Perkins student loans; [k]501 (c) (3) organizations per capita.

TABLE 2   State Scores on Standardized Indices of Civic
Culture and Government Performance

	Civic culture	Government performance
	Index[a]	Index[b]
Vermont	1.52	0.44
Massachusetts	1.05	1.13
Wyoming	0.79	−0.46
Maine	0.78	0.36
North Dakota	0.76	−0.40
New Hampshire	0.75	−0.04
Nebraska	0.73	−0.06
Montana	0.73	0.11
Connecticut	0.64	0.79
Minnesota	0.64	0.76
Iowa	0.63	−0.02
New York	0.60	1.59
Colorado	0.59	0.44
South Dakota	0.50	−0.70
Washington	0.48	0.72
Rhode Island	0.44	0.41
Wisconsin	0.41	0.31
Oregon	0.40	0.81
Kansas	0.39	−0.27
Delaware	0.34	−0.14
Illinois	0.31	0.63
Ohio	0.28	0.80
Idaho	0.28	0.04
Alaska	0.26	—[c]
Indiana	0.25	−0.17
Pennsylvania	0.16	0.67
Missouri	0.10	−0.39
Hawaii	−0.12	—[c]
Virginia	−0.13	−0.65
California	−0.14	1.41
Oklahoma	−0.19	−0.21
New Jersey	−0.29	0.71
Michigan	−0.29	0.87
Maryland	−0.35	0.57
Utah	−0.40	0.32
Nevada	−0.47	−0.76

TABLE 2   (*Continued*)

	Civic culture Index[a]	Government performance Index[b]
West Virginia	−0.50	−0.44
Arizona	−0.51	−0.91
Kentucky	−0.63	−0.43
Arkansas	−0.67	−0.69
North Carolina	−0.75	−0.93
Florida	−0.78	−0.04
Texas	−0.78	−0.52
New Mexico	−0.78	−0.22
Tennessee	−0.87	−0.30
Georgia	−0.93	−1.00
Alabama	−1.09	−1.20
South Carolina	−1.15	−1.45
Louisiana	−1.35	−0.56
Mississippi	−1.53	−1.45

[a]The larger the civic culture score, the more civic the state.
[b]The larger the government performance score, the better the state government performs in terms of policy liberalism, policy innovation, and administrative effectiveness.
[c]Alaska and Hawaii are omitted because of missing data.

variable, the R-square value is only .22, indicating that 78 percent of the variance in the index is left unaccounted for by the six variables. What this suggests is that the civicness of a state, as measured by our index, is not closely associated with the demographics of a state.

How does our index correlate with some political and social indices of the United States? Among the most widely used indicators of the political character of the states is Daniel J. Elazar's trichotomy of subcultures: moralistic, individualistic, and traditionalistic.[3] The moralistic subculture emphasizes good government, which "is measured by the degree to which it promotes the public good and in terms of the honesty, selflessness, and commitment to the public welfare of those who govern."[4] By this description, the moralistic subculture would appear to have much in common with civic culture. In the individualistic subculture, government is concerned not so much with fostering a good society in the moral sense as with promoting and protecting private access to the marketplace.

Government action is usually limited in scope and restricted to the economic realm. The traditionalistic subculture "is rooted in an ambivalent attitude toward the marketplace coupled with a paternalistic and elitist conception of the commonwealth."[5] This subculture would appear to be the least civic of the three subcultures.

As a test of the relationship between Elazar's topology and our index of civic culture, we calculated the mean index score for the states in each of Elazar's categories.[6] The mean for the seventeen states that are considered moralistic is .4708, the mean for the fifteen states that are individualistic is .3049, and the mean for the sixteen states that are traditionalistic is −.8033.[7] This rough comparison provides solid evidence that our index of civic culture is linked to Elazar's subcultures. The moralistic and individualistic states are more civic than average, while the traditionalistic states are substantially less civic. It is interesting to note that the individualistic states are almost as civic as the moralistic states, suggesting that an individualist political subculture is compatible with a civic culture.

Another index of the U.S. states that is commonly used by social scientists is John L. Sullivan's continuum of diversity.[8] This index arrays the states by the diversity of their populations in terms of education, income, occupation, housing, ethnicity, and religion. According to the index, New York is the most diverse state, with a score of .556, and Mississippi is the least diverse, with a score of .230. When the diversity continuum is correlated with our civic culture index, the correlation coefficient is .56. The healthy positive relationship means that the more diverse states tend to be the most civic, thus raising the possibility that diversity and civic culture are causally linked. Perhaps the exposure to the wide range of lifestyles found in some states helps foster civic attitudes. If this is the case, and if civic attitudes promote effective government, then the possibility exists that in some situations, diversity may be an important causal antecedent to government performance. It is also possible, of course, that the most civic states are more diverse because they encourage a multiplicity of attitudes and lifestyles. And, the association between the diversity and civicness of the states may be spurious, the product of a third factor, such as economic development. Still, the correlation deserves further study, especially in light of Putnam's findings that it is civicness that influences economic development, not the reverse.

The third classification of the states that we compared to the civic culture continuum is the 1994 "livability" index, a popular ranking of the quality of life in the states.[9] First developed in 1991, this comprehensive index is calculated annually, using a myriad of factors, ranging from pupil-teacher ratios to highway fatalities involving alcohol. The correlation coefficient between this index and our civic culture continuum is an impressive .73. Apparently, the quality of life in a state is closely tied to its civic culture. It is also noteworthy that a few of the specific indicators used to build the livability index bear resemblance to the measures used by Putnam to construct his index of effective democracy. Although it would be unwarranted to make too much of the similarities between Putnam's measures and the items in the livability index, the occasional parallels raise the possibility that the performance of democratic government in the American states is in part the product of civic culture. We now turn to investigating this potential link more directly.

Government Performance and Civic Culture in the American States

Putnam uses dozens of specific indicators to construct his index of government performance. Almost every one of the indicators can easily be placed into one of the following three categories: policy liberalism, policy innovation, and administrative effectiveness. Policy liberalism refers to the extent to which societies have adopted the types of policies generally associated with modern liberalism, such as extensive welfare systems, progressive tax structures, and consumer protection standards. Putnam inserts a number of liberal measures in his index, including the number of publicly supported day-care centers and family-health clinics in each Italian region. Policy innovation concerns the creative ability of societies to fashion policies to meet pressing needs. Among the innovation indicators used by Putnam is a legislative innovation score based on how quickly the regions adopted twelve different types of creative legislation, ranging from pollution-control statutes to hotel classification standards. Administrative effectiveness is defined as the extent to which governments respond to citizen needs. The administrative effectiveness measures employed by Putnam include a ranking of how quickly and competently the regional governments acted to meet specific citizen's requests.

Following Putnam's lead, we constructed a government performance index for the American states based on indicators of policy liberalism, policy innovation, and administrative effectiveness. For policy liberalism, we relied on a ranking of the states that combines eight policy measures "that reflect the usual ideological divisions between liberals and conservatives."[10] Our measure of innovation is from a comprehensive index of state policy creativity based on more than sixty types of policies.[11] The administrative effectiveness scores were figured by averaging two indices, the Barrileaux, Feiock, and Crew index of the quality of state administra-tions,[12] and the Bowman and Kearney index of the capacity of state government legislatures and governors to make effective and efficient decisions.[13] To produce a comprehensive index of government perfor-mance, we first made certain that the three indices—policy liberalism, policy innovation, and administrative effectiveness—were in standardized form; then we simply calculated the mean score for each state across the indices. The results are shown in column 2 of Table 2, with positive scores associated with states that scored better on the performance index and negative scores with states that scored worse.

The relationship between the civic culture and the government performance indices is displayed in Figure 1. The states form an obvious upward sloping pattern, meaning that the more civic a state is, the more likely it is to have a liberal, innovative, and effective government. To be sure, there are plenty of exceptions. Some of the states that are highly civic have government performance scores that are well below average, and a few of the states that have only average civic values rank quite high on the performance index. Still, the link between culture and performance is indisputable. In formal statistical terms, the correlation coefficient be-

FIGURE 1   Civil Culture and Government Performance

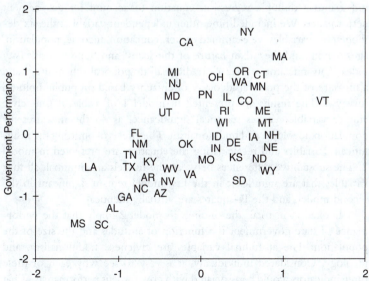

tween culture and performance is .59, and the slope of the best-fitting line is .60, indicating that a one standard-deviation change in the culture index is associated with a six-tenths of a standard-deviation increase in government performance.

Although the strength of the relationship between civic culture and government performance in the states is pronounced, it is not as robust as the correlation of .92 that Putnam reports between culture and performance in the Italian regions.[14] One reason why the American relationship is weaker may be that the range of civic cultures in Italy is much greater than in the United States. Although both Italy and the American states have very civic areas, descriptions of southern Italy suggest that even the least civic American states are far more civic than this region.[15] With the variance in the American index more restricted than in the Italian case, it may be difficult to achieve correlations as strong as those reported by Putnam. Along the same lines, it is possible that Putnam's index of government performance also varies more than our measure, raising the likelihood that his correlations would be stronger.

As interesting as it is to contrast Putnam's findings with our own, the value of civic culture as a concept for understanding government performance in the American states will come not from comparisons with Italy, but from testing the culture index against other explanations of government performance. To initiate this inquiry, we entered our culture index into a multiple regression equation to account for government performance. We included nine other independent variables: the six demographic variables we examined earlier (education, income, population, age, region, and the urban nature of the states) and Sullivan's diversity index,[16] an indicator of Elazar's traditionalistic political subculture,[17] and a measure of the political ideology of citizenry based on public opinion surveys.[18] The results are presented in model 1 of Table 3. Our civic culture variable reaches statistical significance, as do the measures for population, ideology, and traditionalism. The effects of omitting the insignificant variables and recalculating the equation are presented in model 2. The substantive differences between the models are minimal; all four variables that are significant in the first model remain significant in the second model, and the R-squares are virtually identical.

Looked at in total, the findings in model 2 imply that the performance of state government is a function of attitudes and the size of the population. The attitudinal variables are civicness, traditionalism, and ideology. Considered individually, it is easy to see why each of these three indicators would be associated with government performance. What

TABLE 3   Determinants of Government Performance

Independent variables	Model 1		Model 2	
Civic culture	0.37	(2.75)[e]	0.36	(3.08)
Education[a]	—	(0.03)	—	—
Income	−0.00	(−1.15)	—	—
Population	0.73	(4.39)	0.78	(5.71)
Age	−0.03	(−0.84)	—	—
Region	0.11	(0.54)	—	—
Urban/rural	0.01	(1.06)	—	—
Diversity[b]	0.70	(0.34)	—	—
Traditionalism[c]	−1.10	(−1.88)	−1.33	(−3.62)
Ideology[d]	0.02	(2.16)	0.02	(2.18)
R-square		.79		.78
N		48[f]		48

[a]Income inequality was calculated as follows. One measure was created by calculating the percentage of households in each state with incomes above the poverty level and below $75,000. this gives the percentage of households with "mid-level" incomes. A second measure was created by taking the absolute value of the percent of households below the poverty level from the percent earning above $75,000. This gives the inequality between the ends of the income scale. For the final calculation of the variable, these two measures were transformed into z-scores, summed, and averaged. The income data come from the U.S. Government Printing Office, *Digest of Education Statistics* (Washington, D.C.: GPO, 1993), p. 28.
[b]Sullivan's index of diversity for the states.
[c]Morgan and Watson's index of traditionalism for the states.
[d]Erikson, Wright, and McIver's index of ideology for the states.
[e]The values in parentheses are t-scores.
[f]Alaska and Hawaii are omitted because of missing data.

is more interesting is that all of the indices reach statistical significance in the same model. This suggests strongly that they are not mirror images of each other. A closer look at these variables provides some insight into how they might differ. Consider, for instance, the civic culture and ideology measures for the states. The natural expectation would be for states with civic populations to be liberal politically, favoring government initiatives to help the needy and ensure certain standards of equality.

Upon reflection, however, it seems possible for a civic state to be politically conservative. Like all civic people, individuals in these states would be genuinely concerned with promoting the public good, but they would often resist using government for this purpose. These individuals might prefer to build a better society through personal charity and through the organization of volunteer civic groups. As another example, consider civic culture and traditionalism. Traditionalism, as defined by Elazar[19] and Morgan and Watson,[20] has much in common with the values of Christian fundamentalism. To some people, a traditionalism of this type looks suspiciously uncivic. Many fundamentalists, after all, are not particularly tolerant of diverse values and lifestyles. It is also true, however, that fundamentalists are often very compassionate toward those in need, organizing community-service groups and giving generously of their time and money. Thus, it is possible that some very traditionalistic states might rank relatively high on the civic index. These two examples serve to show why the concepts of civic culture, traditionalism, and ideology are related but not identical.

What is of special interest is the significance of the civic culture index. Even pitted against a variety of theoretically relevant explanatory variables, the index remains a powerful predictor of government performance. The coefficient in model 2 indicates that even after controlling for population, traditionalism, and ideology, a one standard-deviation change in the civic index corresponds to a three-tenths of a standard-deviation change in the performance index. This is solid evidence that the strong link between civicness and government performance that Putnam found in the Italian regions is present in the American states, too. If there is such a link, it would be valuable to understand more fully how the components of civic culture influence the components of governmental performance. It is possible, for instance, that civic culture is tightly linked with some dimensions of government performance and not others.

We can make some initial observations in this area with our data. The index of civic culture is correlated with the policy liberalism index at .59, the policy innovation index at .45, and the administrative effectiveness index at .39. All of these relationships are substantial, although the link with policy liberalism is somewhat more powerful. This suggests that civicness may have more to do with encouraging liberal policies than with promoting policy innovation or administrative effectiveness. We can also inspect how the four components of civicness relate to the index of government performance. The results show that the performance index is correlated with the civic engagement index at .59, the political equality index at .57, the solidarity, trust, and tolerance index at .63, and the social structures index at .34. Again, all the relationships are substantial, but the correlation with the social structures index is obviously the weakest. Perhaps social structures of cooperation are less important than the other components of civic culture in influencing government performance.

Conclusion

If civic culture and government performance are coupled in such diverse settings as the United States' states and the Italian regions, the chances are good that the link exists in many other local and regional milieus. Some obvious places to check would be the other major federal democracies, such as Australia, Canada, Germany, and Switzerland. In the United States, municipalities offer another locale for study. The variance in the civic cultures and government performance may be greater across cities than states, providing a fruitful laboratory for investigating the connection between culture and performance. John Kincaid[21] and Joel Lieske[22] have already established that there is a link between political culture and the quality of life in U.S. metropolitan areas, so it seems reasonable that the civic culture of urban areas might influence governmental performance.

Other tasks also await scholarly attention. There is the vexing problem of trying to untangle the causal relationship between civic culture and government performance. Putnam was blessed with an unusual quasi-experimental situation; Italy's regional governments were empowered in the 1970s and endowed with similar resources by the central government. Thus, he could be relatively certain that the quality of the new governments was in part the product of civicness, not the other way around. Researchers looking at other subnational arenas will not be so fortunate. In the United States, for example, the states came into existence at different times and without much in the way of national government resources. Another causal conundrum is between civicness and economic development. Putnam was able to piece together enough indicators of civicness and development for nineteenth-century Italy to conclude that civicness fostered development and that development had little impact on government performance after controlling for civicness. With some effort, it should be possible to replicate his analysis in the United States. Certainly there are adequate indicators of economic development in the states that date back to at least the mid-1800s. Government performance will be more difficult to measure, but some indicators already exist, such as Robert Savage's state-by-state assessment of policy innovation in the nineteenth-century.[23]

There is more work to be done in exploring the link between civic culture and government performance in the American states. Our research addresses the most obvious first question: Is there a link between civic culture and government performance in the states? Our findings provide evidence that such a link exists; by our assessment, civic states do tend to have better governments in terms of the measures of policy liberalism, policy innovation, and effectiveness used here.

Notes

1.   Gabriel A. Almond and Sidney Verba, *The Civic Culture: Political Attitudes and Democracy in Five Nations* (Princeton, N.J.: Princeton University Press, 1963).

2.   Robert D. Putnam, *Making Democracy Work* (Princeton, N.J.: Princeton University Press, 1993).

3.   Daniel J. Elazar, *The American Mosaic* (Boulder, Colo.: Westview Press, 1994).

4.   Ibid., p. 232.

5.   Ibid., p. 235.

6.   We used the political culture scores from Charles A. Johnson, "Political Culture in the American States: Elazar's Formulation Examined," *American Journal of Political Science*, 20 (August 1976):491–509.

7.   Elazar does not categorize Alaska and Hawaii.

8.   John L. Sullivan, "Political Correlates of Social, Economic, and Religious Diversity in the American States," *Journal of Politics*, 35 (February 1973):70–94.

9.   Kathleen O'Leary Morgan, Scott Morgan, and Neal Quinto, eds., *State Rankings 1994: A Statistical View of the 50 United States* (Lawrence, Kan.: Morgan Quinto Corporation, 1994).

10.   Robert S. Erikson, Gerald C. Wright, and John P. McIver, *Statehouse Democracy: Public Opinion and Policy in the American States* (Cambridge, Mass.: Cambridge University Press, 1993), p. 75.

11.   Robert L. Savage, "Policy Innovation as a Trait of American States," *Journal of Politics*, 40 (February 1978):212–224.

12.   Charles Barrileaux, Richard Feiock, and Robert E. Crew Jr., "Measuring and Comparing American States' Administrative Characteristics," *State and Local Government Review*, 24 (Winter 1992):12–18.

13.   Ann O'M. Bowman and Richard C. Kearney, "Dimensions of State Government Capability," *Western Political Quarterly*, 41 (June 1988):341–362.

14.   Putnam, *Making Democracy Work*, p. 98.

15.   Edward C. Banfield, *The Moral Basis of a Backward Society* (Glencoe, Ill.: The Free Press, 1958); Putnam, *Making Democracy Work*.

16.   Sullivan, "Political Correlates of Social, Economic, and Religious Diversity in the American States."

17.   David R. Morgan and Sheilah Watson, "Political Culture, Political System Characteristics, and Public Policies among the American States," *Publius: The Journal of Federalism*, 21 (Spring 1991):31–48.

18.   Erikson, Wright, and McIver, *Statehouse Democracy*.

19.   Elazar, *The American Mosaic*.

20.   Morgan and Watson, "Political Culture, Political System Characteristics, and Public Policies among the American States."

21.   John Kincaid, "Political Culture and the Quality of Urban Life," *Publius: The Journal of Federalism*, 10 (Spring 1980):89–110.

22.   Joel Lieske, "The Correlates of Life Quality in U.S. Metropolitan Areas," *Publius: The Journal of Federalism*, 20 (Winter 1990):43–54.

23.   Savage, "Policy Innovation as a Trait of American States."

9 Mapping the Genome of American Political Subcultures

DAVID Y. MILLER

DAVID C. BARKER

CHRISTOPHER J. CARMAN

MANY STUDENTS OF AMERICAN FEDERALISM have recognized that differences in political culture—the widely shared values, social norms, and institutions that structure and legitimate relationships within a political community—may have profound influence over state politics, policymaking, and representation.[1] However, there has been a paucity of research examining the basic DNA of American political subcultures as expressed in the shared political values of particular communities. We believe it is time to begin mapping this genome. Accordingly, this article proposes a methodology for adequately observing shared political values and provides a preliminary test of this approach with a small pilot study. We hope to provide some tentative steps toward the collective development of a comprehensive, falsifiable theory of American political culture.

Understanding Political Culture

Although culture includes ideational, social, institutional, and technological elements,[2] we consider the ideational element to be a good place to start any reconsideration of culture from the ground up. As such, we are interested in examining shared political values within a community. By "values," we refer to abstract, nonfalsifiable "conceptions of the desirable . . . [rather than] just something to be desired."[3] Indeed, a large body of research has accumulated to suggest that such core visions of "right and wrong" motivate and guide political judgments to a much greater extent than do calculations of "what's in it for me."[4] Furthermore, our focus is on the explicitly political, which we define here as power relationships (1) between citizens and their government and (2) among citizens with regard to public matters. Finally, as students of culture, we are not interested in studying political value priorities for their own sake. Rather, our interest lies in understanding shared value priorities—those "held in common by a particular community."

Perhaps the most notable theoretical contribution to the literature on American political subcultures was made by Daniel J. Elazar.[5] Relying upon historical records of immigration/migration patterns of religious and ethnic groups in the settlement of the American colonies, Elazar theorized that three distinct political subcultures are visible in America— individualistic, moralistic, and traditionalistic. In brief, Elazar argued that the states originally colonized by the Puritans and their progeny developed a moralistic political culture that reflected a commonwealth, where (1) legislation is based on communitarian principles of "good" government, (2) citizenship demands participation, and (3) bureaucracy is isolated from political influence. By contrast, the states originally colonized by those seeking economic opportunity developed an individualistic political culture that approximated a market, where (1) legislation is passed only when the public demands it, (2) politics is seen as a specialized business—not necessarily for all to participate in, and (3) bureaucracy is responsive to elected officials, not independent. Finally, the unique history of the South engendered a traditionalistic political culture, where (1) government activism may take place in order to protect existing power structures, (2) mass democratic participation is often discouraged, and (3) bureaucracies hold very little independent power.

Elazar's influence has been widespread. Indeed, at least one hundred published studies have used Elazar's typology to analyze various political phenomena.[6] Peter Nardulli has even stated that no "self-respecting" analysis concerned with state politics "can ignore" political subcultures.[7] However, Elazar's critics abound. Perhaps the strongest criticism of Elazar has been that the regional cultural distinctions, as originally derived, were not based on any rigorous statistical procedures or empirical data. Indeed, four decades after its introduction, Elazar's typology remains mostly an impressionistic detailing of Elazar's ideas. Although, as noted above, many researchers have subjected the typology to empirical examination (some with considerable success), these works have usually been concerned with whether Elazar's formulation can be applied—observed in the institutions and policy outputs of states/regions—rather than with whether the typology has any empirical foundation in the first place. And although a number of studies have inferred the presence of culture from patterns of specific policy preferences, these efforts have produced evidence that is indirect at best; policy preferences represent the consequences of shared political values—not values themselves. The presence of particular patterns of policy preferences across communities may be consistent with cultural theory; it is impossible to rule out alternate hypotheses without measuring values directly—and almost no extant work on U.S. political subcultures has sought to do this. The two exceptions we were able to identify represent good initial forays into this much-needed exercise.[8] However, these analyses were restricted to data from a single state, thus severely limiting their applicability and external validity. Hence, given that so little scholarship has attempted to directly observe whether the shared value priorities of citizens living within particular geographical communities approximate Elazar's propositions, the large body of work that has been devoted to applying cultural theory to American federalism rests upon an uncertain foundation.

These concerns are all the more evident given dramatic changes in American society in social capital, media/communication, transport, immigration, and religion. Even if the Elazarian framework accurately captured the shared values of particular geographical communities in the United States a generation ago, would it still hold water today, in an America that is increasingly private, mobile, Hispanic, Asian, Catholic, fundamentalist Protestant, racially/ethnically integrated, remote-control dependent, and well traveled along the "information superhighway"? Have new subcultures emerged? Does geography still matter? And if so, is it still related to region? Or has the "red/blue" division between metropolitan America and pastoral America found within most geographic regions obfuscated once salient differences across such regions?

Proposed Research Design and Measurement Strategy

Measuring the ideational element of culture requires capturing individual values as well as the degree to which they are shared. Furthermore, measuring Elazarian subcultures requires an assessment of how those shared values vary according to geographic stratum. Accordingly, the dependent variables involved in any microfoundational assessment of Elazar's thesis must be the value frameworks or priorities of individual citizens. The independent variable of primary interest, then, is the geographical location of one's residence or birth, according to the cultural classifications established by Elazar. We expect citizens born and raised in geographical locations identified as moralistic by Elazar to reveal different value orientations from citizens born and raised in individualistic or traditionalistic geographic locales, and so on.

We would expect citizens raised in communities with moralistic cultures (most New England and northern states, as well as most of the West Coast) to reveal greater communitarianism and populism than citizens who were socialized in individualistic or traditionalistic states.[9] More specifically, such citizens should show a greater tendency to view government (especially local government) as an agent of the public good, to see politics as "clean," and to view bureaucracy as positive. Furthermore, we expect citizens who have been socialized in individualistic states (most mid–Atlantic and Midwestern states and the Southwest) to express more ambivalence toward local government and to view politics as "dirty" and bureaucracy with some disdain. Finally, citizens in traditionalistic states (the traditional South) should view all levels of government and bureaucracy with the most contempt, except when they protect entrenched power structures. Finally, we would expect there to exist a deeper cultural commitment among citizens of moralistic states than among citizens of the other cultures.

Measuring Shared Values

Measuring our dependent variable (individual value orientations) must necessarily be accomplished via a survey instrument, and measuring our independent variable (cultural identity according to geography) requires careful sampling stratification according to various geographic regions and extant cultural theories, as put forward not only by Elazar but by the other cultural mappers as well.

In developing a strategy for measuring the values central to Elazar's political subculture thesis, we begin by referencing cognitive schema theory. Although the concept of a cognitive schema has fallen out of fashion in some circles of political psychology,[10] mainly due to overuse and overzealousness on the part of some early schema theorists, we believe the concept still holds some instructive value for our purposes. Schemata are "tacit theories people hold about the world, enabling them to make sense of an otherwise bewildering array of information."[11] To be sure, in an everchanging world, we would be ineffective in dealing with our environments if we had to begin from scratch on encountering every stimulus. Instead, we tend to rely on cognitive shortcuts, or heuristics, drawn from information previously organized in schemata. This process enables us to process stimuli efficiently.[12]

There are some important attributes of schemata that may inform measurement. One attribute is the concept of balance—combining opposites. People prefer to process stimuli in simple, dichotomous ways. To quote Henry Brady and Paul Sniderman, the more people are able to choose sides, "the more they appreciate the differences between the two sides. What counts, then, is not how people feel toward groups, one by one; rather it is how they feel toward pairs of opposing groups."[13] Indeed, such dichotomous thinking is a heuristic device in itself.

Furthermore, people may not be fully aware of the schemata they use. As David Elkins and Richard Simeon have articulated, "Individuals manifest or express their political culture without generally being aware of it. Political culture consists largely of unconscious assumptions, so taken for granted that . . . members of a culture seldom have occasion to question them."[14] In addition, as Chris Argyris has argued, when considering a particular issue, individuals tend to apply, without even necessarily knowing why, theories about the world that differ markedly from those espoused.[15]

Therefore, given that political culture considerations are deeply imbedded into a person's cognitive framework and may necessarily involve balancing one value against another, developing a way to quantify political culture is a daunting task. Moreover, concerns regarding social desirability complicate this undertaking even further. A measurement technique that may prove quite useful for our purposes is the semantic differential.[16] The semantic differential consists of a series of bipolar adjective scales (word pairs), each of which is conventionally separated into seven categories. The attitude object is placed at the top of the page and respondents are asked to rate this object by checking a category on each of the bipolar scales (e.g., active–passive). Thus, not only is this technique built upon the idea of balance; it also provides a relatively unobtrusive measure of respondent reactions to different concepts. Because respondents are asked to make word associations, rather than overtly indicate the degree to which they agree or disagree with particular statements (such as with Likert scales), the probability of obtaining answers suffering from social desirability bias or other Hawthorne effects becomes reduced with the semantic differential.[17]

In the following section, we describe a pilot study in which we use the logic of the semantic differential in an attempt to measure some aspects of the Elazarian subcultures. We want to stress that this analysis is exploratory and is meant merely to test the efficacy of our proposed methodology.

A Reduced-Form Pilot Study

As an initial foray into analyzing Elazar's theory of political subcultures, student samples were drawn from universities located in states representative of each of Elazar's subcultures. Maine was chosen to represent the moralistic culture, Pennsylvania was selected to represent the individualistic culture, and Mississippi was selected to represent the traditionalist culture. Between 1 January and 1 April 2000, student samples were drawn from political science classes at three similar state universities: Mississippi State University, the University of Southern Maine, and the University of Pittsburgh. Only those surveys where the respondent had been born in the state, had lived in that state for 90 percent of his or her life, and had been born to parents of that state were selected for further analysis. This decision rule left us with viable sample sizes of 37, 42, and 43 students from Maine, Mississippi, and Pennsylvania, respectively. One unforeseen and unexpected misfortune was associated with the sample drawn from the University of Pittsburgh. These students tend to originate from the western part of the state, which Elazar suggested has some secondary elements of the traditionalistic culture within the dominant individualistic environment. This lack of an ideal Pennsylvania sample could potentially mute differences in value orientations between Pennsylvania respondents and Mississippi respondents. As such, particularly given the size of these samples, if statistically significant differences between these two samples do not emerge, we should not necessarily take that as evidence refuting Elazar's hypothesis. Rather, differences between groups of respondents would have only gained statistical significance after swimming upstream against a strong current.

This pilot study focused on respondents' perceptions of three concepts: (1) local government, (2) state government, and (3) the bureaucracy. We chose to concentrate on orientations toward government because, as our definition provided, political culture necessarily pertains to citizens' shared values regarding the proper nature of the relationship between citizens and their government.[18] However, we chose not to measure attitudes toward the federal government because such attitudes are so closely related to left-right ideology, and we considered it of utmost importance to maintain the distinction between measures of traditional liberalism—conservatism and Elazar's conceptualization. Of course, many people might reflexively conceptualize "the bureaucracy" in federal terms. However, although traditional liberalism may envision an active humanitarian role for government, it is formally agnostic with regard to the value and efficacy of bureaucracies. Furthermore, practically speaking, although it may be true that some liberals may look to the bureaucracy as the instrument that administers programs designed to promote the "general welfare," many others may simply see it as a model of inefficiency, antipathy to which does not have an ideological component. Even beyond considerations of distinguishing Elazar's concepts from liberalism–conservatism, we chose to focus particularly on evaluations of state and local governments because the particular shared cultures that we are attempting to measure are hypothesized to reside within particular states and local communities and the institutions that serve them.

The generation of appropriate semantic word pairs started with identifying key ideas that Elazar put forward when distinguishing the three subcultures (see our earlier summary of these).[19] Rather than try to invent appropriate word pairs to represent these perspectives from scratch, we instead searched the lists of semantic word pairs that had been successfully employed for various purposes by C. E. Osgood, his colleagues, and other social psychologists. The following pairs emerged from that review: privilege–right, dirty–clean, disreputable–reputable, free–constrained, sick–healthy, harmonious–dissonant, wise–foolish, refreshed–weary, bad–good, professional–amateur, they–we, duty–voluntary, competitive–cooperative, active–passive, broad–narrow, important–unimportant, weak–strong, closed–open, near–far, and private–public. Based on our reading of Elazar, in which the moralistic culture is portrayed as populist, participatory, and communitarian, we expected citizens from Maine to be the most likely to associate the following words with our three concepts: right, clean, reputable, healthy, harmonious, wise, refreshed, good, professional (with regard to the bureaucracy; unprofessional with regard to state and local government), we, duty, cooperative, active, broad, important, strong, open, near, free, and public. We expected Mississippians to be least likely to choose any of these words to describe the concepts. Finally, we expected the Pennsylvanians to mirror some of the choices of Mainers, but to mirror Mississippians on others. Specifically, we expected them to choose the words right, dirty, disreputable, harmonious, professional, they, voluntary, cooperative, passive, narrow, weak, closed, far, constrained, and private. We also expected more ambivalence overall from the Pennsylvania sample.

In the process of reviewing semantic word pairs, several word pairs surfaced that appeared to cut across the themes identified above. They were added to our list and include the following: groups–individuals, sociable–unsociable, interesting–boring, sensitive–insensitive, awkward–graceful, egotistical–altruistic, simple–complex, and defensive–aggressive. We do not expect patterns to emerge between the different samples with regard to these word pairs, but we have included them for exploratory purposes, to see whether evidence emerges of cultural patterns that are not necessarily predicted by the Elazarian perspective. With these additions, the total list included twenty-eight semantic word pairs that capture the fundamentals of Elazar's three political subcultures. The survey instrument consisted of each of the three concepts, followed by the twenty-eight semantic word pairs. Indeed, one of the purposes of this pilot is to pare down this list to a more manageable set for further analysis.

Figure 1 is an example of what survey respondents saw as they used the semantic differential to consider each concept in light of the word pairs (though, to conserve space, we have only listed five of the word pairs here).

The survey instrument first asks respondents to choose between the adjectives "active" and passive when considering their local government. Scores from 1 through 3 indicate the respondent considers "active" a better descriptor of local government than "passive." A score of 4 indicates neutrality. The instrument then repeats this procedure for the next word pair—"awkward–graceful." After all the word pairs have been considered, the process begins again with the next concept—state government. In the presentation of our results, we have collapsed the data for ease of presentation, aggregating responses of 1 through 3 as representing one pole and 5 through 7 as representing the second pole. To further encourage respondents to "go with their gut" (i.e., their imbedded "theories in use"), we requested that respondents abstain from dwelling or deliberating over their responses, imploring them to work at a fairly high speed and offer their immediate, emotional reaction.

FIGURE 1   Concept of Local Government

ACTIVE	1	2	3	4	5	6	7	PASSIVE
AWKWARD	1	2	3	4	5	6	7	GRACEFUL
BAD	1	2	3	4	5	6	7	GOOD
BORING	1	2	3	4	5	6	7	INTERESTING
BROAD	1	2	3	4	5	6	7	NARROW

Results

Each of the three tables reveals the word pairs where preferences could be statistically differentiated by state. They reveal not only the difference in preferences according to state of birth but also the overall percentage of respondents within each state who agreed that a particular descriptor accurately characterized local government (table 1), state government (table 2), or the bureaucracy (table 3).

As table 1 shows, perceptions of the nature and role of local government are highly differentiated between citizens in the three states. The most striking differences are between the Maine respondents and respondents from the other two states, corroborating early work of Russell Hanson, who showed that the moralistic culture tends to be more deeply imbedded within particular geographic strata than the other two cultures.[20]

Specifically, Mainers' characterization of local government tends to be quite positive. Even though respondents from the other two states sometimes express positive affect toward local government, the frequency of a particular feeling is considerably higher among respondents from Maine. For example, most respondents from Mississippi agree local government is "clean" rather than "dirty," but almost 20 percent more Mainers than Mississippians think that way. Similarly, local government is seen as "strong" by more Mainers than Pennsylvanians. This suggests government is considered to function for the benefit of all, for securing common good. Further, characterizing local government as "interesting," "reputable," and "free" suggests these respondents value the participatory nature of local decision making. All these characterizations resemble remarkably closely Elazar's description of a moralistic political culture.

The cases of Mississippi and Pennsylvania are not quite as clear. First, Pennsylvania respondents rarely agreed upon anything. Agreement by more than 50 percent of Pennsylvania respondents regarding the word pairs was hard to find. Thus, the underlying feeling toward local government is difficult to pin down. However, Pennsylvanians are much more likely to see local government as "passive," "uninteresting," less "reputable," and "dirty," all characteristics of Elazar's individualistic subculture. That said, Pennsylvania respondents also recognize that local government is an important institution. This lack of a consistent pattern of attitudes toward local government suggests a pragmatic attitude—government is there to get done what citizens demand but is not inherently "good" or a commonweal institution. In contrast to the Mainers, and as theorized by Elazar, the Pennsylvanians in our sample did not reveal a penchant for political participation and community activism. In general, this case

TABLE 1   Regional differences in perceptions of local government (significant differences in word pairs)

Word pair	F Sig.	Mississippi	Pennsylvania	Maine
Active–Passive*[c]	0.027	Passive (5%)	Passive (22%)	Passive (8%)
Boring–Interesting*[a,c]	0.008	Interesting (62%)	Interesting (32%)	Interesting (65%)
Clean–Dirty*[b,c]	0.000	Dirty (24%)	Dirty (39%)	Dirty (5%)
Open–Closed*[b,c]	0.007	Closed (22%)	Closed (22%)	Closed (8%)
Defensive–Aggressive*[b]	0.032	Defensive (50%)	Defensive (27%)	Defensive (11%)
Disreputable–Reputable***[b,c]	0.005	Reputable (48%)	Reputable (44%)	Reputable (75%)
Free–Constrained*[b,c]	0.011	Free (45%)	Free (46%)	Free (65%)
Public–Private*[b]	0.025	Private (26%)	Private (20%)	Private (5%)
Right–Privilege*[b]	0.040	Right (48%)	Right (58%)	Right (73%)
Refreshed–Weary**[c]	0.004	Weary (24%)	Weary (34%)	Weary (6%)
Sensitive–Insensitive**[c]	0.011	Sensitive (60%)	Sensitive (44%)	Sensitive (70%)
Healthy–Sick*[b,c]	0.002	Healthy (57%)	Healthy (46%)	Healthy (78%)
Strong–Weak***[c]	0.001	Strong (43%)	Strong (51%)	Strong (73%)

Bonferroni: *sig. 0.05; **sig. 0.01.

[a]Difference between Mississippi and Pennsylvania.
[b]Difference between Mississippi and Maine.
[c]Difference between Maine and Pennsylvania.

also corresponds to Elazar's typology rather well, since the responses are suggestive of an ambivalent and pragmatic attitude toward the relationship between government and citizens.

Mississippi generated the hardest data to interpret. On one hand, Mississippi shares with Maine respondents a hesitancy to see local government as "passive" and a strong sense that local government is "interesting." These views differ sharply from those of the Pennsylvanians, who are four times more likely to use the adjective "passive" and one-half as likely to use the term "interesting." However, Mississippians differ from their Maine counterparts in a manner suggested by Elazar. Mississippi respondents are five times more likely to see local government as "private," almost three times more likely to see it as "closed," and only half as likely to see it as a "right." This suggests that government is the domain of others, presumably the elites, who are more actively engaged in the acts of governing.

Table 2 reveals that moving up one governmental level does little to alter the pattern of responses across states. Just as we observed in the orientations toward local government, aspects of the moralistic culture can be observed in the general positivity Mainers expressed toward state government, as compared with those in Mississippi or Pennsylvania. By contrast, responses by those living in Mississippi and Pennsylvania are difficult to differentiate. Thus, although these data provide clear support for the persistent presence of an Elazarian moralistic culture in Maine that is clearly different from what can be observed in the other two regions represented in this pilot study, we are left without clear evidence differentiating an individualistic culture from a traditionalistic one.

As table 3 shows, with regard to beliefs about the bureaucracy, the differences between the moralistic culture and the other two continue to hold. Although there are not as many statistically significant word pairs as was observed for state and local government, the differences shown here are in some cases much more dramatic. Furthermore, the significant differences are primarily between citizens in Maine and those in Mississippi, with Mississippi respondents tending to report much less warmth toward the bureaucracy than Maine respondents. Such differences comport well with the characterizations of the moralistic and traditionalistic cultures offered by Elazar.

Meanwhile, the attitudes of Pennsylvanians tend to fall neatly in between those of Mainers and Mississippians, displaying orientations that are not easily predictable and are not statistically different from those observed in either Maine or Mississippi. Such ambivalence is characteristic

TABLE 2 Regional differences in perceptions of state government (significant differences in word pairs)

Word pair	F Sig.	Mississippi	Pennsylvania	Maine
Clean-Dirty**[b]	0.006	Clean (40%)	Clean (40%)	Clean (72%)
Open-Closed*[b],**[c]	0.001	Open (60%)	Open (57%)	Open (86%)
Cooperative-Competitive*[c]	0.019	Competitive (60%)	Competitive (62%)	Cooperative (54%)
Reputable-Disreputable***[a],*[b]	0.002	Reputable (52%)	Reputable (48%)	Reputable (69%)
Free-Constrained**[b],*[c]	0.004	Free (45%)	Free (45%)	Free (84%)
Near-Far*[a]	0.045	Near (64%)	Near (43%)	Near (44%)
Public-Private*[b],*[c]	0.007	Private (24%)	Private (26%)	Private (5%)
Sociable-Unsociable*[a],**[b]	0.001	Sociable (71%)	Sociable (45%)	Sociable (73%)
Strong-Weak*[b],*[c]	0.006	Strong (62%)	Strong (62%)	Strong (84%)
Wise-Foolish*[b],*[c]	0.010	Wise (43%)	Wise (52%)	Wise (84%)

Bonferroni: *sig. 0.05; **sig. 0.01.

[a]Difference between Mississippi and Pennsylvania.
[b]Difference between Mississippi and Maine.
[c]Difference between Maine and Pennsylvania.

TABLE 3   Regional differences in perceptions of the bureaucracy (significant differences in word pairs)

Word pair	F Sig.	Mississippi	Pennsylvania	Maine
Good–Bad*a,*b	0.002	Bad (60%)	Good (42%)	Good (57%)
Clean–Dirty*b	0.016	Dirty (62%)	Dirty (42%)	Clean (56%)
Open–Closed*b	0.032	Closed (52%)	Closed (46%)	Closed (25%)
Reputable–Disreputable**b	0.013	Disreputable (57%)	Disreputable (26%)	Disreputable (20%)
Groups–Individuals*a,*c	0.002	Groups (57%)	Groups (86%)	Groups (53%)
Healthy–Sick**b	0.004	Healthy (22%)	Healthy (36%)	Healthy (54%)
Strong–Weak*b	0.021	Weak (43%)	Weak (23%)	Weak (8%)
Wise–Foolish*b	0.016	Wise (31%)	Wise (51%)	Wise (64%)

Bonferroni: *sig. 0.05; **sig. 0.01.
aDifference between Mississippi and Pennsylvania.
bDifference between Mississippi and Maine.
cDifference between Maine and Pennsylvania.

of Elazar's individualistic culture, as is the notion of a bureaucracy beholden to "groups."

Conclusion

In summary, the attitudes expressed by respondents from Maine about different levels of government as well as about bureaucracy were overwhelmingly positive and reflected the value of participation, responsiveness, and common good. In contrast, although respondents from Mississippi did not display overt hostility toward local and state government, they were far less uniform in their praise. More impressive, Mississippians' attitudes about bureaucracy followed Elazar's description almost perfectly: these respondents were much more likely to see the bureaucracy as dirty, unresponsive, and inefficient. With regard to Pennsylvania, the citizen responses were not inconsistent with the individualistic cultural perspective, but clear conclusions cannot be drawn either. Indeed, Pennsylvanians tended to express ambivalence, neutrality, and pragmatism toward government and bureaucracy, much in line with the individualistic culture, but the differences between Pennsylvanian attitudes and Mississippian ones were rarely statistically significant.

This pilot study has several shortcomings. First, the lack of more dramatic differences between Mississippi and Pennsylvania respondents may reflect the fact that the sample was drawn from a region in Pennsylvania that has been purported to contain a substantial secondary element of traditionalism in addition to the dominant individualistic culture. Future efforts should draw samples from the eastern side of the state. Second, the survey respondents were not chosen using random probability sampling techniques. Specifically, the attitudes of university students are probably not fully representative of broader attitudes in Maine, Pennsylvania, and Mississippi. However, it is worth reiterating that the nature of higher education, which emphasizes critical thinking and challenging entrenched assumptions, likely serves to moderate some of the value orientations that students have acquired from their communities prior to enrolling in college. Furthermore, the diversity inherent in most university contexts, as well as the age of most university students, would likely serve to further weaken the local cultural ties to which residents of particular states may feel bound. As such, probability sampling procedures would likely serve to magnify the degree to which values are shared among citizens of particular regions, because more citizens would be sampled who have had more time to "settle in their ways" and who have not been exposed to the diversity of a university setting. Third, the sample size is small. Obviously, we would have been able to make more robust conclusions had the number of surveys been larger.

Future examinations should do a number of things. First, a large, national sample is needed. Second, a broader range of concepts needs to be analyzed, to capture the range of political values purported to be shared in particular communities (e.g., libertarianism, humanitarianism, egalitarianism, individualism, moral traditionalism, and so on). Third, theories pertaining to geographic region do not represent the only prominent model regarding the role of subcultures in contemporary American politics. Indeed, many have argued, even in the face of homogenizing changes in the technologies of transport and communication over the past forty years, that the distinctions between cosmopolitan and pastoral America (i.e., "red" versus "blue") have created a "culture war" largely reflective of differences in religious beliefs transcending region or even class. Thus, future sampling designs should contain another important layer of stratification: respondents should be drawn from separate populations in each of the regions—one urban and the other rural. Finally, it is important to note political culture is not confined to geography (either regional or urban/rural). This has been facilitated by the free flow of information and images due to enhanced selectivity in media consumption and participation in "virtual communities" through talk radio and the Internet. Future surveys should contain questions enabling researchers to evaluate how such communities share values and how these complement or constrain traditional distinctions based on geography.

Notes

1. See Daniel J. Elazar, *American Federalism: A View from the States,* 1st ed. (New York: Crowell, 1966); Michael Thompson, Richard Ellis, and Aaron Wildavsky, *Cultural Theory* (Boulder, CO: Westview Press, *1990);* Robert S. Erikson, John P. McIver, and Gerald C. Wright Jr., "State Political Culture and Public Opinion," *American Political Science Review* 81, no. 3 (September 1987): 797–813.
2. See, e.g., A. L. Kroeber and Clyde Kluckhohn, *Culture: A Critical Review of Concepts and Definitions* (New York: Vintage Books, 1963).
3. C. Kluckhohn, "Values and Value-Orientations in the Theory of Action," *Toward a General Theory of Action,* ed. T. Parsons and E. Shils (Cambridge, MA: Harvard University Press, 1951), p. 395.
4. For a good introduction to this literature, see Stanley Feldman, "Structure and Consistency in Public Opinion: The Role of Core Beliefs and Values," *American Journal of Political Science* 32, no. 2 (August 1988): 416–440.
5. Elazar, *American Federalism,* 1st ed.

6. For a good overview of this literature, see the special issue of Publius: The Journal of Federalism (21, no. 2 [1991]) edited by Frederick M. Wirt.

7. Peter F. Nardulli, "Political Subcultures in the American States: An Empirical Examination of Elazar's Formulation," *American Politics Quarterly* 18, no. 3 (1990): 289.

8. Nardulli, "Political Subcultures"; Ellen M. Dran, Robert B. Albritton, and Mikel Wyckoff, "Surrogate versus Direct Measures of Political Culture: Explaining Participation and Policy Attitudes in Illinois," *Publius: The Journal of Federalism* 21, no. 2 (1991): 15–30.

9. Of course, as Dran, Albritton, and Wyckoff ("Surrogate versus Direct Measures") have made evident, it is overly simplistic to assume that the dominant culture of a given state, as described by Elazar, would accurately describe the culture of any given community within that state. Most states contain elements of all three cultures, in different areas.

10. See James H. Kuklinski, Robert C. Luskin, and John Bolland, "Where Is the Schema? Going beyond the 'S' Word in Political Psychology," *American Political Science Review* 85, no. 4 (December 1991): 1341–1356.

11. Thompson et al., *Cultural Theory*, p. 88.

12. For a good introduction to the literature on heuristic processing, see Paul M. Sniderman, Richard A. Brody, and Philip E. Tetlock, *Reasoning and Choice: Explorations in Political Psychology* (Cambridge: Cambridge University Press, 1991).

13. Henry Brady and Paul Sniderman, "Attitude Attribution: A Group Basis for Political Reasoning," *American Political Science Review* 79, no. 4 (December 1985): 1075.

14. David J. Elkins and Richard E. B. Simeon, "A Cause in Search of Its Effect, or What Does Political Culture Explain?" *Comparative Politics* 11, no. 2 (January 1979): 137.

15. Chris Argyris, *Reasoning, Learning and Action: Individual and Organizational* (San Francisco: Jossey-Bass, 1982).

16. C. E. Osgood, G. J. Suci, and P. H. Tannenbaum, *The Measuring of Meaning* (Urbana: University of Illinois Press, 1957).

17. See Herbert F. Weisberg, Jon A. Krosnick, and Bruce D. Bowen, *An Introduction to Survey Research and Data Analysis,* 2nd ed. (Glenview, IL: Scott, Foresman, 1989).

18. To be sure, a more complete accounting of the various aspects of Elazarian culture would have also examined concepts such as "citizenship," "politics," "political participation," and "political representation." Practical concerns prevented us from exploring as many concepts as we would have liked. Future efforts should fill in these obvious gaps.

19. Daniel J. Elazar, *American Federalism: A View from the States,* 3rd ed. (New York: Crowell, 1972), 100–102.

20. Russell Hanson, "Political Culture, Interparty Competition and Political Efficacy in the American States," *Publius: The Journal of Federalism* 10, no. 2 (1980): 17–36.

PART FOUR

POLITICAL PARTICIPATION AND ELECTIONS

Crucial to the functioning of any democratic polity is citizen participation. However, studies have continually documented a significant difference between the levels of elite and non-elite participation,[1] and the debate continues over the level of participation required of the average citizen if America is to remain democratic.[2] Over the years several groups have pushed for reforms designed to improve the participation of the average citizen, and at the beginning of the 20th century, the Progressives campaigned for a variety of changes in the political system designed with that purpose in mind. Among other changes, they wanted to reform the way candidates for political office were nominated by getting away from a system in which only political party elites chose candidates. Hence, they argued strongly for the adoption of a direct primary in which voters (i.e., average citizens) nominated candidates. Wisconsin was the first state to adopt a direct primary. By now most states nominate candidates by this method, although one of the examples of diversity among the states is the existence of different types of primaries. And most states use the "first past the post," or plurality, system of determining winners in primary and general elections. There are a few exceptions, primarily in the South, where majority runoff rules exist. Election by plurality, gerrymandering, and the existence of single-member districts for most state legislative districts and city councils make it possible for a significant minority, and in some cases, even a majority of citizens to feel that they are not represented because they did not, or could not vote for candidates of their choice. Scholars have often cast a critical eye toward these potentially undemocratic features of American elections, but most of their opinions have been confined to relatively obscure academic journals. In January 1993, however, some of the "obscure" writings on this topic by a law school professor named Lani Guinier elevated these issues to public prominence. That was the year President Clinton nominated her to be the Assistant Attorney General for Civil Rights. In her law journal articles, she had written critically of the principal of majority rule which she argued was tantamount to "majority tyranny" particularly if a situation was created in which a permanent minority of voters was significantly left out of political decision-making in the American political system.[3] She advocated alternative voting systems such as cumulative voting in which voters are able to cast as many votes as there are vacant seats or positions, and can "plump" or stack their votes for particular candidates to enhance their chances of winning. These views were enough to scuttle her nomination even before it got off the ground. She was called the "Quota Queen" in a *Wall Street Journal* op-ed piece by conservative critic, and former Reagan-era Justice Department official, Clint Bolik. Even President Clinton, who took responsibility for withdrawing her nomination, admitted that he had some reservations about her positions on representation and voting.[4]

In the wake of this debacle, Guinier's ideas about alternative voting systems, and particularly cumulative voting, have been widely debated, but the irony is that in their role as laboratories of democracy, the state and local governments have been experimenting with different electoral systems since the beginning of the Republic. The articles included here highlight the issues of representation that are at the heart of this debate and focus our attention on alternatives to the traditional "winner-take-all" plurality system of voting. First, given the new-found prominence of cumulative voting, it is important to weigh its advantages and disadvantages in terms of promoting a more democratic electoral system. In their article examining turnout in local municipal elections, Shaun Bowler, David Brockington, and Todd Donovan demonstrate that cumulative voting increases turnout by about 5 percentage points when compared to plurality-rule elections. Their methodology is worth considering as an example of a careful effort to control for the possible effects of other variables on turnout, and demonstrates how political scientists go about doing research.

One of the issues with trying to switch to alternative electoral systems is whether citizens will understand them. Cumulative voting is particularly susceptible to this concern, but as Robert Brischetto points out in our second article, cumulative voting has been used in several small cities and school districts in Texas since the early 1990s as an agreed upon remedy to claims of minority under-representation in Voting Rights Act litigation. His findings are instructive to other communities considering the system. The city councils and school boards in these Texas communities have become more diverse under cumulative voting, and the evidence from exit surveys indicates that the voters are not confused by the process, even though it is a more complex voting procedure. As several states begin to experience demographic changes over the next several decades, particularly with the rise in Latino and Asian populations, pressure to adopt cumulative voting, or some other alternative, will surely increase.

One of the oft-repeated criticisms of the plurality system of voting that is predominant across the states and localities is the fact that it may, and often does, result in the election of a candidate who does not receive a majority of votes. Run-off elections are used in some places, particularly in the South, to remedy this, but they have been criticized as being discriminatory against racial and other minorities who have a difficult time getting their preferred candidate into the runoff election due to their minority status. As a remedy to this, reformers have pushed for instant runoff voting that is made easier in the age of computers. In their discussion of this system, Steven Hill and Robert Richie describe how it works, and how it has seen considerable success in San Francisco local elections.

One of the most innovative reforms undertaken to increase voter turnout, universal mail balloting, was adopted by the state of Oregon. In his discussion of the history of this election reform, Don Hamilton points out how it developed slowly over time, and by and large, has been successfully administered. The data are not crystal clear about whether turnout has been consistently better in the years since its adoption, and it is also unclear as to whether it has a differential effect on support for either party. Nevertheless, it is extremely interesting to consider the pros and cons of this approach to elections. Also, recalling our discussion of the diffusion of innovation across the states, several states have begun to move in the direction of conducting their elections by mail, although Oregon remains the only state to have adopted it statewide for all elections.[5]

A consistent issue on the public agenda is the role of money in elections and campaigns. The ability to adequately finance a campaign figures significantly in the eventual success of candidates at all levels. From a democratic perspective, if only well-funded candidates are the most successful at winning elections, concerns about equality emerge. On the other hand, as the Supreme Court has determined, spending one's money (for example, by giving to a political campaign) is a form of free speech, and efforts to regulate it tread dangerously on unconstitutional grounds.[6] One way around this potential First Amendment concern is to publicly fund campaigns in order to level the playing field a bit. State and local governments have led the way in this regard. In an examination of this electoral reform, Craig Holman takes an in-depth look at the various public funding provision and stipulations that have been put into effect across the states. A critical point he makes is that the only foray into this arena made by the federal government has been the voluntary public funding of presidential campaigns, and it has not been a very successful effort. In fact, one reason Barack Obama was able to raise so much money in his successful run for president was his decision to forego public funding. Perhaps, once again, the feds can learn from the states.

Notes

1. See, for example, the classic study by Sidney Verba and Norman H. Nie, *Participation in America: Political Democracy and Social Equality,* (New York: Harper & Row, 1972).

2. See John C. Pierce and John L. Sullivan, *The Electorate Reconsidered,* (Beverly Hills, CA: Sage, 1980); M. Margaret Conway, *Political Participation in the United States,* (Washington, D.C.: Congressional Quarterly Books, 1991); and Craig A. Rimmerman, *The New Citizenship,* (Boulder, CO: Westview, 1997).

3. Lani Guinier, *The Tyranny of the Majority: Fundamental Fairness in Representative Democracy,* (New York: The Free Press, 1994), pp. 1–20.

4. David Plotke, "Racial Politics and the Clinton-Guinier Episode," *Dissent,* 42 (Spring, 1995): 221–235.

5. Sam Rosenfeld, "On the Oregon Trail," *The American Prospect.* (May 2006): A9.

6. Buckley v. Valeo, 424 U.S. 1 (1976).

Questions for Review and Discussion

4.1   What is cumulative voting? Do you think it should be more widely used? Why or why not?

4.2   How does instant runoff voting work? How does it contribute to more democratic outcomes?

4.3   What are the pros and cons of mail balloting? Where would it seem to work better? Where would it not work so well? Why?

4.4   What are the pros and cons of public funding of campaigns? What are the differences across the states in this policy? Should it be more widely used? Why or why not?

10 Election Systems and Voter Turnout

SHAUN BOWLER

DAVID BROCKINGTON

TODD DONOVAN

HOW MUCH DO POLITICAL INSTITUTIONS affect levels of voter participation? Typically, this question has been addressed by predicting turnout in the major industrialized countries with models that include measures of electoral rules (Jackman 1987; Jackman and Miller 1995; Powell 1986). Within these studies, the U.S. stands out as a case of exceptionally low turnout. This has generated varying degrees of concern. For some, low or declining levels of turnout are lamentable but not seen as a dramatic threat to democratic processes (Berelson, Lazarsfeld, and McPhee 1954; Polsby 1963). Others, however, believe that low turnout endangers the very legitimacy or fairness of American elections (e.g., Amy 1993; Lijphart 1997; Piven and Cloward 1988; Teixeira 1992).

There are at least two broad, complementary explanations for low participation in the U.S. Individual-level (behavioral) explanations emphasize characteristics correlated with participation and suggest that a sizeable proportion of the electorate lack qualities that might cause them to vote (e.g., Abramson and Aldrich 1982; Leighley and Nagler 1992; Verba and Nie 1972; Wolfinger and Rosenstone 1980). A second category stresses the effects that registration barriers, weak parties, and other rules have on depressing turnout (e.g., Alford and Lee 1968; Caldeira, Patterson and Markko 1985; Jackson, Brown, and Wright 1998; Nagler 1991; Rosenstone and Hansen 1993; Rosenstone and Wolfinger 1978; Rusk 1970).

Our study expands on these explanations by testing if semi-proportional elections are associated with higher turnout when used in the U.S. A number of cross-national studies have found that proportional representation (PR) elections are associated with higher turnout than plurality elections (Blais and Carty 1990; Blais and Dobrzynska 1998; Jackman 1987; Jackman and Miller 1995; Powell 1986). These important studies leave room for further tests of this effect. First, there are too few degrees of freedom to control for many of the place-specific factors that co-vary with plurality rules in cross-national settings. For example, the Powell and Jackman studies use cases that share historical, social, or cultural traits that co-vary with relevant electoral arrangements.[1] This is problematic since one explanation of different rates of turnout is that nations have distinctive "political cultures" that affect their citizens' "subjective orientation to politics" (Verba 1965, 513). Important questions of research design must be addressed in order to demonstrate more conclusively that electoral systems, rather than place-specific factors such as culture, affect turnout. Second, cross-national studies cannot tell us what would happen to participation if a U.S. jurisdiction adopted PR.

What would be ideal, then, is the presence of variation in electoral rules within the same social and cultural context. Current experiments with local elections in the U.S. provide us with such a setting.[2] Moreover, they also provide an opportunity to employ a quasi-experimental research design with a large number of cases. We test if turnout is higher in U.S. jurisdictions that use cumulative voting (CV), a semi-proportional election system, than in jurisdictions using plurality rules. Our research design is structured so that we control for place-specific factors that may confound the impact of electoral system rules. We do this by combining a quasi-experimental case selection with cross-sectional and longitudinal statistical analysis of turnout.

Although nearly all federal, state, and local elections are contested under plurality rules, after the late 1980s numerous U.S. local jurisdictions began experimenting with CV. CV combines multimember districts with a semi-proportional[3] translation of votes to seats and lowers the proportion of votes required to win a seat (Engstrom, Taebel and Cole 1989; Still 1984). At present, about 80 jurisdictions (cities, counties, and school districts) have adopted CV, with most concentrated in a handful of Southern states[4] (Brischetto and Engstrom 1997; Cole and Taebel 1992; Cole, Taebel, and Engstrom 1990; Engstrom and Barrilleaux 1991; Pildes and Donoghue 1995).

CV was adopted on a case-by-case basis locally in response to actual or threatened actions under Section 2 of the Voting Rights Act (VRA). In the vast majority of cases where plaintiffs bring VRA challenges against local election rules, the remedy (reached by consent or by court order) is single-member districting (SMD). However, in a small number of cases, plaintiffs and defendants (local jurisdictions) have agreed to use CV.[5] There is no single reason why some places adopted CV rather than SMD as a remedy, but contributing factors include the preferences of individual attorneys handling the plaintiffs' cases, differences between defendants and plaintiffs over potential districting plans, and local minority-group leaders' willingness to use an experimental system (see Pildes and Donoghue 1995; Taebel, Engstrom and Cole 1988). CV also avoids those difficulties associated with using districts in small communities.[6]

Mobilizing Effects of CV Elections

CV elections could have the same effects on turnout as PR by eliminating the disincentives that plurality rules have on turnout. One probable disincentive for voters in plurality jurisdictions is that some perceive that their votes will be wasted. CV, like PR, allows voters from smaller (if not more) groups the possibility of voting for a winning candidate. CV could also increase voting by raising individual-level political efficacy, particularly among supporters of minority candidates. Cross-national opinion studies illustrate that citizens in PR nations are more satisfied with democracy (Anderson and Guillory 1997), and a panel study of the effects of changing from plurality to PR rules in New Zealand found that minor party supporters demonstrated significant increases in efficacy after the nation's first PR election (Banducci, Donovan, and Karp 1999).

Voters in noncompetitive races can also realize the futility of voting (Amy 1993; Cox and Munger 1989; Guinier 1994, 94–97), and CV elections may be more competitive than plurality elections. For example, SMDs drawn with a majority concentration of any one group could discourage minority candidates from seeking office since they would have a poor chance of winning.[7] Fewer candidates, moreover, might reduce the mobilizing effects of campaigns in plurality jurisdictions.[8] At-large, "first past the post" rules that allow a majority group to sweep all seats (Engstrom and McDonald 1981; Taebel 1978) can have the same effects by discouraging minority candidates from contesting races. But with a lower proportion of votes required to win a seat, CV systems could increase the incentives for candidates to seek office. Cox (1999) has theorized that elites respond to such electoral competitiveness by trying to mobilize more voters.

Recent scholarship presents theoretical and empirical reasons for expecting an increase in voter mobilization efforts under PR (Canon 1999, 357; Cox 1999), and by extension, semi-PR systems such as CV. One key link between election system and turnout, according to Cox, are variations in the mobilization incentives that systems create for elites (Cox 1999, 411; see also Ladner and Milner 1999, 248). Lower thresholds of exclusion mean more candidates from nonplurality groups might seek office. Furthermore, unlike majority-minority SMDs, if the minority share of the participating electorate falls below the threshold of exclusion, minority candidates are not likely to win seats under CV (Brischetto and Engstrom 1997). As noted of CV in Texas, it requires "lots of shoe leather" for a candidate to be elected. "If there is not sufficient local mobilization to get out the minority vote . . . the minority candidate is not likely to win" (Brischetto 1995, 8).[9]

Research Design and Methods

Data on turnout in local elections were requested from the largest jurisdictions in the United States that employed CV. We sought data from all CV places having a 1990 population over 1,000 persons (n = 44). Each place adopted CV in response to conflict over limited (or nonexistent) representation of minorities, and all have sizeable minority populations. We received turnout data from 28 (or 64%) CV places.

Data also were obtained from communities using plurality elections. This set of cases was selected so that each plurality jurisdiction closely matched a specific CV place in key geographic and social characteristics. The 1990 U.S. Census allowed us to identify community-level measures of race and ethnicity, population size, percentage of residents having a high school degree, and median income.[10] Each CV place was matched with a plurality place that was similar on each trait. For example, Rockford, Illinois (1990 pop. 139,426; 16% African American, median income $28,282) is the plurality jurisdiction matched with the CV city of Peoria, Illinois (1990 pop. 113,504; 21% African American, median income $26,074). In the end, we obtained turnout data for 21 of the 28 plurality jurisdictions matched with the CV places from which we received data.

These matched cases supply a control group of plurality places having demographic factors highly similar to the CV places. Each control city is located in the same state and generally in the same county as the "experimental" CV city with which it was matched. If CV school districts or counties were being matched with control cases, then similar in-state jurisdictions were identified in close proximity to the experimental places.[11]

Between 1997 and 1999, local officials in the experimental and control places were contacted by telephone and mail to obtain turnout data from recent elections. Officials in CV places were asked to supply data from their elections held under CV and from their final three plurality elections. This allowed us to conduct a longitudinal analysis of change in turnout within the set of "experimental" communities (pre- and post-adoption of CV), in addition to the cross-sectional analysis of differences in turnout between the experimental (CV) cases and the control (plurality) cases. Overall, 49 different jurisdictions (28 CV and 21 plurality) supplied turnout data on 215 elections.[12] Table 1 reports mean turnout levels for each group of cases and reports means for key independent variables. Cases represent a jurisdiction's election in a specific year.[13] Apart from slight variations in median income, the jurisdictions in each group are

TABLE 1   Descriptive Characteristics: All Cases, Control, and Experimental Groups

Variable	All Elections	Continuous Plurality Elections (Control)	Plurality Elections Prior to CV (Exp Pre)	CV Elections after Switch from Plurality (Exp Post)
Turnout %	19 (14)	17 (16)	18 (12)	23 (13)
Minority %	38 (14)	38 (14)	37 (14)	38 (16)
High School Education %	56 (10)	56 (09)	55 (10)	55 (11)
Median Income $	19,756 (3877)	21,210 (3910)	18,807 (3308)	19,263 (3989)
Total Number of Elections	215	72	74	69

Note: Main entries are means, standard deviations in parentheses. Control groups: Places using plurality elections continuously, matched with demographic and geographic traits of CV places. Experimental pre: Places using plurality contests prior to using new CV system. Experimental post: CV places after switching from plurality.

nearly identical. Our control group (from the matched places) includes results from 72 plurality elections.[14] We also have turnout data for 74 at-large elections held in CV places prior to their adopting CV and 69 subsequent CV elections from those places.

The plurality (control) cases had slightly lower but statistically insignificant differences in mean turnout levels when compared to plurality elections held in the experimental (CV) places. Previous to their adoption of CV, our experimental communities averaged 17.9% turnout, which is comparable to 17.1% turnout for other plurality jurisdictions in our study. In keeping with expectations about the effects of semi-PR rules on participation, turnout was 5.6% higher (23.5%) in the experimental cases after their adoption of CV. An ANOVA test determined that there are significant differences in turnout between these three categories ($F(2,212) = 3.85$, $p = .02$). A dependent samples t-test of the difference between mean turnout levels in the experimental places before and after changing to CV indicates a significant difference ($t = 2.91$, $p = .005$). There is no significant difference between the control and pre-experimental groups.

Hypotheses and Model Specification

We estimate cross-sectional regression models of turnout across all places (control, experimental pre-CV, and experimental post-CV) as well as longitudinal models focusing on places experimenting with CV. Our discussion suggested several testable hypotheses. Clearly, if semi-PR election rules increase elite incentives to mobilize voters, make contests more competitive, or increase voter efficacy, then turnout should be higher under CV. Although we cannot specify the actual mechanism that operates in CV elections to affect turnout, we can isolate the general effect of election rules in a regression equation by using a dummy variable, where 1 = a CV election, and 0 = a plurality election. The coefficient for this term represents the difference in turnout between plurality and CV elections.

Given the controls built into our research design, we can be rather confident that this dummy variable captures differences that stem from election rules. However, since we anticipate that communities with a larger proportion of minority residents might have lower turnout, independent of the election system, our models include a variable that represents the proportion of voting age residents who are nonwhite. In addition to the relative size of the minority population, the specific type of minority is also relevant. Language barriers or citizenship status may mean that

Latinos did not turn out at the same rate as other voters. Indeed, studies have found that Latinos turn out at relatively lower rates than whites and African Americans in various elections (Stanley and Niemi 1995, 79; Uhlaner, Cain, and Kiewiet 1989). We include a dummy variable that represents places where Latinos were the largest minority group.[15] To control for variation in the social composition of these places, we also include a measure of median income. We assume that places with higher median incomes have more residents who have the resources to participate in politics.[16] Since voters may take less interest in school elections, we also include a dummy variable that distinguishes school board from city and county council elections. Participation might also be lower in larger communities for a number of reasons (see Key 1949; Verba and Nie 1972, 231). Since there are few cases in our analysis with populations over 100,000, there is an extreme rightward skew in the distribution of this variable. As a result, we found it necessary to use the log of population as a control.

Cross-Sectional Results

Table 2 reports the results of a set of cross-sectional estimations of turnout that compare plurality places (control and experimental pre-CV cases) to CV places. The first column reports an OLS estimation using data from all 215 elections—72 from plurality control places, 74 plurality elections held in experimental places prior to adopting CV, and 69 from experimental places after adopting CV. The second column lists estimates from a set of cases limited to elections from the experimental and control jurisdictions that were matched demographically.[17] This set includes 63 plurality elections from the control group, 50 plurality elections from places that would end up adopting CV, and 51 CV elections. Cross-sectional comparisons are further refined in the third column with an estimation limited to CV and plurality elections matched by place as well as time.[18] This includes 41 CV elections and 41 plurality elections held in similar places at the same time.

The primary variable of interest is the dichotomous measure that indicates whether an election was run under CV. According to each of our cross-sectional estimates, elections held under CV do result in a turnout rate significantly higher than elections run under traditional plurality schemes. The effect of CV ranges from an increase of 4.7 to 5.2 percentage points, depending on the set of cases being assessed.[19] The substantive impact of CV elections appears modest when we consider

TABLE 2   Cross-Sectional Regression Analysis Models
of Turnout in Local Elections

	All Elections	Matched by Place	Matched by Place and Time
CV Election System	.052**	.050**	.047*
	(.015)	(.019)	(.028)
Minority Population	−.123*	−.098	−.030
	(.075)	(.093)	(.144)
School Board Election	−.028*	−.026	−.007
	(.016)	(.021)	(.034)
Latino Community	−.267**	−.223**	−.264**
	(.032)	(.039)	(.061)
Population (logged)	−.028**	−.029**	−.023
	(.008)	(.010)	(.014)
Median Income	.00002	.00002	.00004
	(.00002)	(.00003)	(.00003)
Intercept	.692**	.605**	.526**
	(.080)	(.097)	(.141)
R^2 (adjusted)	.449	.318	.333
Number of cases	215	164	82

Note: Dependent variable = turnout as a proportion of voting age population. Standard errors in parentheses.
** = significant at $p < .01$ (one-tail)
* = significant at $p < .05$ (one-tail)

that an increase in national turnout of 5 percentage points would be a relatively small proportionate change in participation. The effect is more impressive, however, when the range of local turnout across these cases is considered.[20] For a jurisdiction having the mean turnout (19%), a 5 percentage point increase is, proportionately, a substantial gain.

Several coefficients for control variables are also significant. In the estimation including all elections, there is an independent effect of the type of office being contested. When school board elections are held separately, fewer voters turn out. The log of population is also significant in the first two estimations, with larger jurisdictions having lower turnout. Jurisdictions with Latinos as their primary minority group had lower turnout rates, and the coefficient representing Latino communities is both substantively as well as statistically significant in each estimation. Finally, no estimation demonstrates a significant effect of median income, although the direction of the coefficients suggests wealthier communities have higher participation.

Longitudinal Results

Thus far we have assumed that plurality and CV places were matched on all relevant variables except election system. With perfect matching, the term for CV elections would capture the unique effect of election type. Despite care in matching, however, it is possible that the CV term also captures other factors. Given this limitation, we also estimate longitudinal models of turnout. By looking only at the jurisdictions that experimented with CV, we test for change over time in places that are directly affected by the adoption of CV. Table 3 reports these longitudinal estimates. The CV term represents the intervention of the adoption of CV and thus reflects the increase in turnout after elections were conducted under CV. The first estimation makes use of turnout data from 143 elections in the experimental places—74 were plurality contests and 69 were conducted after switching to CV.

Heilig and Mundt (1984) found that the adoption of new SMD systems can be associated with a short-term surge in turnout due to increased electoral competition, but participation may drop after the first election. A similar effect could occur with CV contests. Likewise, mobilization efforts by local groups could be one-time educational affairs that produce an increase in turnout only after initial CV elections. The second estimation in Table 3 excludes the first two CV elections in each jurisdiction to test if increased turnout is sustained after the first two CV contests. We include a third estimation in Table 3 to take full advantage of our research design. Here, we test if turnout has increased over time in places that did not adopt CV. A dummy variable representing all elections contested after 1993 is included to test this.[21]

Most of the coefficients in Table 3 appear similar to the estimates from the cross-sectional analysis (Table 2). Of primary interest here is that the effects of CV in Table 3 are largely consistent with those reported in Table 2, in the range of 4–5.1 percentage point increase in local turnout after a jurisdiction adopted CV. Overall, the results in Table 3 demonstrate that when a fixed set of jurisdictions in the U.S. switches from plurality to semi-PR election rules, we do see a significant, sustained increase in turnout.[22] Estimates in the second column illustrate that turnout remains 5 percentage points higher than under plurality elections after the second

TABLE 3   Longitudinal Regression Analysis Models
of Turnout in Local Elections

	CV Places, Before & After Adopting CV	CV Places, Before & After, Excluding First Two CV Elections	Non-CV Places Only
Adoption of CV Election System	.040**	.051**	—
	(.016)	(.023)	
After 1993	—	—	−.017
			(.018)
Minority Population	−.125*	−.093	−.143
	(.077)	(.098)	(.098)
Latino	−.247**	−.248**	−.251**
	(.039)	(.046)	(.041)
School Board Election	−.036**	−.027	−.028
	(.018)	(.022)	(.019)
Population (logged)	−.050**	−.047**	−.020*
	(.011)	(.014)	(.009)
Median Income	−.00001	−.00002	−.00001
	(.00003)	(.00003)	(.00002)
Intercept	.889**	.793**	.603**
	(.091)	(.112)	(.103)
R^2 (adjusted)	.447	.446	.438
Number of cases	143	98	146

Note: Dependent variable = turnout as a proportion of voting age population. Standard errors in parentheses.
** = significant at $p < .01$ (one-tail)
* = significant at $p < .05$ (one-tail)

CV contest.[23] Moreover, we find that there was no increase in turnout after 1993 in similar places that never adopted CV.[24]

Conclusion

Our analysis demonstrates that CV is associated with higher turnout than plurality elections in the U.S. CV thus offers the promise of increased representation of minorities coupled with increased participation. The size of the effect appears to be a modest but noteworthy 4% to 5% boost in participation. The jurisdictions examined here adopted CV because their at-large plurality voting plans created barriers to descriptive representation of minorities. When actions are taken against these plans under the VRA, courts typically accept other plurality systems that produce minority representation (e.g., SMDs). Semi-proportionate alternatives to these systems, such as CV, have been found to facilitate minority representation at levels approaching what is found under districting (Brischetto and Engstrom 1997; Cole and Taebel 1992; Pildes and Donoghue 1995). Our results illustrate that the institutional effects of these alternative electoral rules extend beyond just facilitating descriptive representation.

Our quasi-experimental design, controlled case selection, and model estimations demonstrate that the effect of CV on turnout is not an artifact of an analysis that fails to control for place-specific (cultural, social, political, or geographic) factors. All of this suggests quite strongly that some underlying processes associated with CV act to mobilize more voters than plurality elections do. If political reformers are interested in increasing participation in U.S. elections, these findings could be taken as evidence that PR or semi-PR rules could stimulate greater participation, at least in local elections where the potential problem of low turnout is most severe.

Advocates of electoral reform might find satisfaction in the link we find between institutional rules and participation. Yet the findings could also cast a minor shadow over claims advanced by proponents of PR. If we can generalize from local elections in these mostly small jurisdictions, increased proportionality in the electoral formula does not appear to be a magic bullet that will resolve problems of low participation in the U.S.: turnout increased, but it remained low. As noted above, there are numerous behavioral, structural, and institutional factors at play here. Election rules, however, are one of many small pieces of the puzzle of low turnout in the U.S.

The results of this study do lend support to cross-national findings that institutional rules affect turnout. We find that even when cultural and social factors are largely controlled, plurality rules continue to demonstrate a deleterious effect on participation. Indeed, we find about the same effect that Blais and Dobrzynska (1998) identify with cross-national data, and we find results close to the 3%-7% effect that Ladner and Milner (1999) find PR has on local contests in Switzerland. Given this, and the modest effect that semi-PR election rules have on turnout within the U.S., we suggest that attitudinal, behavioral, and other institutional differences explain much of the participation gap between the U.S. and nations that use PR.

Notes

1. For example, plurality SMDs are found in the English-speaking U.S., UK, and commonwealth states (5 of the 19 cases, with an average turnout of 72.4% between 1971 and 1980). PR is present in Scandinavian states (5 of the 19 cases, with a turnout of 83.4% for this period).

2. We "control" for the large variation in American cultural context, in part, by comparing many jurisdictions within the same states.

3. CV does not have rules that allocate seats proportionately to votes. Rather, it reduces the likelihood that a plurality group will win all seats, particularly as district magnitude increases.

4. Nearly all of the CV jurisdictions in this analysis are found in Texas and Alabama. There is one CV jurisdiction each in these data from New Mexico and Illinois.

5. In a number of Texas cases, plaintiffs included the League of United Latin American Citizens (LULAC). In Alabama, they included a black political group, the Alabama Democratic Conference (ADC). Attorneys working for these groups filed cases on behalf of individuals with standing in various communities. LULAC and the ADC in particular each had attorneys who worked to promote semi-PR systems. Local plaintiffs working with different attorneys may have been much less likely to adopt CV. These attorneys' ability to "sell" CV to a local group was one factor affecting if it would be considered for adoption.

6. These include dividing a small population into at least five districts and lowering the candidate pool in very small districts. We thank an anonymous reviewer for noting this.

7. This would be even more certain if we assume that voting is polarized along racial and ethnic lines, as is typically the case in places with VRA actions.

8. Compared to SMD, multimember district elections of any type may be more competitive since when the number of candidates (c) > the number of seats (s), then a minimum of s + 1 candidates are competing against each other for office. Under CV in the U.S., s is always 3 or greater, so a minimum of c = 4 can produce a contest where all 4 might campaign. Under SMD, if s = 3 and c is 4, it is possible that only 2 compete against each other, while 2 others run uncontested.

9. In Atlanta, Texas, for example, African Americans organized get-out-the-vote drives in African-American communities to elect a candidate under CV. In several CV towns with Latino communities, the Southwest Voter Registration Education Project trained activists for local voter mobilization strategies. In another Texas town, a group called Concerned Citizens for Voting began mobilizing voters under the first CV election (Brischetto 1995, 9).

10. Demographic data were drawn either from the 1990 U.S. Census, or, in the case of school districts, from the School District Data Book on CD-ROM published by the U.S. Department of Education.

11. The vast majority of elections follow the municipal model of holding elections in off-year and in odd months. For example, all Texas city council and school

elections included in this analysis are held in early May of each year. Guin, Alabama, which does hold its elections every four years corresponding with presidential elections, does so in August, not November. There are no elections in this analysis that correspond with a national or statewide general election. The practical implication of this is that there are no national or statewide influences on turnout in these data.

12.   Most jurisdictions would provide information on turnout from recent elections. Refusals were greater when data from older elections were requested. Thus, from some places, we have longer time series than others. The majority of these jurisdictions stagger the election of seats, with elections for three or four seats held annually or every two years in many places.

13.   For example, case 1 = election$_{ij}$, where $_i$ is an individual election year and $_j$ is the jurisdiction.

14.   54 of these were conducted under at-large rules, while 18 were conducted under districted elections.

15.   Given the nature of these data, all communities had a sizeable minority population. However, no jurisdictions had a large Latino and African-American population simultaneously. The dummy variable thus = 1 (Latino the largest minority) or = 0 (African American the largest minority). The majority of elections (86%) were contested where Latinos were the predominant minority group.

16.   Likewise, aggregate levels of education could also affect participation. Our measures of income and education, however, are highly correlated (.80), and both are strongly correlated with population (each over .65). To avoid problems of multicollinearity, we omit the measure of education. When education is substituted for income, the substantive results do not change.

17.   This first estimation in Table 2 includes elections from 7 CV places for which we obtained turnout data that lack matching data from plurality jurisdictions.

18.   Since time series for places vary in length, cases are lost when the estimation is limited to when time of election and place are matched.

19.   The size and significance of the effect of election system reported in each estimate in Table 2 remain largely unchanged when dummy variables for year are included in the models.

20.   The dependent variable (turnout) has a mean of .19 and a standard deviation of .14. It ranges from .017 to .682. The distribution has a noticeable but not severe right tail, with only one case lying further than three standard deviations from the mean.

21.   We use 1993 as a break point since half of the non-CV elections were conducted after that year.

22.   Models omitting only the first CV contest produce similar results. The size and significance of the effect of election system also remain largely unchanged when dummy variables for year are included in the models.

23.   We also estimated models using data from the CV elections held in places that had at least two or more contests under CV. We replaced the term for election system with a variable representing the number of times a place had a CV election. Results illustrated that the coefficient for election iteration was trivial (−.009), and not at all significant (p = .52). Thus, the increase in local election turnout demonstrated here does not appear to be the function of some short-lived novelty effect.

24.   We also estimated models for elections in non-CV places using a time-counter,

using dummy variables for individual years, and using other years as break points. The substantive results are unchanged in each estimation.

References

Abramson, Paul, and John Aldrich. 1982. "The Decline of Electoral Participation in America." *American Political Science Review* 76(3): 502–21.

Alford, Robert, and Eugene Lee. 1968. "Voting Turnout in American Cities." *American Political Science Review* 62(3): 796–813.

Amy, Douglas. 1993. *Real Choices, New Voices*. New York: Columbia University Press.

Anderson, Chris, and Chris Guillory. 1997. "Political Institutions and Satisfaction with Democracy: A Cross-national Analysis of Consensus and Majoritarian Systems." *American Political Science Review* 91(1): 66–88.

Banducci, Susan, Todd Donovan, and Jeffrey Karp. 1999. "Proportional Representation and Attitudes about Politics: Results from New Zealand." *Electoral Studies* 18(4): 533–555.

Berelson, Bernard, Paul Lazarsfeld, and William McPhee. 1954. *Voting*. Chicago: University of Chicago Press.

Blais, André, and R. K. Carty. 1990. "Does Proportional Representation Foster Voter Turnout?" *European Journal of Politics* 18(1): 167–81.

Blais, André, and Agnieszka Dobrzynska. 1998. "Turnout in Electoral Democracies." *European Journal of Political Research* 33(2): 239–61.

Brischetto, Robert. 1995. "The Rise of Cumulative Voting." *Texas Observer*, July 28. Pp. 6–18.

Brischetto, Robert, and Richard Engstrom. 1997. "Cumulative Voting and Latino Representation: Exit Surveys in 15 Texas Communities." *Social Science Quarterly* 78(4): 973–91.

Caldeira, Gregory, Samuel Patterson, and Gregory Markko. 1985. "The Mobilization of Voters in Congressional Elections." *Journal of Politics* 47(2): 490–509.

Canon, David. 1999. "Electoral Systems and the Representation of Minority Interests in Legislatures." *Legislative Studies Quarterly* 24(3): 331–86.

Cole, Richard, Delbert Taebel, and Richard Engstrom. 1990. "Cumulative Voting in a Municipal Election: A Note on Voter Reactions and Electoral Consequences." *Western Political Quarterly* 43(1): 191–99.

Cole, Richard, and Delbert Taebel. 1992. "Cumulative Voting in Local Elections: Lessons from the Alamogordo Experience." *Social Science Quarterly* 73(1): 194–201.

Cox, Gary. 1999. "Electoral Rules and the Calculus of Mobilization." *Legislative Studies Quarterly* 24(3): 387–420.

Cox, Gary, and Michael Munger. 1989. "Closeness, Expenditure and Turnout in the 1982 U.S. House Elections." *American Political Science Review* 83(1): 217–31.

Engstrom, Richard, and Charles Barrilleaux. 1991. "Native Americans and Cumulative Voting: The Case of the Sisseton-Wahpeton Sioux." *Social Science Quarterly* 72(2): 388–93.

Engstrom, Richard, Delbert Taebel, and Richard Cole. 1989. "Cumulative Voting as a Remedy for Minority Vote Dilution: The Case of Alamogordo, New Mexico." *Journal of Law and Politics* 5(3): 469–97.

Engstrom, Richard, and Michael McDonald. 1981. "The Election of Blacks to City Councils: Clarifying the Impact of Electoral Arrangements on the Seats/Population Relationship." *American Political Science Review* 75(2): 344–54.

Guinier, Lani. 1994. *The Tyranny of the Majority*. New York. Free Press.

Heilig, Peggy, and Robert Mundt. 1984. *Your Voice at City Hall: The Politics, Procedures, and Policies of District Representation*. Albany, NY: SUNY Press.

Jackman, Robert. 1987. "Political Institutions and Voter Turnout in the Industrial Democracies." *American Political Science Review* 81(2): 405–24.

Jackman, Robert, and Ross Miller. 1995. "Voter Turnout in the Industrial Democracies During the 1980s." *Comparative Political Studies* 27(4): 467–92.

Jackson, Robert, Robert Brown, and Gerald Wright. 1998. "Registration, Turnout and the Electoral Representatives of U.S. State Electorates." *American Politics Quarterly* 26(3): 259–89.

Key, V. O. 1949. *Southern Politics in Nation and State*. New York: Knopf.

Ladner, Andreas, and Henry Milner. 1999. "Do Voters Turn Out More under Proportional than Majoritarian Systems? Evidence from Swiss Communal Elections," *Electoral Studies* 18(2): 235–50.

Leighley, Jan, and Jonathan Nagler. 1992. "Individual and Systemic Differences on Turnout: Who Votes? 1984." *Journal of Politics* 54(3): 635–717.

Lijphart, Arend. 1997. "Unequal Participation: Democracy's Unresolved Dilemma." *American Political Science Review* 91(1): 1–14.

Nagler, Jonathan. 1991. "The Effects of Registration Laws and Education on U.S. Voter Turnout." *American Political Science Review* 85(4): 1393–1406.

Pildes, Richard, and Kristen Donoghue. 1995. "Cumulative Voting in the United States." *The University of Chicago Legal Forum* 1995: 241–312.

Piven, Frances Fox, and Richard Cloward. 1988. *Why Americans Don't Vote*. New York: Pantheon Books.

Polsby, Nelson. 1963. *Community Power and Political Theory*. New Haven: Yale University Press.

Powell, G. Bingham. 1986. "American Voter Turnout in Comparative Perspective." *American Political Science Review* 80(1): 17–43.

Rosenstone, Steven, and Raymond Wolfinger. 1978. "The Effects of Registration Laws on Voter Turnout." *American Political Science Review* 72(1): 22–45.

Rosenstone, Steven, and John Mark Hansen. 1993. *Mobilization, Participation and Democracy in America*. New York: Macmillan.

Rusk, Jerrold. 1970. "The Effect of the Australian Ballot Reform on Split-Ticket Voting: 1876–1908." *American Political Science Review* 64(4): 1220–38.

Stanley, Harold, and Richard Niemi. 1995. *Vital Statistics on American Politics*. 5th ed. Washington, DC: CQ Press.

Still, Edward. 1984. "Alternatives to Single-Member Districts." In *Minority Vote Dilution*, ed. C. Davidson. Washington, DC: Howard University Press.

Taebel, Delbert. 1978. "Minority Representation on City Councils: The Impact of Structure on Blacks and Hispanics." *Social Science Quarterly* 59(1): 142–52.

Taebel, Delbert, Richard Engstrom, and Richard Cole. 1988. "Alternative Election Systems as Remedies for Minority Vote Dilution." *Hamline Journal of Public Law and Policy* 11(1): 19–29.

Teixeira, Ruy. 1992. *The Disappearing American Voter.* Washington, DC: Brookings Institution Press.

Uhlaner, Carole, Bruce Cain, and D. Roderick Kiewiet. 1989. "Political Participation of Ethnic Minorities in the 1980s." *Political Behavior* 11(2): 195–231.

Verba, Sidney. 1965. "Conclusion: Comparative Political Culture." In *Political Culture and Political Development,* ed. Lucian Pye and Sidney Verba. Princeton: Princeton University Press.

Verba, Sidney, and Norman Nie. 1972. *Participation in America: Political Democracy and Social Equality.* New York: Harper and Row.

Wolfinger, Raymond, and Steven Rosenstone. 1980. *Who Votes?* New Haven: Yale University Press.

11 Cumulative Voting as an Alternative to Districting

ROBERT BRISCHETTO

IN JUNE 1995, when the U.S. Supreme Court declared a black-majority congressional district in Georgia illegally drawn to segregate voters on the basis of race, three decades of progress under the Voting Rights Act seemed to begin unraveling. In *Miller v. Johnson*, the high Court ruled that drawing electoral district lines chiefly on the basis of race can be presumed unconstitutional, absent some compelling state interest.

The decision was presaged in 1993 in *Shaw v. Reno*, when the Court called into question a "bizarre shaped" district and warned that "Racial classifications with respect to voting carry particular dangers. Racial gerrymandering, even for remedial purposes, may Balkanize us into competing racial factions; it threatens to carry us further from the goal of a political system in which race no longer matters. . . . "

For voting rights advocates, *Shaw* and *Miller* were bitter pills to take. For almost three decades, they had been drawing districts chiefly on the basis of race in order to level the playing field and allow minorities an opportunity to elect candidates of their own choice. Indeed, the creation of majority-minority districts largely explains why there are 40 African-Americans and 17 Latinos in the U.S. House of Representatives today.

Some analysts predict that as many as a dozen of those seats [might] be invalidated by federal rulings forcing the states to redraw their congressional maps with less attention to race.

In the wake of these Supreme Court decisions, voting rights advocates are seeking solutions that would provide better representation for minorities without resorting to racial gerrymandering. Some have turned to voting systems that approximate the outcomes of single-member districts in multi-seat elections: cumulative voting, limited voting, and the single transferable vote form of proportional representation. . . . Such alternatives were offered earlier by University of Pennsylvania law professor Lani Guinier. In 1993, Guinier's nomination to become Assistant Attorney General for Civil Rights was withdrawn by President Clinton in part because of her "radical" ideas promoting voting schemes that would achieve proportional representation. After *Shaw* and *Miller*, the ideas of the "quota queen"—as she was labeled by politicians and pundits alike—are looking more constitutional.

The search for alternatives to districting has engendered a long-overdue national debate on more basic questions about how well our democracy works and how we choose our elected officials. The United States is one of only a few modern democracies that have not adopted some form of proportional representation. As Birmingham civil rights attorney Edward Still puts it: "Surely any majoritarian system than can leave 49 percent of the people . . . with nothing to show for having gone to the polls except a patriotic feeling is not the answer."

The Cumulative Voting Answer

Cumulative voting is one of several modified at-large electoral systems that might be used to approximate proportional representation in a multi-member elective body. Each voter is allowed as many votes as seats to be filled in a given election. In that way, it is the same as simple at-large systems. However, under cumulative voting, a voter may distribute votes among candidates in any combination, even concentrating all votes on a single candidate.

The system is not new to the American political scene. From 1870 to 1980, Illinois elected members of its general assembly by means of cumulative voting. Each legislative district had three representatives and a voter could cast one vote for each of three candidates, one and one-half votes for each of two candidates, or three votes for one candidate. Cumulative voting also has been used for decades to elect members of many corporate boards of directors. Moreover, during the past decade, some three dozen local jurisdictions in Illinois, New Mexico, South Dakota, and Alabama have adopted cumulative voting as a remedy for minority vote dilution. A federal judge last year [1994] was the first to *order* cumulative voting in a case against Worcester County, Maryland (*Cane v. Worcester County*).

Cumulative Voting in Texas

Since 1991, at least two dozen small cities and school districts in the Texas Panhandle and the Permian Basin have settled Voting Rights Act lawsuits via cumulative voting, most of them brought on behalf of the League of United Latin American Citizens (LULAC). On May 6, 1995, 26 small cities and school districts in Texas held elections under cumulative voting, most for the first time, and all in response to litigation. This event provided a rare opportunity for a researcher to test the effectiveness of that system. In 16 of these jurisdictions, minority candidates were competing against Anglos; in ten jurisdictions, minorities did not file candidacies.

Fifteen of the 16 jurisdictions studied had Latino candidates on the ballot. The Hispanic Research Center at the University of Texas at San Antonio conducted exit polls in these cities and school districts. Bilingual teams of pollsters visited these jurisdictions with bilingual questionnaires, gathering data from 3,615 voters on how they cast their ballots, how well they understood the new system of voting, and how they evaluated it. The Atlanta Independent School District, located in East Texas about 25 miles from Texarkana, held the only election in which a black candidate was running under cumulative voting. The Atlanta ISD survey of 569 voters, a cooperative effort by experts for the plaintiffs and defendants, was conducted by the political science department at Texarkana College.

The study reported in this article analyzes the exit polls of 4,184 voters in the 16 jurisdictions in which minorities ran for office under cumulative voting on May 6. The study addresses several questions:

1.   Was there racially polarized voting? Were there clear differences between minority and Anglo voters in their preferred candidates? Did minorities vote as a bloc?

2.   Did cumulative voting work to elect minority-preferred candidates? If not, why not?

TABLE 1   Cumulative Voting Election Outcomes in Texas Jurisdictions with Minority Candidates, May 6, 1995

| | Total Candidates | Rank of Minority Candidate(s) by: | | Positions Elected | Exclusion Threshold | % Minority Voters | Minority Elected? |
		Minority Voters	Anglo Voters				
Minorities Won:							
Atlanta ISD	5	1	5	4	20%	31	Yes
Anton	8	1	5	3	25	30	Yes
Morton	4	1,2	3,4	3	25	26	Yes, one
Morton ISD	7	1,2	6,7	3	25	23	Yes, one
Roscoe	8	1	6	5	17	17	Yes
Rotan	8	1,2	7,8	5	17	32	Yes, two
Rotan ISD	5	1	5	3	25	25	Yes
Yorktown	2	1	2	2	33	43	Yes
Olton	6	1	6	2	33	22	Yes
Minorities Lost:							
Andrews ISD	7	1	6	3	25%	8	No
Denver City ISD	5	2	4	2	33	4	No
Dumas ISD	7	2	6	2	33	2	No
Earth	6	1,4	5,6	3	25	16	No
Friona	6	1	5	3	25	12	No
Friona ISD	6	1	6	2	33	7	No
Stamford ISD	5	1	4	3	25	7	No

"Minority" refers to African-Americans in the case of Atlanta ISD, where Latinos are fewer than one-half of one percent of the voters. In the other 15 jurisdictions, "minority" refers to Latinos, since blacks are only 1.2 percent of the voters

3. Did voters understand cumulative voting?

4. Did voters accept cumulative voting?

Racially Polarized Voting

Knowing whether voters polarize along racial lines is pivotal in voting rights cases, since in the absence of polarization there can be no claim of minority vote dilution.

In the Atlanta ISD, white and black voters could not have been more polarized in their choices of candidates. Veloria Nanze came in last among white voters, but first among African-American voters. Fewer than 3 percent of white voters cast even one of their four votes for Nanze, while she received 94 percent of all votes cast by blacks.

The same general pattern of polarization between Anglos and Latinos was found in the jurisdictions with Latino candidates, but was less severe. With the exception of two cases, Latino candidates were the top choices of Latino voters and ranked last among Anglo voters.

The Threshold of Exclusion

In the worst case scenario of totally polarized voters, one can predict the outcome for a racial or ethnic group under cumulative voting by simply calculating the "threshold of exclusion": the proportion of votes that any group of voters must exceed in order to elect a candidate of its choice, regardless of how the rest of the voters cast their ballots. It is calculated by one divided by one more than the number of seats to be filled $(1/[1 + n])$.

With four seats up in the 1995 Atlanta School Board election, the threshold of exclusion was $1/(1 + 4)$, or 20 percent. That meant that, even if Veloria Nanze did not receive a single white vote, she could win as long as black voters comprised one more than at least 20 percent of the total voters and concentrated their votes on her.

Blacks comprised 21 percent of the voting-age population in the Atlanta ISD in 1990 and 31 percent in 1995, which means that voter turnout among blacks in this election apparently was much higher than among whites. In next year's election, when three school board seats will become available, the threshold of exclusion will be 25 percent, and it is likely that blacks will elect another representative.

The Results under Cumulative Voting

In the case of the Atlanta ISD, cumulative voting worked as it should have for black voters seeking to elect one candidate. The African-American community not only elected their candidate with almost no white support, but they voted together, placing almost all their votes on Nanze, who came in a close second among five candidates in a race that elected the top four choices.

In the 15 contests involving Latino candidates, on first glance the results seemed mixed: eight wins and seven losses. A closer examination of the contests involving Latinos, however, reveals that cumulative voting worked almost precisely as expected in polarized communities. In each of the seven jurisdictions where Latino candidates lost, there were not enough Latino voters to rise above the threshold of exclusion. For example, in the Denver City school district, Latinos were 36 percent of the total population, but only 15 percent of registered voters and 4 percent of the voters in the May 6 election. Since two seats were open in that election, the threshold of exclusion was set at 33 percent, not low enough for Latino voters to elect their preferred candidate.

In hindsight, all seven losses could have been avoided by lowering the threshold of exclusion or raising the level of minority participation in the election, or both. The thresholds could have been reduced by agreement between the parties designing the cumulative voting system, realizing that the more seats up in an election, the lower the threshold. Since school boards in Texas typically have seven members, if all seats were up at once, the threshold would be $1/(1 + 7)$ or 12.5 percent.

The Key Role of Community Organizing

Raising the level of voter participation through voter registration and education, minority candidate recruitment, and get-out-the-vote efforts is a key winning strategy under cumulative voting. In the Atlanta ISD, blacks launched door-to-door voter education and get-out-the-vote drives in black neighborhoods. In the City of Morton, the Morton ISD, Roscoe, the Rotan ISD, and the City of Rotan, the Southwest Voter Registration Education Project provided training in voter mobilization under cumulative voting. In Yorktown, where Concerned Citizens for Voting had begun mobilizing under their first cumulative voting election in 1992, a Latino was running as an incumbent.

In stark contrast, where Latino candidates lost, minority voter participation was low. The average turnout rate among Latinos registered to vote in the seven jurisdictions in which Latino candidates lost was one-half the turnout rate of non-Latino voters.

Finally, for a group or party to win under cumulative voting in a highly polarized political contest, they must vote together as a group. This may require planning to limit the number of minority candidates so as not to split their strength as a bloc. Placing all of one's votes on a single candidate, or "plumping," is a practice that may enable minority voters to concentrate the strength of their group's vote and improve their chances of electing at least one candidate of their choice. African-American voters in the Atlanta ISD planned their effort very carefully in only a few weeks by agreeing to field only one candidate and by conducting strong voter outreach. The exit poll found that 90 percent of blacks in the Atlanta ISD "plumped" their votes for Veloria Nanze.

Is Cumulative Voting Understood and Accepted?

Ten of the 16 jurisdictions in this study held elections under cumulative voting for the first time; five for only the second time. Beyond documenting the success of minority candidates, this study sought to determine how voters responded to the cumulative voting system. Did they understand the new voting system? How do both Anglo and minority voters perceive cumulative voting?

Since all 16 jurisdictions had been sued for minority vote dilution, it is likely that Anglo voters harbored much resentment at being forced to adopt a settlement over which they had little or no control. Yet, the exit poll found greater understanding and acceptance of cumulative voting than might be expected. More than nine in ten voters of each ethnic group knew they could concentrate all their votes on a single candidate. Asked to compare cumulative voting with previous election systems, more respondents said that cumulative voting was easier than said it was more difficult.

There were large ethnic differences in evaluations of cumulative voting with regard to difficulty. More than twice as many minority as Anglo voters felt cumulative voting was easier compared to other elections in which they had voted; even so, fewer than two in ten Anglos found this election system more difficult than previous voting methods.

Cumulative voting, moreover, was not rejected by the majority of Anglo voters. The poll revealed slightly more agreement than disagreement among Anglos with the statement: "The voting system used today gives everyone a fair chance to elect officials of their choice." Almost nine in ten blacks and eight in ten Latinos agreed that it was a fair system. However, there were a number of Anglos—24 percent—who strongly disagreed with that statement.

Recommendations

This study demonstrates that cumulative voting in Texas has resulted in more diverse city councils and school boards. In a racially polarized context—as was found in all cities and school districts studied—the traditional winner-take-all, at-large elections effectively precluded minority groups from electing candidates of their choice. In those cases where cumulative voting did not result in minority victories, it was not that the method of election did not work, but that it was not applied correctly (that is, to the greatest advantage of minorities). The results of the May 6 elections provide some lessons for those considering the adoption of cumulative voting:

- Before fashioning an alternative to single-member districts such as cumulative voting, one must calculate the relative size of the minority electorate. This proportion determines what "threshold of exclusion" is needed. For Latino communities, voting-age population figures generally will not be an accurate measure of the size of the potential Latino vote; a better indicator is the count of Spanish surnames on the list of registered voters for the jurisdiction.

- After determining the effective size of the minority voting bloc, the number of seats to be filled in any one election is crucial to determining a minority group's ability to elect its preferred candidate or candidates. If the seats are too widely dispersed over several elections, the chance that a minority group can elect a candidate of its choice will be diminished.

- If the size of the minority voting group is large enough to elect, the group must act strategically regarding the number of candidates to field in a given election. Control of candidacies is more crucial in cumulative voting than in other modified at-large systems, such as limited voting and proportional representation, because intra-minority competition can result in minority losses.

- Clearly, cumulative voting is not a minority set-aside program. The ability of minority voters to elect candidates of their choice depends on voter education and solidarity in allocating multiple votes in a manner that will not disperse voting strength. If there is insufficient local mobilization of the minority vote, minority candidates are not likely to win.

• All of the Texas jurisdictions that have adopted cumulative voting are small. The Atlanta ISD was the only jurisdiction with more than 2,000 voters. A modified at-large election system was viewed by election administrators as a desirable alternative to carving their small communities into even smaller single-member districts. Nonetheless, this limited field experiment does not clearly demonstrate whether single-member districts would work as well or better in larger communities.

Conclusion

In view of all the local conditions that must be considered when choosing the type of voting system that best fits the needs of a specific community, the jury is still out on whether cumulative voting should be preferred over single-member districts to solve the problem of minority vote dilution.

Perhaps the answer may be found by returning to a different question, the basic philosophical debate over the kind of democracy we want in the United States. Is it to be a strictly majoritarian system, or should we recognize the democratic principle that the majority has a right to make policy decisions, but a significant minority also has a right to be represented in any decision-making body? Under cumulative voting, if *any group*— racial, gender, country club, "bubbas," the militia—is sufficiently large to meet the threshold and votes as a bloc, it can elect a candidate of its choice. Maybe that's why the system is so controversial, even among civil rights advocates.

12 Success for Instant Runoff Voting in San Francisco

STEVEN HILL

ROBERT RICHIE

IN NOVEMBER 2004, San Francisco held its first election with instant runoff voting (IRV), an important innovation in democracy that could spread to cities and states around the country. IRV was used to elect seven seats on the city's Board of Supervisors and will be used for citywide offices [in 2006]. Although hotly contested—one election in fact drew a remarkable twenty-two candidates—exit polls showed that city voters overwhelmingly liked IRV and found it easy to use, a finding that crossed racial and ethnic lines. All winners were decided either on election night or shortly thereafter. Observers noted how candidates reached out to more voters and engaged in fewer of the negative attacks that plague American politics.

IRV simulates a series of runoffs within a single election. Voters rank candidates in order of choice: first, second, third. These rankings indicate which candidate has support from a popular majority. In each runoff round of counting, the weakest candidate is eliminated. If a voter's first choice gets eliminated, his or her vote goes to that voter's second "runoff" choice. San Franciscans are thus able to vote for the candidates they really like without concern for the dilemma of a "spoiler" candidacy.

Recommended as an option in the Eighth Edition of the National

Civic League's *Model City Charter,* instant runoff voting has been used for decades for national and local elections in Ireland and Australia and recently was adopted for mayoral elections in London and Wellington, New Zealand. Before switching to IRV, San Francisco used to decide the majority winner in a December runoff election, an expensive procedure that the city had to perform each year from 1998 to 2003. With citywide runoffs costing the city more than $3 million, IRV will save millions of tax dollars. Candidates don't have to raise more money for a second election, so independent expenditures have dropped significantly. Winners are now determined in the general election, when voter turnout tends to be highest, receiving far more votes than winners in past city council runoffs. Cities electing leaders in multiple elections would see similar advantages by using the instant runoff instead of a "delayed runoff." It's no wonder that a San Francisco State University exit poll commissioned by the city found that only 13 percent of voters preferred the old runoff system.[1]

These advantages aren't the only reason the nation is watching. To understand the national implications of instant runoff voting, think back to the 2000 presidential election. If the nearly hundred thousand Ralph Nader voters in Florida could have ranked a second candidate as their runoff choice, Al Gore might be president today. Democrats must have wished many times throughout the 2004 presidential campaign that Florida and other battleground states were using IRV. Similarly, Republicans could have responded to Ross Perot's candidacy in the 1990s simply by trying to get as many first- and second-choice votes as they could.

Advocates of IRV say the system is more accommodating to independent-minded candidates, who can run and introduce fresh ideas into electoral debate without spoiling the outcome for another, more popular candidate. These candidates can push important issues that get ignored in this era of poll-tested campaign sound bites and bland appeals to undecided swing voters. Voters are liberated to vote for these candidates, knowing that even if their first choice can't win, their vote will go to a front-running candidate as their second or third choice.

IRV also offers something for those tired of polarized politics and mudslinging campaigns. IRV encourages coalition building among candidates. Because winners may need to attract the second or third rankings from supporters of other candidates, we saw less mudslinging and more coalition building and issue-based campaigning in most of San Francisco's seven council races. A *New York Times* profile of the campaign was headlined "New Runoff System in San Francisco Has the Rival Candidates Cooperating."[2]

Drawing bipartisan support from reform-minded Republicans and Democrats such as John McCain and Howard Dean, legislative bills for IRV have been introduced in twenty-two states. Ballot measures supporting IRV passed by a margin of two-to-one in all three cities where it was on the ballot this year: Berkeley, California; Burlington, Vermont; and Ferndale, Michigan. All three cities are now on a clear path to enact IRV in the coming years. Officials in bigger cities such as New York, Los Angeles, and Seattle are watching San Francisco's successful implementation closely.

San Francisco is leading the United States with modern democratic methods, but we expect more to follow. The main hurdle for many cities has been voting equipment that cannot support IRV. This is starting to change, and whenever the debate is focused on its merits relative to a two-round election or first-past-the-post plurality race, IRV wins.

Did IRV live up to its promise? Let's examine several suppositions posed by advocates of the system.

No More December Runoff Elections

SUPPOSITION   San Francisco voters and election officials will not have to worry about December elections. The Department of Elections will run one fewer election per year, providing more time to prepare for the next election. This will help the department run better elections.

ASSESSMENT   Supposition correct. San Francisco will not hold a December runoff election, for the first time since 1998. Winners were definitively determined in three races on election night, and in the four remaining races on November 5. Winners likely will be identified within twenty-four hours in future races.

Significant Tax Savings

SUPPOSITION   The city will save significant money in eliminating runoff elections. According to figures released by the Elections Commission in 2003, it cost San Francisco taxpayers at least $3 million to administer citywide runoff elections. Administering a runoff election in any one of the eleven supervisorial races cost a prorated amount. By eliminating the delayed runoff, the system will save taxpayers the costs of public financing for supervisor races. Public financing makes available up to $17,000 in public funds to candidates in a runoff election, so the savings is up to $34,000 per supervisor runoff as well as the administrative costs of running the program.

ASSESSMENT   Supposition correct. San Francisco avoided December runoff elections in the four supervisor races in which the candidate did not win an outright majority, so the city saved at least $1.2 million in administration and public financing costs this year alone. Avoiding future runoff elections in the city's annual November elections will quickly repay the one-time costs of implementing IRV ($1.6 million to modify the hardware and software of voting equipment modifications, and $800,000 for voter education), leading to substantial ongoing savings to San Francisco taxpayers.

Increased Votes Cast in the Decisive Election When Winners Are Chosen

SUPPOSITION   More votes will be cast in the decisive election, and winners will receive more votes than winners in the old delayed runoff system. In the previous two non-IRV supervisor elections in 2000 and 2002, relatively high voter turnout elections in November were followed by a sharp decrease in voter turnout in December. The average decline in voter turnout from November to December was 50.5 percent in runoffs in December 2000 and 31.4 percent in runoffs in December 2002.

Winning candidates received a majority of the low turnout December electorate in those two runoff elections. But compared to the total voters who participated in that supervisorial election in November, winning candidates in December received a low of 25 percent and a high of 41 percent of the November turnout, with most races in the low end of this range (see Tables 1 and 2).

ASSESSMENT   Supposition correct. In any runoff system, the winning candidate must win a majority of valid ballots cast in the final round of counting between the top candidates (for example, the "continuing ballots") rather than a majority of total ballots that might have been cast for the race. In this year's IRV elections, all winning candidates won a greater share of the first-choice election turnout than any winning candidate in the December 2000 runoffs.

Here are the numbers for 2004. Every winning candidate in runoffs had a larger vote total and percentage than winners in 2000. All of the

TABLE 1   Board of Supervisor Races, 2000

District	November Election (Total Votes)	December Runoff (Winner's Votes)	Percentage (Winner's Votes in December Compared to Total Votes in November)
District 1	28,194	7,486	26
District 2	38,206	No runoff	NA
District 3	24,860	7,202	29
District 4	27,407	8,453	31
District 5	36,115	10,384	28
District 6	23,425	8,472	36
District 7	33,867	9,333	27
District 8	38,791	9,578	25
District 9	23,765	No runoff	NA
District 10	23,884	5,887	25
District 11	25,023	8,345	33
Supervisor Races, 2002			
District 4	20,452	8,289	41
District 8	31,902	11,096	35

winners were ahead after counting first choices, but in several cases their share of the vote was small—meaning, without an instant runoff we would not have known if they had broad support; in District 5, for example, Mirkarimi received only 28 percent of voters' first choices among the twenty-two candidates. A plurality election can break down this way whenever more than two candidates run, thereby allowing a candidate to win a key office with far less than 50 percent support—including unrepresentative, polarizing candidates who never could have won with a majority.

Comparing the runoff elections in 2000 to the IRV election in 2004, *no* December winner in 2000 had more than 36 percent of the November total. In contrast, *every* winner in 2004 had more than 38 percent of the first count total—and *all but one* (Mirkarimi in District 5) had a percentage greater than 44 percent. Support for winners was significantly higher if determined by the number of people who ranked the winner with at least one of their three rankings. District 5 had twenty-two candidates, but Mirkarimi was ranked by 47 percent of voters. Every other winner drew at least one ranking from at least 53 percent of voters.

TABLE 2 San Francisco Supervisor Races with Runoffs (Votes Counted as of November 10, 2004)

District	Winner	Total Valid IRV Votes	Votes in Final Round	Votes Counted for Winner	Runoff (%)	Winning Votes as Percentage of All Votes	Ballots Ranking Winner	Percentage of All Ballots Ranking Winner
1	McGoldrick	28,011	25,253	13,615	53.9	48.6	16,908	60.4
5	Mirkarimi	34,413	25,681	12,999	50.6	37.8	16,244	47.2
7	Elsbernd	30,838	23,768	13,538	57.0	43.9	16,331	53.0
11	Sandoval	22,789	18,039	10,513	58.3	46.1	12,184	53.5

In sum, San Francisco's first IRV election was a resounding success. Voter understanding will only increase from its current high level. We applaud election officials, city leaders, candidates, and of course the voters for showing how this sensible refinement of plurality and runoff elections makes sense—and showing that it has never been more timely.

Notes

1.   Neely, F., Blash, L., and Cook, C. "An Assessment of Ranked-Choice Voting in the San Francisco 2004 Election: Preliminary Report." San Francisco: Public Research Institute, San Francisco State University, 2004 (http://pri.sfsu.edu/reports.html#23; retrieved Dec. 14, 2004).

2.   Murphy, D. E. "New Runoff System in San Francisco Has the Rival Candidates Cooperating." *New York Times,* Sept. 30, 2004, p. A16.

13 The Oregon Voting Revolution

DON HAMILTON

OREGON'S VOTE-BY-MAIL SYSTEM came of age on a cold, drizzly night in January 1996. It was the night of the special election to replace the disgraced Bob Packwood in the U.S. Senate with Gordon Smith, the charismatic Republican vegetable farmer from eastern Oregon, facing Ron Wyden, the wonkish Democratic congressman from Portland. It was a classic match up of the two men who, as it turned out, would both represent Oregon in the Senate for the next decade after Smith won the state's other seat in November 1996.

This night, famously, was the first Senate election conducted entirely by mail. Oregon's vote-by-mail experiment, which started quietly in 1981 with local races, was facing its biggest test yet. It finally reached prime time.

By most measures, this was going to be Smith's night. The polls looked good and they had momentum, so his campaign blew up balloons, hired a band, and drew several hundred supporters to the ornate third-floor ballroom at the Governor Hotel in downtown Portland. The stakes were high. A Smith win could spark a national Republican trend in 1996, perhaps even portend a GOP upset of Bill Clinton in the fall. They were ready to party.

But when the votes came in, Wyden won. The Republicans were stunned and wanted to blame vote by mail for the loss. "Lots of Republicans went nuts thinking it had somehow been stolen by vote by mail," said Dan Lavey, a top Smith strategist.

Nobody could quite figure out if mail voting favored one party over another but that didn't stop both major parties from trying in the months and years ahead. At one point, Democrats opposed vote by mail because they thought it favored Republicans; later Republicans were sure it favored Democrats. The uncertainty delayed full implementation of mail voting until November 1998, when, through a citizen initiative, Oregon made mail voting the only method for voting in all elections. No more voting booths, polling places, or waiting in line.

New Rituals of Democracy

Today, it's hard to see what the fuss was all about. . . . A 2003 poll by the University of Oregon showed 81 percent of Oregonians preferred mailing their ballot to going to a polling place.

Other states may struggle with multiple methods of voting, doubts about software, and uncertainty over accuracy and recounts, but Oregon has one system and only one system of casting ballots and it leaves a paper trail. Vote by mail has become a routine part of Oregon's political landscape. But it wasn't easy getting there.

Vote by mail, first of all, is nothing more than an absentee ballot sent to everyone. County elections officers mail out packets about three weeks before Election Day. Voters must return their ballot by mail or drop it off by 8 p.m. on Election Day. State officials say it saves money, increases turnout, and makes voting easier for the elderly, busy parents, or anyone who has trouble getting to the polls. Opponents, though, see increased opportunities for fraud and lament losing the ceremony of going to the neighborhood polling place.

Voting, after all, is the secular sacrament of democracy. It's a communal event shared with the neighbors in a school or maybe a church, a community center, or some other symbol of civic virtue. You stand alone in a little booth, make an entirely private, personal, and unedited statement on government. And when you're done you get a little sticker that says "I voted" and you get to wear it all day. It's the merit badge of democracy. Tinkering with these proceedings should never be taken lightly.

Wary Partisans

Vote by mail sneaked up on most Oregonians, and that may be why its arrival went smoothly. In 1981, state lawmakers, with little notice, approved a test program of mail voting for local elections, with the decision left up to county elections officers. In the next few years, a few local races here and there were handled by mail, while the primary and general election every two years remained polling-place elections.

No major changes were being thrust on voters and many may not have seen the practice at first because interest is usually low in local races. Lawmakers, though, liked what they saw and, in 1987, made the vote-by-mail experiment permanent, although still for local elections only. By that year, a majority of counties were using mail ballots for their local elections.

In June 1993, Oregon held its first statewide election entirely by mail, a complicated and boring measure put on the ballot by the Legislature involving voter approval of repayment of urban renewal district bonds. It failed, but turnout was still 39 percent, certainly higher than expected considering the topic.

The system was still untested in the partisan world, but perceptions changed in a 1994 congressional race, even though it was a polling-place election. On Election Night that year, Congresswoman Elizabeth Furse of the 1st District led Republican challenger Bill Witt by 10,000 votes. But as the absentee ballots were counted in the next few days, her lead evaporated to almost nothing. In the end, Furse won but only by 301 votes, one of the closest congressional races in the country that year. The swing to the Republicans came not because people who use the mail somehow favor Republicans but because the party sent absentee ballot requests to all its voters. It was that simple.

But Democrats were wary, suspicious that mail voting—still a new phenomenon on the partisan stage, remember—trended Republican. The Democrats had been whipped in the 1994 elections and were looking everywhere for blame. The 1995 Legislature, controlled by Republicans, approved a plan to extend vote by mail to all elections—primary, general, and a new special March presidential primary. Many Democrats opposed it, among them Democratic National Chairman Donald L. Fowler, who became a prominent voice against mail voting, saying it would reduce participation among poor and less educated voters.

Democratic Governor John Kitzhaber signed the bill for the presidential primary but vetoed the measure extending mail voting to all elections, much to the disappointment of Democrat Phil Keisling, the secretary of state and the state's chief elections officer, an ardent backer of mail voting. Keisling may have been stymied but got his revenge within a few months. In the fall of 1995, Packwood resigned and Keisling, as was his legal right, got to choose the type of election used to fill the seat. And to the surprise of no one, Keisling decided to use mail voting for both the primary and special election, the nation's first such congressional race.

"One of the most delightful moments in my career as secretary of state was letting Don Fowler know that the special election for that open Senate seat would be vote by mail," Keisling said. "He said, 'How can you do that? The governor vetoed the law.' I said, 'Your attorneys don't understand the Oregon law. It's a special election.' He laughed and said, 'I guess there's no way I can talk you out if it,' and I said no."

The Road to Statewide Mail Ballots

Turnout in the December 5,1995, primary was a robust 58 percent. Had Keisling ordered a polling-place primary, the date would have been December 13. On that day, the state was in the throes of a ferocious storm that brought 90-mile-an-hour winds, downed trees, and brought power outages to the populous Willamette Valley, including Portland. The storm would have severely disrupted a polling-place election.

Turnout was even higher, 66 percent, in the January 30, 1996, general election. To be sure, some of that turnout might be attributed to the star power of the race and not to the unique mail voting method. But whatever the reason, turnout was higher than usual. Turnout in the 1994 primary, for example, had been 38 percent. In the end, Wyden won in Portland, as Democrats have to do, while Smith won in rural Oregon, as Republicans have to do. But Wyden edged out Smith in the swing Portland suburbs.

Now Republicans turned against vote by mail. In 1997, a year after the Smith-Wyden race, the Oregon House once again approved a bill extending vote by mail to the primary and general election, but it died in the Republican Senate. This time, Kitzhaber, the Democratic governor, said he would have signed it.

Voters, as it turned out, really liked voting by mail. County elections officers, tired of running a polling-place election every two years and vote by mail for all other elections, let voters permanently request absentee ballots for all elections without having to explain why. And voters signed up in droves. Absentee balloting soon became the most popular voting method in Oregon.

In the May 1996 primary, absentee voters cast 36 percent of ballots, and by the general election six months later, they were casting 48 percent. By the May 1998 primary, 63 percent of all votes cast were absentees, the first time a state cast more votes by mail than at polling places. Polling places were becoming quite lonely.

In November 1998, Oregon put the matter to rest when 69 percent of the voters approved a measure expanding vote by mail to all elections. The question won in all 36 counties. In 2000, Oregon became the first state to vote for a president solely on a mail ballot and today, vote by mail is old news. Opponents are out there but increasingly harder to find.

Here's how vote by mail works. In the three weeks before the election, voters get a packet in the mail. They mark the ballot in blue or black and place it in an anonymous envelope, which is then put in a second envelope. The voter then signs that outer envelope and mails it to the county elections office. The voter pays . . . for the stamp, which doesn't constitute a poll tax, the courts decided, because a voter also may drop it off in person for no charge.

After the ballot arrives, the signature on each envelope is compared with the voter's signature on file from the voter registration card. Voters are called if they forgot to sign the envelope or if the signatures don't match. Ballots cannot be forwarded if a voter has moved.

Ballots are counted by optical scanner. Vote counting can start any-time on Election Day, but no results can be released until 8 p.m. The news media likes this part because by 8 p.m., most of the votes have been counted. The votes in that first tally come from all over. No waiting for late-night rural returns. So the numbers in that first flush of ballots are a far more accurate predictor of the results than the meager numbers that dribble out after the polls close in a polling-place election.

Clearly there was a novelty factor when vote by mail first started. In that 1996 Smith-Wyden Senate race, nearly 60 percent of all ballots had been returned a week before Election Day, according to a study, "Early Voting Reforms and American Elections," by Paul Gronke of Reed College. But old habits returned and, by 2000, half the votes came in on the last two days.

Anyone, in fact, can pick up ballots from voters, something that makes critics nervous. Conceivably, partisans could pick up ballots from opponents and never turn them in. There's nothing in the law to prohibit the practice and no way to tell if it happens unless voters follow up later to make sure if their vote was counted. The Legislature has never addressed the issue, apparently reluctant to stop their campaigns from collecting ballots from supporters. Conceivably, too, someone could pay citizens or coerce them to vote a certain way, given the breach of the traditional secrecy of the voting booth. But there has never been a whiff of any such scandal.

Don't Complain, Organize

So which party does vote by mail favor? Probably neither. Claims to the contrary are based more on hunch than real study. A 1998 University of Michigan study found vote by mail had no bearing on the ability to mobilize more Democrats or more Republicans. Political strategists say vote by mail helps the well-organized, which of course can be said about a polling-place election as well.

"Vote by mail benefits the candidate or party with the strongest political infrastructure in the state," Lavey said. "Vote by mail helps Republicans in southern states with the NRA, the churches, right-to-life. In Oregon, it tends to help Democrats with the unions. Wyden had the edge there in 1996 with women and the environmentalists."

"I truly think it helps neither," Keisling said. "The evidence doesn't show one way or another."

Don McIntire, one of the state's most successful anti-tax activists, sees dangers in vote by mail. He thinks it's designed to help Democrats by helping union workers. "Call me paranoid but what's at stake is an outcome that affects the governing class, the people on the public payroll," he said.

The 2003 University of Oregon survey found no discernable partisan tilt. "Neither of the two major parties have much to lose or gain from vote by mail," the survey said. In the poll, 32 percent of Democrats and 29 percent of Republicans said they vote more often under vote by mail. The Gronke study agreed. "There is no evidence that it changes the composition of the electorate," it said.

It's worth noting, though, that in the vote-by-mail era, starting with the 2000 election, Democrats have won 10 statewide partisan races, the Republicans just one, Smith's 2002 re-election. Republicans, meanwhile, have generally controlled the Legislature. The swing to the Democrats probably has more to do with political changes and the state's strengthening progressive community than the voting method. A similar swing can be seen in near neighbors Washington and California.

A More Discerning Electorate

Civic benefits, however, are easier to substantiate. Turnout was 71 percent in 1996, the last presidential polling-place election, but 86 percent in 2004. Other factors, of course, affect voter interest, like the economy and war. Two of Oregon's highest three voter turnouts—1960, 1992, and 2004—took place before mail voting. In contrast, turnout in the Texas primary this past March barely reached 10 percent.

"Vote by mail increases turnout, perhaps by as much as 10 percent," the Gronke study found. "However, the turnout increases result from the retention of existing voters and not from the recruitment of new voters into the system, and the increase is noticeable only in low-profile contests."

The boost from mail voting appears greater the smaller the election. Supporters of local tax measures look to it as a way to help increase turnout enough to overcome the double majority law, which requires a turnout of at least 50 percent as well as a majority "yes" vote to pass property-tax measures. Today, mail voting may be routine to the voting public, but it's brought dramatic changes for the news media and the campaigns themselves. No longer can a candidate plan on peaking on Election Day. The peak starts when the ballots go in the mail three weeks out and continues until the deadline for turning in ballots. It means campaign workers spend more time on the phone contacting voters and getting out the vote. Who voted is public record; how they voted, of course, is not. So the parties can spend the closing days calling their voters who haven't yet voted and urging them to send in the ballot.

"It increases the cost of campaigning," said Dan Lavey, a former Smith aide. "It took the normal span of activities one would normally prosecute in the final 72 hours and extended it over three weeks. The phone calls, the direct mail. And by the same token, because people could start voting three weeks before Election Day, you need to start your media campaign to have an impact when the first person starts voting as well as when the last person votes. If you think too much money is spent on campaigns, vote by mail is a bad thing."

Vote by mail made life a little more complicated and a lot more hurried for *The Oregonian,* the state's largest newspaper. The paper's policy today is to make sure voters can read in-depth stories of all candidates and ballot measures by the time ballots arrive in the mail. "You don't want any major issue uncovered before the ballots are mailed. You still have the same responsibility to readers," said Bruce Hammond, the paper's politics editor from 2000 to 2005. Reporters use the last three weeks to look at other matters, such as campaign-finance reports and the accuracy of last-minute ads. The policy can mean long delays between publication of a major look in September, say, at a ballot measure—Oregon had a record 26 in 2000—and someone voting in November.

Mail voting does save money, said John Kauffman, elections supervisor for Multnomah County, home to Portland. The 1996 general election—the last presidential race at a polling place—cost $3.31 per vote cast. The county needed 3,000 workers to manage the 1996 election but just 300 for 2004. Postage and supplies are the major expenses but are fairly modest compared to the new machines other states have to buy under the Help America Vote Act. Vote by mail eliminated the logistical hassles and risks of moving the machines, hiring and training the workers, and opening and maintaining the polling places. "I'd dread having to go back to polling-place elections," Kauffman said.

Worries and Safeguards

The mail ballot also simplifies the purging of voter rolls of people who have died or moved away. An undeliverable ballot itself purges the voter rolls of anyone who can no longer receive mail at a particular address. If any of them go astray and are used improperly, the signature match should catch them.

Jitters remain about weakness in the system, a holdover, no doubt, of Florida in 2000, and worries about glitches in the hardware and software in other states. Oregon has its stories of voters receiving more than one ballot or ballots intended for someone else. And there are worries about partisans coming into hospitals or retirement homes and filling out ballots for those unable to manage on their own. No concrete evidence has ever been found of such episodes taking place. Any organized effort to bribe voters would likely come to light.

The most important safeguard may be the voter's signature. The autograph on the outside of the ballot envelope has to match the signature on file from the voter registration card, a comparison done by an elections worker looking at the envelope and a computer screen. It's not blind luck. The same organization that trains the Oregon State Police in signature recognition trains elections workers. When signatures don't match, voters are called and asked to explain. Sometimes there's been a hand injury. Sometimes the signature on the card is old. Signatures change as we age. Sometimes a husband may think it's all right to sign his wife's ballot. It's not. Elections workers threw out more than 1,000 ballots in 2004 because they couldn't verify their signatures.

Duplicate balloting has been one of the few glitches in Oregon's system. It's rare but can happen when, say, someone moves and still receives mail at the old address. Most people who move have mail forwarded and the Postal Service isn't supposed to forward election ballots. One voter did cast two ballots in 2004 but was caught. Most people who actually get two ballots are honest enough to report the problem to the elections office. Vote fraud is, after all, a felony. A statewide voter registration database, mostly up and running this spring, will cancel old registrations once an Oregon voter re-registers in another county.

Motivated criminals have always been able to break elections systems, but fraud is usually discovered or takes place on such a small a scale that it doesn't matter. Large-scale fraud, the kind that might actually make a difference in an election, would probably involve too many people to be kept quiet.

What Oregon Avoids

Attaining perfection in an election system may be unrealistic. Glitches don't matter anyway when the results are decisive. But as we've learned, though, extremely close races may be more common. Washington Governor Chris Gregoire won in 2004 by 129 votes out of 2.7 million cast. And President Bush, of course, won Florida in 2000 by 537 votes out of more than 5.8 million cast. Minutiae can matter.

Perhaps the greatest success of the Oregon system is that it's not what other states are going through. Other states are struggling to upgrade their election systems amid scary stories of botched balloting and fears of vote fraud, corrupt machines, crooked software, and not enough accountability.

Oregon hasn't had a particularly contentious political culture, staying mostly free of big-city political machines like in Chicago or New York. That means no one's political livelihood depended on polling-place elections and the state was flexible enough to shift gears smoothly, although slowly, to a new system. All states, after all, already conduct vote-by-mail elections with absentee ballots. Oregon just made absentee balloting its only method.

The state may have lost some traditional rituals of democracy, but it certainly picked up new ones along the way.

14 The Nuts and Bolts of Public Financing of State Candidate Campaigns

CRAIG B. HOLMAN

THE SYSTEM OF GOVERNANCE in the United States has historically been founded upon two frequently dichotomous forces: the public sphere of democracy, based largely on the principle of equality of opportunity; and the private sphere of capitalism, based largely on individual entrepreneurship. Though these principles are not necessarily at odds, they have created considerable social tension. American history is replete with periods in which economic elites emerged as the dominant force in making public policy (as during the Industrial Age of the robber barons), followed by periods of mass mobilization, in which the populace seized back some control over public policy (as during the Progressive movement). Most periods of American government have fallen somewhere between the two ends of this spectrum.

Campaign finance law is one of the most important modern mechanisms for modulating the influence of economic elites over the formulation of public policy. The unregulated flow of money into politics has often been viewed by the general public as a leading source of disproportionate influence over public policy by wealthy individuals and special interests—and historical experience suggests they do so with good cause. But how best to regulate that flow of campaign cash is a matter fraught with complications, consequences both intended and unintended, evolving social needs, and subjective judgments. In short, there really is no best campaign finance law for all jurisdictions and for all times;[1] an appropriate campaign finance law must be carefully tailored to the needs and objectives of a particular jurisdiction. Nevertheless, many national and state as well as local jurisdictions are experiencing sufficiently comparable trends in campaign financing that they are experimenting with multiple variations of similar laws and regulations, one of which is public financing.

The research in this article examines the historical and contemporary movement toward public financing of candidate campaigns. Several types of public financing programs at the state level are compared and the key elements of each are discussed. By the end, the nuts and bolts of establishing and maintaining a system of public financing of candidates should be fairly evident and provide a basis for evaluating an appropriate model for any particular jurisdiction.

Conceptual Clarity and Evolution of Public Financing of Candidate Campaigns

In publicly funding campaign activity, the federal, state, or local government collects public monies through taxes, fees, or fines and distributes the money to candidates or party committees. Such financing of candidate campaigns is usually offered as an incentive to encourage candidates to voluntarily agree to a spending ceiling. Public financing of party committees is most often offered as a modest means to supplement party activities (such as to help pay for convention expenses) and does not constitute a significant element of campaign finance practices today.

There are two general categories of public financing program: partial public financing and full public financing. In a *partial public financing* program, the government makes public funds available to qualified candidates to pay for a portion, but not all, of campaign expenses. The public grants in a partial program are usually awarded as *matching funds,* a certain amount of public dollars matching private campaign contributions; or as *block grants,* in which the government makes a lump sum payment to candidates who meet specific qualification criteria, such as raising a minimum amount of private campaign contributions.

In a *full public financing* program, the government offers public funds to qualified candidates to pay for nearly all campaign expenses in exchange for candidates agreeing not to accept any private campaign contributions beyond the initial seed money used to start a campaign organization and to meet specific qualification criteria, such as raising a certain number of *de minimus* five-dollar contributions. This type of public financing program is often referred to as a "clean elections" program.

History of Public Financing

Though the clean elections program is frequently seen as the newest and hottest model of public financing of candidate campaigns, it is in fact the oldest—and the original—model.

During the first century of the republic, campaigns were not expensive affairs. Besides the cost of plying potential voters with food and ale and printing hand leaflets, most campaigns were financed on a low budget and did not rely on an extensive base of campaign contributors. It was not until after the Civil War, with the increase in the U.S. population and the rise of industrialism, that money in politics became a concern. Abraham Lincoln was among the first to note the emerging danger of candidates being increasingly in need of campaign funds and wealthy special interests being willing to supply the cash. Lincoln warned: "As a result of the war, corporations have become enthroned, and an era of corruption in high places will follow. The money power of the country will endeavor to prolong its rule by preying upon the prejudices of the people until all wealth is concentrated in a few hands and the Republic is destroyed."[2]

Over the next several decades, matters grew increasingly worse. Industrial capitalists and the robber barons continued to concentrate wealth in the hands of the few, making those individuals the most valued source of campaign money among candidates and officeholders. Charges of corruption became commonplace in American politics. Several state and local governments responded with antibribery laws and disclosure requirements, but these actions accomplished little to restore public confidence in elected officials.

The first time the concept of public financing of candidate campaigns was raised was in 1904. Following allegations of influence peddling in the presidential campaign, Rep. William Bourke Cochran, a Tammany Hall official from Manhattan, proposed that the federal government provide for all candidate campaign expenses. The bill went nowhere.

At the federal level, President Theodore Roosevelt attempted to counter his image of selling out to corporate campaign money by supporting campaign finance reform. Roosevelt joined Congressman Cochran by calling for public financing of party committees in a December 1907 message to Congress. Congress was not ready for public financing of campaigns. Other allies found Roosevelt's new campaign reform programs even more repugnant. One of Roosevelt's wealthiest contributors, Henry Frick, commented: "[Roosevelt] got down on his knees to us. We bought the son of a bitch and he did not stay bought."[3] At least one scholar, however, doubted the sincerity of Roosevelt's newfound commitment to campaign reform.[4]

The idea of public financing did not fade away. A state governors' conference in 1913 debated a proposal for full public financing of state elections. Seven years later, President Woodrow Wilson's treasury secretary, William Gibbs McAdoo, also suggested that the federal government could "purify" politics by paying for all legitimate campaign expenses.[5]

Ironically, the first experiment with public financing of federal campaigns was signed into law by then-President Richard Nixon in 1971. Prior to the sensational outbreak of the Watergate scandal, Congress approved and the president signed the Federal Election Campaign Act (FECA) of 1971, which in part extended public subsidies to the national party committees for campaign activity. The subsequent Watergate scandal led a few years later to Nixon's resignation and amendments to FECA. The most significant feature of the 1974 amendments was creation of a system of partial public financing for eligible presidential primary candidates and full public financing for the major parties' presidential general election candidates—a system that remains in effect to date.

Buckley v. Valeo

Just when the history of campaign finance reform appeared to have evolved to its highest point, the U.S. Supreme Court was invited into the fray. Sen. James Buckley (Republican, from New York) had joined with former Sen. Eugene McCarthy (Democrat, from Minnesota) and General Motors heir Stewart Mott to challenge the constitutionality of the new law. Secretary of the Senate Francis Valeo joined with Common Cause and the League of Women Voters as defendants of the law. In the end, the court struck down several key elements of the law in the landmark 1976 *Buckley v. Valeo* decision.

The *Buckley* decision has set the constitutional standards for all federal, state, and local campaign finance laws ever since. The central question addressed by the court was posed by Justice Potter Stewart: Is money speech and speech money? In other words, does money form the basis for candidates and committees to convey their ideas to the public? A majority of the court ruled that money *as an expenditure* is in essence free speech. Thus, it is unconstitutional for the government to mandate limits on political expenditures. Candidates, committees, special interest groups, and individuals have the constitutional right to spend all the money they wish for campaign advertisements.

However, the court added several important caveats. First, and most important, although money as an expenditure is tantamount to free speech and not subject to mandated limits, money *as a contribution* to others is equivalent to proxy speech—that is, money in the latter case simply serves to help enable someone else to speak on your behalf. As proxy speech, contributions are not entitled to the same constitutional protections as expenditures; the "quantity of the communication by the contributor does not increase perceptibly with the size of the contribution." In this instance, First Amendment considerations are outweighed by the potential for corruption or perceived corruption caused by large contributions. Thus governments may mandate limits on contributions to candidates and committees.

A second important caveat in the *Buckley* decision is that even though governments cannot mandate limits on candidate expenditures, they may offer incentives to encourage candidates *voluntarily* to limit their expenditures. Under FECA, for example, the federal government could offer public funds to candidates in a contractual exchange for the candidates to voluntarily limit spending.

Buckley v. Valeo transformed the nature of campaign finance reform in general and public financing in particular. Although many of the traditional campaign finance reform programs, such as mandatory spending ceilings, found themselves on the ropes under the *Buckley* decision, public financing found new life under the ruling. The most effective tool of campaign finance reform in history was mandatory spending ceilings, but such was no longer to be the case. Now, public financing had to fill the void. Not only was public financing viewed as a means to reduce the importance of private money in elections, but it also became the primary means to achieve some of the most important ingredients of reform, especially implementation of voluntary spending ceilings.

State Public Financing Programs Today

Currently, the federal government, fourteen states, and thirteen local jurisdictions have some form of public financing of candidate campaigns, with these numbers, especially at the local level, regularly in flux (Table 1).[6] Several other states offer minimal public funds exclusively to state

TABLE 1   Public Financing of State Elections

	State	Clean Money?	Statute
All State Offices	Hawaii		HRS §11–217 et seq.
	Minnesota		MS §10A.30(1) et seq.
	Wisconsin		WSA §5.02(23); 11.50(1) et seq.
	Maine	yes	MRSA tit. 21-A §1124 et seq.
	Arizona	yes	ARSA tit. 16, ch. 6, §16–940 et seq.
	Massachusetts	yes	ALM ch. 55A §1A(a)(1) et seq.
Statewide Offices	Florida		FSA §106.30 et seq.
	Rhode Island		GLRI §17–25–19 et seq.
Governorship	Kentucky		KRS §121A.020(a) et seq.
	Maryland		MECA §31–4(a) et seq.
	Michigan		MCL §169.203(1) et seq.
	New Jersey		NSJA §19:44A-27 et seq.
	Vermont	yes	VSA tit. 17, §2856(a) et seq.
Legislative Offices	Nebraska[1]		RSN §32–1603(1) et seq.
Political Party Committees[2]	Idaho		IC §34–2503(a) et seq.
	Indiana		IC §9–7–5.5–8(a) et seq.
	Iowa		IC §56.19 et seq.
	New Mexico		NMSA §7–2–31(A) et seq.
	North Carolina		GSNC §105–159.1(a); 163–278. 41 et seq.
	Ohio		ORCA §3517.16 et seq.
	Texas		EC §173.001 et seq.
	Utah		UCA §59–10–548(1) et seq.

TABLE 1   *(Continued)*

	State	Clean Money?	Statute
Local Jurisdictions with Public Financing for Candidates	Austin, Tex.		(enacted 1994)
	Boulder, Colo.		(1999)
	Gary, N.C.		(2000)
	Cincinnati, Ohio		(2001)
	Long Beach, Calif.		(1994)
	Los Angeles		(1990)
	Miami-Dade County, Fla.		(2001)
	New York City		(1988)
	Oakland, Calif.		(1999)
	Petaluma, Calif.		(2000)
	San Francisco		(2000)
	Suffolk County, N.Y.		(1998)
	Tucson, Ariz.		(1985)

1. Nebraska gives public funds only to candidates whose opponents decline to abide by the spending ceilings. Nebraska's system applies first to the legislature and then to other offices only upon sufficient funding. No public funds were allocated to candidates in the first election cycle. In the last election cycle, one candidate for board of regents qualified for public financing.

2. States that offer public funds only to party committees offer minimal funds, which are usually used to help finance party conventions.

political parties, which are usually used to help finance state party conventions rather than candidate elections.[7]

Although all public financing systems share common essential features, the differences in the nature, scope, and implementation of the programs among the states can be stark. Public financing systems vary from one jurisdiction to another in the number of offices covered by the program, the extent of funding given to candidates, the timing of disbursements, the procedures to determine candidate eligibility, the sources of revenue to pay for the programs, and a host of other factors.

The key components of public financing programs can be generalized into six categories:

1.   Eligible offices and applicable elections

2.   Costs of a public financing system

3.   Sources of public funds

4.   Qualification of candidates for public financing

5.   Allocation of public funds

6.   Voluntary spending ceilings

These key components of public financing programs will be discussed in turn.

Eligible Offices and Applicable Elections

State public financing programs vary in terms of which elective offices are included in the programs and whether the programs apply to primary or general elections or both. Factors such as cost and the competitiveness of primary versus general elections weigh into considering when and where to apply public financing of candidate elections.

Of course, the most ambitious programs apply to all state elective offices and both primary and general elections. Nevertheless, most states have opted to include only some offices and elections in their public financing programs.

Minnesota's public financing program, widely considered one of the most comprehensive at the state level, applies to all state offices but only in the general election. Minnesota has a strong tradition of partisan politics, and the two major parties view the general election as a more critical stage in balancing financial resources between candidates than the primary election. (It is worth noting, however, that this rationale badly backfired for the two major parties in the 1998 gubernatorial election, when public subsidies enabled a third party candidate—Jesse Ventura—to capture the governorship.)

In most jurisdictions, public financing applies only to a few of the most important offices. In Vermont and New Jersey, for example, only candidates for the office of governor are eligible to receive public funds. The precise rationale behind limiting the applicable offices depends on the unique history of the state. Cost is always a factor; it is less expensive to publicly finance only select offices. But political history also counts. In some states, the targeted office may be associated with a specific scandal that did not envelop other offices in the state. Other times, one branch of government may find it acceptable to subject another branch to campaign finance restrictions, but not itself.

Costs of Public Financing Systems

Anytime a state government debates the merits and scope of a public financing program, considerations of cost are front and center. Of course, governments must adopt responsible spending programs when it comes to government policies. But this focus on the cost of public financing of campaigns is largely misplaced. Relative to most other government programs, public financing of candidates is cheap.

Public financing of candidate campaigns generally is not an expensive proposition compared with the overall size of a state budget. Actual costs vary widely from state to state, depending on a number of factors (the size of the state, the costs of campaigning, the amount of public subsidies given to candidates, how many candidates participate, and so on). Minnesota, with a comprehensive partial public financing system for all state offices, budgeted an annual average of $7.6 million for its public financing system in 2000; Wisconsin, also a partial public financing system for all state candidates, budgeted about $450,000 for its program in the same year.

Full public financing programs can reasonably be expected to cost somewhat more, but the price tag still is not intimidating. Since the full public financing programs of Arizona, Maine, Massachusetts, and Vermont are fairly new, accurate cost figures remain elusive for a full public financing program. But current budget allocations suggest that these programs also are not expensive. In the 2000 election cycle, total funds disbursed in these programs amounted to $1.9 million in Arizona, $874,000 in Maine, and about $320,000 in Vermont.

Viewed in a different comparative perspective, such as cost-per-resident or percentage of the state budget, the cost of either a partial or full public financing program does not appear prohibitive. In Minnesota, which has the largest dollar outlay for a public financing program, the cost amounts to roughly $1.50 per resident per year, or 0.06 percent of the state budget. In 2000, Maine's full public financing program cost about $0.68 per resident, or about 0.016 percent of the state budget. Even when a public financing program is fully funded and fully used by all state candidates, it will never cost more than a fraction of 1 percent of the state budget.

For those who still worry that such a program could break the bank, let us point out that it is common for the state statutes establishing public financing to fix a maximum cap on all expenditures associated with the program. If the costs of the program in any particular election near the cap, the available funds are distributed on a pro rata basis and candidates may be permitted to make up the shortfall through soliciting private campaign contributions. This has never yet happened at the state level, though the City of Los Angeles once had to resort to pro rata distribution of funds for its local public financing program.

Sources of Public Funds

The question of where the money for a public financing program will come from is the second most controversial aspect of such programs. Deciding upon the source of revenues to pay for candidate elections is politically sensitive. States have several options, among them allocations from the state general fund, tax check-offs, tax add-ons, tax rebates, lobbyist fees, candidate registration fees, election-related fines, and (a recent innovation) surcharges on civil and criminal fines and forfeitures. As shown in Table 2, most states use some combination of these funding sources.

Though the general fund constitutes the most reliable and fair source of revenues to pay for public financing, it can also be politically problematic. The theme of "taxpayer-funded campaigns" resonates poorly with voters. Survey research has shown that labels mean a great deal in the politics of campaign finance reform. Survey respondents have rather consistently liked the idea of a clean elections program (that is, full public financing), but they tend to be evenly divided over "public financing" of campaigns, and downright opposed to "taxpayer-funded" programs— even though they are all the same thing. Garnering political support for public financing often becomes a game of wordplay in which proponents talk about clean elections and opponents talk about taxpayer dollars.

This is why the federal public financing program and most state programs rely on a voluntary tax check-off revenue source. Taxpayers may choose to dedicate a small portion of their tax dollars to the public financing program. A tax check-off system means that the dedicated dollar or two comes from the general fund and does not add any further tax burden to the taxpayer. Even though the check-off does not cost the taxpayer a dime, the participation rate at both the federal and state levels has been falling dramatically over recent years. In Minnesota, for example, 27.2 percent of taxpayers earmarked dollars for the state public financing program in 1976, but in 1999 it fell to 8.2 percent. In Wisconsin, the participation rate fell from 18.4 percent to 8.3 percent over the same time period.[8]

Proponents of public financing in Arizona, a state known for its fiscal conservatism, sidestepped the whole word game by inventing a new

TABLE 2   Public Financing in the States: Sources of Public Funds

State	Check-off	Add-on	General Fund	Lobbyist Fees	Other
Arizona	$5			X[1]	• 10 percent surcharge on fines • Candidate filing fees • Tax credit
Florida		X	X		• Candidate filing fees • Election fines
Hawaii	$2		Advised by law		• Tax credit
Kentucky			X		
Maine	$3		X	X	• Fines
Maryland		X			
Massachusetts	$1		Advised by law		• Fines
Michigan	$2				•
Minnesota	$5		X		• Property tax check-off • $50 tax rebate
Nebraska	$2		X	X	• Interest
New Jersey	$1		X		
Rhode Island	$5		X		
Vermont		X	X	X	• Business filing fees • Fines
Wisconsin	$1				• Candidate filing fees

1. Arizona's lobbyist fees for financing the public financing program have since been invalidated by the courts.

source of revenues: a 10 percent surcharge on civil and criminal fines. The campaign slogan for Arizona's full public financing program became "Let criminals pay for politicians." Arizona voters overwhelmingly approved the full public financing program on the state's 1998 ballot.

Qualification of Candidates for Public Financing

In all of the contemporary public financing systems, candidates must agree to a spending ceiling and demonstrate some level of viability as a serious candidate to qualify for public funds. Most states also require candidates to limit the use of their own personal funds and have an opponent in order to be eligible for public financing. The greatest difference among states in qualification procedures is in the means of demonstrating viability as a serious candidate.

To qualify for public financing, a candidate must demonstrate that he or she is a serious contender for office and not a frivolous opportunist. This usually involves raising a minimum amount of campaign funds, depending on the level of office. In Hawaii, for example, a candidate for state office other than governor must raise at least $15,000 in private contributions of $100 or less. In Michigan, the fundraising qualification threshold is set at 5 percent of the prescribed spending ceilings, raised in contributions of $100 or less.

Full public financing programs operate somewhat differently. Instead of raising a substantial amount of private contributions to demonstrate viability, a candidate must receive small contributions (usually $5) from a large number of people. Typically, eligible candidates must receive $5 contributions from 2 to 4 percent of the electorate in the last election for that office. Because these are new programs, there is no certainty and little experience in determining precisely how many qualifying contributions are appropriate. Ideally, the appropriate number of required qualifying contributions should meet two objectives. The number should not be so high as to be onerous and disable all but the well-connected candidates from qualifying. At the same time, the number should not be so low that frivolous candidates can qualify and flood the public financing system.

The state-to-state variations in qualification requirements are shown in Table 3.

Allocation of Public Funds

There are two basic forms of allocating public subsidies in public financing programs: matching funds and block grants. Each form of allocating funds must also address the additional issues of amount of disbursement, timing of disbursement, and a maximum cap on disbursements.

Most, but not all, partial public financing systems operate on the basis of a matching fund allocation.[9] Once a candidate qualifies for public subsidies, the candidate may then submit records of private contributions, which the state matches with public funds according to a specified formula. Frequently, a partial public financing program may match a small private contribution on a one-to-one basis or higher. For example, Florida

TABLE 3   Public Financing in the States: Qualification Procedures for Public Financing

State	Procedure
Arizona	1. Agree to voluntary spending ceilings.
	2. No contributions in excess of $100 or a total of $40,000 in the exploratory period.
	3. Receive $5 in-district qualification contributions in the following numbers: governor, 4,000; statewide, 2,500; legislative, 200.
	4. Accept no private contributions thereafter.
Florida	1. Agree to voluntary spending ceilings.
	2. Raise a qualification threshold in private contributions: governor, $150,000; statewide, $100,000.
Hawaii	1. Agree to voluntary spending ceilings.
	2. Raise a qualification threshold in private contributions of $100 or less: governor, $25,000; lieutenant governor, $20,000; other, $15,000.
	3. Have an opponent who also qualifies.
Kentucky	1. Agree to voluntary spending ceilings.
	2. Raise a qualification threshold of $300,000 (governor only).
	3. Have an opponent who also raised $300,000.
Maine	1. Agree to voluntary spending ceilings.
	2. No contributions in excess of $100 for seed money.
	3. Receive $5 in-district qualification contributions in the following numbers: governor, 2,500; senate, 150; house, 50.
	4. Accept no private contributions thereafter.
Maryland	1. Agree to voluntary spending ceilings.
	2. Raise a qualification threshold of 10 percent of the spending ceiling.
	3. Have a viable opponent.
Massachusetts	1. Agree to voluntary spending ceilings.
	2. Accept no private contributions in excess of $100, up to 20 percent of the spending ceiling.
	3. Receive $5 to $100 of in-district qualification contributions in the following numbers: governor, 6,000; statewide, 3,000; senate, 450; house, 200.
Michigan	1. Agree to voluntary spending ceilings.
	2. Limit personal contributions.
	3. Raise a qualification threshold of 5 percent of the spending ceiling in contributions of $100 or less.

TABLE 3   (*Continued*)

State		Procedure
Minnesota	1.	Agree to voluntary spending ceilings.
	2.	Limit personal contributions.
	3.	Raise a qualification threshold in contributions of $50 or less in the following amounts: governor, $35,000; statewide, $6,000; senate, $3,000; house, $1,500.
	4.	Qualify for the general election.
	5.	Receive at least 10 percent of the vote.
Nebraska	1.	Agree to voluntary spending ceilings.
	2.	Have an opponent who does not agree to the spending ceilings.
New Jersey	1.	Agree to the voluntary spending ceilings.
	2.	Raise a qualification threshold of $150,000 (governor only).
Rhode Island	1.	Agree to voluntary spending ceilings.
	2.	Receive a major party nomination.
	3.	Independent candidates raise a qualification threshold of 20 percent of the spending ceiling in contributions of $250 or less.
Vermont	1.	Agree to voluntary spending ceilings.
	2.	Limit aggregate private fundraising, other than qualification contributions, to no more than $500.
	3.	Raise qualification contributions of $35,000 for governor and $17,500 for lieutenant governor in contributions of $50 or less.
	4.	No more than 25 percent of qualification contributors may be from the same county.
Wisconsin	1.	Agree to voluntary spending ceilings.
	2.	Limit personal contributions.
	3.	Raise a qualification threshold of 5 percent of the spending ceiling for statewide offices, and 10 percent for state offices, in contributions of $100 or less.
	4.	Qualify for the general election.
	5.	Receive at least 6 percent of votes cast.

matches each private contribution of $250 or less with twice that amount in public subsidies for participating candidates.

Matching fund formulas are usually set for two distinct purposes: (1) to provide public subsidies so as to reduce the importance of private contributions, and (2) to maximize the importance of small contributions. New York City, for example, exemplifies the second purpose of the matching fund formula. A few years ago, New York modified its matching fund formula from one-to-one for each $1,000 in private contributions to four-to-one public funds for each $250 in private contributions. Theoretically, the same total amount of funds is allocated in the program, but now contributions of $250 or less become more valuable than private contributions in excess of $250.

All full public financing programs deliver their public subsidies to candidates in the form of block grants. Under a block grant formula, once candidates qualify for public financing they receive the public subsidies in one lump sum, or in large chunks according to a set timetable. Full public financing systems could not operate in any other manner, since there are no private contributions to match.

Each method of allocating public funds has advantages and disadvantages. A matching fund allocation system ensures that public funds are awarded only to viable candidates. The disadvantage is that matching funds are awarded unevenly among the candidates, favoring the better fundraisers over others. The block grant system awards an even amount to all qualified candidates early in the campaign, affording an equal footing to all. The disadvantage, of course, is increased likelihood that frivolous candidates could receive substantial public dollars.

Voluntary Spending Ceilings

As shown in Table 4, spending ceilings vary considerably from state to state. Differences in demographics, media expenses, and other election-related factors make a single spending ceiling formula impossible. Some states fix their spending ceiling at an absolute dollar amount, adjusted for inflation. Other states set their ceiling according to an amount-per-resident expenditure, such as Maryland's thirty cents per registered voter. Other states set differing spending ceilings for primary and general elections for the same office.

Setting an appropriate spending ceiling is an important but sometimes overlooked element of an effective public financing program. It is not uncommon for advocates of campaign finance reform to set an unrealistically low spending ceiling in a quest to reduce the amount of money in

TABLE 4   Spending Ceilings Among State Public Financing Programs

State	Spending Ceilings	CPI[1]	Lift[2]
Arizona	Governor: primary, $380,000; general, $570,000		
	Statewide: primary, $80,000; general, $120,000	X	X
	Legislative: primary, $10,000; general, $15,000		
Florida	Governor: $5 million per election cycle		
	Statewide: $2 million per election cycle	X	X
Hawaii	Governor: $2.50 per voter per year		
	Legislative: $1.50 per voter per year		
Kentucky	Governor: primary, $1.8 million; general, $1.8 million	X	
Maine	Average of previous two elections		X
Maryland	Governor: 30 cents per voter		
Massachusetts	Governor: primary, $1.8 million; general, $1.2 million		
	Statewide: primary, $450,000; general, $300,000		
	Senate: primary, $54,000; general, $36,000	X	X
	Representative: primary, $18,000; general, $12,000		
Michigan	Governor: $2 million per election		X
Minnesota	Governor: $1.9 million per year		
	Statewide: $160,000 per year		
	Senate: $43,000 per year	X	X
	Representative: $24,000 per year		
	(Non-incumbents may spend 20 percent more than the ceiling)		
Nebraska	Governor: general, $1.5 million		
	Statewide: general, $150,000		
	Legislative: general, $73,000		
	(Primary election ceilings are 50 percent of general election ceilings)		
New Jersey	Governor: primary, $3.1 million; general, $6.9 million	X	
Rhode Island	Governor: $1.5 million per election cycle		
	Statewide: $375,000 per election cycle	X	X
Vermont	Governor: incumbent, $225,000 per cycle; nonincumbent, $300,000 per cycle		
	Statewide: incumbent, $38,250 per cycle; nonincumbent, $45,000 per cycle		
	Senate: incumbent, $3,600 per cycle; nonincumbent, $4,000 per cycle		
	Representative: incumbent, $1,800 per cycle; nonincumbent, $2,000 per cycle		

TABLE 4   (*Continued*)

State	Spending Ceilings	CPI[1] Lift[2]
Wisconsin	Governor: $1,078,200 per cycle Most statewide: $215,625 per cycle Senate: $37,500 per cycle Representative: $17,250 per cycle	

1. *CPI* denotes that the ceiling is adjusted for inflation.
2. *Lift* denotes that the spending ceiling may be lifted under certain conditions.

politics. Although a low spending ceiling may have some popular appeal, the constitutional framework established by the *Buckley* decision must be kept in mind.

For the time being anyway, spending ceilings may not be fixed by the state and mandated for all candidates. Candidates must voluntarily agree to abide by a spending ceiling. Public financing is a contractual arrangement in which candidates receive public subsidies in exchange for agreeing to limit their spending. Any candidate who does not wish to limit spending—as George W. Bush so declined in the 2000 presidential primary election—may opt out of the public financing program with no penalty (other than forfeiting eligibility to receive public funds).

Opting out can be an attractive strategy to any candidate who can raise and spend more in private dollars than he or she could within the public financing program. This means that if the spending ceiling is too low in a public financing program, or the amount of public subsidies given to eligible candidates are too little, the program is likely to fail. . . .

Spending ceilings should be drawn in accordance with realistic campaign spending practices in prior elections. The average amount spent by the winning candidates for a specific office in, say, the last two election cycles can be calculated, and these figures will offer a useful indicator of an appropriate spending ceiling.

In one particularly innovative public financing program, Minnesota has set its spending ceiling for challengers 20 percent higher than for incumbents. Realizing that incumbents enjoy the additional benefits over challengers of incumbency and name recognition, Minnesota has chosen to allow challengers to spend a little more in attempting to catch up. Despite this seeming structural inequity between challengers and incumbents, the state makes the public financing program so attractive that nearly all candidates opt into its public financing system and play by the rules.

Conclusion: Make Public Financing Work

Perhaps the greatest lesson that can be learned from how the presidential election is financed is that a public financing program must be carefully crafted if it is to work well.

No doubt about it, the presidential public financing system is a failure. Campaign spending in presidential elections has reached an absurdly high level, and a new record is set each election. Campaign fundraising by the presidential candidates never slows, even when the campaign budgets are theoretically paid for in full in the general election, and fundraising consumes most of the candidates' campaign activity. If left unabated, the presidential public financing program will soon collapse in form as well as in substance.

But it need not be so. As can be gleaned from the experiences of some states, public financing can be made to work if the particulars of the program are crafted to fit the needs and objectives of the jurisdiction.

Contribution limits and disclosure requirements are useful tools in ameliorating the corrupting influence of excessive money in politics. Contribution limits help reduce the potential for corruption, and disclosure helps keep the flow of money in public view. But these reforms are no panacea for keeping elections fair and open in a nation largely engulfed in economic inequality

Public financing of candidate campaigns takes campaign finance reform one large step further toward the goal of controlling the influence of money in electoral campaigns. Public financing is not only an effective method of reducing the potentially corrupting pressures of the money chase in politics, but it also enables less endowed candidates to run a viable campaign, provides some semblance of balance in campaign resources among competing candidates, increases voter choice and candidate competition, and places a lid on campaign expenditures. A carefully designed public financing program can offer even more. Some states, such as Arizona, have structured their public financing program to address the problems of wealthy candidates and excessive independent spending by outside groups. If a wealthy candidate plans on exceeding the recommended spending ceiling, or if outside groups make large independent expenditures on behalf of a candidate that in the aggregate exceed the spending ceiling, Arizona's program will give the disadvantaged candidate additional public funds beyond the recommended spending ceiling so as to prevent buying the election.

A solid public financing program should (1) apply to most, if not all, elective state offices; (2) establish reasonable qualification thresholds to allow all viable candidates to participate; (3) make available adequate financial resources so that participating candidates may wage competitive campaigns; and (4) be set within a realistic spending ceiling so as to encourage candidate participation.

Public financing is an inexpensive way to keep elections free.

Notes

1. The viewpoints expressed herein are exclusively those of the author and may not represent those of Public Citizen.

2. Marcel, J. "Still Radical." *Sunday Republican* (Springfield, Mass.), Apr. 9, 1995.

3. Shannon, J. *Money and Politics*. New York: *Random House, 1959*, p. 35.

4. Mutch, R. *Campaigns, Congress, and Courts: The Making of Federal Campaign Finance Law*. New York: Praeger, 1988.

5. Mutch (1988), p. 36.

6. The number of local jurisdictions with public financing programs for local candidates has grown rapidly in recent years. As of 2003, thirteen local jurisdictions have public financing programs, seven of which have been implemented since 1999, with several other localities considering similar programs. Local public financing jurisdictions include Austin (Tex.), Boulder (Colo.), Cary (N.C.), Cincinnati (Ohio), Long Beach (Calif.), Los Angeles, Miami-Dade County (Fla.), New York City, Oakland (Calif.), Petaluma (Calif.), San Francisco, Suffolk County (N.Y.), and Tucson (Ariz.). As of this writing, all of the local programs are partial public financing systems. However, proposals for full public financing systems have been debated in New York, were recently rejected in San Diego (Calif.), and are under consideration in Berkeley (Calif.).

7. The states that offer some public assistance exclusively to state party committees are Idaho, Indiana, Iowa, New Mexico, North Carolina, Ohio, Texas, and Utah. These public allocations tend to be used solely to finance state party conventions.

8. Data on tax check-off rates have been compiled from state elections agencies and are on file with the author.

9. A few states with partial public financing systems, such as Minnesota and Wisconsin, give candidates block grants rather than matching funds. However, the block grants are delivered to the candidate at the conclusion of the election.

PART FIVE

POLITICAL PARTIES

AND INTEREST GROUPS

A key to understanding the diversity of state political parties lies in the notion of decentralization. While the two major parties maintain national committees and organizations, most party activity takes place within each state, and at the local level. What is the linkage, therefore, between these levels of party activity? Writing in the latter part of the 19th century, Lord James Bryce argued that it was the political parties that supplied the steam necessary to drive the machinery of state government. However, with the emergence of the national parties in the early days of the Republic, the state parties were gradually absorbed, preventing the growth of what he called "real state parties" concerned with debating and addressing the issues and problems of each respective state, rather than having an underlying framework of national issues as a basis for existence. Only rarely did such entities emerge. Bryce noted that in the absence of the organizing advantages of "real state parties," the state legislative machinery did not operate as smoothly as it could.[1]

As it turned out, because of the lack of significant competition between "real state parties" in the several states, and as a result of the decentralized nature of American political parties, the parties themselves became "machines" in several states. Concerned only with securing the spoils and advantages of political office, colorful party leaders called "bosses" solidified their power by maintaining a grip on the reins of state government through such mechanisms as political patronage, graft, and corruption.[2] A large portion of this type of party activity and organization occurred at the local level as well, and much of the legendary reputation of the party machines comes from the organizations built in the late 19th century by powerful party leaders in urban areas.[3]

A significant factor leading to the ability of party machines to emerge is the degree of inter-party electoral competition in the states, with lack of competition, or weak competition, opening the door for machines to take control. Indeed, one of the longstanding characteristics of diversity across the states is the relative differences in the strength of the two parties. In the early 1950s, Austin Ranny and Wilmoore Kendall developed a useful typology of party competition in the American states covering the elections of 1914–1954. The typology was based on a four-dimensional measure resulting in an index "derived by averaging the percent Democratic (a) gubernatorial vote, (b) seats in the state Senate, (c) seats in the lower house, and (d) terms for these three offices."[4] Thus, an index of 1.000 indicated total Democratic success, and index of 0.000 indicated total Republican dominance, and an index of 0.500 represented perfect two-party competition. Based on this measure, Ranny and Kendall were able to develop a classification scheme allowing states to fall within five possible categories of One-Party Democratic, Modified One-Party Democratic, Two-Party, Modified One-Party Republican, and One-Party Republican.[5] Several scholars have used this measure, and have updated it through the 1980s. However, in their research, Thomas Holbrook and Emily Van Dunk argue that there are some potential validity problems with the measure proposed by Ranny and Kendall. The most problematic is that it purports to measure the degree of party electoral strength without relying on voting statistics. Holbrook and Van Dunk then flesh out their criticism of the validity of the Ranny/Kendall index, and argue that a better measure of party electoral competition would be based on the results of district-level general election voting patterns averaged for each state. Their research pursues this line of thought and provides such a measure of inter-party competition in the states.[6]

This concern that political scientists have had with measuring state-level inter-party competition stems from the understanding that, by and large, we have a two-party system in the United States, but the relative strength of each party differs across the states. Knowing this helps us better understand state politics. Interestingly, what the data do show about the two major parties is that in recent years they have become more evenly matched in the states.[7]

The close presidential election of 2000 ushered into our political lexicon the oft-mentioned Red State/Blue State distinction. Political pundits, journalists, and other observers latched onto this simple schema to try to explain the election's close outcome. Loosely developed, stereo-typical descriptions of archetypal Red state citizens and Blue state citizens were put forth by several political observers[8] all over the media, and the result was that the color schema were soon taken by many to be valid descriptions of a seriously polarized electorate according to Red-state and Blue-state characteristics. However, as noted already in Part One, careful research has shown that this is not really true at the national level, and that it has been our presidential candidates that have become more polarized in recent years, not the electorate.[9] Our first article provides a less technical argument against any rigid use of the Red/Blue classification at the individual state level as Walter Kirn asks: "What color is Montana?".

Third parties have always existed in the states. Some have been quite successful at getting their candidates elected through the years, and many Americans have become frustrated with the seemingly deadlocked nature of the two-party system. Indeed, slightly over half of the electorate has reported that they believe a major third party is needed.[10] Evidence of third-party successes can be seen in 1998 when Reform Party gubernatorial candidate Jesse Ventura won that seat in Minnesota, and the recent emergence of the Libertarian and Green parties whose candidates have won numerous state and local contests around the country. In light of this third party movement, our next article examines New York's Working Families Party (WFP), and the challenges and successes it has experienced since its creation in 1998. Its strategy is unlike other third parties that try to pull voters away from the two main parties. Rather it relies on a process called "fusion voting" which allows the party to endorse main party candidates, but by doing so under its own WFP label. Fusion voting is only legal in a handful of states, but the WFP is seeking to legalize it in more states.

Conventional wisdom is that interest groups have become extremely powerful players at the state and local level. Political scientists studying them have been interested in the nature of their size, strength, activities, and tactics. Our final two articles take a look at how interest groups operate at the state and local level to influence public policy. One of the dominant findings is that on substantive policy issues, the government leaders, the media, and citizens often rely on interest groups for information and data. This reliance certainly adds to their power.

Notes

1.   James Bryce, *The American Commonwealth,* Vol. 1 (New York: The Macmillan Company, 1921), pp. 571–583.
2.   An example is the Byrd Machine in Virginia. See William Manchester, "The Byrd Machine," *Harper's Magazine,* 205 (November, 1952): 80–87.
3.   For a detailed look at several of the big-city bosses, see Harold Zink, *City Bosses in the United States,* (Durham, NC: Duke University Press, 1930).
4.   Frank B. Feigert, "Postwar Changes in State Party Competition," *Publius: The Journal of Federalism,* 15 (Winter, 1985): 99–112.
5.   Austin Ranny and Willmoore Kendall, "The American Party System," *American Political Science Review,* 48 (June, 1954): 477–485.
6.   Thomas M. Holbrook and Emily Van Dunk, "Electoral Competition in the American States," *American Political Science Review,* 87:955–962.
7.   For example, see Alan Greenblatt, "The Politics of Parity," *Governing Magazine,* January 2002.
8.   For examples of these types of media portrayals see Jill Lawrence, "Values, Votes, Points of View Separate Towns—and Nation," *USA Today,* February 18, 2002: 6; and David Finkel, "For a Conservative, Life is Sweet in Sugar Land, Texas," *http://www.washingtonpost.com,* April 26, 2004.
9.   See Morris P. Fiorina, Smauel J. Abrams, and Jeremy C. Pope, *Culture War? The Myth of Polarized America,* 2nd Edition. (New York: Pearson/Longman, 2006).
10.   Richard L. Burke, "U.S. Voters Focus on Selves, Poll Says," *The New York Times* (September 21, 1994), p. A12.

Questions for Review and Discussion

5.1   What do you think about the Red state/Blue state classification? What is implied by the stereotypes? What are some problems with classifying states this way? What color *is* Montana? Be careful with your response.

5.3   Do you believe we need stronger third parties in the states? If so, how should they proceed to develop their strength? Is fusion voting a viable option? Why or why not?

5.4   What are the roles that interest groups play in state and local politics? Are these positive or negative, in your opinion?

15 What Color Is Montana?

WALTER KIRN

IT HAPPENED IN NOVEMBER [2004] in Montana. Having contracted cancer from his lifelong smoking habit, and suffering from the nausea and loss of appetite that are typical side-effects of chemotherapy, a Marlboro man type (with the blessing of his neighbors, who'd voted to help the ailing old cowboy seek relief from a once-illegal plant) struck a match on his boot heel, cupped the flame, brought it to his lips and lighted a joint.

This development surprised some people.

The people it most surprised were not Montanans, or even Westerners, but Eastern media types—the folks who'd been on TV since the election speechifying about "the values gap" dividing red and blue America. These analysts had reached a consensus that was sweeping in its implications and, if you thought about it for very long, staggering in its simple-mindedness. There are two kinds of voters, the formula said: the easygoing coffeehouse artistes who dwell on the coasts and in small parts of the North, and the uptight white-chapel patriots who live in the South, the middle and the West (or, as geographers put it, "almost everywhere").

Because of its location relative to the Mississippi River and because it voted overwhelmingly for President Bush [in 2004], my home state, Montana, was colored red and tossed on a pile with Wyoming, Utah, Idaho and all those other cattle lands where men are still men, legend has it, and women let them be, leading to rigid behavior in the voting booth. Democrats? Hate 'em. Environmental laws? Them spotted owls are mighty tasty. Firearms? Handy for shooting them spotted owls. Gay marriage? Don't know; I'll have to ask my preacher. Ah, those predictable red Westerners. They're either standing and saluting, kneeling and praying or lying down and breeding.

But sitting and puffing weed? It didn't quite fit—which might have been partly why unruly Montana (which until a few years ago had no daytime speed limit and still permits motorists to drink while driving as long as they're not intoxicated) blurred the national political color code by legalizing medical marijuana at the same time it backed the Republican president. As for the other questions put before them, Montanans didn't just split their ballots; they shredded them. They elected their first Democratic governor in 16 years, upheld a prohibition on toxic mining practices, broke the Republicans' hold on the state Legislature but also amended the state Constitution to ban gay marriage.

One problem with political science is that its laboratories are unsecured, allowing real people to roam around inside them, spitting in test tubes and fiddling with computers. Montanans, and Westerners in general, are especially mischievous in this regard. For starters, they're fond of circumventing the bigwigs by legislating through popular initiatives—a fondness that may explain why of the 11 states where doctors can prescribe cannabis to patients, 9 are in the West. This tendency toward what might be called "vigilante democracy" can make a hash of organized party politics and of electoral models that link past behavior to future results. That's why Arnold Schwarzenegger runs California now.

In Montana, the new Democratic governor, a beefy-looking rancher named Brian Schweitzer, challenged what had become over the years a smug and clubby conservative power structure by choosing a Republican running mate who showed no more reverence for his party's orthodoxies than Schweitzer showed for his. Schweitzer's display of independence worked, and red Montana, like red Wyoming, red Arizona and red Kansas, installed a blue leader, thus turning his state purple—a color the Eastern analysts seem blind to, but which Westerners recognize as the color of sagebrush and, as the song says, of mountain majesties (whatever those are).

Purple is also the color of certain strains of marijuana, particularly the more potent ones. Most Montanans, I'd wager, don't know this from experience, despite having passed last November's initiative with a 62 percent majority—the largest in the history of such votes. And since neither party discussed the issue much during the campaign season, it seems fair to conclude that Montana's decision resulted from independent thinking by thousands of voters. That's not supposed to happen anymore. People vote with their congregation, right? Or against those who belong to congregations.

What were Montanans' reasons for busting out of their assigned political corral? My guess is that they had lots of little private reasons— Grandpa just won't eat since he got lung cancer; the Beatles smoked dope, but they sure did write great songs; the stuff can't be any worse for you than Vioxx—and a handful of larger, more thoughtful reasons linked to concerns about personal liberty, prescription-drug costs and states' rights. When added together, these reasons yielded an outcome: keep your hands off the Marlboro man; the fellow's sick!

For journalists and political professionals, case-by-case outcomes that arise from a welter of motivations won't pay the bills, though. They need every election to have a moral—and, ideally, a chart that supports the moral as well as their authority to propound it. The source of their power is their mania for order, which is why a state like Montana, where people distrust order (and sometimes resist it just because they can), makes such nonsense of their lovely maps. Soon, of course, even this Western ornery streak will be classified and given a color—at which point Montanans may give up being ornery out of sheer, redoubled orneriness and vote to make it illegal to own firearms unless you're married, gay and stoned. Maybe the experts will finally figure out then that the freedom some people cherish most (not only in Montana) is the freedom from being figured out.

16 First Among Thirds

GREG SARGENT

ONE MORNING IN 1989, Dan Cantor was honeymooning in Scotland when his new wife, Laura Markham, looked up from a newspaper article about electoral returns in a European Parliament election. The virtues of European political systems isn't typical pillow talk between newlyweds, but Cantor and Markham were political junkies. She'd been struck by the success that minor parties were having. And she had an idea.

"Why don't you do something useful and start a third party in America?" she asked him.

"You can't do it," he said. "We don't have proportional representation."

As Cantor recalls it, Markham rejoined: "You're a wimp."

He wasn't, as it turned out. Seventeen years later, Cantor's Working Families Party (WFP), based in New York, has become that rare thing in American politics: a progressive success story. It has built itself into a powerhouse on its home turf, and, though you've probably never heard of it if you live outside the state, you may be hearing more about it soon, because it's now on the cusp of going national—and in time may even prove to have an impact on national politics.

Cantor, along with an old friend, union political director Bob Master, and many other colleagues, created the WFP by exploiting the fact that New York is one of a handful of states that allows "fusion" voting—that is, candidates can run on more than one ballot line, and voters can vote for a candidate under more than one party label. Skeptics, take note: The WFP has nothing in common with Green-style third-party politics, which seeks to pull Democrats leftward by running challengers who siphon away votes and are little more than protest candidates. The WFP also seeks to pull Democrats leftward, but it has no interest in merely putting up protest candidates—it does so by "cross-endorsing" Democratic candidates, giving them a second line to capture voters who might like them but might not want to pull the "D" lever: independent voters alienated from both parties, liberals disillusioned with the Democrats' centrist drift, or moderate Republicans who may like a candidate on issues but are loathe to vote Democratic. In New York, the WFP has been successful again and again in pulling extra votes that Democratic candidates might not have received, helping put them over the top in dozens of political races. Indeed, since its birth in 1998, the WFP has overcome much skepticism, steadily growing into a force whose vote pulling has soared, reaching 168,719 for Senator Chuck Schumer's re-election in 2004.

The WFP's focus on Democrats has enabled it to accumulate surprising influence over Democratic officials, yanking them left on economic issues like the minimum wage, which the party was instrumental in helping to raise in New York State, in exchange for its support. Indeed, at a time when Democrats nationally have muted their economically populist rhetoric, the WFP has unfurled a banner of unabashed economic populism. It has managed to get working people of all ideological stripes in New York to listen to its bread-and-butter platform of higher wages, expanded public investment in health care and education, and opposition to shipping jobs overseas.

In coming years, the WFP will begin launching its ambitious plan to channel resources to other states, where local organizers are already hard at work on various efforts to replicate the party's success. . . . If successful, such efforts could eventually help the party influence gubernatorial contests, battles for state legislatures, or, more ambitiously, in congressional and Senate races—a prospect that's already drawing attention from important Washington Democrats.

"They have the organizing capacity to be a triple threat for national Democrats," says Schumer, who heads the Democratic Senatorial Campaign Committee. "They can bring disaffected 'Reagan Democrats' back into the fold, they attract independents, and they provide a place for crossover Republicans. They work very well with Democrats. That's not to say they do everything we want, but they see a common cause." The WFP also plans to try to legalize fusion voting elsewhere—it's legal in South Carolina, South Dakota, Connecticut, Mississippi, and Delaware, in addition to New York. The party hopes to add three or four states by 2008 and another eight to 10 by 2012.

But is the WFP's success really exportable? New York's political culture is unique to say the least, and the obstacles are formidable. The process of getting fusion voting—or "open-ballot voting," as the party prefers calling it—legalized in other states is arduous and expensive. It's awfully tough to persuade political organizers and donors to channel resources into something obscure, tough to explain, and a long way from bearing fruit. What's more, though the numbers show otherwise, WFP officials frequently encounter resistance from institutional Democrats who argue that the WFP doesn't bring in new voters and just moves voters from the Democratic column to their own. Still other Democrats fret that fusion initiatives open the door to similar efforts on the right, making it possible for Republicans to join forces with, say, an anti-tax party or a pro-gun party. The odds are daunting to say the least.

From where Cantor was sitting in that hotel in Scotland 17 years ago, the odds that he'd build a third party from scratch looked pretty daunting, too.

Cantor is rapping his knuckles on the table. He's sitting in a restaurant near the WFP's headquarters in Brooklyn, holding forth on one of his cardinal frustrations: The knee-jerk insistence by Democrats that the WFP is just another Green Party. "This is not Naderism," he says emphatically, in a tone that suggests that he's not exactly thrilled to be repeating the phrase yet again.

To puncture suspicions, Cantor—a slim, energetic 50-year-old with a salt-and-pepper beard—rattles off a long speech about the history of fusion voting in America. Though it's all but disappeared, fusion voting was a big part of post–Civil War political life, fueling some of the great insurgencies in American politics, such as the 19th-century alliance of northern Democrats and Populists, which culminated in 1896 in the candidacy of William Jennings Bryan. He lost to the big business candidate that year, William McKinley.

"If you were a Democrat in the 1880s, you were probably Catholic, possibly an immigrant, urban, and wet—you drank," Cantor adds. "If you were a populist, you were rural, protestant, native-born, and dry. Culturally these things didn't fit together. Politically, it was the worker-farmer alliance of the 19th century."

After Bryan's loss, moneyed interests worked to outlaw fusion voting in many states, almost completely eliminating it by the Depression. In the 1930s, James Farley, a top political operative of Franklin Delano Roosevelt, met with legendary garment workers union chief Sidney Hillman to try to revive fusion voting in New York—again to join culturally diverse constituencies behind a common agenda. "The story" says Cantor, "is that Hillman said to Farley, 'We have a lot of Italian and Jewish Socialist garment workers and they wanna vote for FDR, but they don't wanna do it on a capitalist [Democratic] party line.' Farley said, 'Fine, no problem. Set up your own damn party and we'll just count their votes with ours.'" As it happened, because fusion voting hadn't been used extensively in New York, it hadn't been outlawed.

Many in New York have since used it as a backdoor way of building power. New York's Conservative Party, for example, can give a Republican candidate for governor upward of 300,000 votes—handy to the GOP, since Republican voters are outnumbered in New York State by Democrats by a 5-to-3 majority. The Conservative boss—a tough-talking, ex-Marine-turned-liquor-store-owner named Mike Long—is a major power broker. On the left, there was most notably the Liberal Party, a once-venerable outfit that devolved into a patronage mill for its chief, Raymond Harding, a rotund, Camel-inhaling creature of a vanished era.

By the late 1990s—after they'd tried to launch an ill-fated national minor party called the "New Party" with the help of political operative Joel Rogers—Cantor, Master, and allies like the United Auto Workers and the grass-roots group ACORN had concluded that a local effort was far more likely to succeed, given New York's laws. By then Harding's outfit was so ideologically hollowed out that there was an opening for a real progressive party. Polling convinced them that the best name was the Working Families Party. New York law requires that to become legal, an aspiring party needs to get a minimum of 50,000 votes in a gubernatorial election (established parties have to do this every four years to stay in business). With the 1998 gubernatorial race looming, the WFP gave its line to the Democrat and got to work.

When the votes were first counted on Election Night, the news was grim—the WFP had fallen around 5,000 votes short. At an East Village pizza shop that was serving as party headquarters that night, Master stood up on a chair and delivered a crestfallen defeat speech to a couple hundred young, tearful volunteers. "I think I literally cried that night—and it wasn't from happiness," Cantor says. But several weeks later, they were thrilled to learn from election officials that, with absentee and other ballots, their final tally was 51,325. (The Liberal Party finally expired in

2003, shortly after its gubernatorial candidate, Andrew Cuomo, failed to draw 50,000 votes.)

Over the next few years, the WFP, assisted by Patrick Gaspard, an experienced New York political operative, successfully allied with Democrats in dozens of local races across the state, slowly building a party infrastructure. Visibility and turnout soared with Hillary Clinton's 2000 Senate election. And with the growth of power inevitably came the need for expediency and deal cutting to get things done—such as supporting Republicans whom the WFP deemed good on their issues. Democrats were infuriated a couple years back when the WFP endorsed several Republican state senate candidates who would help override GOP Governor George Pataki's veto of a minimum-wage increase. Some argued that the defeat of one opposing Democrat, a black female, was a blow to progressivism in the broader sense. "At times their focus on particular issues has put them in conflict with the Democratic Party, and even with progressive goals in general," says one top New York Democrat.

WFP allies say, however, that the relentless focus on a few issues has enabled the party to rack up concrete progressive accomplishments—in addition to increasing the minimum wage, the party helped spark the first wave of Rockefeller drug-law reform in decades. "By focusing first and foremost on concrete ways to help the significant percentage of the population that is struggling economically, they've been very successful in arguing substance and ideology to voters," says [former] New York Attorney General Eliot Spitzer. "They've gone against the grain."

So is the WFP's success exportable? It seems clear that the WFP could succeed elsewhere at enticing liberals who want to make a statement against Democratic centrism. But Cantor argues that WFP's real importance is that it can tip close races by luring many independents, young voters suspicious of the major parties, traditional Democrats whose party loyalty has eroded and would thus vote Republican, and even the occasional moderate Republican.

Cantor insists that his party has unlocked the code that will crack what he calls the Democrats' "What's the Matter with Kansas" problem— the recent failure of Democrats to get blue-collar whites to focus on economic issues rather than cultural politics. This is possible, Cantor argues, because minor parties aren't under the same pressure as major ones are to talk about their positions on all issues including hot-button cultural ones. The WFP avoids these issues by and large, and therefore doesn't have the cultural baggage that the Democratic Party does. The WFP's freedom to speak single-mindedly about "kitchen table" issues, Cantor claims, allows it to make a strong case to Republican-trending voters who can vote their economic interest—that is, for the Democrat on the WFP line—without endorsing the Democratic positions that repel them.

"We can say, 'We're not here to talk about guns or abortion. We're only here to talk about wages, health care, and education,'" Cantor says. "That allows us to reach voters who would never self-identify as progressives."

It's easy to be skeptical of Cantor's argument. Why would a nonprogressive turned off by a Democratic candidate's position on social issues suddenly overlook those positions if the candidate's name were on a different ballot line? WFP officials point to a 2002 Long Island congressional race in which Democrat Tim Bishop upset sitting GOP Congressman Felix Grucci by 2,700 votes. Bishop won 2,900 on the WFP line—the margin of victory. Of those, 1,600 voted for Bishop—and here's the key—even as they also backed either GOP Governor George Pataki or Conservative Party candidate Tom Golisano for governor. That means more than half of Bishop's supporters were ticket-splitters—and likely would have backed Grucci without the WFP option. "All we need to do is shift a tiny percentage of voters to completely alter a race's outcome" Cantor argues.

WFP officials also argue that they might appeal to culturally conservative voters who trend Republican because, surprisingly, people are inclined to view the WFP as a centrist party, not a left-wing one. You'd think the WFP's call for expansionist government would leave it easily pigeonholed as a party of the left. But many voters apparently don't see it that way. A recent WFP poll of voters in three battleground states—Ohio, Missouri, and Washington—were asked to rate the party on a scale where 1 was very liberal and 9 was very conservative, after having been told that the WFP fights on "pocketbook" issues "like the outsourcing of jobs to other countries" and "increasing the minimum wage." A surprising 57 percent of voters labeled the WFP at 5 or above.

Still, these numbers don't guarantee national success. For starters, the first and most critical hurdle the party faces—launching successful initiatives to legalize fusion voting—is an uphill one. The WFP says its polling in several states shows majority support for open ballot initiatives, but no one has mobilized against it yet. If the WFP's efforts grow more visible, the GOP and some corporate interests may well channel money into defeating fusion voting, just as they did at the close of the 19th century. And if that happens, the WFP will likely be badly outgunned.

Also, the party may be seen by many as a centrist party when it defines itself. But there's no telling how people would see it should right-leaning commentators and other fusion opponents start painting it as, say, a tool of labor (the source of much WFP funding), or as a redistributionist conspiracy hatched in liberal New York. Finally, it's unclear whether establishment Democrats will lend serious backing to an ambitious effort with an uncertain outcome, particularly since the WFP, while it helps Democrats win elections and strengthens the party's progressive wing, splits candidate loyalty between the two parties.

"The challenge for WFP is to convince institutional Democrats nationally that they should invest resources in something that may take years to bear fruit," says Robert Zimmerman, a top fund-raiser and Democratic National Committeeman from New York. "They also need to show Democrats that they don't dilute the party's institutional control over elected candidates." . . . "Progressives all across the country are fighting huge defensive battles all the time—fending off this attack or that bad referendum," says Master. "We're here to say, 'We're on the offensive in New York because of this party,' and we think we can replicate that across the country. It will be a really potent weapon in the arsenal of Democrats and their allies who want to retake power in America."

17 Interest Groups and Journalists in the States

CHRISTOPHER A. COOPER

ANTHONY J. NOWNES

MARTIN JOHNSON

SCHOLARS HAVE LONG TRIED to understand how interest groups influence the American political system. Traditionally, these scholars have focused their attention on tactics groups use to influence legislators and legislation directly, such as lobbying (Wright 1990). But recent research suggests that interest groups often pursue their policy goals by engaging in more indirect tactics, that is, activities that do not target government officials or institutions directly (Kollman 1998). One of the most commonly cited but least understood means of such outside lobbying involves working through the mass media.

We assume that interest groups attempt to influence the media to slant the news in their favor. If they are successful in doing so, we expect that the content of news coverage will be more favorable to certain groups. Considering the importance of the mass media in setting the public agenda and priming evaluations of politicians (Iyengar and Kinder 1987), knowing how interest groups affect it can help us explain why some groups are more successful than others in advancing their interests.

We examine the interest group-journalist relationship in the context of American state politics. We focus on the states for four reasons. First, although some recent scholarly attention has been paid to the role of interest groups in the states (Gray and Lowery 1996; Hrebenar and Thomas 1987, 1993a, 1993b; Nownes and Freeman 1998), studies of national politics still dominate the literature on interest groups (Baumgartner and Leech 1998; Gray and Lowery 2002). As such, our understanding of interest groups in state politics is still limited. Second, with rare exception (Cooper 2002; Rosenthal 1998), almost no scholarly research has been done on the role of the mass media in state politics. Third, devolution has given state governments increased policy responsibilities, so the states provide substantively more important places to investigate politics. Finally, the American states constitute 50 different institutional, cultural, and political contexts, thus providing a theoretically and empirically rich laboratory for the study of this important subject.

Interest Groups and the Media

Getting a message into the mass media is a form of outside lobbying that can be useful for a politician or interest group in communicating information to the general public, as well as for simply legitimizing their perspective on an issue (Kollman 1998). While interest groups work to influence the public and policymakers in a variety of ways (Baumgartner and Leech 1998), working through the media can be an efficient and highly effective means of agenda-setting. Interest groups can get their messages in the media either by purchasing "advertorials" (Brown and Waltzer 2002) or through making news in some way. Each method has its strengths and weaknesses. While paid media makes it easier to control the content, citizens tend to discount the legitimacy and veracity of paid messages (Shea 1996). Earned media is the distinct opposite of paid media in these respects; while citizens are more likely to trust news reports than paid advertisements, the content of news media coverage is more difficult to control. Earned media coverage can help win elections and influence government decisions, but it may also backfire, with groups, positions, and politicians sometimes not being covered in the best light.

The pitfalls of earned media notwithstanding, many interest groups try to advance their policy and political goals by working with journalists. Indeed, Danielian and Page (1994) find that interest group representatives are the most frequently used sources for major television network news, suggesting a symbiotic relationship between journalists and interest groups. In his seminal work, *Outside Lobbying,* Kollman (1998, 35) reports that 76 percent of his sample of groups at the national level reported "talking with the press" regularly, with this tactic ranking as the third most frequently used lobbying tactic, behind only "contacting Congress personally" and "entering coalitions with other groups." In an earlier study, Schlozman and Tierney (1983, 357) report that 86 percent of the Washington, DC, groups they surveyed "talk with people from the press and the media." Nownes and Freeman (1998, 92) found that large majorities of state-level lobbyists and organized interest groups also "talk to media." Even at the local government level, Cooper and Nownes (2003) find that 92 percent of big-city citizen groups at least sometimes talk to the media (as opposed to never talking to them), while 89 percent of big-city lobbyists do so. The lesson here is clear: lobbyists and groups at all levels of government regularly interact with the media, and it is safe to assume that all this activity is probably thought of by these groups as a form of outside lobbying.

Despite popular press accusations of partisan bias in the media (Goldberg 2001), most scholars believe that any such bias is not the result of the intentional slanting of stories, but rather results from a much more subtle process in which journalists seek to obtain information with minimal costs and tell a clear and concise story (Gans 1979). Interest group representatives who understand this provide factual and timely information to journalists, while perhaps focusing on information that supports their group's viewpoint. If groups can develop goodwill with journalists in this way, they are more likely to have their information used by journalists and, thereby, to have stories reported in a way that benefits their interests. In this sense, a lobbyist's relationship with the news media parallels his or her relationship with legislators (Wright 1996). Providing services leads to goodwill and favorable treatment in subtle but important ways.

How might lobbying for policy preferences through earned media take place in practice? After all, the goal of these groups is to translate their preferences into policy, not simply to gain news coverage. This could be done in two ways, one direct and one indirect. First consider the indirect process. An interest group presents information to a journalist, who records it, interprets it, folds it into a story, and presents it to his or her readers. Citizens then consume this news, interpret it themselves, and either change their minds or (more likely) increase the salience of the issue at hand, potentially inspiring them to express their opinions to policymakers or evaluate candidates based on that issue. Therefore, this process by which interest groups may affect public policy through the media is indirect, complicated, and tenuous, requiring that journalists and citizens receive, accept, and sample the message that originated with the interest group (Zaller 1992). However, we know that the media are an extremely important source of information about state politics and policy for citizens (Delli Carpini, Keeter, and Kennamer 1994), and if policymakers try to reflect the values and preferences of their constituents, then this indirect approach can be effective. Second, stories with an interest group's information may reach policymakers directly, since we know that legislators (and other elected officials) are voracious consumers of the news (Herbst 1998; Weiss 1974). Simply stated, legislators receive interest group information through the media, both directly and indirectly.

Certainly policymakers are influenced by information that comes their way through the media. We know that interest groups provide decisionmaking cues to legislators directly, but the media is also an important source of such cues. For example, Powlick (1995) finds that the media is an extremely important source of information for American foreign policy officials, more important than many overtly political sources, such as interest groups. Kingdon (1973) finds that while it is not as important as some other sources, the media is a source of information for congressional voting decisions, particularly on salient issues. Mooney (1991) also finds that while information from legislators, staff, and other more proximate bodies can be more important, the mass media are still a valuable source of information for many state legislators. Indeed, Herbst (1998) finds that the media are the most important means by which state legislators assess public opinion.

Thus, interest groups may exert more influence on policymakers than we currently understand if they are successful in using the media to transmit their messages both to policymakers themselves and to policymakers' constituents. But many of the linkages in this process are not yet well understood.

Questions and Hypotheses

We work to clarify part of this process by exploring the frequency and types of contacts that journalists have with interest groups. We do this by asking three basic questions about statehouse reporters. First, do journalists have frequent contact with interest groups? Second, how important are interest groups to journalists as news sources compared to other sources? Answering these two questions will help us to better understand how journalists gather information and how interest group representatives stack up to other sources. This analysis will also help us determine whether lobbying the media occurs at the state level to the extent that Kollman (1998) finds it occurring in Washington. If interest groups pursue this outsider lobbying tactic, we should find that journalists and lobbyists have frequent contact. But given that journalists may perceive lobbyists as biased sources and that they tend to focus their attention on public officials (Cook 1989), we expect to find that lobbyists are less important than other more official sources such as legislators.

Finally, we ask whether journalist-interest group interactions are generally initiated by journalists or interest groups. We hypothesize that to the extent to which this relationship is symbiotic, journalists will approach lobbyists as often as lobbyists approach journalists. In the same way that politicians and journalists need each other to achieve their goals, journalists and lobbyists need one another. The degree to which this hypothesis is borne out in the data will indicate the nature of this relationship between journalists and lobbyists. If journalists approach lobbyists more often than lobbyists approach journalists, it would suggest that lobbyists value this relationship less than journalists. Likewise, if lobbyists contact journalists more often, then it is a sign that journalists do not consider the information they receive from lobbyists to be particularly important or useful.

After addressing these basic questions, we delve further into the journalist-interest group relationship by identifying the conditions under which journalists rely more or less heavily on interest groups for information. A careful reading of the state politics literature suggests that variations in at least three aspects of the context of state politics may affect the nature of the journalist-interest group relationship.

First, consider the impact on that relationship of interest group density, that is, the number of interest groups active in a state. The density of the state interest group community has been shown to have a variety of effects on interest group behavior (Gray and Lowery 1995, 1996, 2001), and it may affect their propensity to engage in outside lobbying and, thus, their efforts and success in influencing the media. However, the relationship between interest group density and journalist contact is likely not simple. Rather than a linear relationship, we hypothesize that journalists will interact most with interest group representatives in high- and low-density environments, with medium-density environments producing less interaction. Theories of density dependence suggest that the potential for interest group death is greatest in both low- and high-density environments (Nownes and Lipinski 2005). As such, interest groups should be more likely to seek allies and engage in outside lobbying in these high-risk contexts. Working with the media will be part of this strategy. To test this hypothesis, we operationalize density as the number of groups registered to lobby government in a state in 1999.[1] This density measure ranges from a low of 202 groups (Hawaii) to a high of 2,272 groups (California).

Second, we expect that state legislative professionalism will affect the journalist-interest group relationship. Professionalism should reduce journalists' reliance on interest groups for information because highly professional legislatures offer journalists many other sources of information, especially legislative staffers (Squire and Hamm 2005). In general, we hypothesize that where fewer alternative sources of information exist, journalists turn to interest groups more. To test this hypothesis, we use King's (2000) measure of state legislative professionalism, which is based on a legislature's staff, session length, and legislator salary. We use the scale for the most recent years King reports (1993–94) in which California scores the highest (.900) and New Hampshire scores the lowest (.061).

Finally, we test the effect of overall interest group power in a state on the interest group-journalist relationship. In states where interest groups are more powerful, we expect them to be more closely connected to policymakers and, thus, less reliant on outside lobbying and the media to achieve their policy goals. In states where groups are less powerful, they may need to pursue less direct tactics to achieve their goals, including cultivating journalists to promote their message. Hrebenar and Thomas (2004) have created a system that classifies the general interest group power in a state as either dominant, dominant/complementary, complementary, complementary/subordinate, or subordinate. Dominant states "are those in which groups as a whole are the overwhelming and consistent influence on policy making" (Thomas and Hrebener 2004,121). Alabama, Montana, West Virginia, Nevada, and Florida had dominant interest group systems in their 2002 classification of states' systems. At the opposite end of scale are subordinate states, where groups are "consistently subordinated to other aspects of the policy-making process" (Thomas and Hrebenar 2004, 121). Although no states fell into this bottom category in 2002, Michigan, Minnesota, and South Dakota were scored as complementary/subordinate, the next lowest category.

Data and Methods

The data we use to test our hypotheses on interest group-journalist relationships come from an original survey of statehouse journalists in the American states. As such, we are relying explicitly on journalists' perceptions of the interest group-journalist relationship. We do not have any direct measures of interest group-journalist contact, nor do we have any data on the perspectives of interest group leaders or members regarding this relationship. However, we believe that this perceptual data is a good first step in understanding this relationship.

If these perceptual data bias our results, it would likely be toward finding less contact with lobbyists, that is, working against our hypotheses. After all, journalists may not want to admit that they rely on lobbyists—sources commonly maligned by the public—for information. Given these negative perceptions, it is highly unlikely that they would exaggerate their contact with lobbyists. It is also unlikely that the degree to which journalists lie would vary systematically across states. Because of this, these perceptual data should not bias the results of our multivariate analysis. Furthermore, while analyzing data from both journalists and interest group representatives would be ideal, we believe that given a choice, it is likely that journalists can better help us understand this process than lobbyists. Journalists, not interest group representatives, determine what appears in the news. Interest group representatives would likely exaggerate their influence on the production of news.

Obtaining an accurate list of statehouse journalists to develop our national sample was difficult. We began with a list compiled by the National Conference of State Legislatures. This list was checked for both deletions and additions by telephone calls to each statehouse pressroom. Ultimately, we identified 489 statehouse journalists active as of July 2003. We designed and conducted our survey of these journalists following Dillman's (2000) tailored-design method. We sent the survey to all the journalists on our list in August 2003 and followed up with two waves of reminder postcards. Of the 489 journalists in our initial sample, 35 surveys were returned for incorrect addresses and 19 were returned with notes indicating that the reporter in question did not cover the statehouse. In the end, we received 133 completed surveys from 42 states, for a 31 percent response rate.[2] This outcome is slightly lower than the 36 percent response rate achieved in perhaps the only other survey of statehouse reporters (Boylan and Long 2003), but it surpasses that of many recent surveys of political elites (Abbe and Herrnson 2002; Cooper and Nownes 2003; Kedrowski 1996).

Results

To start our analysis, we turn our attention to our first general question: Do journalists have frequent contact with interest groups? To address this question, we asked our respondents how often they used "interest group representatives as sources when writing political stories." One percent of our respondents replied "never" to this survey item, 5 percent responded "rarely," 49 percent responded "occasionally," and 45 percent responded "often" (n = 130). To delve further into this issue, we asked our respondents to respond to the following statement: "Interest groups use newspapers and other media a great deal in their attempts to achieve their political goals." One percent of our respondents strongly disagreed with this statement, 11 percent disagreed, 68 percent agreed, and 21 percent strongly agreed. In short, these results show that journalists rely on interest group representatives for information to a significant extent and that these journalists overwhelmingly believe that these groups try to use the media for political gain.

How important are interest groups as news sources compared to other sources? We addressed this question by asking our respondents to tell us how useful each of 16 sources of information was in covering the state legislature. As our results in Table 1 show, legislative floor action, printed or draft bills, and legislative staff are the three most useful information sources for our sample of statehouse journalists. Interestingly, while lobbyists' rank tied with another source for seventh among the 16, they were seen by journalists as virtually as useful as rank-and-file legislators and minority party leaders. On average, lobbyists were seen as more useful than governors' press releases, speeches on the floor of the legislature, stories by or conversations with other reporters, and news releases (which, in fact may be another source of interest group information, at least in part). In addition, lobbyists' handouts (written information) were seen as either somewhat or very useful by 62 percent of these respondents. Thus, Table 1 provides further evidence that interest groups and their representatives are important sources of information for journalists covering the statehouse.

To assess who has the upper hand in the interest group–journalist relationship, we asked a series of questions to determine who initiates contact between them. We presented respondents with the six survey items[3] in Table 2 and asked them to reply "never," "rarely," "occasionally," or "often" to each survey item. Several things stand out in Table 2. First, our data show that interest groups contact journalists regularly. For example, 90 percent of respondents said that interest group representatives approached them to "tell their side of the story" at least occasionally, and 83 percent said that interest group representatives come to them with story ideas at least occasionally. But the data also show that this is not a one-way relationship. Specifically, 68 percent of respondents said that they sought out interest group representatives for advice at least occasion-

TABLE 1   Statehouse Journalists' Views on the Usefulness
of Various Sources of Information

		Usefulness			
Information Source	Mean	Not at All Useful	Not Very Useful	Somewhat Useful	Very Useful
1. Printed or draft bills	3.51	1% (1)	3% (4)	40% (50)	56% (70)
2. Legislative floor action	3.50	0% (0)	7% (9)	35% (44)	58% (72)
3. Legislative staff	3.50	2% (2)	2% (3)	40% (50)	56% (70)
4. Conversations with majority party leaders	3.48	1% (1)	3% (4)	43% (54)	53% (66)
5. The Internet/computer based sources	3.42	0% (0)	6% (7)	47% (59)	47% (59)
6. Other ("rank and file") legislators	3.35	0% (0)	7% (9)	50% (63)	42% (53)
7. Conversations with minority party leaders	3.34	1% (1)	10% (12)	45% (56)	45% (56)
8. Lobbyists	**3.34**	**0% (0)**	**5% (6)**	**56% (70)**	**39% (49)**
9. Governor's press conferences	3.02	2% (3)	16% (20)	58% (73)	23% (29)
10. Floor speeches	2.93	2% (3)	21% (26)	58% (73)	18% (23)
11. Stories by other reporters	2.87	2% (2)	22% (28)	63% (79)	13% (16)
12. Legislators' press conferences	2.77	1% (1)	26% (32)	69% (85)	5% (6)
13. News releases	2.67	3% (4)	32% (40)	59% (73)	6% (7)
14. Conversations with other reporters	2.66	6% (7)	30% (38)	56% (70)	8% (10)
15. Handouts from lobbyists	**2.62**	**5% (6)**	**34% (42)**	**57% (71)**	**5% (6)**
16. Committee minutes	2.08	33% (40)	31% (38)	31% (38)	5% (6)

Source: Authors' 2003 survey of 133 statehouse journalists.

Note: Ns vary for individual survey questions due to item nonresponse. Mean scores are based on the following coding: 1 = not at all useful, 2 = not very useful, 3 = somewhat useful, 4 = very useful.

Survey item: "Reporters use a number of sources in covering the legislature. We would like to know what sources are most useful and what sources are least useful to you in covering the legislature. Please rate the following on a four-point scale where 1 means not at all useful and 4 means very useful by circling the number next to the response."

TABLE 2   Journalist-Interest Group Contact Initiation

How often does each of the following occur?	Never	Rarely	Occasionally	Often
1. You use interest group representatives as sources when writing political stories.	1% (1)	5% (6)	49% (64)	45% (59)
2. Interest group representatives come to you to "tell their side of the story" when you are writing political stories.	0% (0)	10% (13)	50% (66)	40% (52)
3. Interest group representatives come to you with story ideas.	0% (0)	17% (22)	52% (68)	31%(40)
4. You seek out interest group representatives for advice on newsworthy issues and topics.	12% (15)	20% (26)	49% (63)	19% (25)
5. Interest group representatives approach you for advice on how best to achieve their political goals through the media.	31% (41)	49% (64)	17% (22)	2% (3)
6. Interest group representatives come to you for advice on political tactics.	61% (80)	30% (39)	8% (11)	1% (1)

Source: Authors' 2003 survey of 133 statehouse journalists.
Note: Ns vary for individual survey questions due to item nonresponse.
Survey item: "How often does each of the following occur—never, rarely, occasionally, or often"

ally. This said, Table 2 suggests that journalists were more likely to report that they had been sought out by an interest group representative than that they had sought one out. Table 2 also shows that interest groups lobby journalists more than journalists ask for advice. While the overwhelming majority of journalists reported being approached by group representatives with story ideas or to tell their side of the story, only 19 percent of respondents said that interest group representatives contacted them "for advice on how best to achieve their political goals through the media" either occasionally or often. And only 9 percent said that interest group representatives came to them "for advice on political tactics" either occasionally or often.

Altogether, the data in Table 2 support the perception that interest groups do not only work to achieve their policy goals through direct lobbying of policymakers, but they also actively engage in what Browne (1998, 343) calls "all-directional" advocacy by targeting the media and, by extension, the public. Our data also suggest that groups' efforts may have stimulated a relationship in which journalists have learned that these groups are a good source of news and relevant information, and therefore, journalists regularly seek them out on their own accord.

What Explains the Extent of Journalist Contact with Interest Groups?

The journalists in our survey differ a great deal in the extent to which they rely on interest groups for information. To explore why some journalists rely on interest group information more than others, we created an additive scale of responses to the six survey items in Table 2. We assigned each "never" response a value of 1, each "rarely" response a value of 2, each "occasionally" response a value of 3, and each "often" response a value of 4. As such, the scale has a theoretical range of 6–24. The Cronbach's alpha for the scale is .64. We used this additive index (which we will call *interest group contact*) as the dependent variable in an ordinary least squares (OLS) regression model with the following independent variables: *density/1000* (number of groups per state divided by 1000),[4] *density/1000 squared, interest group power* (complementary/subordinate = 1, complementary = 2, dominant/complementary = 3, dominant = 4), and *state legislative professionalism* (which we describe above). As discussed above, we expect interest group power and state legislative professionalism to be negatively related to the dependent variable interest group contact. We expect that density has a nonmonotonic relationship with the index, where density has its greatest effect at its highest and lowest values.

As Table 3 shows the estimates for density and interest group power are statistically significant. The hypothesis of a nonmonotonic relationship between density and interest group contact is supported. This support suggests that groups in both high- and low-interest group-density states have more contact with journalists than do groups in medium-density states. As we hypothesized, this is likely because interest group tactics vary with the probability of interest group death. These estimates also show that interest group power is negatively related to interest group contact. This finding suggests that when interest groups can exert influence

TABLE 3   OLS Regression Model for Interest Group Contact

Variable	B (SE)	
Density/1000	−3.35**	(1.60)
(Density/1000)^2	1.69***	(.56)
Interest group power	−.39*	(.21)
State legislative professionalism	−1.48	(1.60)
Constant	18.62***	(1.17)
R^2	.059	
N	129	

*p < 1; **p < .05; ***p < .01 (two-tailed test)

Note: Standard errors were computed by clustering on the state and then adjusted using the technique suggested in Franzese (2005). The dependent variable is the index of the degree of interest group contact reported by a journalist.

directly over government officials, they do so and eschew using the media; but when their power to exert direct influence is blocked, interest groups will look outside government—to the media—in their efforts to influence government decisions.[5]

Conclusion

We have attempted to provide a basic description of the relationship between journalists and interest groups working in and around the state legislature. To summarize, our data indicate the following: (1) interest groups are important sources of information for statehouse journalists; (2) while groups are not the most important sources of information for journalists, they are more important than several other sources, including gubernatorial press conferences, legislative floor speeches, other reporters, and news releases; approximately as important as rank-and-file legislators and minority leaders, and nearly as important as the Internet; (3) a great deal of interest group-journalist contact is initiated by interest groups, but a significant amount is initiated by journalists; and (4) the extent of the contact that statehouse journalists claim to have with interest groups is influenced by the number of interest groups active in the state and the overall level of interest group power in the state.

Our findings have two obvious implications. First, they highlight the importance of learning more about how the journalists who cover state legislatures gather their information. Second, they suggest that interest

group density and interest group power—two variables that figure promi-
nently in the state interest group literature—may influence the nature of
politics in the states in ways that we do not yet understand.

In conclusion, we hope that our data have shed some light on an
important but poorly understood relationship in American politics, the
relationship between interest groups and journalists in the states. Interest
group scholars have long understood the importance of outside lobbying,
but to understand that phenomenon completely, we must gain a deeper
and more theoretical understanding of the way interest groups use the
media to set the agenda and frame the terms of political debate.

Notes

1. Thanks to David Lowery for giving us access to these data.
2. We received no surveys from Indiana, Maine, Missouri, Montana, North Dakota, Rhode Island, Virginia, and Wyoming.
3. On their face, questions 4 and 5 may not appear to be directly relevant to
contact initiation between journalists and lobbyists, but we include them in our
analysis for the following reason. Much of the interaction between journalists and
their sources is relatively informal and may not even relate directly to a specific
story at the time. However these interactions are important for building trust, which
eventually manifests itself in more direct ways, such as direct contact about stories
and information. Building trust is a key precursor to developing sources (Cooper
and Johnson 2006). Sources who are trusted more will find it easier to influence
the news than those who have not built a relationship with a journalist.
4. We divide our interest group density variables by 1,000 to ease interpretation.
5. We also estimated the model using ordinal logistic regression without the last
two questions of the scale in the dependent variable. The substantive interpretation
of the results was similar with the only difference being that interest group power
moved from $p < .1$ to $p < .05$.

References

Abbe, Owen G., and Paul S. Herrnson. 2003. "Campaign Professionalism in State
Legislative Elections." *State Politics and Policy Quarterly* 3:223–45.
Baumgartner, Frank R., and Beth L. Leech. 1998. *Basic Interests: The Importance of
Groups in Politics and in Political Science*. Princeton, NJ: Princeton University Press.
Boylan, Richard T., and Cheryl X. Long. 2003. "Measuring Public Corruption in
the American States: A Survey of State House Reporters." *State Politics and Policy
Quarterly* 3:420–38.
Brown, Clyde, and Herbert Waltzer. 2002. "Lobbying the Press: 'Talk to the People
Who Talk to America.'" In *Interest Group Politics,* eds. Allan J. Cigler and Burdett
A. Loomis. 6th ed. Washington, DC: CQ Press.
Browne, William P. 1998. "Lobbying the Public: All-Directional Advocacy." In

Interest Group Politics, eds. Allan J. Cigler and Burdett A. Loomis, 5th ed. Washington, DC: CQ Press.

Cook, Timothy E. 1989. *Making Laws and Making News.* Washington, DC: Brookings Institution Press.

Cooper, Christopher A. 2002. "Media Tactics in the State Legislature." *State Politics and Policy Quarterly* 2:353–71.

Cooper, Christopher A., and Martin Johnson. 2006. "Politics and the Press Corps: Reporters, State Legislative Institutions, and Context." Presented at the Annual Conference on State Politics and Policy, Lubbock, TX.

Cooper, Christopher A., and Anthony J. Nownes. 2003. "Citizen Groups in Big City Politics." *State and Local Government Review* 35:102–11.

Danielian, Lucig H., and Benjamin I. Page. 1994. "The Heavenly Chorus: Interest Group Voices on TV News." *American Journal of Political Science* 38:1056–78.

Delli Carpini, Michael X., Scott Keeter, and J. David Kennamer. 1994. "Effects of the News Media Environment on Citizen Knowledge of State Politics and Government." *Journalism Quarterly* 71:443–56.

Dillman, Don A. 2000. *Mail and Internet Surveys: The Tailored Design Method.* 2nd ed. New York: John Wiley.

Franzese, Robert J. 2005. "Empirical Strategies for Various Manifestations of Multi-level Data." *Political Analysis* 13:430–46.

Gans, Herbert J. 1979. *Deciding What's News: A Study of CBS Evening News, NBC Nightly News, Newsweek and Time.* New York: Vintage Books.

Goldberg, Bernard. 2001. *Bias: A CBS Insider Exposes How the Media Distort the News.* New York: Regnery Publishing.

Gray, Virginia, and David Lowery. 1995. "Interest Representation and Democratic Gridlock." *Legislative Studies Quarterly* 20:531–52.

Gray, Virginia, and David Lowery. 1996. *The Population Ecology of Interest Representation: Lobbying Communities in the American States.* Ann Arbor, MI: The University of Michigan Press.

Gray, Virginia, and David Lowery. 2002. "State Interest Group Research and the Mixed Legacy of Belle Zeller." *State Politics and Policy Quarterly* 2:388–410.

Gray, Virginia, and David Lowery. 2001. "The Expression of Density Dependence in State Communities of Organized Interests." *American Politics Research* 29:374–91.

Herbst, Susan. 1998. *Reading Public Opinion: How Political Actors View the Democratic Process.* Chicago: University of Chicago Press.

Hrebenar, Ronald J., and Clive S. Thomas, eds. 1987. *Interest Group Politics in the American West.* Salt Lake City, UT: University of Utah Press.

Hrebenar, Ronald J., and Clive S. Thomas, eds. 1993a. *Interest Group Politics in the Midwestern States.* Ames, IA: Iowa State University Press.

Hrebenar, Ronald J., and Clive S. Thomas, eds. 1993b. *Interest Group Politics in the Northeastern States.* University Park, PA: Pennsylvania State University Press.

Iyengar, Shanto, and Donald R. Kinder. 1987. *News That Matters: Television and American Opinion.* Chicago: University of Chicago Press.

Kedrowski, Karen M. 1996. *Media Entrepreneurs and the Media Enterprise in the U.S. Congress.* Creskill, NJ: Hampton Press.

King, James D. 2000. "Changes in Professionalism in U.S. State Legislatures." *Legislative Studies Quarterly* 25:327–43.

Kingdon, John W. 1973. *Congressmen's Voting Decisions.* Ann Arbor, MI: The University of Michigan Press.

Kollman, Ken. 1998. *Outside Lobbying: Public Opinion and Interest Group Strategies.* Princeton, NJ: Princeton University Press.

Mooney, Christopher Z. 1991. "Peddling Information in the State Legislature: Closeness Counts." *Western Political Quarterly* 44:433–44.

Nownes, Anthony J., and Daniel Lipinski. 2005. "The Population Ecology of Interest Group Death: Gay and Lesbian Rights Interest Groups in the United States, 1945–1998." *British Journal of Political Science* 35:303–19.

Nownes, Anthony J., and Patricia Freeman. 1998. "Interest Group Activity in the States." *Journal of Politics* 60:86–112.

Powlick, Philip J. 1995. "The Sources of Public Opinion for American Foreign Policy Officials." *International Studies Quarterly* 39:427–51.

Rosenthal, Alan. 1998. *The Decline of Representative Democracy: Process, Participation, and Power in State Legislatures.* Washington, DC: CQ Press.

Schlozman, Kay Lehman, and John T. Tierney. 1983. "More of the Same: Washington Pressure Group Activity in a Decade of Change." *Journal of Politics* 45:351–77.

Shea, Daniel M. 1996. *Campaign Craft: The Strategies, Tactics, and Art of Political Campaign Management.* Westport, CT: Praeger.

Squire, Peverill, and Keith E. Hamm. 2005. *101 Chambers: Congress, State Legislatures, and the Future of Legislative Studies.* Columbus, OH: The Ohio State University Press.

Thomas, Clive S., and Ronald J. Hrebenar. 2004. "Interest Groups in the States." In *Politics in the American States: A Comparative Analysis,* eds. Virginia Gray and Russell L. Hanson. 8th ed. Washington, DC: CQ Press.

Wright, John R. 1990. "Contributions, Lobbying and Committee Voting in the U.S. House of Representatives." *American Political Science Review* 79:400–14.

Wright, John R. 1996. *Interest Groups and Congress: Lobbying, Contributions, and Influence.* Boston, MA: Allyn and Bacon.

Zaller, John R. 1992. *The Nature and Origins of Mass Opinion.* New York: Cambridge University Press.

18 Perceptions of Power: Interest Groups in Local Politics

CHRISTOPHER A. COOPER

ANTHONY J. NOWNES

STEVEN ROBERTS

WHAT IS THE EXTENT OF INTEREST GROUP ACTIVITY and influence in local politics? Some claim that interest groups are not very active or influential in local politics (Peterson 1981). Others suggest that they can and do exert influence in the local political arena (Fleischmann 1997). Despite a long history of research on power in local politics on the one hand (Dahl 1961; Hunter 1953) and interest group influence on the other (for a review of the literature, see Cigler 1991), the answer to this question remains elusive. This article examines interest group activity and influence in 68 medium-sized cities. The kinds of interest groups that are active in local politics are cataloged, and the effects of institutional structures on interest group behavior are determined. Hypotheses about interest group activity are presented.

Background and Hypotheses

Scholars have identified various types of interest groups that exert influence in the local political arena. First among these are business interests. Ever since the classic works on elitism and pluralism (e.g., Dahl

1961; Lynd and Lynd 1937; Hunter 1953), scholars have debated the role of business interests in local politics. Recent work suggests that business interests—including both individual business firms and trade associations—are the most active interest groups in cities (see, for example, Abney and Lauth 1986; Elkins 1995; Logan and Molotch 1987; Stone 1989). Moreover, case studies of specific regimes show that business interests are supremely important players in city politics (Ferman 1996; Judd 1983; Stone 1989). Recent research suggests that neighborhood organizations are also very active in local politics (Dilger 1992; Elkins 1995). They lobby public officials, mobilize citizens to attend meetings, and are consistently engaged in local governance (Mesch and Schwirian 1996). Berry, Portney, and Thomson (1993) find that neighborhood organizations are good for urban democracy, although they are not a cure-all for the ills of modern urban politics. In addition to business and neighborhood groups, faith-based organizations (Button, Rienzo, and Wald 1997; Sharp 1999; 2003), labor unions (DeLeon 1992; Regalado 1991) and minority groups (Browning, Marshall, and Tabb 2003) seem to be important actors in local politics.

The limited literature on interest groups in local politics suggests three specific hypotheses:

Hypothesis 1: Business groups are the most active and influential types of groups in local politics.

Hypothesis 2: Neighborhood organizations are very active and influential in local politics.

Hypothesis 3: Faith-based organizations, labor unions, and minority groups are also active and influential in local politics but somewhat less so than business groups and neighborhood organizations.

Group Activity in Local Politics

Interest groups are not equally active in all cities. The literature suggests that the structure, culture, and the unique circumstances of each locality produce different levels of group activity and influence. In particular, research suggests that three structures foster interest group activity and influence: mayor-council governments, nonpartisan elections, and the presence of direct democracy. The research also suggests that relatively high levels of interest group activity characterize cities with relatively high levels of citizen interest in politics.

Scholars of local politics have debated the effects of governmental structure for years but have not reached a consensus (DeSantis and Renner 2002). For example, there is an ongoing debate concerning the effects of structure on spending patterns (Clark 1968; Lineberry and Fowler 1967; Lyons 1978; Morgan and Pelissero 1980). A similar debate considers the effects of structure on interest group activity and influence. Clark (1968), Grimes et al. (1976), and Lineberry and Fowler (1967) conclude that reform governments are less susceptible to group activity and influence than nonreform governments. In contrast, Northrop and Dutton (1978) argue that because mayors and managers have different career ambitions, city managers are more susceptible to interest group influence than mayors. Abney and Lauth (1985) ultimately conclude that structure makes no difference.[1] Clearly, there is disagreement among urban scholars regarding the extent of group activity in manager governments.

Another reform structure hypothesized to affect interest group activity is the nonpartisan ballot. When party affiliation does not appear on the ballot, voters rely on other cues to make decisions. As a result, the incumbency advantage is usually strongest in nonpartisan elections (Schaffner, Streb, and Wright 2001). The effects of party do not end at the voting booth. Council members use party identification to identify like-minded members and as a cue for their voting decisions. If they do not have party to guide their voting, they will rely on other cues such as those from interest groups. Research suggests that when parties are not present, interest groups exert more influence (Davidson and Fraga 1988). This conventional wisdom is widely accepted but has not been empirically verified.

Interest groups have recently become major players in initiative and referendum campaigns (Bowler, Donovan, and Tolbert 1998; Bowler and Donovan 1998; Gerber 1999). Most observers of direct democracy now agree that initiatives and referenda lead to relatively high levels of interest group activity. This hypothesis dates from David Truman's (1951) discussion of disturbance theory more than 50 years ago and has been confirmed by numerous empirical studies. Research shows that when policies are put to a vote, interest groups mobilize on both sides to try to influence voters. Cities in which there is a mechanism for direct democracy likely have higher levels of interest group activity than cities without initiatives or referenda.

Structure is not the only factor that may affect interest group activity. In localities in which citizens are active in politics, interest groups likely will find a more hospitable environment. Consequently, citizen interest in politics and interest group activity are hypothesized to be positively correlated.

The literature leads to four additional hypotheses:

> Hypothesis 4: Levels of interest group activity are higher in cities with mayor-council or commission governments than they are in cities with council-manager governments.

> Hypothesis 5: Levels of interest group activity are higher in cities with nonpartisan elections than they are in cities with partisan elections.

> Hypothesis 6: Levels of interest group activity are higher in cities that have referenda and/or initiatives than they are in cities that have neither.

> Hypothesis 7: Levels of interest group activity are higher in cities with relatively high levels of citizen interest in politics than they are in cities with relatively low levels of citizen interest in politics.

Despite substantial attention to interest groups on the one hand and power in American cities on the other, a number of important questions about interest groups in local politics remain unanswered. Among them are the following: (1) What sorts of interest groups are active in local politics? (2) In which policy areas are interest groups most active? and (3) Does governmental structure affect interest group activity?

Data and Methods

To better understand the influence and activity of interest groups in local politics, city council members in 68 medium-sized American cities were surveyed. The sample was determined by identifying every city in the *Directory of City Policy Officials and Resource Guide* (National League of Cities 1998) that had a population of 100,000–300,000. Eighty cities within the larger list of medium-sized cities were randomly sampled.

A random number of councilors were selected from each city. Of the 477 surveys mailed, 161 completed surveys were returned from 68 cities for a response rate of 33.8 percent (see Table 1). This response rate is more than double that considered to be acceptable in marketing research

TABLE 1   Population of Cities in Data Set

City	Population	City	Population
Huntsville, AL	159,789	Bridgeport, CT	142,546
Mobile, AL	196,278	Hartford, CT	139,739
Montgomery, AL	159,789	New Haven, CT	130,474
Anchorage, AK	226,338	Macon, GA	106,612
Tempe, AZ	141,865	Savannah, GA	137,560
Little Rock, AR	175,795	Boise, ID	125,738
Anaheim, CA	266,406	Peoria, IL	113,504
Bakersfield, CA	174,820	South Bend, IN	105,511
Berkeley, CA	102,724	Cedar Rapids, IA	110,000
Chula Vista, CA	135,163	Des Moines, IA	193,187
Concord, CA	111,348	Kansas City, KS	149,767
El Monte, CA	106,209	Topeka, KS	119,883
Escondido, CA	108,635	Lansing, MI	127,321
Fremont, CA	173,339	Livonia, MI	100,850
Glendale, CA	180,038	Warren, MI	144,864
Hayward, CA	111,498	Jackson, MS	196,637
Huntington Beach, CA	181,519	Rochester, NY	231,636
Modesto, CA	164,730	Syracuse, NY	163,860
Moreno Valley, CA	118,779	Yonkers, NY	188,082
Oceanside, CA	128,398	Eugene, OR	112,669
Ontario, CA	133,179	Salem, OR	107,786
Orange, CA	110,658	Allentown, PA	105,090
Oxnard, CA	142,216	Erie, PA	108,718
Pasadena, CA	131,591	Beaumont, TX	114,323
Pomona, CA	131,723	Corpus Christi, TX	257,453
Santa Clarita, CA	110,642	Garland, TX	180,650
Santa Rosa, CA	113,313	Irving, TX	155,037
Stockton, CA	210,943	Laredo, TX	122,899
Sunnyvale, CA	117,229	Lubbock, TX	186,206
Thousand Oaks, CA	104,352	Mesquite, TX	101,484
Vallejo, CA	109,199	Pasadena, TX	119,363
Aurora, CO	222,103	Plano, TX	128,713
Colorado Springs, CO	281,140	Tacoma, WA	176,664
Lakewood, CO	126,481	Madison, WI	191,262

Note: Numbers are populations as reported in the *Directory of City Policy Officials and Resource Guide* (National League of Cities 1998).

(Baldauf, Reisinger, and Moncrief 1999). It also surpasses the response rates of several other surveys of political elites (see, for example, Abbe and Herrnson 2003; Kedrowski 1996). In short, the response rate was adequate for the purposes of this study.[2] Table 2 presents the major characteristics of sample cities and respondents[3].

Three aspects of the research design are worth noting. First, many cities rather than just one were examined. Scholars of state politics have long recognized the advantages of comparative research and have learned a great deal about the effects of institutions and culture on behavior by examining a number of states that vary in theoretically important ways (Jewell 1982; Brace and Jewett 1995). Scholars of local politics, however, have been slower to adopt a comparative approach. Much of what is known about groups in local politics is based on in-depth case studies of one city and/or one policy area.[4] Reflecting a particular place and point in time, single case studies are high in internal validity but low in external validity. Conversely, studies of many cities are higher in external validity but low in internal validity. A comparative approach allows past research to be evaluated and suggests areas for further research on groups in local politics.

Second, the research design relies on the judgment of city council members rather than lobbyists or other group representatives. Studies of city lobbyists show that the city council is the most frequent target of local lobbying (Abney and Lauth 1985). Moreover, research on interest

TABLE 2   Sample City and Respondent Characteristics

Characteristics	Percent
Respondents who come from a city that	
Allows direct democracy	92.0
Has mayor-council system	33.0
Has council-manager system	67.0
Has commission system	1.0
Has nonpartisan elections	85.0
Council members	
Percent male	67.0
Percent white	81.0
Mean age	53.3
Mean number of members on respondent's council	9.2

$N = 161$ (Ns may vary for individual survey items).
Source: Authors' data.

group influence and activity at all levels of government is based almost exclusively on the opinions of lobbyists and/or group representatives (Kollman 1998; Nownes and Freeman 1998; Schlozman and Tierney 1983; 1986; Walker 1991). This approach may introduce some bias, as lobbyists and group representatives have an important but particular perspective on their own influence. Surveying the other side of the influence exchange yields a complementary and oft-ignored perspective on interest group influence.

Third, this study focuses on medium-sized cities, which have been largely ignored in the scholarly literature. Recent work suggests that city size is an important variable that can help explain political activity (Oliver 2000; 2001). Because tens of millions of Americans live in medium-sized cities and city size has a substantial impact on politics, work on medium-sized cities is both theoretically and substantively important.

Results

Over 20 years ago Paul Peterson . . . claimed "local politics is group-less politics" (1981, 116). Although scholars have frequently taken issue with this statement and have identified a few areas in which groups are active, few have asked city council members about group activity in their city. To explore group activity in local politics, respondents were asked if the statement "Interest groups are active in my city" was a good description of their city, a bad description, or in between. For a subsequent multivariate analysis, the responses were combined to form a dichotomous variable (1 = good description and 0 = bad description or in between). Approximately 52 percent of respondents felt that the statement was a good description. Only 2.5 percent chose the bad description response. This finding that interest groups are quite active in local politics calls into question Peterson's conclusion.

The issues on which interest groups are active were then determined. Table 3 presents findings regarding how active interest groups are on a variety of policy issues and how influential they are on the same policy issues.[5] The third column in Table 3 presents a differential score (i.e., the difference between the percentage of respondents who indicate that interest groups are "very active" in an issue area and the percentage of respondents who indicate that interest groups are "very influential" in that issue area). The final column standardizes the differential by dividing it by the percentage of respondents who indicate that interest groups are very active on that issue. The variation suggests that interest groups are not equally

TABLE 3   Policy Areas in Which Interest Groups Are Active and Level of Influence

Policy Area	Level of Activity Not at all	Some- what	Very	Level of Influence Not at all	Some- what	Very	Differ- ential	Ratio
Economic develop- ment	3	29	68	3	39	58	10	.15
Police/law enforce- ment	6	33	62	7	40	54	8	.13
Land-use planning	4	38	59	5	44	51	8	.14
Public safety	6	36	58	5	46	49	9	.16
Zoning	8	36	57	9	45	46	11	.19
Housing	8	43	49	10	61	29	20	.41
Recreation/parks	8	44	47	13	47	40	7	.15
Fire	21	35	45	25	42	33	12	.27
Art/culture	7	50	43	14	56	31	12	.28
Traffic	13	46	41	18	58	25	16	.39
Education	16	44	40	19	50	31	9	.23
Taxes	21	44	36	22	50	29	7	.19
Roads	17	52	31	20	57	23	8	.26
Refuse collection	41	37	22	40	44	17	5	.23
Personal social ser- vices	18	60	22	23	60	17	5	.23
Health	21	60	18	28	57	15	3	.17
Electricity	54	30	17	51	33	16	1	.06
Public transportation	20	55	26	28	55	17	9	.35
Vocational education	57	37	6	55	41	4	2	.33

$N = 161$ (Ns may vary for individual survey items).

Survey item wording: "Below you will find several issue areas in which local governments are active. For each of the issue areas, please indicate whether local interest groups in your municipality are not at all active, somewhat active, or very active. In addition, for each of the issue areas, please indicate whether local interest groups in your municipality are not at all influential, somewhat influential, or very influential."

Notes: Numbers are percentages. Differential = percent "very active" — percent "very influ- ential." Ratio = differential/percent "very active." All entries are rounded to the nearest whole number.

Source: Authors' data.

active on all policy issues. The first row of the table shows that over two-thirds of respondents perceive that interest groups are very involved in economic development issues. Similarly, 58 percent perceive that interest groups are very influential in the area of economic development policy. Despite the differential ratio of .15, economic development is the policy area in which city council members believe interest groups are most active and influential.

The results in Table 3 are contrary to expectations. Sixty-two percent of city council members indicated that interest groups are very active on police/law enforcement issues, and over half reported that interest groups are very influential on police/law enforcement issues. Although there is little extant work on interest group influence in this area,[6] given the increasing importance of homeland security issues, it is fair to conclude that interest group activity has only increased since the data were collected.

The next five policy areas in which interest groups were described as very active are land-use planning, public safety, zoning, housing, and recreation/parks. Lobbying on roads does not appear to be very wide-spread. Despite the perception that city council members deal mostly with "pothole politics," roads do not receive as much interest group attention as many other policy issues. Housing policy has the largest absolute and standardized differential score. This finding indicates that although councilors perceive that interest groups are extremely active in the area of housing policy, they do not view them as particularly influential. In general, there is a correlation between the proportion of respondents who indicated that interest groups are very active in a policy area and the proportion of respondents who indicated that interest groups are very influential in that policy area. ($r = .970$; $p < .01$ [two-tailed test]).

Types of Groups, Level of Activity, and Level of Influence

Types of interest groups active in local politics and the levels of activity and influence of these groups were then examined. The first row of Table 4 shows that councilors view neighborhood associations as the most active and influential types of groups in local politics. The second row indicates that councilors view business associations as second only to neighborhood groups as important players in local politics. These are the only two types of groups that a majority of respondents indicated are very active in local politics. These findings are consistent with Abney and Lauth's work (1985) on group influence in city politics. Rounding out the list of the five most active types of interest groups are public employee

TABLE 4   Types of Interest Groups, Level of Activity, and Level of Influence

Group Type	Level of Activity			Level of Influence				
	Not at all	Some-what	Very	Not at all	Some-what	Very	Differ-ential	Ratio
Neighborhood associ- ations	0	37	64	2	49	49	15	.23
Business associations	3	38	59	2	52	46	13	.22
Public employee unions	17	41	42	19	50	31	11	.26
Cultural/recreational groups	12	54	35	16	57	27	8	.23
Ethnic/minority groups	16	56	28	22	51	27	1	.04
Homeowner groups	21	52	27	22	52	26	1	.04
Environmental groups	17	48	35	23	54	23	12	.34
Antigrowth groups	36	34	30	44	44	12	18	.60
Private-sector unions	35	38	27	40	38	22	5	.19
Single-Issue groups	15	59	26	22	65	13	13	.50
Utilities	34	48	18	34	47	19	−1	−.06
Taxpayer groups	34	48	18	36	53	11	7	.39
Religious/church groups	25	58	17	23	60	18	−1	−.05
Business firms	15	69	16	14	70	16	0	1.00
Women's groups	32	63	6	35	61	4	2	.33
Farm groups	87	12	1	86	11	3	−2	−2.00
Professional associa- tions	73	26	1	70	28	2	−1	−1.00

$N = 161$ (Ns may vary for individual survey items).

Survey item wording: "Below you will find several types of interest groups that are active at the local level. For each type, please specify whether, in your opinion, that type of group is not at all active, somewhat active, or very active. Also, for each type, please specify whether, in your opinion, that type of group is not at all influential, somewhat influential, or very influential."

Notes: Numbers are percentages. Differential = percent "very active" − percent "very influential." Ratio = differential/percent "very active." All entries are rounded to the nearest whole number.

Source: Authors' data.

unions, cultural/recreational groups, and ethnic/minority groups. The data show that councilors view professional associations, farm groups, and women's groups as the least active and influential types of groups.

The largest absolute gaps between activity and influence exist among antigrowth groups, neighborhood groups, business associations, environmental groups, single-issue groups, and public employee unions, all of which appear to be much more active than they are influential. The standardized ratio measure indicates that cultural/recreational groups and taxpayer groups also have fairly high differentials.[7] To determine the overall fit between activity and influence, the correlation between the proportion of respondents who suggested that a type of interest group was very active and very influential was calculated. Once again, it appears the two are highly correlated ($r = .946$; $p < .01$ [two-tailed test]). In general, it appears that the types of interest groups that are most active are also most influential.

Factors Associated with Group Activity

Finally, the factors that lead to varying levels of interest group activity across cities were considered. By examining several cities with varied institutional structures, the variables that lead to active and influential interest groups may be discerned. Cities with initiatives and/or referenda, cities with council-manager governments, and cities with high levels of citizen interest were expected to have relatively high levels of group activity. To test these hypotheses, respondents were asked whether interest groups are active in their city. In the subsequent logistic regression model, the dependent variable represents whether interest groups are active (=1) or not (=0) in the respondent's city. Independent variables were included for whether the city has direct democracy (1 = direct democracy; 0 = no direct democracy), whether the city has council-manager government (1 = council-manager government; 0 = other type of government), whether the city is in California (1 = California city; 0 = not California city), and to what degree citizens in the city take an interest in politics.[8] Also included were three individual-level variables for each respondent— age, sex (1 = female; 0 = male), and race (1 = white; 0 = nonwhite). These demographic variables were included to determine whether different types of city council members view interest group activity in different ways.

Table 5 presents the results of this analysis. The table presents the odds ratios and robust standard errors for each variable. To gain a better understanding of the results, Table 5 also presents the predicted probabilities for the significant variable. These probabilities were computed using

TABLE 5   Logistic Regression Results for Interest Group Activity

Factors	Odds Ratio (SE)
City	
Direct democracy	1.710 (.924)
Council-manager government	.805 (.397)
Nonpartisan elections	.504 (.257)
"Citizens take an interest in politics"[a]	2.38* (.689)
California city	1.710 (.854)
Individual	
Age	.992 (.017)
Female	1.850 (.836)
White	.711 (.328)
Percent correctly predicted	67.9
Proportional reduction in error (PRE)[b]	31.4
chi-square	20.74*
N	140

*$p < .01$ (two-tailed test).
Note: Standard errors are robust standard errors with clustering on city.
Source: Authors' data.
[a]The low-high probability for this variable is .41–.79. It refers to the predicted probabilities of high interest group activity for the low and high value of the independent variable, holding all other variables at their means.
[b]PRE is calculated per Hagle and Mitchell (1992).

CLARIFY, software for interpreting and presenting statistical results, and they represent the predicted probabilities for the low and high values of the independent variable while holding all other variables at their mean (King, Tomz, and Wittenberg 2000; Tomz, Wittenberg, and King 2003).

The results of the model indicate that cities with initiatives and/or referenda do not have higher relative levels of interest group activity. This finding suggests that the presence of direct democracy is less important in local politics than some scholars suggest.

Second, the results suggest that city structure does not influence interest group activity in the hypothesized direction. Cities with council-manager governments are not substantially less likely to see high levels of interest group activity than cities with mayor-council governments. The increased incidence of chief administrative officers (CAOs) who oversee the day-to-day operations of government may have rendered structure less important in local politics.

Third, the data suggest that neither the presence of nonpartisan

elections nor the demographic characteristics of respondents affect perceptions of interest group activity. The hypothesis that cities with nonpartisan
elections would see higher levels of group activity than cities without
partisan elections was not confirmed. The demographic characteristics of
respondents do not appear to affect perceptions of interest group activity.

Fourth, the analyses suggest that cities with high levels of citizen
interest in politics are more likely than cities with lower levels to have
active interest groups. Specifically, the data show that cities with high
levels of citizen interest in politics have a 79 percent chance of being
perceived as having active interest groups, whereas cities with low levels
of citizen interest have a 41 percent chance of being described as having
active interest groups.

Finally, because California is overrepresented in the sample, an independent variable indicating whether a respondent's city is located in
California was included. The odds ratio indicates that California cities
are almost twice as likely as cities in other states to experience high
levels of interest group activity. However, because the coefficient is not
significant, it cannot necessarily be concluded that California cities are,
ceteris paribus, different than cities in other states.

Conclusion

In all, the data provide mixed support for Hypothesis 1 and unqualified support for Hypotheses 2 and 3. While the data suggest that business
organizations are indeed active in local politics, they also indicate that
other types of interest groups are quite active and influential as well. As
for the effects of city characteristics and governmental structure, there is
support for Hypothesis 7. Structure does not seem to affect levels of
interest group influence and activity.

In addition to providing support for many of the hypotheses, the
data also provide new insights into the nature and extent of interest group
activity in localities. The findings show that a multicity approach to the
study of local politics is worthwhile. In order to move beyond description
and develop more broad-ranging theories of local politics in general and
interest group activity in local politics in particular, case studies must be
supplemented with comparative research. Table 3 suggests that issues that
are heavily lobbied for are understudied in political science and urban
studies. In particular, issues of police and law enforcement engender
extremely high levels of interest group activity. Scholars who wish to
understand the influence and behavior of interest groups in local politics

should focus on this understudied policy area. Table 3 highlights a number of other policy areas in which interest groups are active but about which little is known, including recreation/parks, fire, and art/culture.

Recent research suggests that because of the rise of CAOs and other "hybrid offices," city structure may be less important than it used to be (MacManus and Bullock 2003; DeSantis and Renner 2002; Frederickson and Johnson 2001). The findings of this study indicate that city structure is not an important determinant of interest group activity. Conventional wisdom about local politics also is called into question—that is, in cities in which parties are less important, interest groups "pick up the slack." The presence of nonpartisan elections appears to have no effect on levels of interest group activity. Scholars should reexamine this issue, possibly using a more objective measure of interest group activity, such as the number of registered groups per city.

This study highlights a paradox of local interest groups. Specifically, it shows that something that citizens seem to like (an informed citizenry) is associated with something that citizens claim not to like (interest group influence). Political reformers should therefore consider increasing social capital (i.e., the social networks and norms of reciprocity and trustworthiness). Putnam (2000) discusses the ability of groups to promote social capital, but he does not differentiate between politically active interest groups—which Americans claim not to like—and other types of groups. If groups and participation go hand-in-hand as Putnam suggests, then increased interest group activity is a natural feature of cities that are high in social capital.

Notes

1. Abney and Lauth (1985) do find, however, that interest groups in manager cities have less influence over the bureaucracy.
2. For a review of surveys of state legislators, see Maestas, Neeley, and Richardson (2003).
3. The sample is not identical to the overall population; specifically, California is overrepresented. While 27 percent of the population of medium-sized cities is in California, 37 percent of the sample cities are in California. This limitation is inherent to the study design, but California is controlled for in the multivariate model.
4. Many other studies employ this approach (for example, Oliver 2001; Clingermayer and Feiock 1995). The case studies are much more common in the urban politics literature.
5. The data used in this study can be found at paws.wcu.edu/ccooper and web.-utk.edu/~anownes.
6. An exception is Abney and Lauth's (1985) work on interest group influence in cities. Their results are dissimilar to those of this study.

7. Although the standardized differentials are instructive, they are not definitive. Some groups that have very low levels of activity and influence have elevated ratios. For the types of groups near the bottom of the list, the differential may provide a better guide.

8. Respondents were presented with the following statement: "Citizens take little interest in politics in my city." They were then asked to indicate if this was a good description, bad description, or in between. The responses were recoded to make a higher value consistent with a more active citizenry.

References

Abbe, Owen G., and Paul S. Herrnson. 2003. Campaign professionalism in state legislative elections. *State Politics and Policy Quarterly* 3:223–45.

Abney, Glenn, and Thomas P. Lauth. 1985. Interest group influence in city policy-making: The views of administrators. *Western Political Quarterly* 38:148–61.

———. 1986. *The politics of state and city administration*. Albany: State University of New York Press.

Baldauf, Artur, Heribert Reisinger, and William C. Moncrief. 1999. Examining motivations to refuse in industrial mail surveys. *Journal of the Market Research Society* 41:345–53.

Berry, Jeffrey M., Kent E. Portney, and Ken Thomson. 1993. *The rebirth of urban democracy*. Washington, DC: Brookings Institution.

Bowler, Shaun, and Todd Donovan. 1998. *Demanding choices: Opinion, voting, and direct democracy*. Ann Arbor: University of Michigan Press.

Bowler, Shaun, Todd Donovan, and Caroline J. Tolbert, eds. 1998. *Citizens as legislators: Direct democracy in the United States*. Columbus: Ohio State University Press.

Brace, Paul, and Aubrey Jewett. 1995. The state of state politics research. *Political Research Quarterly* 48:643–81.

Browning, Rufus P., Dale Rogers Marshall, and David H. Tabb, eds. 2003. *Racial politics in American cities*. 3rd ed. New York: Longman.

Button, James W., Barbara A. Rienzo, and Kenneth D. Wald. 1997. *Private lives, public conflicts: Battles over gay rights in American communities*. Washington, DC: CQ Press.

Cigler, Allan J. 1991. Interest groups: A subfield in search of an identity. In *Political science: Looking to the future. Vol. 4, American institutions*, ed. William Crotty. Evanston, IL: Northwestern University Press.

Clark, Terry N. 1968. Community structure, decision-making, budget expenditures, and urban renewal in 51 American communities. *American Sociological Review* 33: 576–93.

Clingermayer, James C., and Richard C. Feiock. 1995. Council views toward targeting of development policy benefits. *Journal of Politics* 57:508–20.

Dahl, Robert A. 1961. *Who governs? Democracy and power in an American city*. New Haven: Yale University Press.

Davidson, Chandler, and Luis Ricardo Fraga. 1988. Slating groups as parties in a "nonpartisan" setting. *Western Political Quarterly* 41:373–90.

DeLeon, Richard Edward. 1992. *Left coast city: Progressive politics in San Francisco, 1975–1991.* Lawrence: University Press of Kansas.

DeSantis, Victor S., and Tari Renner. 2002. City government structures: An attempt at clarification. *State and Local Government Review* 34:95–104.

Dilger, Robert Jay. 1992. *Neighborhood politics: Residential community associations in American governance.* New York: New York University Press.

Elkins, David R. 1995. The structure and context of the urban growth coalition: The view from the chamber of commerce. *Policy Studies Journal* 23:583–600.

Ferman, Barbara. 1996. *Challenging the growth machine: Neighborhood politics in Chicago and Pittsburgh.* Lawrence: University Press of Kansas.

Fleischmann, Arnold. 1997. Participation in local politics. In *Handbook of research on urban politics and policy in the United States,* ed. Ronald K. Vogel. Westport, CT: Greenwood Press.

Frederickson, H. George, and Gary Alan Johnson. 2001. The adapted American city: A study of institutional dynamics. *Urban Affairs Review* 36:872–84.

Gerber, Elisabeth R. 1999. *The populist paradox: Interest group influence and the promise of direct legislation.* Princeton: Princeton University Press.

Grimes, Michael D., Charles M. Bonjean, J. Larry Lyon, and Robert L. Lineberry. 1976. Community structure and leadership arrangements: A multidimensional analysis. *American Sociological Review* 41:706–25.

Hagle, Timothy M., and Glen E. Mitchell II. 1992. Goodness-of-fit measures for probit and logit. *American Journal of Political Science* 36:762–84.

Hunter, Floyd. 1953. *Community power structure: A study of decision makers.* Chapel Hill: University of North Carolina Press.

Jewell, Malcolm E. 1982. The neglected world of state politics. *Journal of Politics* 44:638–57.

Judd, Dennis R. 1983. From cowtown to sunbelt city: Boosterism and economic growth in Denver. In *Restructuring the city: The political economy of urban redevelopment,* ed. Susan S. Fainstein et al. New York: Longman.

Kedrowski, Karen. 1996. *Media entrepreneurs and the media enterprise in the U.S. Congress.* Cresskill, NJ: Hampton Press.

King, Gary, Michael Tomz, and Jason Wittenberg. 2000. Making the most of statistical analyses: Improving interpretation and presentation. *American Journal of Political Science* 44:341–55.

Kollman, Ken. 1998. *Outside lobbying: Public opinion and interest group strategies.* Princeton: Princeton University Press.

Lineberry, Robert L., and Edmund P. Fowler. 1967. Reformism and public policies in American cities. *American Political Science Review* 61:701–16.

Logan, John R., and Harvey L. Molotch. 1987. *Urban fortunes: The political economy of place.* Berkeley: University of California Press.

Lynd, Robert S., and Helen Merrell Lynd. 1937. *Middletown in transition: A study in cultural conflicts.* New York: Harcourt, Brace and Company.

Lyons, William. 1978. Reform and response in American cities: Structure and policy reconsidered. *Social Science Quarterly* 59:118–32.

MacManus, Susan A., and Charles S. Bullock III. 2003. The form, structure, and composition of America's municipalities in the new millennium. In *The municipal yearbook, 2003.* Washington, DC: International City/County Management Association.

Maestas, Cherie, Grant W Neeley, and Lilliard E. Richardson Jr. 2003. The state of surveying legislators: Dilemmas and suggestions. *State Politics and Policy Quarterly* 3:90–108.

Mesch, Gustavo S., and Kent P. Schwirian. 1996. The effectiveness of neighborhood collective action. *Social Problems* 43:467–83.

Morgan, David R., and John P. Pelissero. 1980. Urban policy: Does political structure matter? *American Political Science Review* 74:999–1006.

National League of Cities. 1998. *Directory of city policy officials and resource guide.* Washington, DC: National League of Cities.

Northrop, Alana, and William H. Dutton. 1978. Municipal reform and group influence. *American Journal of Political Science* 22:691–711.

Nownes, Anthony J., and Patricia Freeman. 1998. Interest group activity in the states. *Journal of Politics* 60:86–112.

Oliver, J. Eric. 2000. City size and civic involvement in metropolitan America. *American Political Science Review* 94:361–73.

————. 2001. *Democracy in suburbia.* Princeton: Princeton University Press.

Peterson, Paul. 1981. *City limits.* Chicago: University of Chicago Press.

Putnam, Robert D. 2000. *Bowling alone: The collapse and revival of American community.* New York: Simon and Schuster.

Regalado, James A. 1991. Organized labor and Los Angeles city politics: An assessment in the Bradley years, 1973–1989. *Urban Affairs Quarterly* 27:87–108.

Schaffner, Brian F., Matthew Streb, and Gerald Wright. 2001. Teams without uniforms: The nonpartisan ballot in state and local elections. *Political Research Quarterly* 54:7–30.

Schlozman, Kay Lehman, and John T. Tierney. 1983. More of the same: Washington pressure group activity in a decade of change. *Journal of Politics* 45:351–77,

————. 1986. *Organized interests and American democracy.* New York: Harper and Row.

Sharp, Elaine B. 2003. Political participation in cities. In *Cities, politics and policy: A comparative analysis,* ed. John P. Pelissero. Washington, DC: CQ Press.

————. ed. 1999. *Culture wars and local politics.* Lawrence: University Press of Kansas.

Stone, Clarence N. 1989. *Regime politics: Governing Atlanta, 1946–1988.* Lawrence: University Press of Kansas.

Tomz, Michael, Jason Wittenberg, and Gary King. 2003. *CLARIFY: Software for interpreting and presenting statistical results.* Version 2.1. gking.harvard.edu/.

Truman, David B. 1951. *The governmental process: Political interests and public opinion.* New York: Alfred A. Knopf, Inc.

Walker, Jack L., Jr. 1991. *Mobilizing interest groups in America: Patrons, professions, and social movements.* Ann Arbor: University of Michigan Press.

PART SIX

EXECUTIVE LEADERSHIP IN STATE AND LOCAL GOVERNMENT

Executive leadership is critical to public problem-solving. State and local governments need strong leadership from their executives in order to deal with the complex problems they face. As the decade of the 1990s began, several states and numerous cities were facing serious fiscal crises even as they tried to deal with other problems such as inadequate health care, a deteriorating infrastructure, the homeless, and crime. At the dawn of the new century, state governors seemed to be the "Cinderellas" of American politics. Thanks to a booming economy, many states had seen their fiscal crises turn into fiscal surpluses providing opportunities for having the best of both worlds—cutting taxes and increasing spending for key programs. Yet, in the 2008 "credit crunch" period, recessions have returned once again taking a huge bite out of state revenue coffers. Additionally, the continuing devolution of responsibility has created new challenges. Thus, in the new era of state resurgence, governors have had to lead the way in proposing innovative solutions to their states' problems. As they continue to grapple with the numerous issues, citizens and politicians alike look to their government executives for the necessary leadership.

For a long time, governors were seriously hamstrung by constitutional and statutory restrictions on their power to act. This situation was an artifact of the historical distrust of executive authority that helped form the foundation of American constitutional theory, yet it began to be reflected in the constitutions of the states in the form of these restrictions. The most dramatic illustration of this anti-executive philosophy is that only since 1998 has North Carolina's governor had the veto power. In fact, one of the interesting aspects of the diversity of the states is the relative differences in the formal powers of the governors. Indeed, several scholars have attempted to measure the degree of the formal power of governors in order to compare states from weakest to strongest.[1] In spite of the existence of relatively weak governors, one of the most significant changes throughout the states that contributed to their political rejuvenation was the reform and strengthening of the governorship. Reforms have ranged from increased terms of office, to more budget and policy authority,[2] allowing the modern governor to become an important catalyst for policy change and innovation in the American federal system.[3]

Of course, policy making in the American states takes place in the context of separation of powers, and the extent to which governors can influence state policy will depend on their ability to coax legislators to accede to their policy priorities. This fact is often exacerbated by the existence of divided government when one party controls the legislature and the other party controls the executive. Little research has been conducted trying to identify the success of governors in setting the policy agenda and influencing the passage of legislation that helps further the agenda. One major study has concluded that governors have *no* influence on state policy direction.[4] But in our first article, Margaret Ferguson attempts to explain executive leadership in the legislative arena by developing a model of the factors that are key to success. Her comprehensive data set includes all 50 state governors and their efforts to influence state policy making through the state legislature. Her findings suggest that governors do have a significant leadership role in state policy-making.

As creatures of their states, cities are buffeted by a significant number of external and internal forces that present challenging problems for their leaders. Cycles of the economy, movement of capital and jobs, state and federal mandates, strong city councils, interest groups, neighborhood organizations, social conflict, and issues of bi-polarism resulting from a growing underclass make leadership of American cities one of the most difficult tasks in the federal system. Recognizing these realities, The National Commission on State and Local Public Service (the Winter Commission) in 1993 issued a report with recommendations on how executive leadership could be strengthened in the cities. These recommendations came on the heels of the National Civic League's proposed model city charter which contained an even more extensive set of guidelines for improving executive power. The essence of these two sets of recommendations relate to structural changes that are believed to be needed to enhance the mayors' capacity to govern. In our next article, Craig Wheeland assesses the state of the institutional powers of the mayors and their relationship to mayoral leadership. In so doing, he is able to provide a classification of mayoral leadership based on the powers that various city charters grant to their mayors.

Notes

1.   See for example, Thad Beyle, "Governors: The Middlemen and Women in Our Political System," in *Politics in the American States: A Comparative Analysis*, 6th ed., (Washington, D.C.: CQ Press, 1996), p. 237; and Robert Jay Dilger, "A Comparative Analysis of Gubernatorial Enabling Resources," *State and Local Government Review* 27 (Spring, 1995): 118–126.

2.   See Larry Sabato, *Goodbye to Good-Time Charlie: The American Governorship Transformed*, 2nd ed., (Washington, D.C.: CQ Press, 1983); and U.S. Advisory Commission on Intergovernmental Relations, *The Question of State Government Capability* (Washington, D.C.: ACIR, January, 1985).

3.   Thad L. Beyle, "The Governor as Innovator in the Federal System," *Publius: The Journal of Federalism*, 18 (Summer, 1988): 133–154.

4.   Robert S. Erikson, Gerald Wright and John McIver, *Statehouse Democracy*, (New York: Cambridge University Press, 1993).

Questions for Review and Discussion

6.1   What are the factors that are most significant gubernatorial success in the legislative arena? To what extent can governors control these factors, and how does this affect their success?

6.2   What are the classifications of mayoral leadership that Craig Wheeland develops from his research? To what extent is institutional structure key to leadership type? What are some potential problems associated with weak and strong mayor systems? Which one do you prefer? Why?

19 Chief Executive Success in the Legislative Arena

MARGARET ROBERTSON FERGUSON

IN A LEGISLATIVE SYSTEM OF checks and balances as in the United States, what is the leadership role of the chief executive? Are they actually "chief legislators" as some scholars have labeled them (Bernick and Wiggins 1991; Gross 1991; Rosenthal 1990)? Certainly chief executives (particularly at the state level) have moved forward dramatically in the acquisition of formal powers in recent decades. It is possible that these powers enable them to lead their legislatures. However, chief executives function in a complex environment, and there are many other factors that may influence their abilities to lead. For example, state legislatures have also become more institutionally endowed. Perhaps these profession- alized legislatures have moved beyond the need for leadership from the executive branch and merely look to the executive for the final signature. Very little empirical research has been undertaken to flesh out and assess the role of chief executives in the legislative arena. We might ultimately find that the pluralist and multi-access context of American policy-making is such that any individual actor—even one with the resources of a chief executive—is ineffectual in determining the direction of public policy.

In this article, I examine the leadership role of the American state governors in the legislative process by modeling the success of their legislative agendas. Examining my research question in the context of the 50 states offers a variety of benefits. First, the states offer 50 different political, institutional, and economic contexts, allowing me to explore the influence of these on executive leadership. Second, examining 50 individuals allows me to explore the influences of a chief executive's personal characteristics on leadership. Third, the states are a particularly important arena in American government today, given the ongoing devolution revolution (Van Horn 1996; Donahue 1997; Weber and Brace 1999; Hanson 1999), so understanding executive leadership in them is crucial.

I demonstrate that the features of the state legislature largely determine the ability of these governors to achieve success for their legislative goals. Other factors such as political party strength and economic health of the state also affect the legislative success of these executives. On the other hand, despite the fact that prior scholarship has emphasized the formal powers of the governor, I find little evidence of their importance as governors attempt to lead their legislatures.

Modeling the Success of Executive Policy Leadership

The first question to consider about the leadership role of the executive in the legislative arena is, What is leadership? This question has no simple answer. Leadership can be defined as determining what the public wants and what is legislatively and politically feasible, and then advocating for policies to achieve these goals (Edwards 1989; Peterson 1990; Beyle 1983). Leadership is successful when the policies the leader advocated are actually adopted by the legislature and instituted as public policy.

Understood this way, executive leadership must be judged in the context of the actions and motivations of the relevant public and legislators and the broader institutional context in which an executive works. These factors all affect the likelihood of executive legislative success. Chief executives are not discrete actors. To direct law-making, they must interact with the public and the legislature, in nearly all instances. They must consider their political and economic environment and the potential future behavior of legislators and citizens when they make choices about how and when they attempt to lead. Therefore, to understand leadership, we must recognize the strategic nature of the decisions chief executives make. Many factors lead one leader to be successful and another to fail— or even lead one leader to succeed in one instance and fail miserably in another. Thus, personal, political, institutional, and economic factors must all be included in any model that attempts to account for variations in executive leadership and its success.

Personal Factors—The Characteristics and Choices of the Incumbent

At the most basic level, the personal experiences of the person serving as chief executive may affect his or her success in the legislative arena. Consider first the electoral success of the chief executive. The standard political axiom is that chief executives who win their positions by large electoral margins can more easily convince legislators that the public favors their stated policy positions (Edwards 1989). Therefore, electoral success strengthens the executive's bargaining position and should increase legislative success. I measure electoral success as the margin separating a sitting governor from the closest competitor in the preceding election.[1] (See Appendix A for details on the measurement of my independent variables.)

Similarly, positive public approval ratings are believed to provide chief executives with an advantage in dealing with the legislature (Bernick and Wiggins 1991; Beyle 1992; Edwards 1980; Fett 1994; Gleiber and Shull 1992; Kernell 1986; Kingdon 1984; Neustadt 1980; Peterson 1990; Polsby 1978; Simonton 1987). All things equal, legislators concerned with their own reelection will not wish to oppose a popular chief executive, while low public approval ratings may actually decrease the executive's legislative success by encouraging legislators to distance themselves from the unpopular executive's policy agenda (Edwards 1989; Sullivan 1991). I measure gubernatorial public approval using public opinion data compiled by Beyle, Niemi, and Sigelman (2002). Governors are characterized on this measure by the percent of respondents in a sample that agreed that the governor was doing an "excellent," "good," or "above average" job, or who indicated that they "approved" of the governor's job in office (depending upon the coding scheme of the poll).[2]

Public support of chief executives has been found to vary systematically over the course of their terms in office with a high point immediately after an election (the "honeymoon period") and then waning over time (Beyle 1992; Edwards and Wayne 1990; Fiorina 1984; Jacobson 1987; Light 1982; Olson 1985; Ostrom and Simon 1985, 1988; Ragsdale 1993). However, some scholars have argued that such a decline does not inevitably lead to lower legislative success in that executives might become more successful with the passage of time as they acquire experience working with the legislature (Crew 1992; Light 1982; Neustadt 1980). Thus, previous research does not point to a single hypothesis of the effect of the passage of time on legislative success. To help clarify this debate, my model includes two dummy variables for time, one for the first year of the governor's term and one for the last year of the term.

A chief executive's strategic choices may also influence his or her legislative success. One such decision a chief executive must make is size of the agenda to be pursued in the legislature. Multiple considerations likely drive this decision. Probably foremost among these is the desire to gain passage for preferred policies. This requires a chief executive to estimate what the legislature might accept and then adjust his or her agenda accordingly. Other considerations that may influence the size of a chief executive's agenda might include the desires of key constituents, the opportunity to claim credit for having identified an important issue, and the desire to lay the groundwork for proposals that might pass in the future. Therefore, the size of the agenda is partially, but not wholly, determined by the executive's assessment of what is feasible. But regardless of the causes of an executive's decision to limit or expand the legislative agenda, the scope of this agenda may well affect the executive's legislative success. Some argue that leaders possess a limited amount of political capital, and to be successful, they must pick priorities carefully, focusing on only a few key issues (Bond and Fleisher 1990; Edwards 1989; Peterson 1990; Pfiffner 1988; Sullivan 1991). Therefore, the scope of the chief executive's agenda is hypothesized to be negatively related to legislative success. I measure the scope of a governor's legislative agenda as the number of broad policy areas (such as welfare, health care, and crime) addressed in his or her most recent State of the State address.

Many of the more personal and idiosyncratic characteristics that may affect leadership, such as charisma, public speaking ability, and intelligence, are not amenable to measurement, but other such factors can be accounted for in my model of gubernatorial legislative success. First, those chief executives whose terms are marked by scandal will likely see their influence in the legislature reduced as law-makers feel freer to oppose them and may even gain political advantage by doing so (Simonton 1987). I compiled data for a dummy variable on scandal from information in *State Capital Reports* (a reporter contained in Lexis-Nexis).[3] I define a "scandal" as significant, numerous, or persistent legal or financial questions.[4]

Finally, I try to assess the impact of the political skill of a chief executive on legislative success. Chief executives who have held prior elective office may be more politically skillful, and thus more likely to succeed, since they may have allies already in place and need to spend less time learning to serve in the crucial first months of their terms (Bernick and Wiggins 1991;

Crew 1992). On the other hand, some empirical research has found little support for the impact of political skill on chief executive success (Edwards 1989). I try to resolve this debate by including two dummy variables in my model, one for whether the governor has held the governor's office previously and one for previous legislative experience.

Each of these personal factors may help to predict a chief executive's legislative success. No matter what formal powers are available to a chief executive, if he or she lacks the personal inclination or skill to use them effectively, legislative success will not follow. Conversely, a chief executive with strong skills and a popular mandate may still have a hard time overcoming institutional and political handicaps. It is to the institutional resources and handicaps for legislative success that I turn next.

Institutional Factors

Legislative success may also be a function of the office a chief executive holds and the legislature with which he or she must work. Strong institutional powers of a chief executive's office may be a necessary, but not sufficient, condition of legislative success (Bernick 1979; Bernick and Wiggins 1991; Beyle 1990, 1996; Brudney and Hebert 1987; Dilger, Krause, and Moffett 1995; Ferguson 1993, 1994; Gross 1991; Kingdon 1984; Mueller 1985; Neustadt 1980; Schlesinger 1965; Sigelman and Dometrius 1988). Serving in an institutionally strong office will give a chief executive leverage to become involved in the legislature's policy debate since legislators will need the executive's support for a variety of policy decisions. I include four measures of formal powers in my model of gubernatorial legislative success: tenure potential, appointment power, budget proposing power, and veto power.

If a chief executive may run for re-election, legislators deciding whether to support the executive's agenda operate with uncertainty as to future encounters with him or her. As such, and typically being risk-averse regarding their own re-election (Mayhew 1974), legislators may be more likely to support the chief executive's position. Executives who are prevented from seeking another term of office, or lame ducks, may be seen as weaker politically and as having few benefits to offer those who support their legislation (Beyle 1990). Thus, lame duck status should reduce an executive's legislative success. I measure this with a dummy variable coded 1 for governors who are not allowed by law to seek re-election.[5]

While appointment power is not directly related to the legislative process, it is a means of breaking the legislative-bureaucratic alliances by which policy in legislatures is often made. To the extent that chief executives are able to place individuals who share their philosophy and goals into key administrative positions, the fortunes of their legislative proposals ought to benefit. This power offers governors access to information in the executive branch and influence over the regulatory decisions made by executive agencies. It also increases the likelihood that agency heads will share the policy goals of the governor, which will aid the chief executive as these state agency heads often work closely with legislators to direct the formulation of legislation (Hebert, Brudney, and Wright 1983; Ferguson 1993, 1994; Wright 1967). I measure a governor's appointment power as the degree of authority the governor possesses for the appointment of administrators in 37 different functional areas. For each functional area, a score ranging from 0 (no official role for the governor) to 5 (the governor had sole authority for appointing the official) is assigned depending on the amount of influence the governor exerted (Beyle 1990). The score for each state is the average score across the 37 offices.

Chief executive responsibility for preparing the state's budget is a third element of formal powers that may influence legislative success. Legislatures typically have unlimited power to shape and enact budget bills, but the president and governors in all but six states possess broad authority to propose and implement the budget. This power may benefit the success of other elements in the executive's legislative agenda by improving the bargaining position of the chief executive in the legislative arena (Beyle 1990). I measure gubernatorial budget-making power as a dummy variable coded 1 if the governor possesses sole responsibility for preparing the budget, and 0 otherwise.

Finally, my model of gubernatorial legislative success includes a measure of veto power. The president possesses only a package veto, but gubernatorial veto powers vary in quality and strength. Chief executives can use the veto or its threat as a bargaining tool to help secure passage of their preferred legislation (Bernick and Wiggins 1991; Wiggins 1980). I measure veto power as a dummy variable coded 1 when the governor possesses the strongest veto power defined by the Schlesinger (1965) index (item veto with a super-majority required to override), and 0 otherwise.

Beyond the formal powers of the office, chief executives' legislative success may also depend on their information-gathering resources and lobbying operations. These "enabling resources" (Dilger, Krause, and Moffett 1995) of the office can combine with its formal powers to promote an executive's pursuit of a legislative agenda. Therefore, my model includes a variable for size of the governor's staff.

In addition to the characteristics of the chief executive's office, the characteristics of the legislature can influence the executive's legislative success. First, legislatures that meet more days out of the year and whose members receive higher salaries, have more extensive staff, and are more likely to stay in office long enough to develop policy expertise probably face the executive on a more equal footing (Bowman and Kearney 1988; Moncrief and Thompson 1992; Moncrief et al. 1992; Mooney 1995; Squire 1992). The state legislatures vary dramatically in the degree to which they are professionalized in these ways, although most state legislatures have become increasingly professional in the past generation (Brace and Ward 1999; Hamm and Moncrief 1999). Thus, the degree of legislative professionalism should influence executive success at policy leadership, assuming the executive and legislature have differing legislative priorities. However, it remains unclear in the current literature how this change has interacted with governors' growing formal power (Bernick and Wiggins 1991; Gross 1991; Jewell and Whicker 1994; Peterson 1990). I employ an indicator drawn from Squire (1992) who measures legislative professionalism as the closeness of pay, staff, and annual days in session of a state legislature to that of Congress.

Finally, my model of a chief executive's legislative success needs to control for the general tendency of the respective legislature to pass bills. Like in Congress, the vast majority of state legislation does not become law. However, legislatures vary significantly in the number of bills considered each session and the proportion of those bills that pass. In states that tend to pass many or most of the bills introduced, one would certainly not be surprised if many or most of the governor's initiatives passed. Including a variable for overall rate of bill passage helps to control for this legislative tendency. Therefore, I calculated the overall percentage of "non-governor" bills passed in each state's legislature during the 1993–94 legislative session and included it in my model. Although this measure may reflect several underlying and unmeasured constructs, it helps to capture an important legislative tendency that could affect the passage rate of gubernatorial proposals.

Political Factors

Various factors that help define the political context are likely to influence a chief executive's legislative success. Perhaps most important among these is political party. Where one or both chambers of the legislature are controlled by the chief executive's party, executive legislative success should be enhanced because it gives the executive a built-in core of support (Beyle 1996, 1992; Bond and Fleisher 1990; Bowling and Ferguson 2000; Crew 1992; Gleiber and Shull 1992; Kingdon 1984; Morehouse 1981, 1994, 1998; Peterson 1990; Rivers and Rose 1985). I assess this effect of party with dummy variables for two types of divided government—simple divided government (where both chambers of the legislature are controlled by the opposition party) and compound divided government (where the legislature itself is divided, with the chambers controlled by different parties).[6] Bowling and Ferguson (2000) found that it is the condition of compound divided government that makes law-making most difficult. In addition, the governor's initiatives must be formally proposed by legislators, who themselves may be able to draw upon party loyalties. I account for this effect in my model with a dummy variable coded 1 where the proposal sponsor is a member of the majority party in that chamber.[7]

The presence and activity of interest groups is another political condition that might affect the ability of a chief executive to achieve legislative goals. Previous research suggests that political systems with more interest groups and broader domains of interests represented will see diminished executive influence over policy-making (Berry 1989; Gais, Peterson, and Walker 1984; McFarland 1992; Schlozman and Tierney 1986). Complex and dense interest group systems may make it more difficult to pass any legislation, whether supported by the chief executive or anyone else (Bowling and Ferguson 2000; Gray and Lowery 1995). I measure the interest group environment with two variables developed by Gray and Lowery (1996), one for interest group density and the other for interest group diversity. Interest group diversity is measured with a Herfindahl index of concentration across 10 categories of interest groups.[8] Interest group density is the number of groups registered to lobby in the state. Both of these variables are hypothesized to be negatively related to the likelihood of gubernatorial legislative success.[9]

Economic Factors

The condition of the economy is also likely to influence the legislature's response to a chief executive's proposals. I use the unemployment rate as a proxy for overall state economic conditions, since it is highly visible and colors state legislators' impressions of the economic conditions facing the state (Crew 1992; Peterson 1990). When a weak economy cuts into a state's resources, legislators will feel pressure to make cuts and new proposals that require additional funds will be less likely to pass. Poor economic conditions will also have a more general negative effect on the governor's position of leadership as governors are to some extent held responsible for the economic performance of their states (Crew 1992; Dilger, Krause, and Moffett 1995; Peterson 1990). I control for this factor with both the change in monthly unadjusted unemployment rate in the state at the time of final bill action compared to the previous month and the rate of unemployment at the time of final bill action. These measures are hypothesized to be negatively related to gubernatorial legislative success.

Data

Testing hypotheses of chief executive leadership success at the national level has always been problematic because of the small number of presidents and the lack of variation in many variables of interest, particularly the institutional variables (Peterson 1990). Examining presidents over time addresses this problem to some extent, but it raises validity questions about the effect of the historical period. Instead, I test these hypotheses with data on governors from a single year in all 50 states. This allows for substantial variation in executive personalities, institutional and political arrangements, and economic conditions. Using Lexis-Nexis, I gathered data for all bills with final legislative action in each state in 1994.[10]

My dataset contains 89,678 pieces of legislation.[11] The information for each bill includes a bill synopsis, committee referral and action, floor action (in the originating chamber and the other chamber), bill sponsorship, and a series of subject labels that I used to categorize bills into policy areas. I converted this Lexis-Nexis information into the variables for my model of gubernatorial legislative success.

To develop my dependent variable—gubernatorial legislative success—I first identified gubernatorial policy proposals. In some states, these bills were easy to identify because, unlike the president, governors can introduce legislation directly in a few states. In other states, the legislative leadership routinely submits legislation on behalf of the governor (Rosenthal 1990). But in other states, identifying gubernatorial bills was more difficult. Most governors do not offer formal legislative plans to their legislatures for consideration, and there is no state version of *Congressional Quarterly* that monitors gubernatorial position-taking uniformly across the states.

One approach to staking out a legislative agenda that is common to all governors is the State of the State address. I used these addresses to identify gubernatorial proposals. Given the limited amount of time available for a State of the State address, and the limited attention span of the audience, governors usually choose to focus on the items they believe to be most important for their states (Herzik 1991; Light 1982). Therefore, although the address may not include all of the governor's proposals, it can be expected to include the ones most important to the governor that year. Research on governors and on presidential State of the Union addresses indicates that these speeches constitute valid and reliable indicators of executive policy goals (Crew 1992; Herzik 1991; Light 1982). Herzik (1991, 31) asserts that "as these addresses generally come at the outset of legislative sessions and contain specific policy and budgetary proposals the governor will pursue, they best approximate the governor's actual policy agenda." Similarly, Rosenthal (1990, 7) calls the State of the State address "the vehicle that announces to all what policies and programs the governor will pursue and gives the legislature its first strong indication of what the governor has in mind." These addresses constitute public documents that have been offered for many years and are generally consistent across the states in the time they are made and the goals inherent in them. For these reasons, I use governors' State of the State addresses to identify the proposals that constitute their policy agendas.[12]

After identifying specific proposals from each State of the State address, I used the Lexis-Nexis subject categories to code them. I then used a computer algorithm to tag bills introduced in the legislature in these policy areas as potential gubernatorial bills. I then reviewed the synopsis of each of these bills to verify as well as possible its match with the governor's enunciated preferences. Where multiple bills matched the governor's goals, I coded each as a "governor" bill.[13] Using this method, I had identified 1,092 governor-endorsed bills, although 79 of these were excluded from my final dataset due to missing data.[14] Appendix B shows the number and percentage of bills from each state. These governor bills are my unit of analysis.

Having identified the bills in each state that were congruent with the governor's policy preferences, I characterized whether they were successful. I define gubernatorial legislative success as the passage of legislation endorsed or sponsored by the governor. I derived this information from Lexis-Nexis. A bill was deemed to be passed when it 1) was signed by the governor, 2) became law without the governor's signature, or 3) was adopted by both chambers of the legislature and was not vetoed by the governor. This measure is a dichotomous variable for each governor bill indicating whether it became law (coded 0 for failure and 1 for adoption).[15]

Results

Since my dependent variable, gubernatorial success on a bill, is dichotomous, I employ logistic regression analysis to test my hypotheses, using the data described above and in Appendix A. The results of the estimation of my model are displayed in Table 1. These results offer some support for my hypotheses, but there are also some unexpected findings. Taken together, these results tell us much about the factors that lead to the success or failure of chief executives' legislative agendas.

Thirteen of the model's 22 independent variables have estimated coefficients with the expected sign and that achieve statistical significance ($p < .05$). However, five have the unpredicted sign, contradicting the expectations of the extant literature. The remaining four variables' coefficients have the expected sign but fail to achieve statistical significance at conventional levels. In this section, I examine each of the statistically significant findings and suggest reasons for the non-significant and unexpected findings. In addition, I have converted the logistic regression coefficients into example probabilities to examine the substantive effects of each variable on gubernatorial legislative success.

Factors associated with a governor personally are found to be of mixed importance. Governors in my dataset apparently could not make effective use of an electoral mandate, as the electoral margin variable coefficient exhibits an unexpected (although not statistically significant) negative sign.[16] To the extent that this negative sign has meaning, it may result from the length of time that had passed since the electoral margin variable was measured, with election effects being on the wane in most states in my dataset. In 1994, most governors were well into their terms and many were on the verge of new elections. Furthermore, this finding is in keeping with the findings of some other empirical work that shows that electoral margin has little effect on legislative success (Peterson 1990).

Gubernatorial popularity performs in a similarly unexpected fashion. Although some scholars of executive politics have viewed public approval to be an important informal resource (Bernick 1979; Crew 1992; Rosenthal 1998, 1990), my analyses show no support for this hypothesis, in keeping with some empirical work in this area (Bond and Fleisher 1984; Collier and Sullivan 1995; Mouw and MacKuen 1992; Peterson 1990). However, it just may be that governors have to achieve higher levels of popularity than the fairly unpopular governors serving in 1993–94 for this effect to be felt.

As noted, the effect of the passage of time on gubernatorial legislative success is not a settled question in the literature. I find that governors in

TABLE 1   Model of Executive Leadership Success in the States, 1993–94

Independent Variable	B (standard error)		Probability at 1 s.d. < mean (dummy = 0)	Probability at 1 s.d. > mean (dummy = 1)
Personal Factors				
Electoral margin	−2.083	(1.252)		
Gubernatorial popularity	−0.018	(0.010)		
Scope of governor's agenda	−0.132**	(0.046)	.29	.13
First year of governor's term	0.344	(0.516)		
Last year of governor's term	−0.773**	(0.274)	(.29)	(.16)
Scandal	−0.690*	(0.371)	(.22)	(.13)
Prior term as governor	0.818**	(0.349)	(.14)	(.27)
Prior legislative experience	0.073	(0.269)		
Institutional Factors				
Appointment power	0.018	(0.012)		
Strong veto power	0.521	(0.371)		
Budget responsibility	−0.568	(0.287)		
Staff support	0.544*	(0.301)	.17	.24
Lame duck status	0.093	(0.374)		
Legislative professionalism	2.448**	(1.076)	.15	.26
Non-governor bill passage rate	7.136***	(0.810)	.07	.44
Political Factors				
Simple divided government	−0.706*	(0.385)	(.22)	(.13)
Compound divided government	−0.694*	(0.347)	(.23)	(.13)
Majority party status of bill sponsor	0.492**	(0.211)	(.15)	(.22)
Interest group density	−0.001**	(0.000)	.27	.14
Interest group diversity	−4.991	(16.810)		
Economic Factors				
Unemployment rate	−0.374***	(0.083)	.32	.11
Change in unemployment	−3.784***	(0.811)	.29	.13
Constant	0.518	(2.442)		

TABLE 1   (*Continued*)

Independent Variable	B (standard error)	Probability at 1 s.d. < mean (dummy = 0)	Probability at 1 s.d. > mean (dummy = 1)
Goodness of fit statistics:			
Percent predicted correctly	81%		
Proportional reduction in error	22.4%		
Model chi-square	222.64***		
N = 1013			

Maximum likelihood estimates for logistic regression.

*p < .05; **p < .01; ***p < .001 (one-tailed tests, except for measures of the year in the governor's term and legislative professionalism, which are two-tailed.)

Note: To calculate probabilities, all other variables were set at their mean values. Probabilities in parentheses are for dummy variables. For interval variables, I report the probability of bill passage at one standard deviation below and one standard deviation above the mean. Predicted probabilities are reported only for those variables whose effects are statistically significant at the .05 level or less.

the last year of their terms are less successful in achieving their legislative goals than are governors earlier in their terms.[17] The dummy variable for a governor's first year has a positive coefficient, but it is not statistically significant.

On the other hand, gubernatorial strategic decisions as to the scope of the agenda do have the expected effect on gubernatorial legislative success. I find that governors who pursue broad agendas have a significantly harder time achieving their goals than governors who pursue more tightly constrained agendas. For example, a governor who proposes an agenda one standard deviation smaller than the mean has more than double the probability of passage for each element of that agenda than proposals of a governor with an agenda one standard deviation larger than the mean (13 percent probability of passage versus 29 percent). Governors who attempt to tackle too many issues may find that the success of their entire agenda suffers. Experience as a former governor (but not as a state legislator), whether it indicates skill or established relationships, improves the governor's legislative success, as expected. Proposals offered by experienced governors have a 27 percent probability of passing as compared to only a 14 percent probability for first-term governors. Conversely, involvement in a major scandal significantly hampers a governor's legislative success, reducing the probability of a bill's passage from 22 percent to 13 percent.

The findings for the effect of institutional factors on gubernatorial legislative success are also mixed. Despite the amount of attention paid to them in the state politics literature, the variables representing the formal powers of the governor contributed little to explaining my dependent variable. Indeed, budget power is estimated actually to hamper the passage of a governor's bills. The coefficient estimate for the lame duck status of a governor carries an unpredicted positive sign, but it does not achieve statistical significance. Thus, my results provide no real support for the idea that formal powers or tenure limitations affect a governor's ability to succeed in the legislative arena. On the other hand, gubernatorial enabling resources, measured as access to staff support, apparently do assist the governor in the legislative arena. For example, proposals from a governor with one standard deviation fewer staff than average have only a 17 percent probability of passage, while proposals offered by a governor with one standard deviation more staff than average have a 24 percent probability of passage.

The institutional qualities of the state legislature appear to have more impact on a governor's success than those of his or her own office. Legislative professionalism is positively related to gubernatorial legislative success in my model, to a statistically significant degree. While the existing literature is inconclusive on this effect, I find that the substantive effects here are noteworthy. Proposals offered by governors working with very professional legislatures have a 26 percent chance of adoption, as compared to only a 15 percent chance in less professional bodies. This synergistic relationship between empowered governors and professionalized legislatures needs to be more fully examined by state politics scholars (Dilger, Krause, and Moffett 1995). The general tendency of a legislature to pass bills also has a statistically significant and positive effect on the likelihood of a governor's bill passing. As I suggested above, this variable is probably a proxy for several forces that are currently missing from the model. The probability of passage varies dramatically with changes in this variable, from 7 percent in states where the legislature adopts one standard deviation fewer than average bills to 44 percent in states where this figure is one standard deviation higher than average. Taken together, these results confirm the idea that much of the success of gubernatorial proposals can be attributed to the characteristics of the legislature rather than to the actions and characteristics of the governor and his or her office.

Political environment factors behave largely as predicted in my model, with political party proving particularly important. Both simple and compound divided government hamper a governor's legislative success by 9 and 10 percentage points, respectively. Majority party status of the proposal sponsor is estimated to improve the chances of the bill achieving passage by 7 percentage points. My hypothesis of the effect of interest group density was also supported, although the variable for interest group diversity does not perform as expected. Denser interest group systems reduced the odds of gubernatorial legislative success to a statistically significant degree. In a state with a one standard deviation denser interest group system than average, a governor's bill has only a 14 percent probability of passage, while in a system that is one standard deviation less dense than average, the chance for passage rises to 27 percent.

Finally, economic factors are also important in accounting for gubernatorial legislative success. Both a state's unemployment rate and the trend in unemployment at the time of final bill action have the expected negative influences. Poor economic conditions do not bode well for gubernatorial legislative success, and the substantive impact of these effects is dramatic. Both above average and fast growing unemployment result in a low probability of bill passage (11 percent and 13 percent, respectively), while lower than average unemployment and unemployment growth are associated with much better prospects of passage (32 percent and 29 percent, respectively).

Discussion and Conclusions

Understanding chief executives' legislative leadership role clearly requires that these officials be viewed in the multiple levels of the context in which they attempt to lead. The goals and characteristics of the executive, and their institutional, political, and economic environments are all important in determining the success (or lack thereof) that attends their leadership in the legislative arena.

I found that executive success wanes over time, since being in the final year in the governor's term is negatively associated with success. This supports the traditional "bank-account" theory of chief executive clout, and President Johnson's advice to act quickly in pursuing legislative agendas might in fact serve chief executives in good stead (Pfiffner 1996). On the other hand, I also found evidence that experience improves chief executives' chances of achieving legislative success and that limiting the size of their legislative agendas is a good strategic decision. To the extent possible, a chief executive should avoid major scandals, assist their partisans in gaining election to the legislature, and encourage members of the majority party in a legislative chamber to sponsor his or her bills.

However, unfortunately for chief executives, I found that most of the forces that influence their legislative success are those over which they have little control. While personal strategic choices and some characteristics of the governors themselves do have an effect, political, institutional, and economic factors are the most important influences on executive success in the legislative arena.

Despite the overall importance of the institutional context, my findings are not exactly what the extant literature leads us to expect. First, while strong formal powers are widely viewed as a necessary condition for the exertion of gubernatorial leadership (Schlesinger 1965; Dye 1969; Beyle 1990; Dometrius 1987; Mueller 1985), my findings do not support that view in the legislative context. This points to the importance of understanding which formal powers and resources are important in which arenas of executive action. For example, it should not be particularly surprising that appointment power is not influential in the legislative arena, even though other research has shown its importance in the administrative arena (Hebert, Brudney, and Wright 1983; Ferguson 1993, 1994; Wright 1967). Furthermore, budget proposal power may in fact be a vital gubernatorial influence in the budget process itself, if not in the broader legislative arena. These results show the wisdom of studying individual elements of gubernatorial power rather than examining the traditional power index as a whole, as is common in much gubernatorial research.

My second important finding on institutional influences is that the characteristics of the legislature are just as important in determining gubernatorial legislative success as the characteristics of the governor and his or her office. Prior research has given some hint of this (Bernick and Wiggins 1991; Gross 1991; Jewell and Whicker 1994; Peterson 1990), but the direction of the influence I found for legislative professionalism was not fully predicted by the existing literature. Professional legislatures actually bolster the legislative success of the governor, indicating that policy-making power in the states is not a zero-sum game. This synergy between professionalized legislatures and modern, institutionally empowered governors' offices is certainly fertile ground for future examination.

Of course, this study has certain empirical limitations that must be recognized. First, my findings are isolated to a single point in time, and so they may be time-bound and fail to capture fully the dynamism of these forces. Second, the data identify gubernatorial initiatives at the point of initiation and cannot account for whether amendments to the legislation were adopted or whether governors favored those amendments. Third, the dataset does not include budget bills. These were not available in Lexis-Nexis, but even if they had been, they would have been problematic because of the different conventions surrounding budget-making in the states.

Notwithstanding these empirical caveats, this study offers important insights into the nature of executive legislative policy leadership. If governors (and by extension, presidents) are expected to be "chief legislators" in our political system (Bernick and Wiggins 1991; Gross 1991; Rosenthal 1990), my study shows that they are only partially equipped to fulfill this role based on their own skills and experiences. Larger forces, which are mostly outside the control of the chief executive, have much to do with whether a governor is legislatively successful. Taken together, my findings also raise some significant questions about the conventional understanding of executive leadership and point the way for future research to examine these questions further.

APPENDIX A   The Measurement of Independent Variables

Independent Variables	Measurement	Source	Expected Effect on Executive Legislative Success
Personal Factors			
Electoral margin	% vote in last election	Barone (1996)	+
Gubernatorial popularity	% giving governor a positive job rating in survey closest to final bill action	Beyle, Niemi, and Sigelman (2002)	+
Scope of governor's agenda	Number of policy issues addressed in the State of the State address	State of the State addresses	–
First year of governor's term	In 1994	Council of State Governments (CSG) (1994, 50–1)	?
Last year of governor's term	In 1994	CSG (1994, 50–1)	?
Scandal	Serious and persistent criminal investigation, financial problems, etc.	State Capital Reports	–
Prior term as governor	Served previously as governor	CSG (1994, 50–1)	+
Prior legislative experience	Served previously as legislator	Thad Beyle, UNC-Chapel Hill	+
Institutional Factors			
Appointment power	Average power of governor over appointment of administrators in 37 state function areas	CSG (1994, 72–6)	+
Strong veto power	Item veto with super-majority required to override	CSG (1994, 55–6)	+

APPENDIX A   (*Continued*)

Independent Variables	Measurement	Source	Expected Effect on Executive Legislative Success
Budget responsibility	Sole responsibility for preparing the budget	CSG (1994, 55–6)	+
Staff support	Size of governor's staff divided by number of state employees	CSG (1994, 53)	+
Lame duck status	No opportunity to seek re-election	CSG (1994, 50–1)	–
Legislative professionalism	Index based on member pay, staff members per legislator, and total days in session	Squire (1992)	?
Non-governor bill passage rate	Percentage of non-governor bills that passed in 1993–94 sessions	Lexis-Nexis	+
Political Factors			
Simple divided government	Both chambers of legislature controlled by opposition party	Bowling and Ferguson (2001)	–
Compound divided government	One chamber of legislature controlled by opposition party	Bowling and Ferguson (2001)	–
Majority party status of bill sponsor	Majority party status in chamber	Lexis-Nexis	+
Interest group density	Number of groups registered to lobby	Gray and Lowery (1996)	–
Interest group diversity	Herfindahl index of concentration across 10 categories of interest groups	Gray and Lowery (1996)	–

APPENDIX A   *(Continued)*

Independent Variables	Measurement	Source	Expected Effect on Executive Legislative Success
Economic Factors			
Unemployment rate	Rate of unemployment at time of final bill action	U.S. Dept. of Labor (1994)	–
Change in unemployment	Change in unemployment from previous month at time of final bill action	U.S. Dept. of Labor (1994)	–

APPENDIX B   Number and Percent of Bills per State in Dataset

The second column (# of bills) indicates the number of bills proposed by each governor in the dataset. The third column (% of dataset) indicates the percent of the total number of governors' bills in the dataset from each state. This table illustrates that these bills are well distributed across the states.

State	# of bills	% of total dataset
Alabama	15	1.4%
Alaska	15	1.4%
Arizona	13	1.2%
Arkansas	6	0.5%
California	29	2.7%
Colorado	14	1.3%
Connecticut	19	1.7%
Delaware	13	1.2%
Florida	19	1.7%
Georgia	19	1.7%
Hawaii	37	3.4%
Idaho	12	1.1%
Illinois	39	3.6%
Indiana	21	1.9%
Iowa	13	1.2%
Kansas	12	1.1%
Kentucky	16	1.5%
Louisiana	85	7.8%

APPENDIX B   *(Continued)*

State	# of bills	% of total dataset
Maine	12	1.1%
Maryland	90	8.2%
Massachusetts	9	0.8%
Michigan	17	1.6%
Minnesota	35	3.2%
Mississippi	10	0.9%
Missouri	27	2.5%
Montana	10	0.9%
Nebraska	8	0.7%
Nevada	9	0.8%
New Hampshire	7	0.6%
New Jersey	9	0.8%
New Mexico	27	2.5%
New York	54	4.9%
North Carolina	17	1.6%
North Dakota	9	0.8%
Ohio	11	1.0%
Oklahoma	23	2.1%
Oregon	6	0.5%
Pennsylvania	21	1.9%
Rhode Island	22	2.0%
South Carolina	25	2.3%
South Dakota	8	0.7%
Tennessee	4	0.4%
Texas	29	2.7%
Utah	5	0.5%
Vermont	12	1.1%
Virginia	70	6.4%
Washington	27	2.5%
West Virginia	42	3.8%
Wisconsin	32	2.9%
Wyoming	8	0.7%

Notes

1. Chief executives who succeeded to office have no electoral mandate to draw upon. In my dataset, these governors were Folsom of Alabama, Tucker of Arkansas, and Miller of South Dakota. Their electoral margin is set to zero.
2. If more than one survey was taken in the same month, I averaged their results.

These gubernatorial approval data are available at: http://www.unc.edu/-beyle/jars.html.

3. *State Capital Reports* gathers information from major news sources and offers weekly reports of news highlights. "Scandals" are a regular feature of *State Capital Reports*.

4. Scandals coded in my dataset were legal investigations surrounding the financial dealings and campaign practices of Jim Folsom of Alabama, Arkansas's Jim Guy Tucker's implication in the Whitewater investigation (later indicted and convicted), charges that New Jersey's Christine Whitman's campaign paid black voters to stay away from the polls, Oklahoma's David Walters' 17 indictments for various campaign finance violations, and various allegations against Rhode Island's Bruce Sundlun.

5. One might suspect that the negative impact of lame duck status would be most dramatic in the last year of a governor's term. I tested this idea by creating an interaction term between these two variables. The interaction term performed essentially the same as the dummy variable for lame duck status.

6. Since Nebraska is unicameral and non-partisan, the governor can never benefit from party unity, and so I coded Nebraska as compound divided government. Coding Nebraska as unified government does not substantively change my results.

7. The names of proposal sponsors were drawn from the Lexis-Nexis data. Sponsors' party identifications were found in the *Election Results Directory*, 1994 edition. Where more than one sponsor was listed in the Lexis-Nexis file, I used the party identification of the first sponsor.

8. A high value indicates low group diversity, with groups concentrated in only a few categories.

9. Ideally, the model would also account for the number of groups lobbying in the policy area of each of a governor's bills. However, such data were not available for this study.

10. Six state legislatures did not meet in session in 1994: Arkansas, Montana, North Dakota, Texas, Nevada, and Oregon. North Carolina Governor Jim Hunt, did not address the legislature in 1994. For these seven states, I used 1993 data.

11. This includes bills introduced in the 1993–94 sessions, as well as those remaining active from previous sessions. More than half of the states allow carryover of bills (within defined periods) from one session to the next, and bills often require more than one session to progress to final action.

12. In New Jersey, I employ the agenda that the incoming governor, Christine Whitman, identified in her inaugural address. Schaefer of North Dakota and Mc-Wherter of Tennessee offered their legislative plans in their Budget Addresses. Thus, I use these addresses in these two states.

13. There are several reasons that multiple bills of similar content might be introduced in a legislature, and there are various strategies a legislature might employ to address such duplication. A single piece of legislation may serve as the vehicle for addressing the policy issue (allowing the rest to die), or multiple pieces of legislation might be consolidated into a single bill. My method may result in an overcounting of governor bills and, therefore, an underestimation of gubernatorial success. However, my model also controls for a legislature's tendency toward bill passage, which helps account for this method a legislature might use to cope with multiple introductions of similar or identical bills. Thus, the inclusion of the bill passage rate variable reduces the potential bias caused by an overcounting of governor bills.

14. These bills are fairly evenly distributed across all 50 states. To test for the

sensitivity of the findings to data from a particular state, I re-estimated my model removing data from the three states with bills each making up more than 5 percent of the total. There were no substantive differences from my conclusions based on the entire dataset.

15.   This measure has limitations due to data availability. If a bill became law as a result of being attached as an amendment to another bill, my measure will not account for that. Furthermore, my measure cannot account for amendments to governor bills or whether the governor supported those amendments. The likely bias of my measure is that it underestimates gubernatorial legislative success. But since this bias is probably uniform among the states (or at least randomly distributed), this likely does not bias the tests of my hypotheses.

16.   The three governors in my dataset who succeeded to the office were coded as having an electoral margin of zero. Setting these governors' electoral margin to that of the governor whom they replaced did not change the sign or statistical significance of this estimated coefficient.

17.   Since these data encompass only a single point in time, I am unable to compare a single governor's success in one year to his or her success in a previous year. I leave this analysis to future research.

References

Barone, Michael. 1996. *The Almanac of American Politics*. Washington, DC: National Journal.

Bernick, E. Lee. 1979. "Gubernatorial Tools: Formal vs. Informal." *Journal of Politics* 41:656–64.

Bernick, E. Lee, and Charles W. Wiggins. 1991. "Executive-Legislative Relations: The Governor's Role as Chief Legislator." In *Gubernatorial Leadership and State Policy*, eds. Eric B. Herzik and Brent W. Brown. New York: Greenwood Press.

Berry, Jeffrey M. 1989. *The Interest Group Society*. Boston, MA: Scott, Foresman and Company.

Beyle, Thad. 1983. "Governors." In *Politics in the American States*, eds. Virginia Gray, H. Jacob, and Kenneth N. Vines. 4th ed. Boston, MA: Little Brown.

Beyle, Thad. 1990. "Governors." In *Politics in the American States*, eds. Virginia Gray, H. Jacob, and R. B. Albritton. 5th ed. Boston, MA: Little Brown.

Beyle, Thad. 1992. "New Governors in Hard Economic and Political Times." In *Governors and Hard Times*, ed. Thad Beyle. Washington, DC: Congressional Quarterly.

Beyle, Thad. 1996. "Being Governor." In *The State of the States*, ed. Carl E. Van Horn. 3rd ed. Washington, DC: Congressional Quarterly Press.

Beyle, Thad, Richard G. Niemi, and Lee Sigelman. 2002. "Approval Ratings of Public Officials in the American States: Causes and Effects." *State Politics and Policy Quarterly* 2:215–29.

Bond, Jon R., and Richard Fleisher. 1990. *The President in the Legislative Arena*. Chicago: The University of Chicago Press.

Bond, Jon R., and Richard Fleisher. 1984. "Presidential Popularity and Congressional Voting: A Reexamination of Public Opinion as a Source of Influence in Congress." *Western Political Quarterly* 37:291–306.

Bowling, Cynthia J., and Margaret R. Ferguson. 2001. "Divided Government, Legislative Gridlock and Policy Differences: Evidence from the Fifty States." *Journal of Politics* 63:182–206.

Bowman, Ann O'M., and Richard C. Kearney. 1988. "Dimensions of State Government Capability." *Western Political Quarterly* 41:341–62.

Brace, Paul, and Daniel S. Ward. 1999. "The Institutionalized Legislature and the Rise of the Antipolitics Era." In *American State and Local Politic,* eds. Ronald E. Weber and Paul Brace. Chatham, NJ: Chatham House.

Brudney, Jeffrey L., and F. Ted Hebert. 1987. "State Agencies and Their Environments: Examining the Influence of Important External Actors." *Journal of Politics* 49: 186–206.

Collier, Kenneth, and Terry Sullivan. 1995. "New Evidence Undercutting the Linkage of Approval with Presidential Support and Influence." *Journal of Politics* 57: 197–209.

Council of State Governments. 1994. *The Book of the States*, Vol. 30. Lexington, KY: Council of State Governments.

Crew, Robert E. 1992. "Understanding Gubernatorial Behavior: A Framework for Analysis." In *Governors and Hard Times,* ed. Thad Beyle. Washington, DC: Congressional Quarterly.

Dilger, Robert J., George Krause, and Randolph R. Moffett. 1995. "State Legislative Professionalism and Gubernatorial Effectiveness, 1978–1991." *Legislative Studies Quarterly* 20:553–71.

Dometrius, Nelson C. 1987. "Changing Gubernatorial Power: The Measure vs. Reality." *Western Political Quarterly* 40:319–33.

Donahue, John D. 1997. *Disunited States.* New York: Basic Books.

Dye, Thomas R. 1969. "Executive Power and Public Policy in the States." *Western Political Quarterly* 22:929–39.

Edwards, George C., III. 1980. *Presidential Influence in Congress.* San Francisco, CA: Freeman.

Edwards, George C., III. 1989. *At the Margins: Presidential Leadership of Congress.* New Haven, CT: Yale University Press.

Edwards, George C., III, and Stephen J. Wayne. 1990. *Presidential Leadership: Politics and Policy Making.* New York: St. Martin's Press.

Fenno, Richard F. 1986. "Observation, Context and Sequence in the Study of Politics." *American Political Science Review* 80:3–15.

Ferguson, Margaret R. 1993. "Assessing Perceived Gubernatorial Influence Over State Administrators: 1978–1988." Presented at the Annual Meeting of the American Political Science Association, Washington, DC.

Ferguson, Margaret R. 1994. "Institutional Determinants of Administrative Control and Oversight." Presented at the Annual Meeting of the Southern Political Science Association, Atlanta, GA.

Fett, Patrick J. 1994. "Presidential Legislative Priorities and Legislators' Voting Decisions: An Exploratory Analysis." *Journal of Politics* 56:502–12.

Fiorina, Morris. 1984. "The Presidency and the Contemporary Electoral System." In *The Presidency and the Political System,* ed. Michael Nelson. Washington, DC: Congressional Quarterly Press.

Gais, Thomas L., Mark A. Peterson, and Jack L. Walker. 1984. "Interest Groups, Iron Triangles, and Representative Institutions in American National Government." *British Journal of Political Science* 14:161–85.

Gleiber, Dennis, and Steven A. Shull. 1992. "Presidential Influence in the Policymaking Process." *Western Political Quarterly* 45:442–68.

Gray, Virginia, and David Lowery. 1995. "Interest Representation and Democratic Gridlock." *Legislative Studies Quarterly* 20:531–52.

Gray, Virginia, and David Lowery. 1996. *The Population Ecology of Interest Representation: Lobbying Communities in the American States*. Ann Arbor, MI: University of Michigan Press.

Gross, Donald. 1991. "The Policy Role of Governors." In *Gubernatorial Leadership and State Policy,* eds. Eric B. Herzik and Brent W. Brown. New York: Greenwood Press.

Hamm, Keith and Gary F. Moncrief. 1999. "Legislative Politics in the States." In *Politics in the American States: A Comparative Analysis,* eds. Virginia Gray, Russell L. Hanson, and Herbert Jacob. 7th ed. Washington, DC: Congressional Quarterly Press.

Hanson, Russell. 1999. "Intergovernmental Relations." In *Politics in the American States: A Comparative Analysis,* eds. Virginia Gray, Russell L. Hanson, and Herbert Jacob. 7th ed. Washington, DC: Congressional Quarterly Press.

Hebert, F. Ted, Jeffrey L. Brudney, and Deil S. Wright. 1983. "Gubernatorial Influence and State Bureaucracy." *American Politics Quarterly* 11:243–64.

Herzik, Eric. 1991. "Policy Agendas and Gubernatorial Leadership." In *Gubernatorial Leadership and State Policy,* eds. Eric B. Herzik and Brent W. Brown. New York: Greenwood Press.

Jacobson, Gary. 1987. "Running Scared: Elections and Congressional Politics in the 1980s." In *Congress: Structure and Policy,* eds. Matthew McCubbins and Terry Sullivan. New York: Cambridge University Press.

Jewell, Malcolm E., and Marci Lynn Whicker. 1994. *Legislative Leadership in the American States*. Ann Arbor, MI: University of Michigan Press.

Kernell, Samuel. 1986. *Going Public: New Strategies of Presidential Leadership*. Washington, DC: Congressional Quarterly Press.

Kindgon, John W. 1984. *Agendas, Alternatives and Public Policies*. Boston, MA: Little, Brown and Company.

Light, Paul. 1982. *The President's Agenda*. Baltimore, MD: Johns Hopkins University Press.

Mayhew, David. 1974. *Congress: The Electoral Connection*. New Haven, CT: Yale University Press.

McConnell, Grant. 1966. *Private Power and American Democracy*. New York: Vintage Books.

McFarland, Andrew S. 1992. "Interest Groups and the Policymaking Process: Sources of Countervailing Power in America." In *Politics and Interests,* ed. Mark P. Petracca. Boulder, CO: Westview Press.

Moncrief, Gary F., and Joel A. Thompson. 1992. "The Evolution of the State Legislature: Institutional Change and Legislative Careers." In *Changing Patterns in State Legislative Careers,* eds. Gary F. Moncrief and Joel Thompson. Ann Arbor, MI: University of Michigan Press.

Moncrief, Gary F., Joel A. Thompson, Michael Haddon, and Robert Hoyer. 1992. "For Whom the Bell Tolls: Term Limits and State Legislatures." *Legislative Studies Quarterly* 17:37–47.

Mooney, Christopher Z. 1995. "Citizens, Structures, and Sister States: Influences on State Legislative Professionalism." *Legislative Studies Quarterly* 20:47–67.

Morehouse, Sarah McCally. 1981. *State Politics, Parties and Policy.* New York: Holt, Rinehart and Winston.

Morehouse, Sarah McCally. 1994. "The State Party and the Legislative Party: The Linkage." Presented at the Annual Meeting of the Southern Political Science Association, Atlanta, GA.

Morehouse, Sarah McCally. 1998. *The Governor as Party Leader.* Ann Arbor, MI: University of Michigan Press.

Mouw, Calvin, and Michael MacKuen. 1992. "The Strategic Configuration, Personal Influence, and Presidential Power in Congress." *Western Political Quarterly* 45: 579–608.

Mueller, Keith J. 1985. "Explaining Variation and Change in Gubernatorial Powers, 1960–1982." *Western Political Quarterly* 38:424–30.

Neustadt, Richard. 1980. *Presidential Power.* New York: Wiley.

Olson, David M. 1985. "Success and Content in Presidential Roll Calls: The First Three Years of the Reagan Administration." *Presidential Studies Quarterly* 15:602–10.

Ostrom, Charles W., Jr., and Dennis M. Simon. 1985. "Promise and Performance: A Dynamic Model of Presidential Popularity." *American Political Science Review* 79: 334–58.

Ostrom, Charles W., Jr., and Dennis M. Simon. 1988. "The President's Public." *American Political Science Review* 32:1096–119.

Peterson, Mark. 1990. *Legislating Together.* Cambridge, MA: Harvard University Press.

Pfiffner, James P. 1988. *The Strategic Presidency.* Chicago: Dorsey.

Polsby, Nelson. 1978. "Interest Groups and the Presidency: Trends in Political Intermediation in America." In *American Politics and Public Policy,* eds. Walter Dean Burnham and Martha Wagner Weinberg. Cambridge, MA: MIT Press.

Ragsdale, Lyn. 1993. *Presidential Politics.* Boston, MA: Houghton Mifflin.

Rivers, Douglas, and Nancy Rose. 1985. "Passing the President's Program: Public Opinion and Presidential Influence in Congress." *American Journal of Political Science* 29:183–96.

Rosenthal, Alan. 1990. *Governors and Legislatures: Contending Powers.* Washington, DC: Congressional Quarterly Press.

Rosenthal, Alan. 1998. *The Decline of Representative Democracy.* Washington, DC: Congressional Quarterly Press.

Schlesinger, Joseph A. 1965. "The Politics of the Executive." In *Politics in the American States,* eds. Henry Jacob and Kenneth N. Vines. Boston, MA: Little, Brown.

Schlozman, Kay Lehman, and John J. Tierney. 1986. *Organized Interests and American Democracy.* New York: Harper and Row.

Sigelman, Lee, and Nelson C. Dometrius. 1988. "Governors as Chief Administrators: The Linkage Between Formal Powers and Informal Influence." *American Politics Quarterly* 16:157–70.

Simonton, Dean Keith. 1987. *Why Presidents Succeed: A Political Psychology of Leadership.* New Haven, CT: Yale University Press.

Squire, Peverill. 1992. "Legislative Professionalization and Membership Diversity in State Legislatures." *Legislative Studies Quarterly* 17:69–79.

Sullivan, Terry. 1991. "The Bank Account Presidency: A New Measure and Evidence on the Temporal Path of Presidential Influence." *American Journal of Political Science* 35:686–723.

United States Department of Labor, Bureau of Labor Statistics. *Employment and*

Earnings. Monthly editions, 1993–94. Washington, DC: U.S. Government Printing Office.

Van Horn, Carl E. 1996. "The Quiet Revolution." In *The State of the States,* ed. Carl E. Van Horn. 3rd ed. Washington, DC: Congressional Quarterly Press.

Weber, Ronald E., and Paul Brace, eds. 1999. *American State and Local Politics: Directions for the 21st Century.* New York: Chatham House.

Wiggins, Charles W. 1980. "Executive Vetoes and Legislative Overrides in the American States." *Journal of Politics* 42:1110–7.

Wright, Deil. 1967. "Executive Leadership in State Administration: Interplay of Gubernatorial, Legislative and Administrative Power." *Midwest Journal of Political Science* 11:1–26.

20 An Institutionalist Perspective on Mayoral Leadership

CRAIG M. WHEELAND

THE FACTORS THAT INFLUENCE EFFECTIVE mayoral leadership are still not well understood. There is continuing debate in the academic literature over theories of mayoral leadership,[1] and many communities debate ways to change their form of government to influence how their mayor provides leadership. In this essay, I use James . March and Johann Olsen's institutionalist theory of politics to guide my interpretation of how the formal structure of municipal government can influence mayoral leadership style.[2] I refine James Svara's two models of mayoral leadership—the executive mayor and the facilitative mayor—to describe the styles supported by the formal rules found in the charters or statutes used in the forty largest cities in the United States.[3] Three facilitative mayor subtypes (council leader, community leader, and partial executive) and four executive mayor subtypes (strong leader, constrained leader, legislative leader, and weak leader) can be identified and ranked according to the formal resources available to support their efforts. These findings have implications for the practice of city politics and for the development of a theory of mayoral leadership.

An Institutionalist Theory of Mayoral Leadership

March and Olsen suggest that "political institutions define the frame-work within which politics takes place."[4] They argue that rules are the means by which an institution affects behavior. Rules are the "routines, procedures, conventions, roles, strategies, organizational forms, and tech-nologies around which activity is constructed."[5] Rules also include the "beliefs, paradigms, codes, cultures, and knowledge that surround, support, elaborate, and contradict those roles and routines."[6] They explain that rules "define relationships among roles in terms of what an incumbent of one role owes to incumbents of other roles. "[7] They argue that the "logic of appropriateness associated with obligatory action" shapes how individuals follow the rules supported by the political institutions in which they work.[8] In other words, an official shapes his or her action by defining the situation, determining his or her role, assessing the appropriateness of different actions in the situation, and carrying out the most appropriate one.[9]

Of course, discretion exists in using rules, because they are not monolithic and may be contradictory and ambiguous, so conformity to as well as deviation from rules can occur in a political institution. They conclude that trust, "a confidence that appropriate behavior can be ex-pected most of the time," supports the network of rules and rule-bound relations[10] Deviation from the rules (violating the "logic of appropriate-ness") undermines trust among officials and potentially erodes support for the political institution as well.

Research on mayoral leadership recognizes the contextual relevance of the municipal institution, although the relative weight given to institu-tional features varies among scholars. Svara has developed a theory of mayoral leadership that emphasizes the formal institutions of govern-ment.[11] He argues theories of mayoral leadership should begin with "the form of government in which the mayor's office is located," because the form of city government defines the basic "roles and types of leadership" to be offered by the mayor.[12] He suggests that the two main forms of city government (strong mayor–council and council–manager) establish the formal preconditions for mayoral leadership styles—an executive-style leader and a facilitative-style leader, respectively. He argues that a mayor increases the chances of being successful if he or she adopts a leadership style compati-ble with the form of city government in which the mayor serves.

The implication here is clear: using a particular form of government creates a set of institutions whose formal rules can structure behavior in the ways March and Olsen suggest. Although it is possible for a mayor to use a leadership style different from the one supported by the formal rules, doing so may violate the logic of appropriateness and potentially erode the trust that supports the formal institutions in the city's political system.

Svara based his model of the executive mayor on mayors in forms of government marked by the principle of separation of powers, as in a strong mayor-council city. This principle is the foundation for a conflict pattern of interaction among officials, especially elected officials, who have incentive to compete with one another to accomplish their agendas. Svara suggests that "by establishing direction, forging coalitions, galvanizing the bureaucracy—in general by managing and resolving conflict in all dimensions of the governmental process—the Executive Mayor becomes the driving force in this form of government."[13] Indeed, the successful executive mayor draws power from formal and informal sources to become the dominant actor in city government.

Svara's facilitative mayor model is based on governmental forms marked by the unification-of-powers principle, such as the council-manager city, in which the city council has the legislative and executive powers of government. This principle is the foundation for a cooperative pattern of interaction among elected and appointed officials (the city manager being an example of the latter). The facilitative mayor has ample authority to act as the "guiding force in city government who helps insure that all other officials are performing as well as possible and that all are moving in the right direction.[14] Like the executive mayor, the facilitative mayor can act as a "policy initiator," helping to set the agenda and develop policies to address problems facing the community.[15] However, the facilitative mayor need not pyramid resources to be successful. Instead, he or she "accomplishes objectives through enhancing the efforts of others. . . . Rather than seeking power as the way to accomplish tasks, the facilitative mayor seeks to empower others."[16]

The research presented here builds on Svara's work in two ways. First, since the particular formal powers of a mayor can vary within each form of government, it is possible to refine Svara's models by identifying subtypes of executive and facilitative mayors. Second, it is possible to link other formal institutional features, such as full-time status of the mayor and design of the electoral system, to Svara's theory to develop a more complete institutionalist perspective on mayoral leadership.

Types of Mayoral Leadership

There are twenty-six mayor-council cities, thirteen council-manager cities, and one commission city (Portland, Oregon) among the forty largest cities in the United States.[17] All forty mayors have the formal power to perform ceremonial activities, which gives them the opportunity to cultivate a positive image with the public. Aside from this common feature, the form of government used in each city creates rules that serve as an incentive for a leadership style. Using Svara's two models of mayoral leadership, the twenty-six mayor-council cities generally support an executive mayor, and the thirteen council-manager cities along with the commission city generally support a facilitative mayor. Within these two basic types of mayoral leadership, additional distinctions can be made to refine Svara's classification. These subtypes capture the variation in key formal institutional features affecting the ability of the mayor to perform as an executive or as a facilitator.

FACILITATIVE MAYOR   Interpretation of the data on the thirteen council-manager cities and one commission city presented in Table 1 [page 284] suggests three types of facilitative mayor: council leader (CL), community leader (CML), and partial executive (PE). The CL (as an example, San Antonio) is defined as a mayor who is a voting member of the council and the presiding officer at council meetings. The CML (as in San Diego) is distinguished from the CL by a charter provision that empowers the mayor to present a legislative program addressing the needs of the city (that is, an annual state-of-the-city speech) or by the power to review and comment on the budget prepared by the city manager before it is submitted to the council (the "first review" power). The PE is a facilitative mayor who has one or more powers of the executive mayor, such as veto power (Charlotte, Long Beach, and Kansas City) or the power to prepare the budget (Portland and San Jose). Of the fourteen cities with facilitative mayors, five have CLs, four have CMLs, and five have PEs.

On the basis of the extent to which the institutional design supports facilitative leadership, the CMLs are most likely to be successful, followed by the CLs and then the PEs.[18] The CML may find it easier than the CL to draw attention to specific problems facing the city, offer a proposed course of action, and influence allocation of resources in the budget because these are charter-based responsibilities. The power to propose a legislative program or first-review the city manager's budget allows the mayor to provide leadership without necessarily undermining the prerogatives of the council or the city manager; indeed, it can enhance the mayor's ability to guide the policy-making process. Of course, mayors may choose to offer a state-of-the-city speech, undertake efforts to offer a legislative program, and influence budgetary priorities even if they do not have a charter-based responsibility to do so (as in the case of San

Antonio). If the practice becomes routine and part of the informal set of expectations (that is, "informal" rules), then the CL can be just as successful a facilitative mayor as the CML.

The PE has greater obstacles to overcome than the CL in performing as a facilitative-style leader. The power to veto ordinances, or to initiate the budget process and prepare the budget, creates rules more appropriate for an executive style of leadership. Because the PE's role is not clearly defined as a guiding force, the PE's actions could produce tension and conflict among council members and appointed officials rather than promote cooperation and teamwork. Salary appointment powers, reporting responsibility, and the electoral system are other formal institutional features that also can affect how these three types of facilitative mayor perform.

The mayors' salaries can influence the amount of time the official is willing and financially able to devote to duties. The salaries vary from part-time (Oklahoma City pays $2,000 per year) to half-time (Austin pays $35,000 per year) and full-time (San Jose pays $87,550 per year). The full-time salaries offered in Kansas City (PE), San Diego (CML), Long Beach (PE), Portland (PE), and San Jose (PE) are for these mayors a formal incentive to spend most of their time performing their duties. Half-time mayors, as in Austin (CL), Virginia Beach (CL), Tucson (CML), and Phoenix (CML); and part-time mayors, in Oklahoma City (CL), San Antonio (CL), Fort Worth (CL), Dallas (CML), and Charlotte (PE), lack this incentive.

Appointing the members of boards, commissions, and authorities, as well as being permitted to appoint assistants to form a mayoral staff, can increase the potential of a facilitative mayor to emerge as a guiding force in city politics.[19] The power to appoint members of boards, commissions, and authorities enhances the mayor's status as the official with the best opportunity to establish relationships with the city's public, private, and nonprofit leadership. The power to appoint assistants who work on policy and management topics increases the mayor's ability to influence policy and coordinate council members and the city manager.

In twelve of the fourteen cities with facilitative mayors, the mayor has at least one of the two types of appointment power. In nine of the twelve cities—Oklahoma City (CL), San Diego (CML), Tucson (CML), Phoenix (CML), Charlotte (PE), Long Beach (PE), Portland (PE), Kansas City (PE), and San Jose (PE)—the mayor has both types of appointment power. For example, San Diego's mayor has the most extensive appointment power of any facilitative mayor: she appoints members of some boards, commissions, and authorities with council approval and appoints

TABLE 1   Facilitative Mayors

City	Formal Institutional Features						Type of Mayoral Leader
	Member of Council	Votes with Council	Presiding Officer	Proposes Legislation	General Veto Power	Prepares Budget	
Oklahoma City	yes	yes	yes	no	no	no	Council leader
Austin	yes	yes	yes	no	no	no	Council leader
San Antonio	yes	yes	yes	no	no	no	Council leader
Virginia Beach	yes	yes	yes	no	no	no	Council leader
Fort Worth	yes	yes	yes	no	no	no	Council leader
San Diego	yes	yes	yes	yes	no	no	Community leader
Dallas	yes	yes	yes	yes	no	no	Community leader
Tucson	yes	yes	yes	yes	no	no	Community leader
Phoenix	yes	yes	yes	yes	no	no	Community leader
Charlotte	no[1]	no[2]	yes	yes	yes	no[3]	Partial executive
Portland	yes	yes	yes	no	no	yes[3]	Partial executive
Long Beach	yes	no	yes	yes	yes	no[4]	Partial executive
San Jose	yes	yes	yes	yes	no	yes[5]	Partial executive
Kansas City	yes	yes	yes	yes	yes	no[6]	Partial executive

Notes:

1. The mayor is not formally a member of the council primarily because of voting status and administrative prerogatives.

2. The mayor does not vote with the council except for three decision types: to break ties, on the appointment or dismissal of the city manager, and on controversial amendments to the zoning ordinance.

3. The mayor usually is the commissioner in charge of the office of finance and administration. The mayor then may appoint the city's financial officer and direct the budget process. Indeed, during the budget process all departments are brought back into the mayor's portfolio.

4. The city manager is responsible for preparing the budget and submitting it to the mayor, who then submits the budget to the council; however, the mayor may attach comments, recommendations, and amendments to the budget for the council to consider.

5. The mayor initiates the budget process. The mayor's budget director and staff work with the city manager's budget director and staff to prepare the budget. Any differences are worked out before the budget is submitted to the council. The mayor is recognized as the leader in budgetary matters, which is an understanding firmly grounded in the formal language used in the charter; therefore differences are usually resolved to reflect the mayor's priorities. Note that this is different from the first-review approach used in Kansas City and Long Beach.

6. The city manager prepares the budget and submits it to the mayor for first review. The mayor forwards the budget to the council along with a letter of transmittal in which the mayor discusses his or her recommendations and endorsements.

thirty staff members, eight of whom work on policy and management topics. San Antonio (CL) and Dallas (CML) are the only two cities that permit the mayor to appoint citizens to serve on some boards, commissions, and authorities, but not to appoint assistants. Austin (CL) is the only city that permits the mayor to appoint assistants, but not members of boards and commissions. Austin's mayor appoints four staff members, two of whom work on policy and management topics. Only the mayors in Virginia Beach and Fort Worth have neither appointment power.

Having a charter-based responsibility to prepare reports and submit them to the council can also increase the potential for the facilitative mayor to emerge as a guiding force in city politics. This power to report enhances the mayor's opportunity to set the public agenda via press conferences, council meetings, and various appearances before community groups. Of course, a mayor may prepare reports and submit them to the council and to the public even if there is no official responsibility, but the seriousness with which these reports are received may be less than if the mayor routinely did so as part of his or her official duties. None of the charters in the five cities with CLs grant the mayor this power. The mayors in two of the four cities with CMLs (Tucson and Phoenix) and three of the five cities with PEs (Charlotte, Portland, and San Jose) have formal reporting responsibilities.

In twelve of fourteen cities with a facilitative mayor, two of the four features found in electoral systems—direct election and nonpartisan election—support the mayor as a guiding force in city politics. All fourteen cities permit direct election of the mayor by the voters, and in all but Tucson (CML) and Charlotte (PE) elections are nonpartisan. Direct election gives a facilitative mayor the visibility in the community and contact with voters across the city needed to build an electoral coalition that supports his or her efforts to work as a guiding force once in office. Nonpartisan election is also compatible with an effort to work as a guiding force, rather than a driving force, although there may be some undesirable effects, such as low voter turnout, a middle-class or business bias, low-quality policy debates, and a high rate of reelection for the incumbent.[20] The main advantage of a nonpartisan election is not having to engage voters initially as a Democrat, Republican, or other party's candidate. The opportunity exists, therefore, to create an identity that, at the very least, appeals beyond party labels and supports a mayoral candidate's effort to build an inclusive electoral coalition.

Two other features of electoral systems, the length of the mayor's term and term limits, vary across the fourteen cities. A mayor who serves a longer term and who can seek reelection to more than two terms has the potential to nurture relationships with voters, other public officials, and interest group leaders, all of which enables the mayor to emerge as the guiding force in city politics. Two of the five CLs (Oklahoma City and Virginia Beach), two of the four CMLs (Tucson and Phoenix), and one of the five PEs (Portland) serve four-year terms without a limit on the number of terms served. These six mayors enjoy a formal advantage over other facilitative mayors with shorter terms or who are limited to two terms.

Consideration of additional formal institutional features—salary, appointment powers, reporting responsibilities, and the electoral system—complicates the effort to rank mayors because their use varies widely. Rather than attempt to assess the myriad combinations of these features in all fifteen cities, for each type of facilitative mayor I offer a profile of one who is advantaged by these additional formal features:

> Among the CMLs, the mayor of San Diego is well positioned to be successful because he or she earns a full-time salary; serves a four-year term; and has the power to appoint members of boards, commissions, and authorities (without council approval) as well as assistants (without council approval).

> Among the CLs, the mayor of Austin is well positioned to be successful because he or she earns a half-time salary and has the power to appoint assistants (without council approval).

> Among the PEs serving in council-manager cities, the mayor of Kansas City is well positioned to be successful because he or she earns a full-time salary; serves a four-year term; has the power to appoint members of boards, commissions, and authorities (without council approval) and assistants as well (without council approval).

Fort Worth's (CL) mayor is least advantaged of the fourteen cities when considering these additional features, because he or she receives part-time pay, serves a two-year term, and does not have either formal appointment powers or formal reporting responsibility

The complete set of formal features used in Charlotte (PE) place its mayor in the least favorable position to emerge as a guiding force. Charlotte's mayor is part-time, serves a two-year term, is elected in a partisan election, may vote with the council only in rare circumstances, has a general veto power (one of only three mayors out of the fourteen to have this power), may be "active in enforcing the law," may require members of city departments to meet with him or her for consultation and advice, and may hire "experts to examine the affairs of any department." This combination of institutional features increases the potential for a conflict pattern to emerge between the mayor and Charlotte's other officials (council members and the city manager), in part because of the ambiguity in the rules defining the mayor's role. Following the logic of appropriateness is difficult for all PEs, but especially for Charlotte's mayor.

EXECUTIVE MAYOR   Interpretation of the data on the twenty-six mayor-council cities presented in Table 2 [page 290] suggests four types of executive mayor: strong leader (SL), constrained leader (CSL), legislative leader (LL), and weak leader (WL). All twenty-six mayors have the power to propose legislation; submit reports on their government's performance; execute the law; appoint assistants (only Indianapolis requires council approval of these appointments); and appoint many, if not all, members of boards, commissions, and authorities (in some cities, without council approval). Five other formal powers that vary across the twenty-six cities are used to distinguish the four types of executive mayor: presiding at council meetings, vetoing ordinances, preparing the budget, appointing department heads, and appointing a chief administrative officer (CAO). The SL (New York, for instance) is defined as a mayor who prepares the budget, who can veto ordinances, and who appoints department heads (and in some cities a CAO) without council approval.

The CSL (as in the case of Baltimore) is distinguished from the SL by the requirement that appointment of department heads (and in some cities the CAO) must be approved by the council (in St. Louis, the mayor's power to prepare the budget is constrained by the existence of a board of estimate and apportionment). The LL is distinguished by serving as presiding officer at council meetings and having the power either to vote as a member of the council (Houston) or to vote under special circumstances such as to break a tie (El Paso and Chicago). The WL is distinguished by using boards and commissions to appoint some department heads, especially key department heads such as the police chief (Los Angeles) and fire chief (Milwaukee). Of the twenty-six cities with executive mayors, nine have SLs, twelve have CSLs, three have LLs, and two have WLs.

On the basis of the extent to which the institutional design supports exercising executive-style leadership, SLs are more likely to succeed than the other mayoral types, especially WLs.[21] The SLs' appointment powers give them formal control over the executive branch, which can help them emerge as the driving force in city government. As presiding officer of the council, an LL may find it easier to influence the council's agenda and development of policy in comparison to the other types of executive mayor, especially if the LL also has veto power (El Paso and Chicago). Yet all three LLs, like CSLs, appoint department heads with council approval, which potentially reduces their control over the executive branch. The WLs face the greatest institutional obstacles to becoming the driving force in part because boards and commissions are given direct authority over some department heads. Therefore, the rank order of mayors from highest to lowest is (1) SLs, (2) LLs with a veto power, (3) CSLs, (4) LLs who lack a veto power (Houston), and (5) WLs. Two other formal institutional features—salary and the electoral system—may also affect whether any of these subtypes of executive mayor emerges as the driving force in city politics.

In twenty-five of the twenty-six cities with executive mayors, the mayor earns a full-time salary, ranging from $75,000 in Nashville to $170,000 in Chicago. The full-time status of these twenty-five mayors gives them the formal incentive to devote the time needed to emerge as the driving force in their cities. This is not the case for El Paso's mayor, an LL who earns a half-time salary.

All twenty-six mayors are directly elected by the voters and all but two serve a four-year term; the mayors in Houston and El Paso serve two-year terms. The same rationale supporting direct election of a facilitative mayor holds for election of an executive mayor. Direct election bestows on them the visibility in the community and the contact with all voters across the city needed to build an electoral coalition that supports his or her effort to emerge, in this case, as a driving force.

Two other electoral features vary across the twenty-six cities: term limits and partisan elections. Mayors in fourteen cities have term limits, which is a disadvantage in comparison to the other mayors who can extend their influence over a longer period of time. Mayors in eleven of the fourteen cities are limited to two terms: New York (SL), Philadelphia (SL), New Orleans (SL), Denver (SL), Atlanta (CSL), Jacksonville (CSL), Albuquerque (CSL), Oakland (CSL), San Francisco (CSL), Washington (CSL), and Los Angeles (WL). The mayors of Nashville (SL) and Houston (LL) are limited to three terms, and the mayor of El Paso (LL) is limited to four terms. Houston and El Paso's mayors serve two-year terms, so they are limited to a maximum of six and eight years, respectively. Partisan elections are used in only seven cities: two have SLs (Philadelphia and New York) and five have CSLs (Baltimore, Indianapolis, St. Louis, Pitts-

TABLE 2 Executive Mayors

City	Presiding Officer	General Veto Power	Prepares Budget	Appoints Department Heads Without Council	Appoints CAO Without Council	Type of Mayoral Leader
		Formal Institutional Features				
Philadelphia	no	yes	yes	yes[1]	yes	Strong leader
New York	no	yes	yes	yes[2]	yes	Strong leader
Nashville	no	yes	yes	yes[2]	n/a	Strong leader
Boston	no	yes	yes	yes	yes	Strong leader
Detroit	no	yes	yes	yes[3]	n/a	Strong leader
New Orleans	no	yes	yes	yes	yes	Strong leader
Denver	no	yes	yes	yes	n/a	Strong leader
Columbus	no	yes	yes	yes	n/a	Strong leader
Cleveland	no	yes	yes	yes	n/a	Strong leader
Memphis	no	yes	yes	no	no	Constrained leader
Atlanta	no	yes	yes	no	no	Constrained leader
Jacksonville	no	yes	yes	no[4]	yes	Constrained leader
Seattle	no	yes	yes	no	n/a	Constrained leader
Pittsburgh	no	yes	yes[5]	no	n/a	Constrained leader
Baltimore	no	yes	yes[5]	no	n/a	Constrained leader
Indianapolis	no	yes	yes[6]	no	n/a	Constrained leader
St. Louis	no	yes	yes[6]	yes	n/a	Constrained leader
Albuquerque	no	yes[7]	yes[8]	no	no	Constrained leader
Oakland	no	yes[7]	yes[8]	no	no	Constrained leader

TABLE 2   Executive Mayors (*Continued*)

| | Formal Institutional Features | | | | | |
City	Presiding Officer	General Veto Power	Prepares Budget	Appoints Department Heads Without Council	Appoints CAO Without Council	Type of Mayoral Leader
San Francisco	no	yes	yes	no[9]	no	Constrained leader
Washington	no	yes	yes	no	yes	Constrained leader
El Paso	yes	yes	yes	no	no	Legislative leader
Houston	yes	no	yes	no	yes	Legislative leader
Chicago	yes	yes	yes	no[10]	no	Legislative leader
Milwaukee	no	yes	yes	no[10]	n/a	Weak leader
Los Angeles	no	yes	yes	no[11]	no	Weak leader

Notes:

1. The mayor appoints the managing director, director of finance, and the city representative without council approval. Other department heads, such as the police commissioner, the fire commissioner, and the recreation commissioner, are appointed by the managing director with the approval of the mayor. By custom, mayors traditionally have exerted control over these appointments.

2. Only the director of finance and the director of law require council approval.

3. The CAO appoints department heads with the mayor's approval.

4. Most appointments require the council's approval.

5. The board of estimate, which consists of the mayor, the council president, the comptroller, the city solicitor, and the director of public works, establishes fiscal policy, so the mayor's power is constrained formally. However, because the mayor appoints the director of public works and the city solicitor, he controls three of the five votes; therefore the budget reflects the mayor's priorities.

6. The board of estimate and apportionment, which consists of the mayor, the comptroller (an elected official), and the council president, prepares the annual budget and submits it to council, so the mayor's budget authority is constrained.

TABLE 2   Executive Mayors (Continued)

Notes (Continued)

7. Because Measure X, which passed in November 1998, was not clear on how the mayor's new veto power would work, the mayor, city council, and city attorney agreed to follow these procedures: (1) the mayor has no input on resolutions, so a simple majority rules; (2) for an ordinance, the mayor may vote to break a tie; on a five-to-three vote, the mayor has the option of sending the bill back to the council and demanding a six-to-two vote in order to pass.

8. The mayor is "responsible for the submission of an annual budget to the council which shall be prepared by the City Manager under the direction of the Mayor and Council." At the time of the budget submission, the mayor submits a "general statement of the conditions of the affairs of the city, the goals of the administration, and recommendations of such measures as he may deem expedient and proper to accomplish such goals."

9. The mayor appoints and removes a controller with council approval. With the mayor's approval, the city administrator appoints the heads of four departments: administrative services, public works, solid waste, and public guardian and administration. The heads of other departments are appointed by the mayor according to this procedure: boards or commissions, such as the fire commission and the police commission, submit a list of at least three qualified applicants to the mayor, and if the mayor rejects this list, then the board or commission submits another list.

10. The mayor appoints with council approval the commissioners of public works, health, building inspection, city development, and others as well. The major exceptions are the chiefs of police and fire, who are appointed by the fire and police commission. The mayor appoints the members of the fire and police commission, with the council's approval, to staggered five-year terms.

11. In addition to the CAO, the mayor appoints (with council approval) the purchasing agent, treasurer, city clerk, and the director of planning. The mayor appoints with council approval the boards of commissioners that control these departments: airports, harbors, libraries, pensions, recreation and parks, water and power, animal regulation, personnel, fire, police, building and safety city planning, municipal courts, public utilities and transportation, social services, and traffic. Board members serve five-year staggered terms. The mayor, with council approval, appoints a chief administrative officer for each of these departments, except for the chief of police. The mayor appoints, with council approval, the chief of police from a list of qualified candidates prepared by the board of police commissioners.

burgh, and Washington). These seven mayors can use the political party as a means to contest an election, shape a legislative program, and organize government so that they become the driving force in governing the city.

Consideration of the mayor's salary and the design of the electoral system suggests how to refine the ranking of executive mayors. The mayors serving in Baltimore, Indianapolis, St. Louis, and Pittsburgh (all CSLs) are advantaged by these other formal features, because they earn a full-time salary, serve a four-year term without term limits, and are elected in a partisan, election. If one discounts the impact of being limited to two four-year terms, then the mayors of New York (SL), Philadelphia (SL), and Washington (CSL) could be added to this list of advantaged mayors. The mayor of Los Angeles, already disadvantaged by being a WL, also is disadvantaged by the use of nonpartisan elections and term limits. El Paso's mayor is most disadvantaged by these other formal features, because the mayor is an LL who earns a half-time salary, serves a two-year term with a four-term limit, and is elected in a nonpartisan election.

Implications of This Research for Practice

For those reform-minded political leaders and their supporters who think formal institutional features are preventing their mayor from offering the kind of leadership needed in their city (either the executive or the facilitative style), this research offers two options.

Option one is to change the institutional design to use the strongest version of mayoral leadership appropriate to the form of government and adopt one or more of the other institutional features that enhance the mayor's formal position, such as a full-time salary. For example, in November 1995 San Francisco voters approved Measure E, which altered the city charter by giving the mayor more control over appointing and removing the city administrator and department heads as well as increasing the mayor's influence in the budget process.[22] These changes made San Francisco's mayor a constrained leader rather than a weak leader.

There is, however, a risk in using this option. Some changes may lead to a package of formal institutional features that do not consistently support either the executive or the facilitative style of leadership. For example, giving the mayor a general veto power in a council-manager city (Charlotte, Long Beach, Kansas City) or giving the mayor control over the budget (San Jose) rather than the power of first review (Kansas City) creates rules that are inconsistent with the facilitative style. Similarly, leaving in place rules such as vesting the city manager with the power to appoint department heads inhibits the mayor from developing an executive style of leadership. This lack of consistency in the rules generates ambiguity that can inhibit an official's ability to interpret his or her role. In other words, following the logic of appropriateness is more difficult and the potential to erode trust among officials and with the public increases. As Protasel argues, "injecting the idea of the separation of powers into the council-manager system would seem to put the directly elected mayor on a collision course with both the council and the city manager. Policymaking deadlock—a continual threat in mayor-council systems—could be expected to occur periodically. . . ."[23]

Option two is to change the form of government to create the formal institutional incentives needed for another style of mayoral leadership (executive or facilitative) and pattern of interaction among officials (conflict or cooperation) to emerge. Several of the cities in this study have explored this option in recent decades—San Diego,[24] Kansas City,[25] Dallas,[26] Washington,[27] and Oakland[28]—but these efforts were not fully successful, in part because of voter opposition. Although changing the basic form of government is difficult to accomplish, it is preferable to producing a hybrid set of formal institutional features that inhibit the efforts of all city officials to follow the logic of appropriateness.

Oakland is an example of a city that first pursued option one and then moved on to option two. In 1968–69, Oakland's mayor received a part-time salary and had three secretaries and one administrative assistant, a package, Pressman felt, that helped explain why the city manager was so dominant in that era.[29] By the 1990s, Oakland's mayor received a full-time salary and could appoint a number of assistants, among them a chief of staff, an assistant for media relations, an assistant for economic development, and an assistant for environmental policy. These changes established formal features that were consistent with the rules supporting a facilitative style of leadership. Yet some city officials, especially the mayors, and community leaders continued to push for changing the mayor's powers. In November 1998, Oakland's voters were asked to approve changes in the mayor's powers that would essentially establish a mayor-council form of government.[30] This time, by a vote of three to one, Measure X passed. The change is not permanent, however. A provision in the measure requires citizens to vote to approve it again in six years or the council-manager form will be restored.

Implications of This Research for Theory

This research suggests how an institutional perspective constitutes a needed foundation for developing a theory of mayoral leadership.

By beginning with an institutional perspective, we are more likely to:

Recognize the two main models of mayoral leadership, the facilitative mayor and the executive mayor

Develop an appreciation for each style of leadership

Recognize the subtypes of facilitative and executive mayor

Understand the impact other institutional features, such as salary and the design of the electoral system, have on mayoral leadership

Understand how contextual variables (political culture, fiscal resources, economic elite activity, and interest group activity) and proximate variables (the mayor's skills, personality, vision of the job, and legislative program) combine with formal institutional features to affect a mayor's performance

Regarding this last point, the mayors of San Diego and Philadelphia have the formal institutional features needed to be successful facilitative and executive mayors, respectively; yet whether they are successful depends on the influence of the other contextual variables and proximate variables.

Finally, this analysis suggests five questions to guide future research. First, how much of an effect do the distinguishing features defining the subtypes have on mayoral performance? Second, what happens to values such as trust among city officials when the mayor chooses to act in ways that are not compatible with the type of leadership defined by the city's form of government? Third, how much of an effect do other formal institutional features, such as salary and the electoral system, have on the mayor's performance? Fourth, does governing a large city require the executive style of mayoral leadership (and therefore use of the strong mayor–council form), or can a facilitative-style mayor (and therefore the council-manager form) successfully be used in a large city? Fifth, should a theory of mayoral leadership begin with the primacy of the formal institutional design before other contextual and proximate variables are considered?

Conclusion

The mayors in the forty largest cities in the United States increase their chances to be successful (1) if they act in ways that are compatible with the formal institutional features defining their jobs, because doing so follows the logic of appropriateness and therefore preserves trust among officials and citizens; (2) if they have the strongest version of either type of mayoral leadership; and (3) if they are supported by other formal institutional features, such as a full-time salary. It is hoped that the conceptual framework and data presented here stimulate further research on the effects that institutions have on mayoral leadership. Although formal institutional features alone do not determine mayoral performance, an institutional perspective is the foundation needed to guide the practice of politics and to develop a complete theory of mayoral leadership.

Notes

1.   For three excellent reviews of the literature as well as three important theories of mayoral leadership, see Kotter, J. P, and Lawrence, P. *Mayors in Action*. New York: Wiley, 1974; Ferman, B. *Governing the Ungovernable City*. Philadelphia: Temple University Press, 1985; and Svara, J. H. *Official Leadership in the City*. New York: Oxford University Press, 1990.

2.   March, J. G., and Olsen, J. P. *Rediscovering Institutions*. New York: Free Press, 1989.

3.   Svara (1990).

4.   March and Olsen (1989), p. 18.

5.   March and Olsen (1989), p. 22.

6.   March and Olsen (1989), p. 22.

7.   March and Olsen (1989), p. 23.

8.   March and Olsen (1989).

9.   March and Olsen (1989).

10.   March and Olsen (1989), p. 38.

11.   Svara, J. H. "Mayoral Leadership in Council-Manager Cities: Preconditions Versus Preconceptions." *Journal of Politics*, 1987, 49, 207–227; Svara (1990).

12.   Svara (1990), p. 87.

13.   Svara (1990), p. 26.

14.   Svara (1990), p. 27.

15.   Svara, J. H., and Associates. *Facilitative Leadership in Local Government*. San Francisco: Jossey-Bass, 1994, p. 225.

16.   Svara (1990), p. 87.

17.   The data on mayoral powers and other formal features in the forty largest cities (1990 population) in the United States were secured from three sources: (1) charters and statutes, (2) interviews with city officials, and (3) a follow-up letter and survey asking each mayor to verify the accuracy of the information. The data are accurate as of 1998.

18.   The seventh edition of the Model City Charter offers several recommendations for designing the council-manager form of government, along with a commentary explaining the reasoning supporting each one. See National Civic League. *Model City Charter*. Denver: National Civic League Press, 1989. Numerous academics, elected officials, and professional managers worked on the seventh edition. I use the Model City Charter as one of the sources to guide my interpretation of the

importance of (1) the mayor delivering a state-of-the-city speech; (2) the mayor's power to appoint citizens to boards, commissions, and authorities; (3) the mayor's power to vote as a member of the council (so no veto power); and (4) direct election of the mayor.

19.   The commentary supporting the Model City Charter also suggests that (1) a mayor should be a part-time official and (2) should not have the power to appoint assistants. Any staff support needed by a mayor should be provided by the city manager, because creating an "independent staff could lead to the mayor's encroachment on the executive responsibilities of the manager." See National Civic League (1989), p. 26.

20.   See Banfield, E., and Wilson, J. Q. *City Politics.* New York: Random House, 1963, pp. 151–167. See also Bledsoe, T. *Careers in City Politics.* Pittsburgh: University of Pittsburgh Press, 1993.

21.   Although the National Civic League endorsed the council-manager form in the seventh edition of the Model City Charter, it also "recognized that some cities, if properly organized, can strengthen their operations with the strong mayor and council form." See National Civic League (1989), p. 77. If a strong mayor–council form is preferred, then the National Civic League endorses allowing mayors to appoint department heads without council approval in order to prevent "provincialism and political pressures" from influencing the council in such a way as to undermine the mayor's effort to recruit personnel from other cities on the basis of professional competence. It also rejects using boards and commissions to appoint department heads, because this "dilutes" the mayor's authority and prevents him or her from acting as a "genuinely responsible executive." This argument along with other sources—including Pressman, J. L. "Preconditions for Mayoral Leadership," *American Political Science Review* 66 (June 1972): 511–524; Ferman (1985); and Svara (1990)—support my interpretation of how these two features can influence mayoral leadership.

22.   See King, J. "Prop. E Would Rewrite S. F Charter: Revision Gives More Power to Mayor, Supervisors." *San Francisco Chronicle,* Nov. 1, 1995. See also McCormick, E. "Proposition Results Seen as Call for Reform, Efficiency" *San Francisco Examiner,* Nov. 8, 1995.

23.   Protasel, G. J. "Leadership in Council-Manager Cities: The Institutional Implications." In H. G. Frederickson (ed.), *Ideal and Practice in Council-Manager Government.* Washington, D.C.: International City/County Management Association, 1995.

24.   Sparrow, G. W "The Emerging Chief Executive 1971–1991: A San Diego Update." In Svara and Associates (1994).

25.   Blodgett, T., and Crowley, J. C. "The Position of the Mayor in Large Council-Manager Cities." *National Civic Review,* July–Aug. 1990, 79, 332–336.

26.   Reed, S. R. "Dallas Dilemma: Headstrong Bartlett Stuck in City's Weak Mayor System." *Houston Chronicle,* July 11, 1993.

27.   Bonilla, H. "Close to Home: A City Manager for the District." *Washington Post,* July 16, 1995.

28.   DelVecchio, R. "Uneven Voter Turnout Sank Oakland's Strong-Mayor Proposal." *San Francisco Chronicle,* Nov. 12, 1996.

29.   Pressman (1972).

30.   DelVecchio, R. "The Oracle of Oakland: Jerry Brown's Style Is Less Tyrannical than Visionary" *San Francisco Chronicle,* Nov. 5, 1998.

PART SEVEN

LEGISLATIVE INSTITUTIONS AND POLITICS

The institutions that received the most criticism forty-five years ago, but have probably seen the most improvement, are the state legislatures. It seems the reform of the legislatures lagged behind the changes in the executive branches by about twenty years.[1] Commentaries on the woeful state of affairs in capitols across the states pulled no punches in pointing out the problems. The former president of the American Bar Association, Charles S. Rhyne, described the situation in this way: "Our legislatures try to solve jet-age problems with horse-and-buggy methods, and in their failure they're *inviting* federal intervention."[2]

Most reformers agreed at the time that three major problems caused the legislatures to be unrepresentative, inefficient, and ineffective.[3] First, legislators weren't paid enough. Only the independently wealthy in many states could afford to give up time to serve in the legislature. Second, most legislatures were severely understaffed. James Miller described this as the "sickest aspect of our sick legislatures."[4] Without good research and bill-writing personnel, legislation was bound to suffer. Finally, legislatures did not meet often enough to be very effective. During the 1950s and 1960s, legislatures typically met only three to six months, and many met less often. Factor in travel time back to their districts for legislators each week, and it is easy to see that not a lot of time was spent on policymaking.

In light of these problems, the legislatures were pressured to reform themselves in these three areas. And reform they did. State legislatures have now become much more professional. With higher salaries, longer sessions, and more full-time staff personnel, they are in a much better position to deal with the modern complex problems facing state and local governments.[5]

Given this history, our first selection is an insightful autobiographical account of Stewart Bledsoe, a former rural state legislator from Kittitas County, Washington. He captures the essence of the legislative process from the point of view of the part-time citizen legislator prior to the professionalizing reforms of the 1970s. He hints at the problems mentioned above with his statement that:

> [i]n many states you'd get a better crew if the pay were better. And that better crew could do a whale of a better job with enough staff to research facts and bring in unbiased information on which intelligent decisions can be made.

With many of the reforms behind them, the state legislatures had been rejuvenated. However, there is still significant variation (i.e., diversity) in the degree of legislative professionalism across the states, and one of the continuing efforts by scholars in this field has been to develop a useful measure of legislative professionalism in order to be able to compare the states on this factor. Most measures have utilized data relative to the three areas of concern noted above (salaries, session lengths, and staffing), and the most commonly used measure is one developed by Peverill Squire in the early 1990s. Our second article is by Squire who discusses his measure, brings it up to date, and provides a good historical examination of the differences in the degree of state legislative professionalism across the country.

One of the most controversial state legislative reforms in recent years has been term limits. Proponents of term limits decried the lack of turnover, consistent political cronyism, and unresponsive legislatures, while opponents claimed term limits would solidify power in the hands of unelected bureaucrats and lobbyists by forcing experienced legislators to step down. In the midst of this controversy, several states adopted legislative term limits, and twenty states currently have put them in place. The obvious question is who was more correct about the effects of term limits, the proponents or the opponents? The next article, by John Straayer, explores the answer to this question in the context of Colorado's experience with term limits. As the author notes, there have been consequences, but they may not have been intended.

In our final two selections, we take a look at local legislative institutions. Most cities are governed by elected city councils, or city commissions, whose members have to balance a difficult number of duties as they fulfill their elective roles. In her piece titled "Playing the Political Game," Kate Wiltrout takes us through a typical day in the life of the Savannah, Georgia, city council from informal lunches, to formal meetings, to after-hours constituency service. Similar days are experienced by city council members all around the country.

Finally, one elected legislative official rarely discussed or written about is the township trustee. Most New England and Midwestern states have political subdivisions in unincorporated areas called townships which provide essential services such as trash removal, fire protection, and road maintenance. These political subdivisions are governed by a board of trustees, usually consisting of three elected members. Just what does a township trustee do? Well, as Brian Williams suggests, it certainly is not white-collar work.

Notes

1. Ann O'M. Bowman and Richard C. Kearney, *The Resurgence of the States* (Englewood Cliffs, NJ: Prentice-Hall, 1986), p. 76.
2. Quoted in James Nathan Miller, "Our Horse-and-Buggy State Legislatures," *Reader's Digest* 86 (May, 1965): p. 50, emphasis in original.
3. On this point, see ibid. pp. 51–53; and Citizen's Conference on State Legislatures, *The Sometimes Governments: A Critical Study of the 50 American Legislatures,* 2nd ed., (Kansas City, MO: Citizen's Conference on State Legislatures, 1973).
4. Miller, p. 52.
5. Bowman and Kearney, pp. 88–92.

Questions for Review and Discussion

7.1 What have been the changes in the level of professionalism of your state legislature? Has it seen more or less change than the average state?

Do you think your state legislators have adequate resources to make good public policy? Why or why not?

7.2   Ask a local city councilmember if you can follow him/her around for a day to see what the job entails. What conclusions do you draw from this?

21 I Spent a Winter in Politics: Confessions of a Farmer after His First Season in the Statehouse

STEWART BLEDSOE

IT'S ANOTHER WORLD. You wear a suit every day. You lay out the day's work without first checking the weather. You swap hand calluses for writer's cramp and pick up ten sloppy pounds around the middle.

This and a lot more happened to me at the State Legislature last winter. And I learned something that we'd better understand in rural America—how the machinery works from the *inside!*

Some neighbors started it. "Come on. Give politics a try." A reluctant "Yep" from me, and we took off.

Several months, scores of speeches, thousands of doorbells, and tens of thousands of mailings later, the election was over—but not for me. Had to count the absentees, so slim was the margin. They call me "Landslide" hereabouts for finally chalking up that teensy win. Nothing keeps the hat size down like having 10,000 neighbors who *don't* think you're the people's choice.

My first look at law-making was a jolt. What a lot to learn in a hurry. Like taking your first riding lesson on a bucking bronco. The chute pops open, and you're out there riding for your life.

My learning process began *fast*. One day I was tapped as a fill-in luncheon speaker. "Tell 'em how it looks to a freshman legislator," I was instructed. So I did. Specifically. Bluntly. It made the front page: "Bledsoe Raps Legislature." My confreres awarded me a muzzle, no foolin'. I'd wear it, I said, as soon as I got my foot out of my mouth.

I had to learn a new language—the kind lawyers use. When I introduce a bill, I'm proposing to write a law. It has to add up, legally. But you soon learn to think in "whereas-es."

Issues are seldom as simple or clear-cut to a legislator as to you. He must instinctively consider all sides—not just your point of view. You might remember that next time you approach him.

Legislators aren't suddenly transformed into supermen. Just because you elect them and pack them off to the statehouse and entrust your law-making to them doesn't make them any smarter than they were back home. Some are superior people, some sadly inadequate.

In many states, you'd get a better kind of crew if the pay were better. And that better crew could do a whale of a better job with enough staff to research facts and bring in unbiased information on which intelligent decisions can be made.

LOBBYISTS   Till I worked alongside 'em, I was as skeptical as you about what goes on behind the scenes. The good ones do a needed job, give facts and straight answers even if it doesn't help their case.

Another type, less lovable, points a political gun square at you. He and his "thousands of followers" openly intend to "support their friends, defeat their enemies." They don't threaten, but you get the message.

The lobbyist who buys and sells legislators in wholesale lots is mostly fictional. I never did meet one.

One day on the floor I got help from an unexpected kind of lobby. I was heading the floor fight for a sales tax exemption on artificial insemination. With a little understanding of the issue, my nonrancher colleagues were about to play "funny." The bill could have been lost in the hilarity. Just as the funsters unlimbered quips about my "sex tax," the gallery filled with a delegation of nuns. Silence. The bill passed. *There's* lobbying.

FLOOR SPEECHES?   Window dressing, mostly. A lot of people sitting in the galleries think they're seeing laws being made. They're wrong. A good share of the speeches are for the record, and the newspapers. The real work goes on in committees.

Big issues are pretty well decided before hitting the floor. Disillusioning? Shouldn't be. Think of the chaos if important policies were all settled during impassioned floor debate. In committee you can study facts, go deeper, do a better job. And here's where you line up the basic support for a bill, too. A farmer's experience in dickering is handy here. You learn that compromise isn't necessarily a dirty word.

Biggest jolt I got out of my winter in politics was to learn that farmers are so obviously a minority—just how much of a minority will become big news as the urban population starts rearranging our rural lives for us.

The city dweller understands our problems poorly. Too often we beg for his sympathy. That's a mistake. It gets nowhere and only demeans farmers. Much better express our problems in *his* main-street dollars. Then they get the message!

Who states our case? You do. Organizations are fine. They can represent you with lobbyists, paid hands. The punch comes when *you* do something about it. Only then.

A letter in your own hand: Great! Do it right, though. Not vague or vindictive like "No more taxes, you spendthrift!" Abusive letters get nowhere. Make yours friendly, thoughtful, and above all, specific. "Hold the line on taxes by cutting back on _____." (You fill in the blank.) He'll read that one.

If your organization meets, passes resolutions, and goes home, you've wasted your time. Make sure they're pressed home. They're meaningless sleeping in the minute book.

WANT TO BE REALLY EFFECTIVE?   Pick up the phone. You're busy. So's your legislator. You can state your case—probably get an answer, all in one clatter. Try it. It worked on me, and I know it has on others.

Petitions? Forget 'em. Holler down the rain barrel, instead. It's just as effective and more fun. En masse visits to the statehouse can work if someone has done the advance work. Angry faces packing the gallery don't do much. Scheduled meetings with legislators and two-way discussions can.

Arrange for a small group to have a special breakfast with their own legislators—and pay for it yourselves. That kind of thing gets somewhere.

The most effective route of all: Find a candidate who states your principles, then snuggle up to him when *he's* seeking help—during the campaign. Put his bumper sticker on your truck, put up his signs, work for him. You'll have his attention when you state *your* case.

YOU'RE TOO BUSY?   Well, friend, you'd better find time for politics. Look at your last tax statement if you need incentive.

Once home from the Legislature, rewarding to me was the rare comment, "Nice going, Thanks for what you did." Puzzling was the one: "How did you like it back at the Congress in Washington, D.C.?"

Baffling was the close neighbor who asked, "Where you been, Stew—haven't seen you for months?

Fame—it's wonderful!

22 Measuring State Legislative Professionalism

PEVERILL SQUIRE

MEASURES OF LEGISLATIVE PROFESSIONALISM are intended to assess the capacity of both individual members and the organization as a whole to generate and digest information in the policymaking process. Professionalism is typically associated with unlimited legislative sessions, superior staff resources, and sufficient pay to allow members to pursue legislative service as their vocation. The concept has been hypothesized to influence a wide range of behaviors, both within and outside the legislature, from the adoption of various internal rules and procedures to specific policy outputs. Given the concept's importance across a wide spectrum of academic research, the method of measurement for legislative professionalism is an important question to address.

Measures of legislative professionalism have been around since the early 1970s. The first indices were created by John Grumm (1971) and the Citizens Conference on State Legislatures (1971) to measure legislative policymaking capacity. Since then, a number of alternative measures of professionalism have been devised for various purposes, but all have tried to tap into the same general concept (Berkman 1993; Berry, Berkman, and Schneiderman 2000; Bowman and Kearney 1988; Carey, Niemi, and Powell 2000, 694–7; King 2000; Moncrief 1988; Morehouse 1983). In this article, I revisit a widely used measure of legislative professionalism that I developed 15 years ago (Squire 1992a). I discuss how I conceived of the measure and the theoretical concept of legislative professionalism. I then explain the mechanics of the index and assess its reliability and validity, in part by examining scores for 1979, 1986, 1996, and 2003. Next, I consider a potential criticism of my measure and, in response, provide revised scores for 1979 and 2003 that allow for its use in dynamic studies. I conclude with a few final thoughts on the measure.

Developing a Measure of Professionalism

The Grumm (1971) and Citizens Conference on State Legislatures (1971) measures were based on what each identified as ideal characteristics of a professionalized body. They both offered a definition of legislative professionalism and then proceeded to measure it. I approached measuring professionalism differently; rather than starting with a definition, I began with an example. My starting point was an observation that Nelson Polsby had made about the legislative professionalization movement:

> One favored place to begin has been for reformers quite consciously to adopt as their model the United States Congress. In American state legislatures this has meant a movement toward the establishment of a respectable pay scale, provision for independent staff services, and increases in the time allowed for legislatures to sit. (Polsby 1975, 297)

This comment suggested establishing Congress as the archetypical professional legislature. Accordingly, I devised a professionalism measure using relevant attributes of Congress as a baseline against which to compare those same attributes of other legislative bodies (Squire 1992a). Specifically, I compared an index of Congress's pay to members, average days in session, and average staff per member to an index composed of those same attributes in other legislatures. In essence, the measure showed how closely a legislature approximated these characteristics of Congress on a scale where 1.0 represented perfect resemblance and 0.0 represented no resemblance. Almost every other professionalism measure has also incorporated data on member salary, time demands, and staff resources (Carey, Niemi, and Powell 2000, 694; Thompson and Moncrief 1992, 199); the use of Congress as a baseline against which to compare the state legislatures was the novel element of my index.

Conceptualizing Legislative Professionalism

Ironically, while there has been general consensus about how to measure legislative professionalism, there has not been complete consensus about the underlying concept. Most notably, Rosenthal (1996, 175) argues that "professionalism as a concept ought to be restricted to the legislature, and not extended to include the members who comprise it." Rosenthal thinks that most measures and conceptualizing on this subject conflate an institutional concept and an individual-level concept. He argues that time demands and staffing levels are characteristics of the legislature as an institution and that member salary represents a characteristic—careerism—of legislators as individuals. Rosenthal sees these concepts as related, but distinct. Viewed in these terms, the accepted three-component measure of legislative professionalism creates somewhat different implications for legislators and legislatures. I suggest some of these implications in Table 1.

The implications of professionalism for legislators demonstrate that the concept is only partly related to careerism. Certainly, as salaries in-

TABLE 1   Implications of Legislative Professionalism for Legislators and Legislatures

Professionalism Component	Implications for Legislator	Implications for Legislature
Salary and benefits	• Increased incentive to serve, leading to longer tenure • Increased ability to focus on legislative activities	• Leads to members with longer tenure, creating a more experienced body • Attracts better qualified members
Time demands of service	• Reduced opportunities to pursue other employment and increased need for higher salary to compensate for lost income • Increased opportunity to master legislative skills	• Increased time for policy development • Increased time for policy deliberation
Staff and resources	• Increased ability to influence policymaking process • Increased job satisfaction • Enhanced re-election prospects	• Increased policymaking influence relative to the executive

crease, legislators have greater incentive to continue service in the legislature, a relationship at the heart of careerism. But increasing pay has an additional, more subtle, consequence for legislators in that it allows them to focus their energies exclusively on their legislative activities rather than having to juggle them with the demands of their regular occupations. Importantly, this second implication holds whether a member seeks a career in a legislature or intends to serve only for a brief period.

Furthermore, the implications of time demands for legislators condition the impacts of legislator pay. On one hand, when few demands are made, legislators do not need much money to compensate for their time. When legislative demands are low, legislators may not have to sacrifice much time from their regular jobs to serve in the legislature. On the other hand, full-time legislators must be paid enough to allow them to support themselves and their families without income from outside occupations. Thus, at the extremes, the relationship between time demands and salary needs is simple. But in the middle range, where legislatures meet for several months each year, the situation becomes more complicated. In these states, the point at which legislative salary suffices to compensate for lost income is subtle, clouding these characteristics' implications for careerism (Maddox 2004).

Time demands also have a second implication for legislators. The limited legislative socialization literature (Bell and Price 1975) suggests that the more days each year that a legislature meets, the better legislators understand the intricacies of the legislative process. Thus, beyond any implications for careerism, longer sessions give members a better chance to master arcane rules and procedures.

The level of staff resources in a legislature has several straightforward implications for legislators. First, a greater number of staff members leads to better-informed legislators, allowing members to have greater influence in the policymaking process. Second, with more impact on policymaking, legislative job satisfaction likely increases with staff resources (Francis 1985). Finally, a larger staff base likely improves re-election prospects by enhancing legislators' ability to provide constituent services. Greater job satisfaction and enhanced re-election prospects clearly promote careerism. But the contribution that staff makes to a legislator's ability to affect policymaking remains independent of careerism.

Thus, this examination of the theoretical implications of the three components of professionalism for legislators shows that only some of them are clearly linked to careerism. Others imply that professionalism will increase legislators' policymaking capacities without necessarily requiring longer tenures. Consequently, even at the level of the individual legislator, the concept of professionalism is not equal to the concept of careerism.

The institutional implications of legislative professionalism are generally clear-cut and well understood. First, higher salaries allow legislators to devote more time and energy to lawmaking by freeing them from the distraction of another occupation, which can lead to longer-serving, and therefore more informed and effective, legislators (Squire 1988a). Second, higher salaries attract better-qualified legislators, in terms of academic credentials, occupational status, and the like, a prominent notion in European legislative studies (Eliassen and Pedersen 1978; King 1981; Saalfeld 1997) but overlooked in American legislative studies. Third, meeting for more days each year provides legislators with more time to develop legislative proposals and more time to deliberate on them, thereby improving legislative output (Rosenthal 1996, 171). Fourth, increased staff resources make the legislature a more equal partner with the executive branch in policymaking (Rosenthal 1996, 171–2).

Thus, the components of the traditional legislative professionalism measures have somewhat different implications for legislators than for the institutions in which they serve. In combination, however, these components constitute a concept not captured by each of them individually. Conceptually, professional legislators are not just longer serving, they are also better equipped as policymakers for reasons beyond their longevity. Additionally, professional legislatures are stronger competitors in the policymaking process for more reasons than just their being composed of veteran members.

Finally, it is important to note that the potential impact of term limits on legislative professionalism is apt to be limited. Term limits do not alter the number of days a legislature meets, the salary its members earn, or the staff that is provided. Instead, term limits potentially truncate the legislative career, reducing the benefits gained from experience. Only in a handful of the 15 states with term limits—arguably California, Michigan, and Ohio—do they have any significant implications for professionalism because it is only in those few state legislatures that limits force the bulk of members to leave earlier than they might have otherwise (Moncrief, Niemi, and Powell 2004; Moncrief, Thompson, Haddon, and Hoyer 1992). Even in these few states, only the lower chamber is significantly impacted regarding member experience because with term limits the upper chamber typically becomes populated with former members of the lower chamber (Moncrief, Niemi, and Powell 2004, 369–70). Notably, even before the imposition of term limits, most members of the professional California Assembly opted to serve for only a few terms (Squire 1988a, 1988b, 1992b). All of these observations suggest that a professional legislature need not necessarily be a career legislature.

The Mechanics of Measuring Legislative Professionalism

My professionalism index, like virtually all other measures of this characteristic, includes indicators of pay, session length, and staff resources, and measuring each of these components presents challenges.

Measuring Legislator Salary and Benefits

Two significant aspects of member remuneration must be considered when developing an indicator: salary from legislative service and retirement or health care benefits. Only the former has ever been included in legislative professionalism measures, including my own. But as I argue below, employment benefits may affect a legislator's re-election decision.

A valid measure of state legislative salaries presents at least two challenges. First, although Congress and most state legislatures pay their members an annual salary, legislators in nine states only receive per diems or weekly salaries while the legislature is in session. Fortunately, it is reasonably straightforward to calculate annual remuneration for these nine states, at least when the session length can be determined accurately.

Second, a state legislator's total income is difficult to gauge accurately because just over half of the states provide their legislators with unvouchered (or functionally unvouchered) expense reimbursements. We can assume that vouchered expense reimbursements compensate legislators only for real expenses they incur in serving and, therefore, should not be counted as income. In contrast, unvouchered expense reimbursements often become vehicles for boosting legislators' salaries without drawing public attention. While it is relatively easy to calculate how much money a state's legislators receive in unvouchered expenses, short of accessing legislators' tax returns, it is impossible to distinguish between compensation for real expenses and supplementary income.

Thus, as other such measures have done, my professionalism index uses the base legislative salary figure in a state, which provides a good approximation of overall compensation (Carey, Niemi, and Powell 2000, 696; Squire 1988a, 69). Would including unvouchered expenses change the measure in any appreciable way? In a handful of states, the salary figure would change considerably if unvouchered expenses were included.

The most notable case is Alabama, where in 2005, for example, the $10 per diem paled in comparison to the unvouchered expense payments of $2,280 per month, plus an additional $50 per day for three days during each week that the legislature met. But even if adding unvouchered expense reimbursements changed salary figures noticeably in a few states, the impact on the overall legislative professionalism measure is minor, especially because salary represents one of three equally weighted components. For example, my professionalism measure for 2003 using the simple base salary measure correlates at .99 with the same year's measure substituting a salary figure that includes even the generous unvouchered expense reimbursements, as calculated by the National Conference of State Legislatures (NCSL).

Finally, it is worth considering whether the availability and generosity of pensions and healthcare coverage should be included in the legislative income calculation. For example, even with its high salary, the appeal of legislative service in California may have been reduced since voters abolished the legislative pension plan in 1990. On the flip side, Texas legislators are paid an annual salary of only $7,200, but they may find their body's generous pension plan—which is tied to state judicial salaries and provides an annual pension of $34,500 after 12 years of service—worthy of continuing in office. Thus, employment benefits may need to be incorporated in future legislative professionalism measures.

Measuring the Time Demands of Legislative Service

The number of days, state legislatures meet is reported in one of two ways: calendar days and legislative days. Calendar days generally represent the number of days between the opening and closing of the legislative session, including days when the legislature does not actually meet. Legislative days signify the number of days the legislature actually meets. In my view, the relevant consideration for legislative professionalism is how many days a legislator must be in the state capitol to conduct legislative business, and thus, be unavailable for other business and personal activities. Therefore, I use the number of legislative days in computing my professionalism measure. This method requires a conversion for those states that report only calendar days. I use a simple and rough calculation, deflating the number of calendar days by five-sevenths to approximate the number of legislative days in a state for a given year. This process assumes that a legislature meets five days per week while in session and may overestimate the number of days the legislature actually met. Where state legislatures operate under strict session limits, I use the maximum number of meeting days in my measure, since legislatures that have such limits routinely bump up against them. Fortunately, most state legislatures report legislative days. But even coding legislative days can be tricky. For example, in the *Book of the States 2005* (Council of State Governments 2005, 168–9), the Illinois House of Representatives lists meeting for 94 legislative days in 2004, but a note admits that "34 [legislative days] were perfunctory," suggesting little legislative business was conducted on those days.

My measure does not take into account the time demands made on legislators by special sessions, but this likely does not damage its validity or reliability. Special sessions intrude on a member's time significantly only if they are used routinely as a device to evade session limits. In such a case, they could add substantially to the number of days a legislature actually meets each year. But special sessions are rarely, if at all, used in this fashion. Indeed, in 18 states, the legislature does not even possess the power to call a special session. The vast majority of state legislative special sessions are limited in scope, with agendas devoted to only a few issues, making them substantively different from regular sessions.

In practice, adding the number of days in special session makes virtually no difference to my legislative professionalism measure. For example, for 2003 my index correlates at .99 with the same measure with special session days added. Indeed, the NCSL surveyed legislators in 2003 ask, among other things, how much time they devoted to their legislative service, broadly construed (Kurtz et al. 2006). Even though such self-reports are prone to exaggeration and encompass any activity related to legislative service, the responses to that survey question aggregated by state legislature correlate with my measure of time demands for that year at .59.

Measuring Legislative Staff Resources

To measure a legislator's staff resources, I use legislative staff figures gathered by the NCSL (2004). They report three sets of numbers: permanent staff, session-only staff, and total staff during the session. I use the last of these because I am interested in how much assistance legislators receive during a session. Thus, the NCSL's staffing numbers (measured in 1979, 1988, 1996, and 2003) tap directly into the concept I want to measure. Unfortunately, valid and reliable data on state legislative staff are difficult to find for years in which the NCSL did not conduct its surveys. Therefore, some researchers have opted to use annual budget figures for a state legislature as a surrogate for staff resources (Berry,

Berkman, and Schneiderman 2000; Carey, Niemi, and Powell 2000; Moncrief 1988). However, legislative expenditures are potentially confounded by the inclusion of legislator salaries, the cost of building maintenance, and other housekeeping items unrelated to staffing, depending on what a state legislature includes in its budget. But scholars can take comfort from the fact that legislative expenditures and staffing levels are highly correlated (Carey, Niemi, and Powell 2000, 696) and that legislative professionalism measures incorporating either legislative expenditures or staffing numbers produce remarkably consistent state rankings (Berkman 2001, 675; Maestas 2003, 448; Mooney 1994).

Evaluating the Squire Legislative Professionalism Index

Using these data and coding rules, I calculated professionalism scores for each state legislature for 1979, 1986, 1996, and 2003, as shown in Table 2. To compute these values, I divided the score for each state legislature on each of the three dimensions by the parallel score for Congress (averaged for both chambers) for the same years. I added the scores for the three components and divided by three. Thus, each of the three components is equally weighted. This calculation yields a score for each state that can be interpreted as the percentage of professionalism that its legislature had compared to Congress that year. An examination of the scores in Table 2 provides some insight into the index's reliability and validity.

Reliability

A cross-year comparison of the scores in Table 2 for each state suggests that the measure is reliable. The scores do not bounce around much from year to year, which is what we should expect, given that during this time period state legislatures did not undergo radical changes in their professionalism. Furthermore, almost no state moves up or down much in rank from year to year. Overall, these figures indicate a highly reliable measure.

Validity

The validity of the measure can be assessed in two ways. First consider its face validity. The scores in Table 2 parallel nicely with both qualitative assessments of state legislative professionalism (Hamm and Moncrief 2004, 158; Rosenthal 1993, 116–7; Kurtz 1992, 2) and other quantitative mea-

TABLE 2   State Legislative Professionalism—1979, 1986, 1996, and 2003

State	1979 Rank	1979 Score	1986 Rank	1986 Score	1996 Rank	1996 Score	2003 Rank	2003 Score
CA	1	.526	3	.625	1	.570	1	.626
NY	3	.407	1	.659	3	.515	2	.480
WI	16	.249	12	.270	4	.459	3	.439
MA	4	.386	4	.614	5	.332	4	.385
MI	2	.463	2	.653	2	.516	5	.342
PA	6	.345	5	.336	8	.283	6	.339
OH	5	.355	6	.329	7	.315	7	.304
IL	7	.344	8	.302	11	.236	8	.261
NJ	30	.175	13	.255	6	.320	9	.244
AZ	11	.269	15	.250	18	.185	10	.232
AK	8	.320	7	.311	12	.232	11	.227
HI	17	.246	11	.276	9	.252	12	.225
FL	19	.224	13	.255	10	.249	13	.223
CO	9	.284	9	.300	21	.172	14	.202
TX	24	.191	20	.210	13	.215	15	.199
NC	25	.190	22	.203	28	.149	16	.198
WA	21	.212	18	.230	14	.198	17	.197
MD	14	.252	21	.204	16	.189	18	.194
CT	23	.200	17	.233	20	.178	19	.190
OK	15	.249	15	.250	17	.188	20	.187
MO	13	.266	10	.297	15	.198	21	.174
IA	12	.266	19	.225	23	.164	22	.170
MN	22	.211	23	.199	19	.179	23	.169
NE	20	.216	25	.186	22	.172	24	.162
OR	18	.233	27	.183	25	.153	25	.159
DE	28	.179	24	.192	26	.151	26	.148
KY	47	.078	44	.101	41	.087	27	.148
VT	39	.130	36	.145	33	.117	28	.144
ID	29	.179	41	.119	36	.110	29	.138
NV	40	.130	31	.160	24	.161	30	.138
RI	38	.142	35	.148	35	.113	31	.133
VA	32	.164	29	.170	27	.150	32	.131
LA	35	.150	26	.185	29	.144	33	.129
KS	31	.169	34	.152	37	.067	34	.125
WV	33	.150	40	.125	34	.116	35	.125
SC	10	.281	28	.178	30	.135	36	.124
GA	37	.142	39	.133	38	.107	37	.116
TN	34	.149	38	.135	32	.117	38	.116

TABLE 2   (*Continued*)

State	1979 Rank	1979 Score	1986 Rank	1986 Score	1996 Rank	1996 Score	2003 Rank	2003 Score
NM	44	.092	45	.098	49	.053	39	.109
MS	26	.185	31	.160	31	.127	40	.107
AR	41	.115	43	.105	39	.104	41	.106
IN	36	.143	37	.139	39	.106	42	.102
ME	27	.180	30	.161	41	.098	43	.089
MT	42	.114	42	.110	43	.073	44	.076
AL	45	.085	33	.158	45	.067	45	.071
UT	46	.082	47	.082	44	.067	46	.065
SD	43	.104	46	.083	46	.065	47	.064
WY	49	.075	49	.056	48	.057	48	.054
ND	48	.077	48	.075	47	.058	49	.051
NH	50	.062	50	.042	50	.034	50	.027
Mean		.209		.221		.182		.185
Median		.188		.186		.152		.154

Note: A state legislature's professionalism score is based on its legislator pay, number of days in session, and staff per legislator, all compared to those characteristics in Congress during the same year.

Sources: The scores for 1986 are from Squire 1992a. The scores for 1996 (with a slight revision for Nevada) are from Squire 2000. The member pay and days in session data for the 1979 and 2003 measures are calculated from the appropriate volumes of the *Book of the States*. The staff data for state legislators is from the National Conference of State Legislatures reports, "Size of State Legislative Staff: 1979, 1988, 1996, and 2003," dated May 6, 2004. Congressional data are taken from Dwyer 2004, Congressional Quarterly 1993, and Ornstein, Mann, and Malbin 2000 and 2002,

sures (Mooney 1994). Second, and perhaps more importantly, the measure has predictive validity. That is, it has performed as expected in many studies of state politics and policies, given hypotheses of the causes and effects of legislative professionalism. For example, several studies have found a state's population to have a strong positive relationship with state legislative professionalism as measured by this index (King 2000; Mooney 1995; Squire 2005; Squire and Hamm 2005). Membership turnover has shown to decline as professionalism increases (Moncrief, Niemi, and Powell 2004). Legislators in more professional legislatures have more contact with their constituents (Squire 1993) and are more attentive to constituent concerns (Maestas 2003) than are their counterparts in less professional legislatures. Legislative efficiency—the percentage of bills passed and the number of bills enacted per legislative day—is positively related to professionalism (Squire 1998). The inclination to reform government personnel practices increases with legislative professionalism (Kellough and Selden 2003), as does the willingness to adopt increasingly complex and technical policies (Ka and Teske 2002). Per capita government spending also increases with the level of legislative professionalism (Owings and Borck 2000). Each of these hypotheses of the causes and effects of professionalism was supported using my measure, demonstrating its predictive validity.

Professionalism as a Moving Target

One potential problem with my measure of legislative professionalism is that the congressional baseline continually moves. In other words, as Congress changes over time, the standard by which I measure state legislative professionalism changes. It is as if the state legislatures are in a race to become like Congress, but Congress keeps moving the finish line. Consider the effect of this phenomenon on New Hampshire's relative standing on my index over time. New Hampshire shows this moving standard effect well because its absolute value on the indicators that compose my measure barely change at all. The state constitution set legislative pay at $200 per biennium in 1889, and it has not changed since then. The legislature meets for essentially the same number of days per year as a century ago and still employs only a small staff. In effect, New Hampshire's legislature could serve as an alternative baseline for professionalism because of its lack of change.

But how has the New Hampshire legislature's professionalism standing compared to Congress changed over time? Evidence presented elsewhere shows that from 1935 to 1960, New Hampshire scored higher than it has in more recent decades (Squire 2005; Squire 2006). As shown in Table 2, New Hampshire places last in every time period from 1979 to 2003, and more importantly, its scores drop with each succeeding period, albeit by a small amount. Thus, New Hampshire's scores document that the standard by which a professional legislature is measured in my index has become more stringent over time. Simply by not changing its legislature, New Hampshire has fallen further and further behind the professionalism standard set by Congress.

As a result, is it fair to keep moving the standard? For example, a legislature could increase staffing from one point in time to the next but appear to lose ground because Congress improved its staffing even more. Because Congress serves as the baseline, it if changes its session length, staffing, and pay over a given period, then the scores from my index could be inappropriate for use in analyses involving professionalism over that time period.

One way to explore the extent of this potential problem is to anchor the professionalism standard set by Congress and recalculate my measure. I did this by calculating the grand mean for Congress on each of the three professionalism indicators using data from the late 1970s and the early 2000s, converting the earlier salary figures to 2003 dollars to control for inflation. Then, I recalculated the state legislative professionalism scores for 1979 and 2003 using these congressional grand means. The results, presented in Table 3, reveal an important substantive finding. The mean and median scores indicate that, measured against the anchored congressional score, state legislatures made modest progress in their professionalism between 1979 and 2003. This finding contradicts the storyline suggested by the data in Table 2 that use the single-year congressional baseline, which shows a slight decline in professionalism over that time period. However, the differences between the two grand professionalism scores and their counterparts reported in Table 2 are small. The correlations among the professionalism scores in Tables 2 and 3 are presented in Table 4. The two grand mean scores correlate at .99 with the regular professionalism scores using the single-year baseline for their respective years. Indeed, all of these professionalism scores are highly correlated with each other, with the expected pattern that the correlations are somewhat smaller for those scores that are further apart. These correlations provide additional confirmation of my professionalism index's reliability.

Why do the grand mean legislative professionalism scores change so little from their regular one-year baseline score counterparts? The answer is that on two of the three dimensions of professionalism, Congress did not change much between 1999 and 2003, and the congressional baseline barely changed. This lack of change is no surprise. Staffing levels have changed little in Congress in recent decades. If anything, congressional staff has been reduced slightly since 1995 (Ornstein, Mann, and Malbin 2000, 132). And while Congress has both greater ability and greater will to increase its salary than do most state legislatures, the actual salary changes in Congress were not large between 1979 and 2003. In constant 2003 dollars, members of Congress were paid $145,730 in 1979 compared to $154,700 in 2003. Only the number of days in session changed markedly between the two years, with Congress meeting longer in 2003, However, as already noted, any change in one component of my professionalism measure will not greatly affect the scores since it has three equally weighted components.

TABLE 3   State Legislative Professionalism Measured against
Congressional Grand Mean—1979 and 2003

State	1979 Rank	1979 Grand Mean Score	2003 Rank	2003 Grand Mean Score
CA	1	.469	1	.675
NY	3	.379	2	.513
WI	11	.227	3	.513
MA	4	.319	4	.444
MI	2	.400	5	.367
PA	5	.309	6	.356
OH	7	.304	7	.345
IL	6	.305	8	.285
AZ	12	.225	9	.256
AK	8	.266	10	.249
NJ	25	.158	11	.247
HI	16	.218	12	.239
NC	26	.155	13	.232
FL	18	.208	14	.229
CO	9	.235	15	.227
CT	24	.165	16	.217
WA	21	.189	17	.213
MD	15	.219	18	.212
OK	17	.209	19	.208
TX	23	.175	20	.205
MO	13	.224	21	.198
IA	14	.221	22	.197
MN	20	.190	23	.186
NE	22	.179	24	.182
OR	19	.205	25	.176
VT	41	.104	26	.174
KY	46	.066	27	.163
DE	27	.151	28	.163
ID	30	.142	29	.161
RI	39	.109	30	.149
KS	32	.134	31	.147
NV	38	.110	32	.145
SC	10	.228	33	.143
VA	29	.145	34	.141
WV	34	.127	35	.140
LA	36	.122	36	.138
TN	33	.129	37	.132
MS	28	.151	38	.127

TABLE 3 *(Continued)*

State	1979 Rank	1979 Grand Mean Score	2003 Rank	2003 Grand Mean Score
GA	35	.123	39	.127
NM	44	.076	40	.115
IN	37	.120	41	.114
AR	40	.104	42	.114
ME	31	.139	43	.104
MT	42	.091	44	.089
AL	45	.070	45	.078
SD	43	.085	46	.076
UT	47	.066	47	.075
WY	48	.059	48	.062
ND	49	.059	49	.059
NH	50	.046	50	.033
Mean		.178		.203
Median		.157		.175

Note: A state legislature's professionalism score is based on its legislator pay, number of days in session, and staff per legislator, all compared to those characteristics in Congress averaged for 1978–79 and 2001–02. Salary figures are converted to 2003 dollars.

Sources: The member pay and days in session data are calculated from the appropriate volumes of the *Book of the States*. The staff data are from the National Conference of State Legislatures report, "Size of State Legislative Staff: 1979, 1988, 1996, and 2003," dated May 6, 2004. Congressional data are taken from Dwyer (2004).

TABLE 4 Professionalism Score Correlations

	1979 Score	1979 Grand Mean Score	1986 Score	1996 Score	2003 Score
1979 Grand Mean Score	.996				
1986 Score	.916	.921			
1996 Score	.862	.888	.908		
2003 Score	.863	.885	.890	.949	
2003 Grand Mean Score	.866	.884	.881	.943	.994

Note: All scores are statistically distinct from zero at p ≤ .01, using a two-tailed test.

Concluding Thoughts

The evidence presented in this article suggests that my state legislative professionalism index is a reliable and valid measure. Moreover, the measure is easy to understand and intuitively appealing. However, I have two cautionary comments about its use in statistical analysis. First, rank ordering of state legislative professionalism, while perhaps of some cursory interest, provides limited analytical use. For example, looking at the scores for 2003 in Table 2, one would be hard pressed to make the case that there was any significant difference in the policymaking capacities or professionalism generally of the Texas, North Carolina, and Washington state legislatures. After all, a small tweak in the way salary is calculated or days in session are counted could easily re-order their positions in these rankings. Second, scores of the sort presented in Table 4 may be preferred for dynamic analyses. Overall, however, I conclude that my index of state legislative professionalism, first presented 15 years ago, is robust and appropriate for use in a wide variety of studies.

References

Bell, Charles G., and Charles M. Price. 1975. *The First Term*. Beverly Hills, CA: Sage.

Berkman, Michael B. 1993. "Former State Legislators in the U. S. House of Representatives: Institutional and Policy Mastery." *Legislative Studies Quarterly* 18:77–104.

Berkman, Michael B. 2001. "Legislative Professionalism and the Demand for Groups: The Institutional Context of Interest Population Density." *Legislative Studies Quarterly* 26:661–79.

Berry, William D., Michael B. Berkman, and Stuart Schneiderman. 2000. "Legislative Professionalism and Incumbent Reelection: The Development of Institutional Boundaries." *American Political Science Review* 94:859–74.

Bowman, Ann O'M., and Richard C. Kearney. 1988. "Dimensions of State Government Capability." *Western Political Quarterly* 41:341–62.

Carey, John M., Richard G. Niemi, and Lynda W. Powell. 2000. "Incumbency and the Probability of Reelection in State Legislative Elections." *Journal of Politics* 62:671–700.

Citizens Conference on State Legislatures. 1971. *State Legislatures: An Evaluation of Their Effectiveness*. New York: Praeger.

Congressional Quarterly. 1993. *Congress A to Z*. Washington, DC: Congressional Quarterly.

Council of State Governments. 2005. *The Book of the State, 2005*. Vol. 37. Lexington, KY: Council of State Governments.

Dwyer, Paul E. 2004. "Salaries of Members of Congress: A List of Payable Rates and Effective Dates, 1789–2004." CRS Report for Congress 97–1011 GOV.

Eliassen, Kjell A., and Mogens N. Pedersen. 1978. "Professionalism of Legislatures: Long-term Change in Political Recruitment in Denmark and Norway." *Comparative Studies in Society and History* 20:286–318.

Francis, Wayne L. 1985. "Costs and Benefits of Legislative Service in the American States." *American Journal of Political Science* 29:626–42.

Grumm, John G. 1971. "The Effects of Legislative Structure on Legislative Performance." In *State and Urban Politics,* eds. Richard I. Hofferbert and Ira Sharkansky. Boston, MA: Little, Brown.

Hamm, Keith E., and Gary F. Moncrief. 2004. "Legislative Politics in the States." In *Politics in the American States,* eds. Virginia Gray and Russell L. Hanson. 8th ed. Washington, DC: CQ Press.

Ka, Sangjoon, and Paul Teske. 2002. "Ideology and Professionalism—Electricity Regulation and Deregulation over Time in the American States." *American Politics Research* 30:323–43.

Kellough, J. E., and S. C. Selden. 2003. "The Reinvention of Public Personnel Administration: An Analysis of the Diffusion of Personnel Management Reforms in the States." *Public Administration Review* 63:165–76.

King, Anthony. 1981. "The Rise of the Career Politician in Britain—And its Consequences." *British Journal of Political Science* 11:249–85.

King, James D. 2000. "Changes in Professionalism in U.S. State Legislatures." *Legislative Studies Quarterly* 25:327–43.

Kurtz, Karl T. 1992. "Understanding the Diversity of American State Legislatures." *Extension of Remarks* (June):2–5.

Kurtz, Karl T., Gary Moncrief, Richard G. Niemi, and Lynda W. Powell. 2006. "Full-Time, Part-Time, and Real Time: Explaining State Legislators' Perceptions of Time on the Job." *State Politics and Policy Quarterly* 6:322–38.

Maddox, H. W. Jerome. 2004. "Opportunity Costs and Outside Careers in U.S. State Legislatures." *Legislative Studies Quarterly* 29:517–44.

Maestas, Cherie. 2003. "The Incentive to Listen: Progressive Ambition, Resources, and Opinion Monitoring among State Legislators." *Journal of Politics* 65:439–56.

Moncrief, Gary F. 1988. "Dimensions of the Concept of Professionalism in State Legislatures: A Research Note." *State and Local Government Review* 20:128–32.

Moncrief, Gary F., Richard G. Niemi, and Lynda W. Powell. 2004. "Time, Term Limits, and Turnover: Membership Stability in U.S. State Legislatures." *Legislative Studies Quarterly* 29:357–81.

Moncrief, Gary F., Joel A. Thompson, Michael Haddon, and Robert Hoyer. 1992. "For Whom the Bell Tolls: Term Limits and State Legislatures." *Legislative Studies Quarterly* 17:37–47.

Mooney, Christopher Z. 1994. "Measuring U.S. State Legislative Professionalism: An Evaluation of Five Indices." *State and Local Government Review* 26:70–8.

Mooney, Christopher Z. 1995. "Citizens, Structures, and Sister States: Influences on State Legislative Professionalism." *Legislative Studies Quarterly* 20:47–67.

Morehouse, Sarah McCally. 1983. *State Politics, Parties and Policy.* New York: Holt, Rinehart, and Winston.

National Conference of State Legislatures. 2004. "Size of State Legislative Staff: 1979, 1988, 1996, and 2003." http://www.ncsl.org/programs/legman/about/staff count2003.htm (January 6, 2007).

Ornstein, Norman J., Thomas E. Mann, and Michael J. Malbin. 2000. *Vital Statistics on Congress, 1999–2000.* Washington, DC: AEI.

Ornstein, Norman J., Thomas E. Mann, and Michael J. Malbin. 2002. *Vital Statistics on Congress, 2001–2002.* Washington, DC: AEI.

Owings, Stephanie, and Rainald Borck. 2000. "Legislative Professionalism and Government Spending: Do Citizen Legislators Really Spend Less?" *Public Finance Review* 28:210–25.

Polsby, Nelson W 1975. "Legislatures." In *The Handbook of Political Science,* eds. Fred I. Greenstein and Nelson W. Polsby. Reading, MA: Addison-Wesley.

Rosenthal, Alan. 1993. "The Legislative Institution: In Transition and at Risk." In *The State of the States,* ed. Carl E. Van Horn. 2nd ed. Washington, DC: CQ Press.

Rosenthal, Alan. 1996. "State Legislative Development: Observations from Three Perspectives." *Legislative Studies Quarterly* 21:169–98.

Saalfeld, Thomas. 1997. "Professionalisation of Parliamentary Roles in Germany: An Aggregate-Level Analysis." In *Members of Parliament in Western Europe: Roles and Behavior,* eds. Wolfgang Muller and Thomas Saalfeld. London: Cass.

Squire, Peverill. 1988a. "Career Opportunities and Membership Stability in Legislatures." *Legislative Studies Quarterly* 13:65–82.

Squire, Peverill. 1988b. "Member Career Opportunities and the Internal Organization of Legislatures." *Journal of Politics* 50:726–44.

Squire, Peverill. 1992a. "Legislative Professionalism and Membership Diversity in State Legislatures." *Legislative Studies Quarterly* 17:69–79.

Squire, Peverill. 1992b. "The Theory of Legislative Institutionalization and the California Assembly." *Journal of Politics* 54:1026–54.

Squire, Peverill. 1993. "Professionalism and Public Opinion of State Legislatures." *Journal of Politics* 55:479–91.

Squire, Peverill. 1998. "Membership Turnover and the Efficient Processing of Legislation." *Legislative Studies Quarterly* 23:23–32.

Squire, Peverill. 2000. "Uncontested Seats in State Legislative Elections." *Legislative Studies Quarterly* 25:131–46.

Squire, Peverill. 2005. "The Contours of American Legislative Professionalism, 1910–2003." Presented at the Annual Meeting of the Western Political Science Association, Oakland, CA.

Squire, Peverill. 2006. "The Professionalization of State Legislatures in the United States over the Last Century." Presented at the 20th International Political Science Association World Congress, Fukuoka, Japan.

Squire, Peverill, and Keith E. Hamm. 2005. *101 Chambers: Congress, State Legislatures and the Future of Legislative Studies.* Columbus, OH: Ohio State University Press.

Thompson, Joel A., and Gary F. Moncrief. 1992. "The Evolution of the State Legislature: Institutional Change and Legislative Careers." In *Changing Patterns in State Legislative Careers,* eds. Gary F. Moncrief and Joel A. Thompson. Ann Arbor, MI: University of Michigan Press.

23 Colorado's Term Limits: Consequences, Yes. But Were They Intended?

JOHN A. STRAAYER

COLORADO'S LEGISLATIVE TERM LIMITS of eight years per chamber were adopted in 1990 and thus have impacted . . . every member who was in place at the time of the 1990 adoption. And the result? There are numerous observable consequences, but they are not always what term limits proponents said they wanted.

Along with Oklahoma and California, Colorado was one of the first states to adopt term limits. The measure was an initiated constitutional amendment. It passed with 71 percent approval and majorities in every county in the state. In 1994, voters followed up by imposing similar term limits on every Colorado local government as well.

Colorado now limits legislators to eight years per chamber, and members are free to move from House to Senate or vice versa and serve another eight. They may also sit out for four years after being limited, and then return.

Among the arguments advanced by term limit proponents were these: turnover would be increased, there'd be more opportunities for minorities and women, political careerism would be curtailed and legislatures would take on more of a "citizen" quality, and candidate dependence on special interest money and support would decrease. We would, in short, replace professional politicians with regular folk.

Opponents warned of dire consequences. Legislating would become amateur hour and power would flow to lobbyists and staffers. The legislatures would lose institutional memory and expertise. They would also lose independence, as the power of the executive would grow.

So, what has happened in Colorado? Many of the promises of proponents are yet unrealized, but some of the fears of opponents are too. What follows is an early assessment of the impact of term limits, based upon roughly 50 interviews conducted in 2000, two dozen more in 2002, continuous personal observation of Colorado's General Assembly and examination of some available documentary materials.

Membership Turnover and Experience

Turnover has increased since term limits, but not dramatically. The overall level of membership experience has dropped some, more in the House than in the Senate. But perhaps most significantly, the number of members with lengthy tenure has plummeted.

In the years preceding term limits, legislative turnover hovered in the 20–30 percent range. It rose to 36 percent in 1998, 36 percent in 2000 and 26 percent in 2002—increases to be sure, but not dramatic. The average number of years of legislative experience at the start of sessions declined from 3.85 in the House in 1967 to 2.4 in 2003, and 8.51 in the 1967 Senate to 7.0 in the 2003 Senate. Again, meaningful declines, but not dramatic. But the number in the House of 65 members with six or more years of experience fell from 18 in 1997 to 8 in 2003 and in the 35 member Senate the numbers went from 18 in 1997 to 9 in 2003. The conclusion? Historic turnover patterns are such that term limits have had some, but not dramatic, impacts on the overall level of member experience. However, the limits have drained the chambers of what had previously been a relatively small cadre of long-term veterans. And what do informed observers say are the consequences? Those relatively few long-term veterans who carry the institutional memory, transmit norms, provide role models, lead the defense of the institution, share stories of policy history and act as "policy champions" in long-term pursuit of solutions to tough policy problems—they are gone and both the institution and public suffer as a result. Further, the new and limited members rush to make their policy mark, sometimes with trivial and/or poorly thought-out measures.

Leadership

The impacts on leadership follow from the impacts on turnover and experience. The two Speakers before term limits served eight and ten years respectively. For the three pre-limits Senate Presidents the numbers were six, 10 and seven years. Just as importantly, their pre-leader tenure was generally quite lengthy, ranging from six to 14 years. Since the limits hit in 1998, the House has had three Speakers, each serving just two years and with an experience base of six years each. The first post-limits Senate President served two years after 20 years in the two chambers, the second served two years following six in the Senate and the third begins his 2003 presidency after four years of legislative experience.

The consequences? There is broad consensus that leaders, lame ducks from the get-go, are weaker. As soon as they are selected, the contest to succeed them begins, and thus the campaigns for leader slots are continuous. Contestants seek to build coalitions early and strengthen them further by wooing candidates during campaigns. Formal leaders are less important as commitments and votes are cued by the dynamics of the ongoing leadership contests. Predictability declines.

Committees

While committee membership has turned over at a rate apace to overall institutional membership change, chairmanship turnover jumped dramatically at first, then settled back. From 1993 to 1995, before term limits, five of the 10 House chairmanships and three Senate chairmanships changed hands. From 1997 to 1999, as the limits first hit, nine of ten House chairs and seven of ten Senate chairs were new. But as of 2003, eight of the eleven House chairs returned. Party control changed hands in the Senate in both 2000 and 2002, bringing in all new committee chairs. But of the 10 2003 Senate chairmen, seven have House experience and six of the 10 have previously chaired committees in one of the chambers.

The result? Term limits have brought a little more inexperience to House committees, in terms of both members and chairmen. But in the Senate, in spite of oscillation in party control, the limits have done little to shrink experience. Some observers report weakened bill screening and some procedural disorder, mostly in the House. But that view is not universal. Questions and answers during hearings reveal less familiarity with existing statutory law and constitutional bounds, a condition linked more to overall experiential decline than to chairmanship turnover.

The Lobby

The lobby has been impacted, but not in the manner anticipated by term limit opponents. The general consensus among members, lobbyists and others is that the overall influence of the lobby corps may have grown, but not a lot. The internal dynamics of the lobby have changed, however, with a "leveling" of the proverbial "playing field." Many long-term veteran lobbyists have seen their influence depart along with the legislative veterans with whom they had developed close ties. For newer and often younger lobbyists it has become a more open game.

Some observers argue that ethics have taken a hit. Departing legislators may be treated with less respect, there is some revisionist history with respect to decision understandings and policy, commitments are sometimes broken, candor as to both the pros and cons of bills has suffered. It appears, thus, that the impact of limits is more on the dynamics of the lobby operation than on the lobby's clout.

Staff

Here too, the worst nightmares of term limited opponents have not been realized. Colorado's legislators do not have individual staffers, save for scant hourly aids and office help for leaders. There is a session-only pool of clerical help and two major centralized nonpartisan staffing units. One does research and provides clerical help to committees and the other drafts the bills and amendments, reviews the statutes and advises the legislature on questions of law and constitutionality.

Before and after term limits these units were nonpartisan in both theory and fact. Their influence has grown slightly on matters of process, as they are asked more often to answer procedural questions. However, they have self-consciously backed away from the business of offering policy advice. With the vastly reduced reservoir of experience and policy history among members, the potential for more staff clout is clearly present. But so far that has not occurred.

Legislative Demographics

The predictions and hope by some term limit advocates that the departure of many long-term incumbents would pave the way to a higher proportion of women and minorities has proven illusory in Colorado. In the 1997–98 sessions, 36 percent of the membership was female and there were seven Hispanics and three African-Americans. During the immediate post-limits sessions in 1999–2000, the female percentage declined to 34. There were nine Hispanics and, again, three African-Americans. As the 2003 session began, 33 percent are women, eight are Hispanics and the African-American contingent has grown to five. So while the numbers have changed a bit, term limits have triggered nothing dramatic.

Budgeting

Term limits have had a clear impact on budgeting. Colorado has a six-member Joint Budget Committee (JBC) with its own staff of 15 analysts. Colorado has traditionally been a strong legislature state and the JBC has been its power center.

This is changing. In the two sessions before term limits hit, the six members had collectively logged 57 years of legislative experience and 28 years on the JBC itself. By the 2003 session those numbers had fallen to 27 in the legislature and just eight on the JBC. This has increased the influence of the JBC staff. Further, many of the new legislators come with scant understanding of the complex budget process and are unhappy with their own lack of influence.

Collectively then, term limits seem to have increased the staff influence on the JBC, and the JBC's influence within the legislature, and heightened members' discontent with their own lack of influence. It is a stretch to attribute these shifting dynamics to term limits completely, however, as recently adopted constitutional and statutory revenue and spending limitations are additional and important factors.

Institutional Power

The Colorado Legislature's policy making latitude has been significantly constrained in recent years, primarily by constitutional revenue limitations and expenditure earmarking. But term limits, too, have contributed. The impacts which are at least partially attributable to term limits include a power shift away from the legislature and toward the governor.

Other than the central staffing units, legislators have very little help while the governor has sizeable policy and budget staffs. The diminished levels of experience exacerbate the legislative staffing and informational disadvantages and the current governor has showed an unambiguous inclination to tilt the power balance in his direction.

Further, members facing term limits look for opportunities in other elective positions, or in the executive branch. In their search, the governor can help or hurt them and thus inclinations to defend the institution against the executive in circumstances of conflict sometimes diminish. Members in the governor's party face temptations to become party loyalists first, legislators second, and this can be especially the case for newer members who have yet to internalize the need to defend the legislature within the separation of powers context.

In summary, the general consensus is that term limits are one of several factors which have tilted the power balance away from the legislature and toward the executive. This is manifest in the budget process and in the establishment of the legislative agenda.

A Citizen Legislature?

Term limit proponents may have hoped for more of a "citizen legislature," but that's not what they got. Political ambition and careerism thrive. Virtually none of the limited members are returning to private life. Since the limits hit in 1998, members have run for the state senate, congressional seats, local offices, become lobbyists or moved to the executive branch. In 1998, and for the first time in 24 years, Colorado elected a Republican governor, Bill Owens, and Owens has filled much of his administration with former legislators. One count shows that of the 58 members ousted by the limits in the past three election cycles, just seven have not yet sought and/or acquired another office, appointment or political position.

The Summary Picture

In Colorado neither term limit advocates nor opponents were entirely correct with their predictions. Turnover has increased, but not dramatically. The overall experience level has dropped a good deal in the House, but not much in the Senate. There is some indication that committee work is less orderly and bill screening less effective, but not all observers agree. The lobby core is changed some, but neither the lobby nor the staff has experienced the predicted major jump in power. Anyone hoping that term limits would eradicate political ambition and careerism should be badly disappointed.

The major impacts which should be of concern to lovers of legislatures are the loss of institutional memory and the power tilt toward the executive. No longer can a lawmaker work an important issue over the course of a decade, slowly but surely refining policy, educating colleagues and the relevant public, and building a winning coalition. These "policy champions" are now booted by term limits and the search for effective remedial public policy is left to the less experienced. Inexperience also leaves members vulnerable to revised and re-revised versions of policy history.

And as to the separation of powers, a legislature with rapidly rotating leadership and continuous leadership campaigns, which meets just 120 days each year, whose members lack the individual staff which the governor possesses, and with many members who have little legislative experience and many more looking at the executive branch as one way to extend a political career, is vulnerable to executive dominance. Colorado's governor is not yet king, but the General Assembly is wise to guard its flank.

24 Playing the Political Game

KATE WILTROUT

12:50 P.M. Thursday

OVER FRIED CHICKEN, collard greens, biscuits, and sweet tea, eight aldermen and the mayor are gathering as a group for the first time in two weeks.

They sit at a broad mahogany table in the conference room on the second floor of City Hall, tucked between the mayor's office and the council's chambers. The room overlooks the intersection of Bull and Bay Streets and the shade of Johnson Square.

With the city attorney and the city manager at the table, space is tight. Other city employees, holding maps, spreadsheets, background documents, jockey with journalists and caterers for seats on the perimeter of the crowded room.

This isn't the actual city council meeting—that's next door in about an hour. The working lunch is a chance for council members to run through the agenda, feel out issues, and bring up concerns they've heard in the past two weeks.

The air-conditioned room is frosty—so cold some regulars come equipped with cardigans—but the tone of the conversation is warm.

Before business, aldermen ask about each other's spouses, their vacations, their grandchildren. At one end of the table, a few talk about being berated by residents furious about the latest round of property tax assessments.

The banana pudding phase of the meeting ends; business begins. An eight-page agenda is the conversation's rudder.

One alderman questions a $20,500 bid to replace a monument at Colonial Cemetery damaged when the city removed a tree. The topic sparks concerns from another alderman about vandalism at another city cemetery. A third mentions flooding problems there; they move on after noting that the council should set aside money for cemetery maintenance during the fall budget process.

Before the informal session adjourns, the council runs through a host of other issues; updates on the June flood, concerns about people popping covers off manholes and causing sewage backup, drivers who ignore the barricades on flooded streets. A few minutes before 2 P.M., the police department passes out a plan for a new pet ordinance. Debate is heated as time runs out and the council packs up and heads next door.

2:05 P.M. Thursday

The scene inside the city council chambers is a high school civics lesson come to life. Four aldermen take their seats to the right of the mayor, four to the left.

Being a council member isn't a lucrative activity—aldermen will earn $10,000 a year next term. The mayor will earn more—$42,000 annually. As the members settle into tall, swiveling leather chairs behind desks fitted with microphones and a switch that lights up their vote on the wall, the job seems to have its perks.

Council's chambers are impressive, from the waist-high, semicircular wooden railing that separates them from the public seats, which are sometimes occupied by students on field trips or official foreign guests, to the high ceilings, the large state and U.S. flags, the wooden parquet floor.

The laid-back, off-the-cuff tone at lunch switches into a more serious, official one as a visiting clergyman gives the invocation and everyone in the room recites the Pledge of Allegiance. Then it's down to the nuts and bolts of governing Savannah.

For the uninitiated, the meeting might seem strange and ritualistic. It's peppered with snippets of legislating lingo like "Do I hear a second?"

and "Motion to continue discussion in two weeks" and "Move to approve items 8.1 through 16, excepting item 11."

Governing is slow business, and though campaign talk is heavy on vision and issues, the daily grind is far less glamorous. The meeting has five basic parts: voting on alcoholic beverage licenses, zoning issues, traffic engineering reports, bids for city projects, and miscellaneous petitions.

By the time the meeting ends, the council has—among other things—voted to put a yield sign at a southside intersection and spend $106,664 on street sweeper parts, granted three new liquor licenses, approved the transfer of four cemetery plots, and delayed a decision on the broken monument in Colonial Cemetery.

After Hours

Welcome to the other half of an alderman's job, the half that has nothing to do with catered lunches and leather swivel chairs. Most aldermen say they spend about half their official time—which is supposed to be 10 hours a week but can sometimes run double that—responding to the citizens who put them in office.

A constituent is calling an alderman to complain about a bad pothole in front of his house. He's called the city's traffic engineering department but thinks he got a runaround. Could he make a call and try to speed up the process? He grabs a pen, writes down the name and address, and says he'll call the department in the morning.

Council members receive calls of all kinds. One constituent called her alderman after she inherited some land she didn't have any real use for. Then she learned she had to pay taxes on it that she couldn't afford. Was there anything he could do to help?

The alderman asks some questions. Where is the property? She tells him it's near a neighborhood playground. He has an idea. Would she like to deed the property to the city to expand the playground? That way, kids would get a bigger sandbox, the city would get the property, and the woman wouldn't have to pay any property taxes on it. A few weeks later, the item is one of the many the council approves at its bimonthly meeting.

25 Being a Township Trustee Isn't a White-Collar Job

BRIAN WILLIAMS

CLARK COUNTY'S [Ohio] 10 townships each have three elected trustees and an elected clerk, but aside from those four officials, township payrolls vary greatly. Some townships, such as Springfield Township, have as many as eight full-time workers to patch roads, pick up brush, and mow grass at cemeteries. But some less-populous townships do not have full-time workers.

MOOREFIELD TOWNSHIP   Population: 10,000. Budget: $1 million. Full-time Employees: Two. Fire and Rescue Volunteers: 50. Fire Stations: Two. Miles of Roads: 52.

Moorefield Township does not have quite the urban proximity of Springfield Township, but it has a similar diversity. It has public lands (Buck Creek State Park), industry (most notably Navistar's assembly plant), farms, and a city-sized residential subdivision (Northridge). Of the 10,000 township residents, 7,000 live in Northridge, [primarily a housing area for Navistar workers].

Trustees don't do road repairs themselves, but their position is more of a shirtsleeves than strictly a white-collar job. On a . . . [spring weekend day in 1990], Township President Robert Mounts was on hand as volunteers in one of the township's fire trucks placed a decoy owl in a North-ridge tree to keep away blackbirds that descend upon the neighborhood. "Anything in the township that we can help a resident with, we try to do," Mounts said. That includes going to bat for township homeowners who don't want their property annexed by [the nearby city of Springfield]. Township clerk Gayle Arthur said Moorefield is not involved as regularly as Springfield Township in annexation disputes with the city [of Springfield], but takes a stand in particular cases if a resident requests help.

"Any township doesn't like annexation," Mounts said. "The services [the city] offers do not compete with the township. We have more of a personalized service, and a smaller government. We do not like annexation."

The services in Moorefield Township, in addition to installing decoy owls, include road maintenance and leaf and brush pickup. Residents who trim trees and want the branches hauled away can tell the township to do it. But they do not need to call to have maintenance crews . . . remove leaves from the roadside.

"Our main thrust is to take care of our roads and keep our fire and ambulance services at a good level,"Arthur said. "We have a very dedicated and highly trained fire staff and emergency medical staff."

Mounts said Moorefield Township officials have no major new goals for the coming year, but want to "maintain the service, and the quality of work we do in the township."

HARMONY TOWNSHIP   Population: 3,236, including [the village of] South Vienna. Budget: $225,000. Full-time Employees: None. Fire and Rescue Volunteers: 45. Fire Stations: One. Miles of Roads: 33.5.

The term "politician" usually evokes images of legislators wearing three-piece suits while bickering over legal details or posing in photo opportunities. A good photo opportunity might be an elected official getting his hands dirty doing an honest day's work, like [Harmony Township president] Porter Gardner and his fellow Harmony Township trustees do. "We do the roads ourselves," he said. "We do it to have something to do. And it makes us save on funds."

Harmony Township has no full-time employees. With [about] 34 miles of roads and a budget of less than a quarter million dollars, saving on funds is important. And that can mean busy days for part-time trustees who are always on call for their constituents. "We try to resurface one-third of these roads every year," said Gardner. But narrow roads in rural townships don't get expensive asphalt paving. The roads are chipped and sealed—pea gravel spread over tar. Trustees don't do all the work themselves, of course. They hire contractors for the bigger jobs. "We're supposed to get some money from Issue 2 to widen New Love Rd. from the [Conrail] tracks north to U.S. 40," he said. "That's about the only project for this year we have now."

Trustees are also responsible for maintaining five cemeteries. That makes for a lot of work in the summer, so they hire part-time workers to help with mowing.

Like his counterparts in other townships, Gardner is proud of the local firefighters. The 45 fire and emergency volunteers work out of the township-run fire station in South Vienna.

Among other concerns of trustees are reduction of waste and finding new landfill space for the area's trash. "I don't know what the answer is, but something has to be done," Gardner said. He said illegal dumping in Harmony Township "isn't too serious yet, but it's getting worse."

And like farmers and officials in neighboring Madison Township, he is hoping the Grand Trunk Western Railroad line near the South Charleston Landmark grain elevator can be preserved so rail shipping will still be available to farmers in the eastern part of Clark County.

MADISON TOWNSHIP   Population: 2,700 [including the village of South Charleston]. Budget: $160,000. Full-time Employees: None. Fire and Rescue Volunteers: 25 fire, 7 township rescue volunteers. Fire Stations: One. Miles of Road: 24.2.

In Madison Township, South Charleston is a metropolis. Other than that single village, the township is entirely rural. Its $160,000 budget is the smallest among Clark County's 10 townships, and its 24.2 miles of local roads is fewer than any township except Pleasant.

"We usually try to clean up some of the berms," said C. David Sprague, the township vice president. "Last year we did two miles [on each side] to let excess water get off the roads."

Madison Township, like Harmony Township to the north, has no full-time employees, which means trustees drive dump trucks and wield shovels. They replace signs, clean culverts, and inspect the roads for chuckholes. They hire contractors for plowing, mowing, and road resurfacing. Sprague said the township has applied for state Issue 2 funds to resurface Clifton Rd., but does not know yet if the project will be approved.

Township Clerk Vicki Hines said the township gets a little bit of help on some maintenance projects. Each spring, the South Charleston Baseball Commission organizes a fundraising project in which young athletes pick up trash along some of the county roads. That helps clean up some of the remnants of illegal dumps of the sort that also plague other townships. She said one of the township's goals this year is to upgrade the township's rescue vehicle and fire contract.

Sprague explained that Madison Township contracts with an individual private fire company for fire protection, and pays for it through the township fire levy. He said the township would like to see a few additional volunteers in the company. "We've lost some people," he said. "The state is requiring more and more hours of training. [Firefighters] have to go back and be recertified every three years. We try to reimburse them for mileage to training sessions." He said recruiting is done by handbills, phone solicitation, and notices on a bulletin board at the South Charleston library.

In a township where farming is the major business, the threatened loss of rail service to the Landmark grain elevator at South Charleston is a major concern.

"It's on the minds of everybody," Sprague said. "If we lose that rail, that means everything has got to be trucked. It'll cost the farmers a lot of money—farmers in Madison, Green, Harmony, Springfield, and other townships, too."

Clark County Commissioners have earmarked $200,000 as their contribution toward a public-private consortium to buy the section of the Grand Trunk Western Railroad between [the city of] Springfield and [the village of] Washington Court House. The group, which includes grain shippers, Clark and Fayette counties, and the Ohio Department of Transportation, hopes [to] buy the line if the railroad is allowed to abandon it.

PLEASANT TOWNSHIP   Population: 2,500. Budget: $245,000. Full-time Employees: Two. Fire and Rescue Volunteers: 25. Fire Stations: One. Miles of Roads: 18.75.

Pleasant Township president David Locke, who has been a trustee for about 10 years, is the only veteran on a board that added newcomers Dana Bumgardner and Dick Gaus after the November [1989] election. But he sees no continuity problem on the board.

"We've got two new trustees this year," he said. "I think we're making the right decisions and meeting the needs of the community." Most of the needs are the same as last year's.

"We continually improve and update our road system," he said. "Our road budget is low, but we do a good job according to what we have. We chip and seal (resurface) three to five miles every year, so every road is redone every five years. That's our goal."

He said the township plans to seek some state Issue 2 money for other road projects. "And we want to try and strengthen, maintain, and improve our fire department," he said. "We want to keep these people up with necessary equipment."

Like trustees all over the county, Locke and his fellow members want to see an integrated county policy for trash reduction and disposal. "It should be on the mind of everybody in the county," he said. "It's going to have to take some hardcore decisions in the next few years. We are discovering an increase in people just throwing trash out on the road— used furniture and appliances dumped along gravel roads. On all of our roads, we get trash, pop bottles thrown out."

Locke said the township's two employees are vigilant about ordinary litter, as well as larger illegal dumpsites. He said they walk the roadsides looking for trash each time they mow in the summer.

Pleasant Township's only other workers are the 25 volunteers at the Catawba-Pleasant fire station. "They're doing a fantastic job," Locke said. But he acknowledges that keeping up staffing levels "is a continual problem." Given the increasing state standards that firefighters must meet, "it gives you a good feeling about these volunteers." Locke said they are always recruiting new volunteers by word of mouth or placing notices on local bulletin boards.

PART EIGHT

BUREAUCRACY,
BUREAUCRATS, AND
ADMINISTRATORS

The principal function of bureaucracy is the implementation of public policy. A bureaucracy is composed of both appointed officials and permanent career civil servants who usually obtain their position through a system of merit employment, which uses performance and training criteria for promotion and hiring. The merit system has replaced the old patronage, or spoils system in most states and cities, although remnants of it hang on across the country.[1] Even though most people would prefer that civil servants be hired and promoted on the basis of merit, considerable criticism has been leveled against the merit systems in the last few decades. The critics allege that the criteria used for merit are biased against women and minorities, and that once hired, it is practically impossible to fire unproductive and ineffective civil servants. Moreover, the ability of elected executives to push their policy agendas rests greatly on having key supporters appointed to policymaking and implementation positions in bureaucracy. Consequently, there is always a tension between those who favor expanded merit systems versus those who favor greater patronage opportunities.

Related to the complaint about the difficulty in firing poor employees due to their merit protections, a few states have ventured into controversial territory by choosing to eliminate all or most merit protection for civil servants. The first state to do this was Georgia when in 1996 the state legislature there passed, and Governor Zell Miller signed, SB 635 which stipulated that after July 1, 1996, all employees hired by the state will not have civil service protection. They can be promoted, transferred, or demoted instantly, and their raises are based on performance only. While the new hires would be offered the same basic benefit package, their terms of employment would be radically different than previous hires in that they would essentially be "at will" employees. Five years later, the state of Florida pursued a similar policy with the passage of the "Service First" law which put into effect a massive overhaul of its civil service system characterized by three key changes: 1) the elimination of seniority, 2) the creation of a large class of positions that would no longer have civil service protection, and 3) the establishment of a system-wide reclassification of positions with regard to pay and responsibilities. The tension between patronage and merit continues to present challenges to state and local governments as they struggle to develop administrative systems that are responsive to policy changes, but at the same time take advantage of the expertise that bureaucrats bring to their jobs.

A common complaint by citizens is that bureaucracy and bureaucrats are inefficient and unproductive, and reformers are constantly proposing ways to change state and local governments in order to make them more efficient and responsive to citizens. Examples include the privatization of public services, the creation of charter agencies that are given freer rein to make service delivery decisions by being released from red tape, and the use of technology to enhance citizen participation and communication. Our first article takes up one of these examples of reform—the use of charter agencies in Iowa. You'll want to pay particular attention to what is meant by the term "charter agency" as it is being touted quite positively these days as a successful innovative reform to state and local bureaucracy.

Powerful demographic changes point to an impending crisis: Many government positions are being vacated by baby-boom retirees and not enough younger workers are emerging to replace them. As our final article details, this is particularly true at the local level, and in rural areas especially.

Note

1.   Raymond Wolfinger, "Why Political Machines Have Not Withered Away and Other Revisionist Thoughts," *Journal of Politics* 34 (May,1972): 365–398.

Questions for Review and Discussion

8.1   What do think about the relative effort to do away with civil service merit protection? What are the pros and cons of having patronage versus merit systems of employment for government agencies?

8.2   What is a charter agency? Is this a good idea? Can you think of any potential problems with creating a greater number of these types of agencies across the states?

8.3   Have you thought of state or local government service as a possible career option? Go to *www.localintern.org* to find out more about what the International City/County Management Association (ICMA) is doing to encourage the next generation of local government managers, and how you might be able to pursue a career in local government.

26 Beyond Bureaucracy with Charter Agencies

JIM CHRISINGER

BABAK ARMAJANI

A DEER AND A DEPARTMENT OF CORRECTIONS CAR met on a winding southern Iowa road. Neither survived. Corrections would have waited 15 months for a replacement vehicle following the normal procurement procedure. Reclassifying a corrections position through the personnel system usually took a couple of months. But because the Department of Corrections is an Iowa Charter Agency, they picked up a new car in less than two weeks and they turned around a reclassification in a few days.

What's going on here?

Iowa is testing the hypothesis that state agencies can accomplish more for the people they serve if they can focus more effort on achieving results and less on complying with rules. Put another way, Iowa is exploring the trade-off between getting something done and making sure we do nothing wrong.

A New Deal

Four years of budget cuts sent Iowa through the usual paces: across-the-board cuts, early retirement incentives, top-to-bottom reviews, reorganizations and layoffs. While these moves kept the budget balanced,

Gov. Tom Vilsack and Lt. Gov. Sally Pederson realized that they would not solve the structural imbalance. "Government as usual" is simply not sustainable in this fiscal and political climate. In response, the Iowa Reinvention Partnership hatched the idea of charter agencies and asked for volunteers.

How are charter agencies different? Charter agencies are all about achieving results for Iowans. Easy to say. But agency directors who put results first know they will encounter barriers in the form of the state's administrative systems. These systems were not designed to achieve results; they exist to minimize risk, at the expense of innovation. Procuring cars and reclassifying positions are but two good examples. Here's another: seven separate signatures required for a travel authorization ironically means no one actually feels accountable for the decision.

So in addition to putting results front and center, charter agencies take on bureaucracy's web of rules. Government's usual "must follow the rules above all else" mentality both frustrates the public and stifles those working in government.

The charter agency invitation was (1) spend less time and money on paperwork and low-value-added rule compliance, so you can (2) redirect that energy into innovation to achieve the results Iowans most value.

Instead of relying on the Governor's Office and the Department of Management to drive change and improvement, the charter agency deal would kindle ongoing improvement from within each agency. The Governor's Office and Management change roles, shifting from command and control to become enablers and barrier busters (see text box).

The main "central control" agencies also contributed to the flexibilities, allowing charter agencies to:

Purchase goods and services outside General Services contracts, provided the charter agency can document the cost benefit, including authority to purchase travel tickets directly instead of using the state's travel contractor;

Access technical assistance from experts on innovation and public entrepreneurship at Public Strategies Group, at no charge;

Retain 80 percent of all new entrepreneurial revenues generated; and

Utilize streamlined contracting requirements for capital projects.

In more detail, here is the Iowa charter agency "deal" that was offered to all Iowa agencies, except Management and Administrative Services. Charter agencies commit to:

- Produce measurable benefits—and improvements in those benefits—for the people they serve.

- Help close the current years budget gap, through contributed savings or additional revenues. Additional revenues should be entrepreneurially achieved, not raised through new taxes or fees. Charter agencies must collectively come up with at least $15 million each year.

In return, charter agency enacting legislation provides:

1. Charter agency directors may stand in the shoes of the director of administrative services to "exercise the authority granted to the department of administrative services" in three areas: "personnel management concerning employees of the charter agency," "the physical resources of the state" and "information technology."

2. Charter agency directors may "waive any personnel rule," "waive any administrative rule regarding procurement, fleet management, printing and copying, or maintenance of buildings and grounds" and "waive any administrative rule regarding the acquisition and use of information technology."

3. Charter agencies are exempted from required Executive Council approval for out-of-state travel, convention attendance, and professional organization memberships.

4. Charter agencies may retain the proceeds of capital asset sales.

5. Charter agencies may retain half of year-end appropriation balances.

6. The governor may authorize a bonus for a charter agency director of up to 50 percent of the director's salary. Similarly, a charter agency director may authorize employee bonuses of up to 50 percent of the amount of the director's salary.

7. During the period of FY04 through FY06, charter agencies are exempt from mandatory across-the-board budget cuts.

8. Charter agencies are not subject to FTE caps.

9. Charter agencies are eligible for part of the $3 million Charter Agency Grant Fund to foster innovation.

Also, charter agencies are exempted from many requirements. For example, charter agencies no longer need to:

TABLE 1 Iowa Charter Agencies Savings and Revenue Reporting, FY 2004

Department	Expenditure reduction commitment	Actual expenditure reduction	Revenue increase commitment	Actual revenue increase	Total FY 2004 commitments	Actual FY 2004 total	FY 2005 commitments
Human Services	$1,000,000	$1,000,000	...	...	$1,000,000	$1,000,000	$1,000,000
Corrections	500,000	500,000	...	...	500,000	500,000	500,000
Natural Resources	50,000	50,000	150,000	154,665	200,000	204,665	300,000
Revenue	...	683,073	1,000,000	633,705	1,000,000	1,316,778	1,500,000
Veterans Home	...	...	1,300,000	1,300,000	1,300,000	1,300,000	1,300,000
Alcoholic Beverages Division	...	...	1,250,000	9,788,598	1,250,000	9,788,598	5,000,000
Uncommitted Grant Funds	1,750,000	...	...	...	1,750,000	...	0
Lottery	...	...	8,000,000	8,400,000	8,000,000	8,400,000	10,990,000
All Departments Total	...	...	8,000,000	8,400,000	15,000,000	22,510,041	20,500,000

File travel claims when expenses are paid by an outside entity;

Submit pre-contract questionnaires for contracts valued at $1,000 or less; or

Submit pre-contract questionnaires for corporate or governmental vendors, provided they obtain the information needed to meet audit requirements.

Finally, Gov. Vilsack, Lt. Gov. Pederson, and Department of Management Director Cynthia Eisenhauer made their support unequivocally clear.

Despite all of the above, many directors and staff remained skeptical. Many did not want to gamble on the new deal because they were unsure it was "real." Some felt they could not justify the fiscal obligation. Others had not made transformation into a results-based organization a priority.

But six directors, who were running into roadblocks on the road to results, saw enough potential to literally pay for charter status with budget cuts or new revenue contributions. They perceived net value.

Jeff Vonk, director of the Department of Natural Resources (DNR), was already pushing entrepreneurship and change, challenging his department to be a "world-class organization." Charter agencies fit naturally with his vision. In addition to the DNR, five others stepped forward in July of 2003: the Departments of Corrections, Human Services, and Revenue, the Alcoholic Beverages Division of the Department of Commerce, and the Iowa Veterans Home. The Iowa Lottery has its own, similar new deal.

All commitments to the new deal are documented in the charter agency legislation and in annual Charter Agency Agreements for each agency, negotiated and signed by the agency director and governor. Each agreement leads with a list of the agency's specific and quantified performance goals and special projects. The agreements also include a list of flexibilities, the fiscal obligation and other terms.

Note that charter agency status does not infringe on collective bargaining agreements. Charter agencies have worked successfully with our unions as they exercised flexibilities that touched union interests. For example, the Department of Revenue used their flexibility to rehire a retiree at a higher salary because the person had recently become a CPA. Union approval was needed, and obtained after a good discussion.

So Far, So Good

If the new deal is ultimately about better results for Iowans and less bureaucracy for agencies, the first round of reporting is positive. Achievements include:

Reduced turnaround time for air quality construction permits from 62 to six days; for wastewater construction permits from 28 months to 4.5 months, both without sacrificing environmental quality;

Reduced stays in Child Welfare shelter care by 20 percent, or 10 days;

Increased the number of children with health coverage by 12 percent this year;

Improved the rate of income tax returns filed electronically from 55 percent to 63 percent, first nationally;

Reduced the failure rate for probations by 17 percent;

Reduced the number of Veterans Home residents who have moderate to severe pain from 18.5 percent to 9 percent;

Provided good work experiences for 50 percent more women inmates than before charter agencies;

Saved $200,000 by developing a new pharmaceutical bidding process and negotiating drug costs;

Replaced that wrecked car in two weeks, instead of 15 months;

Saved $38,281 by bringing contracted work back in;

Saved money on air tickets, e.g. Des Moines–San Antonio for $444 instead of $656;

Eliminated the M-40 form, speeding intern hiring from 10 days to one day;

Waived an administrative rule to correct a pay equity mistake; and

Reduced turnaround times on personnel actions from months to days.

These results benefit Iowans. They also lift morale inside government. "It's exciting to be part of an effort that focuses on results and enables us to report those results to a legislative oversight committee that wants to hear from us," reports Jim Elliott, the charter agency staff lead at the Veterans Home. DNR Deputy Director Liz Christiansen adds, "We have been able to eliminate paperwork and undertake entrepreneurial efforts. And I feel like we're just getting started."

Bill Gardam of the Department of Human Services points to employees' ability to make their own travel reservations as not only resulting in lower costs, but also enabling "employees to have a personal life because now they can better fit their work travel into the rest of their lives." The bottom line, as the Department of Revenue's Cindy Morton puts it, is that charter agencies "show that this administration is committed to results for Iowans."

State budget savings and revenue contributions for FY04 totaled more than $22 million, $7 million more than the $15 million target. Most of the $22 million came from increased revenues, especially from the Alcoholic Beverages Division. Charter flexibilities sparked their entrepreneurial spirit. One of their first and most productive moves was to switch from a uniform markup on their products to variable pricing, which increased revenues without significantly increasing alcohol consumption. The Division's leader, Lynn Walding, says charter agencies "helped us be creative. It also helped me implement ideas I've had for a long time, especially to pursue the business side of our organization. It prompted us to go the extra mile."

Charter Agencies are also helping agencies absorb budget cuts, in addition to benefiting the General Fund. "Cost savings ideas are percolating up now; these will save us money," observes Corrections' Deputy Director John Baldwin.

Revenue's Morton put it this way, "As a charter agency, we are able to promote out-of-the-box thinking and then act on it." Baldwin also appreciates that his agency now has "more control over what we do, especially purchasing and classifications. Our agency works more smoothly when we don't have to go through the bureaucratic process. We now have choice." DNR's Christiansen echoed this benefit, appreciating "more of a sense of control over our day-to-day activities."

The achievements above were expected, at least hoped for. But charter agency staff also described the unexpected. They reported a liberating and energizing effect beyond specific flexibilities. For example:

> Corrections is in discussions with a local casino/racetrack and the Animal Rescue League to create two thoroughbred retirement farms to provide excellent work opportunities and rehabilitation for inmates and more humane treatment for the horses.

> The Veterans Home and Corrections are partnering to turn an old kitchen area into an outpatient clinic.

Neither of these actions was impossible pre-charter, but charter spark and momentum are making them happen.

In interviews for this article, many of the agencies focused on the connection between creativity and charter agency status. "We want to use charter agencies to tap into the creativity of our people," asserts Liz Christiansen. "Charter agency status has given us an opportunity to try new ideas, share planning and strategies with other charter agencies, and to promote innovation. It has also given us recognition, that we are a proactive department that seeks ways to improve," according to Jim Elliott of the Veterans Home. Lynn Walding also noted the impact of the spotlight on charter agencies, "Encouragement breeds enthusiasm and improvement."

The charter agency grant fund has also fostered improvements. Walding notes that "in the past, we would have to go to the legislature to get improvement money. This freedom [through the grant fund] will allow us to provide better service to customers: a new licensing system, automated order ehtry, and tax payments, all online. So we can redirect staff, reduce operating expenses, and provide better services."

Grant money enabled DNR to create an internal revolving fund to be a self-lender for future improvements. Liz Christiansen also reports "many new suggestions to save money" that the revolving fund can enable.

When asked now "what's the first word that comes to mind when you think of Charter Agencies?" the lead charter agency staffers replied with: proactive, innovation, opportunity, flexibility and potential.

Overcoming Inertia

For all the promising results, the charter agency concept still faces barriers. A few in Iowa government are still wondering whether the new deal will last. Most are believers now, however. The big conversion happened in October 2003, when a reduced revenue forecast triggered a 2.5-percent across-the-board cut—part of the charter arrangement was that these agencies would be exempt from any across-the-board cuts. Agencies held their breaths, assuming that the governor—or later the legislature—might ask them to take their share of the cut anyway. They did not, which meant that all the other agencies took a larger hit than they would have if the cut had been shared among all agencies. From then on, charter agencies knew the new deal was real.

Although the law gives charter agencies sweeping authority, agency staff approached this opportunity gingerly. They have seen prior experiments fail. They learned their craft in government's "above all, do not make a mistake" culture. As one deputy put it, "you're wondering about how far you're allowed to go and what the consequences may be for testing the boundaries." Charter agency staff are also genuinely concerned about potentially causing harm to their agency and themselves by rashly acting in an area without much experience. But as they try on their new powers, they are appreciating the results. Walding reports that his people "were initially resistant but are now excited." And so far at least, there have been no pitfalls. This fact encourages everyone to take the next step.

The Department of Human Service's Bill Gardam suggests that charter authority and flexibilities would be better utilized if agencies had "more clarity on abilities and expectations." Jim Elliott also noted, "a challenge for us was educating the staff on the benefits that would offset the portion of the appropriation that was given back. We needed to develop strategies to deal with the loss of funds." Baldwin concurred, "We need to spend more time educating staff as to the power, flexibilities, and possibilities."

Iowa's Department of Administrative Services "owns" many of the rules and policies being tested by charter agencies. DAS staff have been cooperative and supportive, while also cautioning charter agencies about possible problems. Charter agencies present an opportunity for DAS to transform part of its role from "control" mode to "support and guide."

Where Next?

Ultimately, this experiment poses the question of whether all agencies should become charter agencies. Should this form of doing business be adopted across state government? Iowa is not yet ready to answer. These changes are big and new enough that it will take some time for all involved to reach a comfort level. "Slowly, people are accepting charter agencies for what they are. With time, charter agency status will be even more useful," Baldwin predicts.

Legislators' reactions have been positive. When told by the Department of Corrections about replacing the car in two weeks instead of 15 months, one representative's first question was about the price paid. The answer was that the price was the same, because either way it was purchased off the same high-volume contract. The legislator's next comment was, "maybe all agencies should be purchasing their cars this way."

For now, Management is working with charter agencies to explore the potential and limits of the current pilot. All agree that there is more potential than is being realized. Gardam reports that DHS is continuing to work to "get everybody on board, get our people to think creatively, and then implement their ideas."

"The more trust they are willing to put into the hands of the employees, the greater the potential for success and the better the results for Iowans," the Veterans Home's Jim Elliott concluded.

The new deal is changing minds in charter agencies. As the cynicism fades and staff realize that the new deal is real, they are becoming more creative, assertive, entrepreneurial, and even excited. Iowans benefit.

27 Does Age Matter? Local Governments in the Post-Baby Boom Era

TODD TUCKER

IN THE UNITED STATES TODAY, approximately 12 percent of the population is over the age of 65. By 2010, 10,000 Americans will turn 65 every day. U.S. Census Bureau mid-range estimates for the year 2030 are that 20 percent of the U.S. population will be 65 years of age or older. This projection is likely underestimated, however, because of the population's increased longevity.[1]

This ballooning population of eligible retirees will result in service changes across the nation. Although it is generally understood that demographic changes will create an increased demand for aging services, there is greater uncertainty about how an aging population might affect local governments. This article, which reflects the results of a research project conducted at the University of Colorado in 2006 titled *Local Government in the Post-Baby Boom Era,* presents the potential effects of an aging population on county governments along the Front Range of Colorado.

Variables of Aging

Five indicators were measured to determine the potential impact of the aging population: (1) the percentage of elderly individuals as part of the population projected to the year 2030, (2) the percentage of the county government workforce eligible for retirement, (3) the anticipated service demand by county department or division, (4) the anticipated level of attrition for the county government workforce by department or division, and (5) employee training, development, and recruitment programs and priorities.

After assessment of these indicators, it was determined that rural counties will experience the greatest change in age distribution and, consequently, the greatest challenges in meeting service and labor demands (see Figure 1). These projections are due to the expected percentage of elderly, a low or negative rate of population growth, increased longevity, a limited population pool to draw from, and a trend for the aging and elderly to remain in their existing homes as long as possible. Also, rural counties do not always provide their employees with adequate development opportunities to prepare them for the challenges of the future. These rural counties, however, are not alone.

The Colorado Example

Currently, most counties in Colorado have an elderly population that constitutes less than 10 percent of the population. By 2030, however,

FIGURE 1   Percentage of Population Age 65 and Older for Selected Populations, 2002, 2010, 2020, and 2030

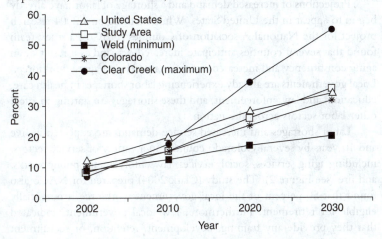

Source: U. S. Census Bureau, 2005. Note: Projections 2010 through 2030 assume the 2001–2004 rate of population change remains constant and mortality at 85 years of age.

the average percentage of elderly within the 10 counties along the Front Range that were studied will be nearly double the U.S. census national estimate of 20 percent. In some instances, as much as 55 percent of the county population will be age 65 or older.

The implication of a change from 10 percent to 30 to 55 percent of a county population over the age of 65 is significant, particularly in rural counties with small and dispersed populations, such as Clear Creek County, Colorado. For counties that are experiencing a high rate of population growth, such as in parts of Weld County, Colorado, the impacts of an aging constituency and nation may be less dramatic because younger people have been the primary driver of continued growth, but even fast-growing counties will experience challenges related to service increases for the elderly and worker shortages.

Furthermore, high rates of population growth may not result in a balance in the age distribution in Colorado counties because Colorado is a destination for mobile retirees.[2] Thus, projections for the percentage of elderly for all counties in Colorado could well be low. Similar projections also indicate that the census mortality estimates for those aged 65 and older are high.

While there are advantages to continued growth and an increasing population of retirees, there will also be challenges for local governments and businesses, including potential increases in demands for services for the elderly, shortages of skilled labor, and reductions in revenues and federal funding assistance for local governments.

Projections of increased demand and a shortage of labor have already begun to appear in the United States. While working on a 2004 research project for the National Association of Counties (NACo), a study team found that several counties anticipate increased demand as a result of an aging constituency and increased attrition caused by an aging workforce.[3] Local governments are already experiencing labor shortages in health care, education, and law enforcement, and these shortages are starting to affect other labor sectors across the nation.

Labor shortages and increased service demands are expected in five and 10 years by several Colorado counties in a variety of service sectors, including aging services, social services, law enforcement, public works, and fire (see Figure 2). The study (Clark 2004) prepared for NACo also found that 50 percent of the local government workforce is potentially eligible for retirement. Furthermore, few local governments indicated that they provide any training, development, retention, or recruitment programs for their more junior employees.

Although not the focus of this Colorado case study, it was observed

FIGURE 2   Percentage of County Departments in the Front Range of Colorado That Expect Workforce Shortages and Increased Service Demand in Five and 10 Years

Department	Workforce shortages		Increase in service demand	
	In five years (%)	In 10 years (%)	In five years (%)	In 10 years (%)
Sheriff	43	29	43	43
Social services	43	14	86	43
Public works	43	43	29	0
Fire	14	43	43	14
Revenue and taxation	14	43	14	14
Court system	14	43	14	14
Transportation	14	14	57	29
Utilities	14	29	29	14
Aging services	14	14	100	57

that global shifts in demographics will also affect the revenue stream for the federal government in the United States, which will result in funding reductions for local governments. In other words, as the global population ages, particularly in the industrialized nations of North America, Europe, and much of Asia, global production will decline.[4] This trend will impact the global economy adversely.

The demand for qualified workers also will increase as nations struggle to maintain historic productivity levels and provide services for their populations. If this observation is realized, revenue allocations and reductions will dilute government resources around the globe.

Another study prepared for NACo shows that a shortage of skilled labor in the United States has affected efforts to promote new economic development and the expansion of an existing economic base in the private sector.[5] Reductions in the economic base can result in a leveling or reduction in revenues for local governments by affecting sales tax returns and property valuations. Studies also suggest that to maintain historic levels of economic productivity and domestic output, the U.S. workforce will have to increase by 58 million during the next 30 years.[6]

These studies further indicate that the number of available workers will increase by less than half that amount. In addition to the short supply of labor, the education and skills necessary to maintain historic levels of productivity are also in doubt, exacerbating the labor and revenue deficit.[7]

Furthermore, although 76 million young people will be moving into the U.S. workforce over the next 20 years, the longevity of earlier generations with a combined population of 191 million will increase the elderly dependency ratio (the number of working-age individuals compared with the number of retirees) from the current level of 5 to 1 to a level in 2030 of 2.6 to 1.

In other words, by 2030, there will be 2.6 people between 15 and 64 for every person over the age of 65; and in some industrialized nations this ratio will be reduced to nearly 1 to 1. This level has changed significantly since the 1960s, when the number of workers to retirees was 7 to 1 in the United States. What's more, this figure does not include the child dependency ratio that further reduces the number of workers to nonworkers. As a result of the changing demographics caused by increased health and longevity and the increased cost of health care, it is expected that there will not be enough workers in the generations succeeding the baby boomers to adequately fund and provide services or to meet historic productivity levels.[8]

Consequently, the burden of welfare programs will increase for these future workers; and unless the productivity of the average worker can increase significantly over the next 20 years, the overall productivity output in the United States and other industrialized nations will decline as there will not be enough qualified labor to meet the demand.

The effects of a decline in productivity will include reductions in revenues, which in turn create fiscal challenges for local governments. These fiscal challenges could lead to significant social implications, including potential cuts to Medicare and Medicaid. Although the National Governors Association is working to limit federal cuts to Medicare and Medicaid,[9] expert testimony before Congress indicates that the financial burden for these programs combined with debt service payments will unduly constrain the federal budget over the next 10 to 20 years.[10]

As a result of these growing budgetary constraints, funding for these programs will likely shift from the federal government to state and local governments, stretching already thin budgets.

Challenges

Local governments will confront generational and fiscal challenges as the global and national populations age. These challenges will increase over time and across the nation. For Colorado, the challenge may be greater than in other parts of the country because of the projected increase of elderly residents, which is expected to be nearly double the projected national average of elderly for 2030. So, despite improved health and longevity, labor and funding resources will be diluted as the population continues to mature locally, nationally, and globally. Therefore, to maintain historic levels of domestic productivity, the competition for skilled labor will be even greater, with an ever-dwindling pool of qualified applicants to draw from in Colorado and across the country.

In the short term, some labor supply and economic impacts may be softened by delayed retirement and a greater participation in the workforce by women and immigrants or by increased use of aging employees as volunteers or as part-time or outsourced employees. However, the size and projected longevity of those aged 65 and older will result in service demands that stretch the country's ability to meet the need, which, in turn, will affect local government in Colorado.

Effects will be felt in the form of slower economic growth; a lower standard of living and persistent structural unemployment for the elderly, the unskilled, and minority groups; income redistribution caused by the purchase of foreign goods and services; further erosion of the industrial base caused by a limited pool of skilled labor; wage-push inflation for the available skilled labor; and reductions in federal funding assistance for local governments.[11]

Local Government Action

In addition to the challenges described above, most local governments do not appear to be addressing or adapting to generational differences in work values and service expectations or implementing competitive programs equally among the generations for employee retention, job satisfaction, and employee development. Should the predictions of slower economic growth come to pass, local governments will contend with reductions in revenues from sales tax and other funding sources, including reductions in assistance from the federal government as the demand for services increases. Thus, local governments will be required to do more with much less, and it is critical that local governments partner with their employees to ensure adequate service provision and retain or develop critical skills.

Fortunately, a few county governments in Colorado and in other areas have begun to implement measures to address attrition, labor shortages, skills deficits, and increases in service demands. Some local governments, for example, are crossing political boundaries to form partnerships and aggregate services for the elderly; one example is Adams County, Colorado, which also services portions of Arapahoe County through its Senior Hub program. Still other governments, such as Ajo, Arizona, with its arts and culture program, are combining compatible services between the elderly and youth. Yet more must be done.

Local governments can also reduce service and contact demands as they create or expand on self-service systems to include online bill payments or payment assistance, service scheduling for such elder care assistance as meals-on-wheels, and more online resources and information, like applying for government assistance or unemployment insurance. They can even expand on such remote monitoring systems as photo radar, site security, and computerized systems for acquiring building permits. In addition, new partnerships with surrounding jurisdictions, agencies, and nonprofit organizations or even the privatization of some services may be useful for meeting service demands and cutting aggregate costs.

Perhaps local governments can also borrow concepts from the private sector for employee retention and morale and create programs such as flextime, job sharing, or hiring retirees back part time or as consultants in order to retain aging workers. It also will be increasingly important to provide opportunities for junior workers to participate in decision making and mentoring and development programs.

Boulder County, Colorado, for example, has developed a year-long employee leadership program called the Public Service Institute to provide training in self-efficacy and organizational awareness. Encouraging, retaining, developing, and training existing employees in such a manner may offset the impacts of an aging population by providing current employees with the skill sets, resources, and knowledge necessary to fill the gaps.[12]

Current literature focuses primarily on programs to retain retiring employees and to enhance youth development. It is rare to find articles or studies of government employers that place equal emphasis on providing senior, junior, and sophomore workers with training, retention, development, and quality-of-life opportunities. Current literature suggests that younger workers have commitment levels, work values, and career goals different from their predecessors, possibly caused by divergent generational values.[13]

Career goals could have as much to do with opportunity as they have with divergent generational values. As older government employees delay retirement, younger employees may find limited opportunities for advancement and critical skills development, and, as a result, may exhibit withdrawal behaviors leading to decreased productivity and commitment as well as the desire to seek fulfillment and opportunity elsewhere.[14]

Consequently, as the pool of qualified candidates shrinks, leadership voids may result when vacancies occur. This may result in more outsourcing, the recruitment of employees who need specialized training, and the retention of employees with less experience than may be desired.

The wide array of challenges that face the nation over the next 20 years or so may cause local governments in particular to work closely with younger workers to develop their abilities and learn to become successors with the requisite values to manage greater diversity, the ethics to make balanced decisions, and the skills to meet the eminent challenges of tomorrow.

Notes

1. Laurence J. Kotlikoff and Scott Burns, *The Coming Generational Storm: What You Need to Know About America's Economic Future* (Cambridge, Mass.: MIT Press, 2004), 1–72.

2. J. Westkott (Colorado state demographer), interview on "Local Matters," National Public Radio, Boulder, Colo., September 2005.

3. Richard L. Clark, "Counties Face the Senior Boom: A Survey of the Effect of an Aging Population and an Aging County Workforce on County Services," prepared for the National Association of Counties (Athens: University of Georgia, Carl Vinson Institute of Government, February 2004), www.naco.org/contentmanagement/ContentDisplay.cfm?ContentID=13923.

4. Stanley Kurtz, "Demographics and the Culture War: The Implications of Population Decline," *Policy Review* (Hoover Institution), no. 129 (February–March 2005), www.hoover.org/publications/policyreview/3431156.html.

5. City Policy Associates, "Urban Worker Survey" (Washington, D.C., National Association of Counties, 2001), www.naco.org/Content/ContentGroups/Publications1/Surveys1/Urban/UrbanWorkerSurvey.pdf.

6. Donald M. Atwater and Aisha Jones, "Preparing for a Future Labor Shortage: How to Stay Ahead of the Curve," *Graziadio Business Report* (Pepperdine University) 7, no. 2 (2004), http://gbr.pepperdine.edu/042/laborshortage.html.

7. Employment Policy Foundation, "Future Labor and Skills Shortage Jeopardize American Prosperity" (Washington, D.C.: Employment Policy Foundation, 2001), http://www.epf.org/research/newsletters/2001/ef20011025.pdf (June 12, 2005).

8. Ralph C. Bryant and Warwick J. McKibbin, "Issues in Modeling the Global Dimensions of Demographic Change," Brookings Discussion Papers in International Economics, no. 141 (Washington, D.C.: Brookings Institution Press, December 1998), www.brook.edu/views/papers/bryant/141.pdf.

9. Kathleen Hunter, "Bush Budget Short on State Aid," Stateline.org, February 6, 2006, www.stateline.org/live/printable/story?contentId=86488.

10. David M. Walker, "21st Century: Addressing Long-Term Fiscal Challenges Must Include a Re-Examination of Mandatory Spending; Testimony before the Budget Committee, House of Representatives," Report no. GAO-06-456T (Washington, D.C.: U.S. Government Accountability Office, February 15, 2006), www.gao.gov/new.items/d06456t.pdf; and David M. Walker, "Medicare: Program Re-

form and Modernization Are Needed but Entail Considerable Challenges; Testimony before the Special Committee on Aging, U.S. Senate," Report No. GAO/T-HEHS/AIMD-00-77 (Washington, D.C.: U.S. General Accounting Office, February 8, 2000), www.gao.gov/archive/2000/h100077t.pdf.

11.   Walker, "21st Century: Addressing Long-Term Fiscal Challenges Must Include a Re-Examination of Mandatory Spending."

12.   NACo recently described additional efforts in a special supplement on succession planning; see "Hot Topics, Succession Planning," special supplement to *County News* (NACo), December 11, 1006, www.naco.org/Template.cfm?Section=Labor_and Employment&template=/ContentManagement/Content Display.cfm&ContentID=21985.

13.   Lynne C. Lancaster and David Stillman, *When Generations Collide: Who They Are, Why They Clash, How to Solve the Generational Puzzle at Work* (New York: HarperCollins, 2002).

14.   Lakshmi Ramarajan and Sigal G. Barsade, "What Makes the Job Tough? The Influence of Organizational Respect on Burnout in the Human Services," November 2006, http://knowledge.wharton.upenn.edu/papers/1327.pdf.

PART NINE

STATE AND LOCAL

COURT SYSTEMS

A continuing controversy relative to state and local court systems is the question of whether judges should be elected or appointed, and if appointed, by whom. One of the best examples of diversity across the states is the variation in the manner in which judges are selected. In about half the states, judges obtain their office either by partisan or nonpartisan election. In the other half, judges are appointed by the legislature, the governor, or *via* the merit system, whereby a judicial nominating commission presents a slate of candidates (usually three) to the governor, who must choose one candidate from the list.

To attempt to keep electoral politics out of the selection process as much as possible, reformers in most states would prefer the merit plan. They question the utility of judicial elections by arguing that, quite simply, citizens often do not know who the better-qualified candidates are in a judicial election. Indeed, research has shown that judicial elections tend to have low salience among voters.[1] One consequence of the public's ignorance of judicial candidates and elections was illustrated quite poignantly in 1990 in the state of Washington when State Supreme Court Chief Justice Keith Callow was defeated by the upstart, and inexperienced attorney Charles Johnson.[2] On the other hand, proponents of judicial elections argue that in order to keep judges democratically accountable they must be subjected to popular elections.

A critical question scholars have asked about the issue of judicial selection is whether the selection method has any effect on the type of judges chosen and on judicial decision making. In our first article, Damon Cann explores answers to this question by examining whether selection method has any effect on how states judges grade the quality of decisions rendered by their state courts. His results provide support for those favoring merit-based appointment systems.

Jury duty is an important civic responsibility, and two basic expectations we have about our democratic system is that persons charged with crimes have the right to a jury trial and that the jury will be representative of the community. Unfortunately, the representativeness of juries is largely a myth, and many citizens have easily avoided jury duty across the states. This has resulted in several state and local courts imposing fines and other methods of increasing the pool of potential jurors for their trials. In our next article, James Levine and Steven Zeidman, take a look at the efforts made by the state of New York to reform its jury system and to make jury service less onerous. The changes did not come easily, and only a handful of states have experienced similar success.

Our final article focuses our attention on local courts and the oft-reported lack of professionalism of small town courts and judges. Focusing on the state of New York's system of "justice courts" in small rural towns, William Glaberson's article details several areas of concern about the judges who sit on the bench in these courts and the decisions they render. The article certainly makes you wonder about the paradoxical name of the courts themselves.

Notes

1.   On this point, see Charles A. Johnson, Roger C. Shaefer, and R. Neal McKnight, "The Salience of Judicial Candidates and Elections," *Social Science Quarterly* 59 (September, 1978): 371–378.

2.   Hugh Bone, "Washington Primary: Judicial Politics," *Comparative State Politics* 11 (December, 1990): 45–48.

Questions for Review and Discussion

8.1   How does your state select and retain state and local judges? Can you name one or more members of your state's highest court?

8.2   What are the ways that jury duty can be avoided in your state or locale? Are the examples of reform from New York worthy to pursue in more areas? Why or why not?

8.4   What are the problems with the small town "justice courts"?

28 Judicial Selection and State Court Performance

DAMON CANN

POLITICAL SCIENTIST DOUGLAS RAE has shown that the method by which governmental officials are selected can have profound political consequences.[1] It thus behooves judicial scholars to evaluate the quality of justice obtained under different selection plans. Not only could the results of such studies have important ramifications for states, they can also inform the nascent debate on whether federal judges should be elected rather than appointed.[2]

Political pressures on judicial candidates led many states to abandon judicial elections in favor of merit selection plans (among which the Missouri Plan is the most prominent) where judges are appointed to an initial term of office by the governor (who chooses from a list prepared by a nonpartisan nominating commission). After these judges serve their initial term, they must stand for a retention election. A host of "good government" groups, as well as the American Judicature Society, have relentlessly advocated reforming state courts by adopting such merit-selection plans nationwide.

Proponents of merit selection contend that the merit-based system is an ideal compromise between two conflicting ideals for judicial selection plans—independence and accountability. Independence is protected because judges are initially appointed, generally serve longer terms, raise and spend little money on campaigns, and do not face other candidates when they stand for retention elections (and thus campaigns tend to focus on qualifications rather than ideology). Still, the retention elections allow for a measure of accountability by providing a means for the public to remove a judge whose decisions are unacceptable.

Some have contended that the popularity of merit selection is unwarranted because limited empirical evidence exists supporting the claim that merit selection actually preserves independence while promoting accountability. I contend that the scholarly obsession with independence and accountability has led scholars to overlook the overall quality of outcomes under different selection systems. This article reviews criticisms of common modes of selection and the empirical evidence behind those criticisms, and recommends a new way to evaluate the overall performance of a state court system based on the evaluations of the judges within the system. Judges in states with certain modes of selection may rate the overall quality of justice in their state at a higher level than judges in states with other modes of selection.

Empirical Studies

Perhaps the most striking factor in existing empirical studies of judicial selection mechanisms is the lack of support for reformers' claims. While reformers have contended that merit selection plans yield more qualified judges, the bulk of the evidence suggests this is not the case. For example, one study examining the personal characteristics of judges sitting on state courts of last resort shows that the method of selection has little or no impact on the percentage of judges selected with strong educational and professional qualifications.[3] A follow-up study shows that in spite of a jump in the number of states using merit selection plans between the 1960s and the 1980s, there was (at best) only a trivial increase in the qualifications of state judges over that same time period.[4] In short, existing evidence does not support the contention that any method of judicial selection is more successful than another in selecting experienced and well-educated judges.

Merit selection has also been praised as a way to insulate the judiciary from political pressures. However, a path-breaking study by Melinda Gann Hall demonstrates that levels of partisan competition in a state not only affect the proportion of the vote received by the incumbent, but also outcomes in nonpartisan and retention elections. This implies that voters are able to identify the ideology of candidates—even in retention elections—and cast their vote accordingly.[5]

Not only have these promises of merit selection been unsubstantiated, many of the criticisms of election-based systems appear to be unwarranted. For example, reformers have claimed that the large sums of money raised in judicial elections threaten the integrity of the judiciary. However, empirical studies have failed to establish that campaign contributions lead judges to vote in a particular way. A study of the Wisconsin Supreme Court (which is selected by nonpartisan elections) shows that there is no relationship between attorney contributions to judges and the probability of that attorney winning the case.[6] Additionally, while a study of the Alabama Supreme Court finds a correlation between campaign contributions and outcomes in arbitration decisions, its author readily admits that he cannot establish that the contributions caused the judges to vote in a particular way.[7]

It is equally plausible that contributors decide to donate to judges who already support their views (rather than giving money to someone they disagree with in hopes that their contribution will change a judge's mind). The latter possibility is in harmony with studies of the link between campaign contributions and votes in Congress that show that the correlation between votes and money is best understood as ideological groups supporting candidates who are already disposed to vote with the group rather than aggressive donors trying to buy the votes of legislators.[8] In short, available evidence does not show that campaign fundraising leads to a general decline in the integrity of judges.

Elections have also been faulted for failing to promote accountability—the very virtue they are purported to provide. Indeed, judicial elections have been characterized as low-profile campaigns with low rates of participation and little discussion of issues.[9] However, more recent evidence challenges this notion. A study of Ohio voters finds that citizens are able to link judicial candidates to a political party and use that information in casting their votes, even though party affiliation does not appear on the ballot in Ohio judicial elections. The study also shows that ideology influences voting behavior in judicial elections.[10] Further, voters seem to have particularly high levels of participation and understanding when voter guides and other independent sources of campaign information are available.[11] Additionally, a landmark multi-state study shows that voters in elections (notably *including* retention elections) are aware of issues in elections and that those issues influence electoral outcomes.[12] Whatever judicial elections may have been in the past, the bulk of empirical evidence suggests that the key ingredients for accountability are present in contemporary judicial elections.

The general interpretation of these studies has been that elections may be no worse than merit selection in terms of accountability and independence. However, the actual findings may be more concisely summarized by saying that evidence shows that elections do, in fact, promote accountability and that retention elections do not provide as much insulation from external political forces as had been hoped.

Regardless of the interpretation, the problem faced by the literature on accountability and independence is a general failure to link the results to conclusions about overall court performance. After all, the reason we are concerned about accountability and independence is that we think systems with accountable and/or independent judges will yield better overall outcomes. This being the case, explorations into the value of the sundry judicial selection systems would be better carried out by directly examining the quality of outcomes rather than examining independence, accountability, or other intermediary factors leading to quality overall outcomes.

View from the Bench

Any empirical study of the overall quality of court outcomes runs into one major obstacle: Defining and measuring the quality of a state court system outcomes. A unique, nationwide survey of 2,428 state court judges conducted by the Justice at Stake Campaign provides some traction on this difficult issue.[13] The sample includes judges from state supreme, appellate, and trial courts.

The survey asked judges to list the most important duties of courts and judges. The four responsibilities judges chose as the most important were "making impartial decisions," "ensuring fairness under law," "defending constitutional rights and freedoms," and "providing equal justice for rich and poor." The survey also asked judges how well courts and judges in their state perform their duties. This question regarding how well state courts perform their duties can function effectively as a measure of the quality of justice.

This indicator of the quality of justice is particularly valuable because it is based on the views of judges. Judges are uniquely positioned to evaluate the quality of justice in their state. They are very familiar with court operation procedures and are well-versed in the decisions generated.

Additionally, the face validity of the measure is strong because it represents a broad conception of how well a state's court system works rather than measuring a single, specific aspect of quality.

Having established a method of measuring the quality of general court outcomes, we can move on to consider whether mode of selection affects the quality of outcomes in a state. If partisan elections (or even nonpartisan elections) diminish the quality of justice in a state, judges in merit selection or appointment states should rate the quality of justice in their state higher than judges in states using partisan or nonpartisan elections.

Data

The survey asked judges to rate how well courts and judges in their state perform their duties (rating the quality of performance as excellent, good, fair, or poor). I propose to explain judges' responses using three principal sets of factors: Characteristics of the court system, characteristics of the judge, and the surveyed judge's opinion of other judges in the state.

Among the characteristics of a court system, the method of selecting judges stands as a prominent potential influence on the quality of court performance. To incorporate selection mechanisms into the empirical model, I use a set of dichotomous indicators for the mode of selection by which most judges in the state are selected—*Nonpartisan, Merit Selection*, and *Appointment*, with partisan elections being the baseline category. This allows us to compare the quality of court performance in each type of system relative to a partisan election system. Based on the claims of reformers, I expect judges in merit selection and appointment states to have higher evaluations of the quality of work done by courts and judges in their state.

While this classification is used by the American Judicature Society and employed throughout the scholarly literature[14] it poses two possible problems. First, some states are difficult to classify. This is problematic for states like Ohio and Michigan, which are classified as nonpartisan because party identifications are not on the ballot but where parties nominate candidates and the affiliation of the candidates is widely known. To address this, I also present results from a model that uses a single dummy variable. *Appointment or Merit System*, coded 1 for systems using appointment or merit systems and 0 for states using competitive elections (either partisan or nonpartisan).

Second, a few states (18 percent) use different selection systems to select judges at different levels of the system (e.g. nonpartisan elections for the supreme court, partisan elections for all other courts). To address this problem, this analysis focuses on the method of selection for *most* judges in the state. Re-running the analysis excluding states with multiple selection systems makes no substantive difference in the outcome. Similarly, re-running the analysis using the method of selection for the state high court (the most salient elections in a state) produces similar results. Thus, while this operationalization of mode of selection may be imperfect, the results are robust to several different operationalizations.[15]

Additionally, state courts with more resources may be able to better carry out their work. Thus, I include an index measuring the *professionalism* of a state's courts.[16] While the items in this index bear most directly on state supreme courts (salary of supreme court judges, staff for the high court, and similar items), the professionalism of state high courts and lower courts is likely highly correlated, so the index at hand serves as a proxy for the professionalism of the entire system.

The characteristics of the judge responding to the survey may also have bearing on his or her evaluations of the quality of justice. To control for the possible effect of race, I include a set of dichotomous indicators for *African-American, Hispanic,* and *Other Non-white*; white is the baseline category. In addition to the respondent's race, the respondent's gender may also affect their views of state court performance. Accordingly, the variable *Male* is coded 1 for male judges and 0 for females.

Judges' length of service on the bench may affect their attitudes toward the quality of their state courts. While the survey did not directly ask respondents how long they had served on the bench, it did ask their age. Age should be correlated with length of service on the bench (though not perfectly). Moreover, age of itself may affect judges' attitudes toward their state courts. Accordingly, I include a variable for *age* in years at the time of the survey.

One final characteristic of the judges must be considered—judges serving on higher level courts may have different attitudes about their state courts than judges serving on lower level courts. Accordingly, I include a variable for respondents who serve on their state *supreme court* and state *appellate courts,* with trial courts being the baseline category.

Finally, a judge's views of other judges in the state may affect the way he or she evaluates how well state courts and judges perform. As such, I include a measure of the respondent's assessment of the ideological extremity of other judges in the state. *Very Extreme* is coded 1 for judges who think judges in their state are either very liberal or very conservative.

Somewhat Extreme is coded 1 for judges who think judges in their state are either somewhat liberal or somewhat conservative. Judges who think their state has a moderate judiciary constitute the baseline category.

Results

Because the dependent variable consists of four ordered categories (excellent, good, fair, and poor), I use an ordered probit model for the statistical analysis.[17] Some judges did not respond to several questions, leaving us with a usable *n* of 2,230. The key result is that judges in states where most judges are elected by merit selection or appointment rate their state court system significantly higher than judges in states where most judges are elected in partisan elections. The results also show that judges' evaluations in nonpartisan states do not differ significantly from the evaluations of judges in partisan states. In short, the data show that judges selected in traditional elections (whether partisan or nonpartisan) rate their state court systems lower than judges in states that use a merit selection or an appointment system.

Because the model with the full typology of selection systems provides more detailed information, our interpretation of results will focus on that model, though the results from both models were substantively similar.[18] Figure 1 shows the relationship between mode of selection and

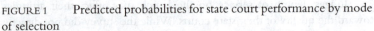

FIGURE 1   Predicted probabilities for state court performance by mode of selection

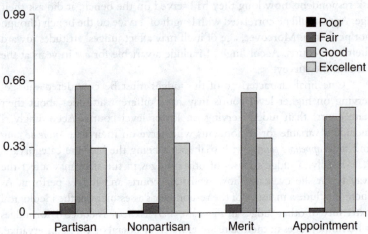

judges' ratings of their state court systems graphically using predicted probabilities.[19] These figures represent the probability of a judge with specific characteristics rating their system at each of the 4 levels—excellent, good, fair or poor. The difference between partisan and nonpartisan systems is negligible. However, judges in merit selection states have a 37 percent chance of rating their state courts as excellent compared to just 32 percent chance in partisan states. Remarkably, judges in states where judges are appointed by the governor or legislature have a probability of about .5 of rating their state courts as excellent. As the predicted probability of being in the "excellent" category increases (moving from partisan toward appointment plans), the probability of being in the "good," "fair," or "poor" categories decreases. While there is substantial variation across systems in judges evaluations of performance, it is worth noting that it is very unlikely for judges in any system to rate their state courts as "poor."

The court professionalism index has no significant impact on how judges rate their state courts. Two possible explanations exist. First, when evaluating the quality of justice in their states, judges may evaluate the extent to which judges do the best they can given available resources. If evaluations are indeed made in this way, the resources available to judges would not likely affect the ratings. Second, it may be that if the index captured the professionalism of lower courts as well as it assesses state supreme courts then one would find a significant effect.

The characteristics of the judges answering the survey also affect the way they evaluate the quality of justice in their state. Relative to white judges, African-American judges rate the performance of their state courts lower. However, Hispanic judges and judges of other races do not differ significantly from white judges in their evaluation of state court performance. Not only does race affect judges' evaluations of the quality of justice in their state courts, but gender does as well. Male judges tend to rate the performance of their state courts higher than female judges. Age and the level of court a judge serves on do not have significant effects on judges' evaluations of the quality of their state courts.

Finally, a judge's assessment of the extremity of other judges in their state court system has a strong, significant effect on their evaluations of their state courts. Judges who view the other judges in their state as too extreme rate the performance of their state courts much lower. Figure 2 graphs the predicted probabilities of rating state court performance varying judges' evaluations of the extremity of judges in their state, holding the method of selection constant as merit, selection.[20] Judges who consider their state judiciary to be ideologically moderate have a .41 probability of rating their state courts as excellent. In contrast, for judges who see

FIGURE 2   Predicted probabilities for state court performance by extremity of state judges

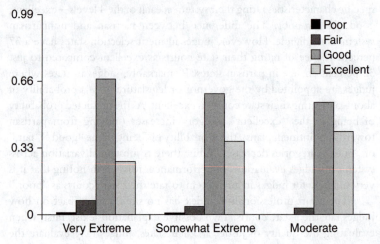

their state judiciary as somewhat extreme or very extreme, the probability of an "excellent" rating drops to .37 or .26, respectively. It appears that a judge's assessment of the ideology of judges in his or her state affects their assessment of the quality of justice about as strongly as the mode of selection.

Discussion

While some have criticized reformers for advancing their cause without empirical evidence of its effectiveness, this analysis provides strong empirical evidence that merit selection and appointment plans are superior to partisan and nonpartisan elections. In states where most judges are chosen by merit selection or appointment, judges rate the quality of the work done by their state courts higher than judges in states where most judges are selected through partisan or nonpartisan elections.

We began with a discussion of the two issues that have characterized the debate over judicial selection mechanisms—accountability and independence—and noted that empirical research has supported the notion that elections maximize accountability. However, even if citizens are well-informed and able to use elections to maximize accountability, the evidence here shows that, on balance, using elections to select judges actually diminishes the overall performance of state courts (as measured in the two ways considered in this article). It may be that accountability is not the key to an effective judiciary. Alternatively, while accountability could be desirable, it may be impossible to obtain it without the negative side-effects inherent to elections.

More research is necessary to target the specific reasons why judges in merit selection and appointment states rate their courts higher than judges in election states. One possibility is that judges are concerned that the politicization of judicial campaigns may be damaging the legitimacy of the judiciary in their state. Scholars should consider how the mode of selection effects citizen perceptions of the courts. Another possibility lies in campaign finance. Judges may view fundraising and campaigning as a tremendous burden. Further, while there is scant evidence that campaign contributions effectively "buy" judges' votes, it is possible that the very appearance of *quid pro quo* exchanges makes people uncomfortable.

An additional avenue for fixture exploration is the measurement of the quality of justice. While the measure used here based on judges' evaluations of their state court systems has strong face validity, future work should consider alternative measures of the general quality of court outcomes. This will allow researchers to test the robustness of these results.

Ultimately, this research provides solid empirical evidence that the campaign to move toward merit selection systems and away from election systems is both warranted and desirable. While judicial elections may not be uncompetitive events with uninformed voters, merit selection and appointment states appear to achieve better overall court performance. Reformers should continue to press for their cause knowing that the general outcomes of court systems using merit selection or appointment plans are superior to systems using partisan or nonpartisan elections.

Notes

1. Rae, POLITICAL CONSEQUENCES OF ELECTORAL LAW (New Haven, CT: Yale University Press, 1967).

2. Richard Davis, ELECTING JUSTICE: FIXING THE SUPREME COURT NOMINATION PROCESS (London: Oxford University Press, 2005).

3. Bradley Canon, *The Impact of Formal Selection Processes on the Characteristics of Judges—Reconsidered*, 6 LAW & SOC'Y. REV. 579 (1972).

4. Henry Glick and Craig Emmert, *Selection Systems and Judicial Characteristics: The Recruitment of State Supreme Court Justices*, 70 JUDICATURE 228 (1987).

5. Hall, *State Supreme Courts in American Democracy: Probing the Myths of Judicial Reform* 95 AM. POL. SCI. REV. 315 (2001).

6.   Damon Cann, *Campaign Contributions and Judicial Behavior*, 23 AM. REV. POL. 261 (2002).

7.   Stephen J. Ware, *Money, Politics, and Judicial Decisions: A Case Study of Arbitration Law in Alabama*, 25 J. L. POL. 645 (1999). McCall and McCall also find an association between contributions and decisions but do not attempt to substantiate a causal relationship. *See* Madhavi M. McCall and Michael McCall, *Campaign contributions, judicial decisions, and the Texas Supreme Court: Assessing the appearance of impropriety*, 90 JUDICATURE 214 (2007).

8.   For a comprehensive discussion, see John R. Wright, INTEREST GROUPS AND CONGRESS: LOBBYING, CONTRIBUTIONS, AND INFLUENCE (Boston, MA: Allyn and Bacon, 1966).

9.   For examples, see Patrick W. Dunn *Judicial Selection and the States: A Critical Study with Proposals for Reform*, 4 HOFSTRA L. REV. 285 and Phillip Dubois, FROM BALLOT TO BENCH: JUDICIAL ELECTIONS AND THE QUEST FOR ACCOUNTABILITY (Austin, TX: University of Texas Press, 1980).

10.   Larry Baum, *Explaining the Vote in Judicial Elections: The 1984 Ohio Supreme Court Elections*, 40 WEST. POL. Q. 361 (1987).

11.   Nicholas Lovrich and Charles Sheldon, *Voters in Contested, Nonpartisan Judicial Elections: A Responsible Electorate or Problematic Public?* 36 WEST. POL. Q. 241 (1983).

12.   Hall, *supra* n. 5.

13.   The survey took place November 2001–January 2002. The response rate for this mail survey is unknown because the survey firm did not report it. However, it is possible to estimate *minimum* response rates for the survey based on the number of judges in each state. While it would be easy to survey all state supreme court judges (there are 334 of them), it would be a mammoth task to survey all state trial court judges (there are nearly 10,000). The survey contains responses from 188 supreme court judges, 527 appellate court judges, and 1713 lower (trial) court judges. By dividing the number of responses at each level by the number of all judges at each level, I estimate *minimum* response rates as 56.3% for supreme court level, 57.1% for the appellate level, and 18.2% for the lowest level. Considering the healthy response rates for the higher levels, it appears that not all lower court judges were surveyed. Thus, 18.2% is a *minimum* response rate; the true rate is likely much higher. Judges from New Jersey were advised by their state not to participate in the study, so New Jersey judges were dropped from the sample. Because there are fewer supreme court judges than appellate court judges, and more trial court judges than appellate and supreme court judges combined, the raw data overwhelmingly reflect the attitudes of lower courts. To address this issue, I weight the data by level so that the opinions of judges at all levels have equal weight.

14.   *See, e.g.,* Christopher Bonneau, *What Price Justice(s)? Understanding Campaign Spending in State Supreme Court Elections* 5 STATE POL. & POL'Y Q. 107–125 (2005); Deborah Goldberg and Samantha Sanchez, THE NEW POLITICS OF JUDICIAL ELEC-TIONS 2002. (Washington, DC: Justice at Stake Campaign, 2003); and Laura Langer's State Supreme Courts Natural Courts Database www.u.arizona.edu/~llanger/NSFSESLANGER.htm from which these data were obtained.

15.   A third possible problem is that many states fill mid-term court vacancies through appointment even in elective states. Still, these individuals must ultimately fact election, which could still affect judges' evaluations of how well their court system functions.

16.   The index is developed in Paul Brace and Melinda Gann Hall, *"Haves" versus*

"Have Nots" in State Supreme Courts: Allocating Docket Space and Wins in Power Asymmetric Cases, 35 L. & SOC'Y. REV. 393 (2001).

17.   A table containing the statistical results is available at http://deann.myweb.uga.edu/judres.pdf.

18.   Further, a likelihood ratio test shows that this model fits the data significantly better than the model with the elected/appointed dummy.

19.   In an ordered probit model, the effects of a variable are conditional upon the values of all other variables in the model. To generate these predicted probabilities, I varied the mode of selection while setting state court professionalism and age to their respective means and assumed a state judiciary that is somewhat extreme (the modal category), and a respondent who is a white male trial court judge (again reflecting the modal categories).

20.   To generate these predicted probabilities, I varied the extremity of the state judiciary while setting state court professionalism and age to their respective means mean and assumed a merit selection system (the modal category), and a respondent who is a white male trial court judge.

29 The Miracle of Jury Reform in New York

JAMES P. LEVINE

STEVEN ZEIDMAN

ACCEPTED WISDOM HAS IT that reforming courts is like moving mountains—a Herculean task that is well-nigh impossible. The reasons
are many: court autonomy, deep-seated traditions, lethargy, cynicism,
institutional fragmentation, vested interests, and just plain ineptitude.
Political scientist Malcolm Feeley, after studying many unsuccessful attempts to change the functioning of courts, concluded with the following
despairing words:

> Scholars are finding that many innovative programs fail in their
> implementation. This book suggests that the picture is bleaker; the
> causes of failure are found at every stage of planned change. Often
> failure is rooted in conception, in a fundamental misunderstanding of
> the nature of the problem, the dynamics of the system, the nature of
> the change process, and attention to detail at the service delivery level.[1]

It is thus truly remarkable that New York State was able to radically
transform its jury system in the space of a decade. Against all odds, an
abundance of initiatives were successfully put into place to accomplish
two goals—democratizing jury service and easing juror burdens. We call

this dramatic reconstruction of a jury system that had resisted change for a century the miracle of jury reform.[2]

This article analyzes how such monumental change was accomplished. Six major participants in the process were interviewed at length: Judith Kaye (Chief Judge of New York State), Jonathan Lippman (Chief Administrative Judge of New York State), Colleen McMahon (Federal District Court judge and the former chair of a judicially appointed commission charged with reviewing jury service in the state and making recommendations for improvement), Judge James Lack (former chair of the New York State Senate Judiciary Committee), Chester Mount, Jr. (Director of Research and Technology, New York State Unified Court System, Office of Court Administration), and Anthony Manisero (Manager, Statewide Jury Support, New York State Unified Court System, Office of Court Administration). We also had an exchange of correspondence with Marc Bloustein, counsel for the New York State Office of Court Administration. These interviews were supplemented by a search of media coverage of the jury reform process and review of reports prepared by the courts.

The Reforms

A number of reforms were put into place to expand the pool of available jurors. Master source lists were expanded and improved to include public assistance and unemployment compensation rolls.[3] Special postal service lists on changes of address were incorporated into databases of prospective jurors. An automated system was put into place to help go after those ignoring jury summonses. A list of "permanently qualified" jurors, which resulted in the same individuals being called repeatedly, was abolished. Perhaps most significant of all, legislation granting automatic exemptions to 20 occupations, including pharmacists, embalmers, lawyers (including judges), and police officers, which had resulted in the removal from jury service of more than a million people statewide, was repealed.

To reduce the burden of jury service, a number of conveniences and amenities were implemented. All persons summoned to service on a particular date were given the unqualified opportunity to receive one automatic postponement to a date of their choosing within six months by utilizing a computerized telephone system. Courthouse facilities were upgraded: more telephones were installed; inspections and cleaning of bathrooms were regularized; public address systems were updated. Assistance and information given to jurors were enhanced: a new juror orientation video narrated by well-known newscasters was created; a juror handbook was published, including a statement of jurors' rights and responsibilities, as well as a glossary of legal terms; a juror newsletter (*Jury Pool News*), with lively stories and even a crossword puzzle, was developed to help jurors endure the boredom of waiting periods; and a juror hotline accessible by a toll-free number was put into place to field complaints and answer questions about jury service.

More substantive devices aimed at making the juror's experience less onerous included instituting a one day/one trial system, except in New York City, whereby no one serves for more than one day or one trial; increasing jurors' pay from $12 to $40 per day; and requiring that employers with a minimum of 10 employees pay at least three days of employees' wages while the employees serve as jurors. The voir dire process to ferret out unacceptable jurors was made less demanding by including written questionnaires for pre-screening, making provision for screening of complete arrays for obvious challenges for cause, and imposing time and relevance restrictions on questioning. As a result, the average length of voir dire in civil cases dropped from 9.3 hours in 1995 to 4.3 hours in 2000.[4]

Arguably, the most burdensome practice of the pre-reform jury system in New York was mandatory sequestration of jurors during deliberation in *all* felony trials, a requirement that differentiated New York from all of the other 49 states and the federal court system. In May 2001, this stressful and disorienting legal provision was lifted, except in capital cases. Thereafter, New York judges, like their counterparts elsewhere, were given discretion to order sequestration only if warranted by massive publicity and media coverage.

Not all of the changes sought materialized. The plan to drastically limit peremptory challenges in criminal cases foundered, although the number of such exclusions not requiring a rationale was reduced in civil cases. But this failure is overshadowed by the transformation of so many facets of jury service—what one court official called a "sea change in court administration."[5] What follows is an attempt to understand both the successes and the disappointments in the effort to ameliorate the jury system's woes. In a nutshell, what made jury reform work?

Transformational Leadership

Across the board, when we asked those involved how change was accomplished, we received a four-word answer: Chief Judge Judith Kaye. Although Kaye herself modestly disclaimed such personal power, there was unanimous agreement among those interviewed that her determination to reform the jury system upon being named chief judge in 1993 was the force that turned the tide. She took a very active role in crafting the proposals for change and seeing them to fruition. In the words of one respondent, she was a "fairy godmother" with a "magic wand;"[6] in the words of another, jury reform was "her story."[7]

But her work was not magic. Rather, she carefully employed an approach known in the field of public administration as transformational leadership. Rather than relying primarily on the promise of rewards or the threat of punishments to get others to act responsively, she made attempts to get those whose support was necessary for accomplishing goals to "buy into" the desired course of action and embrace the mandates being put forward. This style of leadership occurs "when leaders broaden and elevate the interests of their followers, when they generate awareness and acceptance among the followers of the purposes and mission of the group, and when they move followers to transcend their own self-interests for the good of the group."[8] To accomplish these ends, transformational leaders utilize charisma, inspiration, intellectual stimulation, and individualized consideration.[9]

This characterization of leadership fits Judge Kaye to a tee. Once having decided to make jury reform her highest priority, she relentlessly crusaded on its behalf. Relying heavily on public relations, she gave countless speeches to bar associations and good government groups. At an annual meeting of the New York State Bar Association, she emphasized that the judiciary alone could not effect change, and exhorted the bar association, lawyers, and the public to each do their part: "[D]emanding only change by the courts, perpetuating and entrenching everyone else's old habits, simply will not get the job done. If it is to be more than facial, jury reform requires change on the part of everyone, including the public."[10] Judge Kaye also used large portions of her annual "State of the Judiciary" addresses to make the case for jury reform: "For too long, in many areas of the State, jury service has been a burden falling unfairly on too few of our citizens, whose time is often spent unproductively and in cramped, neglected facilities. The citizens of this State deserve better.[11]

She relied on charm, charisma, oratory, political sagacity, and self-assurance, making legislators, administrators, bar associations, and the general public feel that if they joined in, they would be on the side of the angels. In sounding a clarion call for action, she not only sold people on the righteousness of the cause, but also displayed a fierce determination that had an infectious effect on those hearing the call. Pointedly refusing to take credit for changes being accomplished, she allowed others to bask in the glory of the reform effort.

It must also be noted that an amendment to the state constitution passed in 1977 gave the chief judge substantial formal administrative authority over the courts. This enabled Judge Kaye to wield significant influence over lower court judges, court clerks, and jury commissioners, as well as the Office of Court Administration, which controls many aspects of judicial functioning.[12] So, besides relying on nonstop proselytizing, Kaye was able to utilize a degree of authority; she gave some "marching orders."[13] As Judge McMahon observed: "Kaye uses an iron fist in a velvet glove."

Establishing Legitimacy

Part of Judge Kaye's strategy was to create a climate favorable to jury reform among interested parties and the public. She created a special commission (The Jury Project) to study flaws in the jury system and to make recommendations for improvement. Its mandate was to survey the legal terrain to discover how New York was at variance with prevailing national practices, to garner empirical data about the actual functioning of the system, and to seek citizen input about sources of dissatisfaction with jury service. The aim was to propel change by obtaining credible information about the system's shortcomings and by making persuasive arguments for remedial measures.

Judge Kaye was fully engaged with The Jury Project. To enhance the likelihood that she would have a voice in the commission's deliberations, and to increase the chances that the recommendations of the final report would be to her liking, she selected as chair Colleen McMahon, a highly respected lawyer whom she had known for some time. Not only was McMahon someone who could be trusted, but as a partner in a very successful law firm (Paul, Weiss, Rifkind, Wharton and Garrison), she could channel substantial resources into the project. The firm spent upwards of $100,000, and McMahon herself devoted more than 50 percent of her time over a year-long period on the project.

McMahon and Kaye handpicked the rest of the commission, seeing to it that various stakeholders on jury issues were represented and sizing up in advance the potential members' commitment to reform. The commission reflected a balanced mix of viewpoints: upstate and downstate, criminal and civil, prosecution and defense.[14] According to Chief Administrative Judge Jonathan Lippman, a calculated gamble was placing potential naysayers from within the court system on the commission in the hope that they would succumb to the reform-minded majority. In the end, it was not surprising that the report advocated all the major reforms desired by Judge Kaye except for drastic reductions of peremptory challenges in criminal cases.[15]

Because the commission was composed largely of pillars of the legal establishment, it had a gravitas that enabled it to speak with the voice of authority.[16] The impressive auspices of the report gave it credibility, enabling Judge Kaye herself to take a behind-the-scenes role in the struggle, in keeping with her august judicial position which precluded bare-bones public engagement in the political process.

The commission did not just canvass the legal literature. Rather, it assembled a vast amount of empirical data pertinent to reform—including statistics on the impact of undeliverable jury summonses on the skewing of the jury pool, surveys of jurors about their experiences, and financial assessments of the cost of mandatory sequestration. The final report eschewed pretentious rhetoric but instead relied on factual points to buttress the case for reform. It wound up being a balanced piece of policy analysis that had intellectual credibility.

An additional force for change was the research provided by the National Center for State Courts and the American Bar Association's jury standards efforts.[17] Both of these sources provided invaluable information about sensible reform based on years of painstaking scholarship.[18] The jury commission did not have to re-invent the wheel but could utilize materials already in place, produced by two highly respected bodies.

Yet another means of legitimating proposed changes was significant plying of the press. The chief administrative judge and the Office of Court Administration routinely supplied information about the reform process to the print media, and a LexisNexis search indicates nothing but uniform support for reform initiatives. Thus, newspapers across the state advocated that mandatory sequestration of jurors during deliberations be abolished in all but notorious cases. The *Buffalo News* headlined an editorial, "State Should Lock Up Criminals, Not Jurors," and the *New York Times* opined: "Let Our Jurors Go." While jury reform is not generally considered a high-salience issue, such media focus provided a positive political environment for lawmakers taking the lead on reform.[19]

Administrative Perseverance

Judge Kaye recognized early on that one source of jury system backwardness was the outdated and unexamined administrative practices of the state's far-flung jury system. While the Office of Court Administration in Manhattan was staffed by sophisticated officials inclined toward reform, it had little power in comparison with local jury commissioners and clerks, many of whom saw their domains as fiefdoms immune from outside interference.[20] Reform meant more work, learning new routines, and embracing modern technology—a host of demanding new burdens. Chester Mount, director of court research at the Office of Court Administration, was asked about the challenges posed by an entrenched judicial bureaucracy:

> Question: Was there resistance to change?
> Answer: Yes.
> Question: From whom?
> Answer: From everyone.

How was the resistance overcome? Chief Judge Kaye brought her zeal for reform into the administrative apparatus of the court system, exciting those at the top about her mission and enticing them into coming on board. She transformed their way of thinking, and they in turn devised a game plan for fomenting changes that did not require legislative approval. Using a "roll up the sleeves" approach, they ventured out to many of the state's 62 counties, urging change and providing the wherewithal to accomplish it, including state-of-the-art information technology that could help to better identify a broader pool of potential jurors and to better track those being summoned. They first went to the more sympathetic clerks and commissioners, who with prodding and encouragement engineered change. These reforms were then held up as models to the recalcitrants, who were embarrassed into following suit.

Two tactics were crucial. The first was flexibility; there was substantial trial and error in changing longstanding practices and a realization that reforms had to be adapted to local circumstances. Over a several-year period, the central office became an on-site presence, providing the technical expertise necessary to modify the modus operandi of individual court systems. Court administrators went "into the field" to help local officialdom work out the kinks and glitches of new approaches. There was an implicit recognition that to improve jury functioning one size does not fit all.

Second, the art of effective interpersonal relations was put to good use in converting the skeptical rank-and-file. By coming across as decent human beings with a capacity for empathy and warmth, central office personnel were able to overcome the ostracism that initially confronted them. As Tony Manisero of the Office of Court Administration put it: "We engaged in endless schmoozing" [a Yiddish word widely used in New York City more or less meaning "small talk"]. This had the effect of breaking through the adversarial relationship that is often occasioned when outsiders come in and tell locals how to run their affairs. It also mitigated the negative impact of the almost endless cajoling of such personnel that was essential to keep them focused and on track; they were "lured" into going along. Putting a human face on outside intrusion was an important means of gaining cooperation.

Not coincidentally, the style of transformational leadership employed by the chief judge was emulated by court administrators. By humanizing and individualizing their dealings with jury system officialdom, rather than relying on the bureaucratic chain of command, they were able to convert jury commissioners, clerks, and administrative personnel into key collaborators in the jury reform effort.

Politicking

While the chief judge can, and did, implement many changes herself pursuant to her rule-making authority over the courts, several of the proposed reforms required legislative approval.[21] Put another way, the legislature still retains control over many aspects of court organization and administration.[22]

In no small measure, old-fashioned use of politics was what helped the major reforms needing legislative enactment to succeed. While the chief judge's transformative leadership did light fires under people to spur action, lobbying, bargaining, compromise, and some degree of brinksmanship were needed to bring initiatives to fruition. The politics were a bit more muted than normal, as it would have been inappropriate for the top judge of a state to court individual legislators. But in the final analysis, standard political activities were instrumental in securing necessary legislation.

The chief judge's motto was incrementalism, an understanding that change could not happen all at once.[23] While she remains devoted to this day to a full gamut of court reforms (some of which have as yet eluded her),[24] she decided to "take a crumb, then two crumbs, then half a loaf" rather than push an all-or-nothing approach.[25] Thus, although she is unequivocally committed to the complete elimination of peremptory challenges because of their potential for creating skewed juries and their negative impact on jurors who are struck on this basis, she reconciled herself to the fact that the stiff opposition from both prosecutors and the defense bar to eliminating such challenges precluded passage of such a measure. Likewise, the staunch resistance from the court officers' union, whose members benefited enormously from the overtime pay secured from the escorting and guarding of sequestered jurors, prompted her to at first accept the intermediate reform of eliminating mandatory sequestration only in the case of non-violent felonies. The point is that political realism prompted the embracing of gradualism as the only navigable road to jury reform.[26]

One of the puzzling questions about the reform process was how the legislature was to be successfully wooed. One means of so doing was garnering the governor's support. Colleen McMahon's standing in the Republican Party enabled her to arrange a meeting between Republican Governor George Pataki and Judge Kaye early into the crusade for jury reform. Kaye had been appointed by the previous governor, Democrat Mario Cuomo, so she had no direct connections with Pataki, who had defeated Cuomo in his bid for reelection. Pataki, after his meeting with Judge Kaye, accepted jury reform in principle and held a press conference expressing his general support. The governor's backing was not only useful in obtaining bipartisan approval of reforms, but it gave assurance that the bills that were passed would be signed into law. Unlike her predecessor, who had an acrimonious relationship with his governor, Judge Kaye's rapport with the governor also led to the wholesale adoption of a succession of annual judiciary budget requests.[27]

Our interviews uncovered specific mechanisms for influencing legislators. Jonathan Lippman (the chief administrative judge of the state), a trusted confidant of the chief judge and a career practitioner of court administration, did the lobbying. His expertise in the details of the courts ("the nuts and bolts that don't fit"[28]) was of inestimable value in winning legislators over as he "worked the halls" of the state capitol. Armed with a vast knowledge of the jury system and a persuasive set of answers to frequently asked questions, he persuaded key members of the legislature to become sponsors and supporters of reform measures.[29]

Specifically, Lippman was able to forge an alliance with James Lack, chair of the State Senate Judiciary Committee, who (among other things) agreed to "take the bill" eliminating exemptions—a commitment that Judith Kaye called "immensely beneficial."

As a veteran lawmaker with years of experience and a leading Republican in the state, Lack was able to take the right procedural steps to push the bill forward. He was advantaged by the fact that most of the measures entailed no political party cleavages; they were not "hot button" items.

Nonetheless, formalities were involved: Lack's staff engaged in independent research; Lack held hearings; and he got proposals on the legislative
calendar for formal votes. Lack also worked with his counterpart in the
state assembly to get the support of that body. At the end of the day,
some of the changes, such as increasing juror pay, passed because there
was no vocal and concerted opposition. What was needed was the attention and activity of a respected legislator who could shepherd the bills —
which is what Senator Lack provided.

There were two issues that required more complex political maneuv-
ering. Eliminating occupational exemptions did trigger protests from some
groups about having their preferred status abolished. Police officers, firefighters, and physicians made many calls to legislators about the inconve-
nience of jury service and the way it would intrude on their work. The
Catholic Church of New York was especially vehement, protesting not
only on the grounds that priests needed to be "on call" at all times, but
also on the basis of potential moral dilemmas that they would face if their
religious precepts were at variance with the law. So fervid was their
objection that Cardinal John O'Connor, the archbishop of New York,
personally interceded to oppose getting rid of exemptions for clerics.

How was this hurdle overcome? First, it was decided by both legislative and judicial leaders that they would have to "take an absolutist
approach" regarding the abolition of all exemptions; there could be no
sacred cows.[30] To give in to one vested interest would create a Pandora's
Box, opening the door to others wanting similar concessions. In contrast
to the "rounding of the edges" of other proposals to enhance their political
attractiveness, it was decided that the line would have to be held with
respect to eliminating the right to exemptions in order to prevent the
entire initiative from falling through.[31]

A second, somewhat contradictory stratagem was to provide assurances that the plights of individuals in some of the previously exempted
categories would be considered on a case-by-case basis by individual jury
commissioners. Cardinal O'Connor in particular was told that word would
go out that priests feeling compromised would get a sympathetic ear.
While these informal understandings had no legal standing, they did
assuage the concerns of those who were most adamant. In the end, the
resistance collapsed and the bill passed unanimously.

The second issue requiring deft political handling was abolition of
mandatory sequestration; it was a hard nut to crack. The court officers'
union, which had opposed even the modest curtailment of sequestration
approved in 1995 because of a projected loss in officers' remuneration,
remained categorically opposed in 2001 when complete abolition was

under consideration (except for capital cases). To overcome this ardent opposition, a bargain was brokered by Judge Lippman and the union's lobbyist: in exchange for the union's agreement to reverse its position and support an end to automatic sequestration, new duties were given to court officers that would keep their salaries at preexisting levels. Officials with the union were quoted as having struck a "win-win" deal under which the state's 3,000 uniformed court officers would be deployed to provide additional courtroom security, and were given the extra task of escorting jurors to train and bus stations at late hours. The bottom line was that no overtime pay would be lost as jurors were relieved of the disliked burden of sequestration.

Once the accord was reached, the bill was approved unanimously by both houses of the legislature and signed by the governor; it took effect immediately upon passage. Judge Lippman hailed "an enlightened union leadership" for serving the public interest, and Judge Kaye also chimed in with praise.[32] Another part of the negotiation thus played itself out in the ensuing spin: union officials were spared the criticism of appearing self-serving and crassly materialistic. This was the concluding phase of the savvy political machinations guided by top officials in the state's judiciary, resulting in the abolition of mandatory sequestration which had survived in New York for 120 years.

Moral of the Story

The moral of this remarkable story about recalcitrant agencies being turned around, and reluctant lawmakers being prodded into action to change dubious practices of a jury system, is the efficacy of vigorous, enlightened judicial leadership. The inspiration and aggressiveness of Chief Judge Judith Kaye in rallying both administrative and legislative troops to her call for reform is a testament to what the highest-ranking judge of a state can accomplish. Revamping of antiquated courtroom practices, which are often anchored in tradition and sustained by narrow self-interests, may well require judges to depart from their customary reactive nature. Jury reform in New York State happened because a chief judge took charge.

But good intentions are not enough. Judge Kaye prevailed because she used politics, the art and science of influence, to further the desired ends. While never forsaking proper judicial protocol, she developed a strategy to secure acquiescence to her position and then methodically implemented her plan. Flexibility, toughness, charisma, and persistence were all put to good advantage in turning people around; transformational leadership carried the day. In truth, judges aiming to overturn deeply entrenched courthouse status quo may be well advised to function simultaneously as politicians in robes.

Notes

1. Feeley, COURT REFORM ON TRIAL: WHY SIMPLE SOLUTIONS FAIL 205 (New York: Basic Books, 1983). Indeed, even New York State Chief Judge Judith Kaye has stated, "I know how hard it will be to effect real change within the court system, where traditions are long, resources short and daily demands enormous." Kaye, *It Is Time to Reform the Jury System*, N.Y. L. J., January 25, 1995, at S1. *See also* Hansen, *New York Tackles Jury Standards: After Years of Stubbornly Resisting Change, State May Be Ready for Reform*, 80 A.B.A. J. 22 (January 1994) (quoting Tom Munsterman of the National Center for State Courts that some of New York's jury practices "have been around since the days of Alexander Hamilton").

2. Only a few other states have been able to achieve significant reforms of their jury systems. *See* Landsman, *Appellate Courts and Civil Juries*, 70 U. CIN. L. REV. 873, 879 (2002) (singling out New York, Arizona, California, and Colorado).

3. Prior to that, jurors were tabbed from only three sources: voter registration, the Department of Motor Vehicles, and tax records.

4. New York State Unified Court System, CONTINUING JURY REFORM IN NEW YORK STATE 17 (January 2001).

5. Interview with Chester Mount, March 26, 2002.

6. Interview with Colleen McMahon, July 22, 2002.

7. Interview with Jonathan Lippman, May 14, 2003. Lippman added: "The jury is her [Kaye's] signature; it's her legacy."

8. Seltzer & Bass, *Transformational Leadership: Beyond Initiation and Consideration*, 16 J. MGMT 693–694 (1990).

9. Bryant, *The Role of Transformational and Transactional Leadership in Creating, Sharing, and Exploiting Organizational Knowledge*, 9 J. LEADERSHIP & ORGANIZATIONAL STUD. 31, 36 (2003).

10. Kaye, *supra* n. 1.

11. Kaye, "The State of the Judiciary" 7 (1994).

12. As Jonathan Lippman noted, "The key was a strong Chief Judge working in a system that allowed her to be strong." *Supra* n. 7.

13. *Supra* n. 5.

14. *Supra* n. 6.

15. "The Jury Project: Report to the Chief Judge of the State of New York," March 31, 1994.

16. Marc Bloustein, counsel for the New York State Office of Court Administration, stated that the prestige of the commission helped make passage of at least some reforms "inevitable." E-mail to Steven Zeidman, July 31, 2002. For the record, it should be noted that Zeidman, one of the authors of this article, was a member of the commission.

17. ABA Comm. on Jury Standards, STANDARDS RELATING TO JUROR USE AND MANAGEMENT (1993).

18.   For a general overview of jury reform issues and efforts, see Munsterman & Hannaford, *Reshaping the Bedrock of Democracy: American Jury Reform During the Last Thirty Years*, 36 JUDGES' J. 5, 5–7 (1997); Ellsworth, *Jury Reform at the End of the Century: Real Agreement, Real Changes*, 32 U. MICH. J.L. REFORM. 213 (1999).

19.   One of the authors of this article played a small role in the media campaign to promote reform. James Levine wrote an academic article reviewing relevant empirical literature, which concluded that sequestration normally does more harm than good. Levine, *The impact of sequestration on juries*, 79 JUDICATURE 266–272 (1996). Based on this research, he published a letter to the editor in *The New York Times* in which he said that "it is time to stop making jurors prisoners of the court." N.Y. Times, March 12, 1997, at A22.

20.   New York State's 57 commissioners of jurors presented many potential, and real, obstacles to reform.

21.   Most notably, occupational exemptions and jury sequestration were statutory regulations.

22.   *See generally* New York Judiciary Law. Note, too, that to the extent he can, and did, exert influence over legislators, the governor, too, affects court administration.

23.   Indeed, Jonathan Lippman referred to jury reform as "a decade-long quest." *Supra* n. 7.

24.   Schwartz, *Chief Judge's Reform Efforts Just Go Bust*, N.Y. Daily News, December 9, 2003, at 41.

25.   Interview with Judith Kaye, April 21, 2003. Judge Kaye's commitment to jury reform is ongoing. In April 2003 she formed the Commission on the Jury to determine how the court system could better utilize jurors' service, and in May 2003 she launched the Jury Trial Project, a statewide initiative charged with experimenting with a variety of reforms to improve juror comprehension (e.g., permitting jurors to take notes, allowing jurors to submit written questions for witnesses, etc.).

26.   Other examples of jury reform gradualism, or incrementalism, include phasing in changes over several years (e.g., the increase in juror pay) and using pilot projects (e.g., with respect to changes in civil voir dire).

27.   In 1991, Governor Mario Cuomo substantially cut the judiciary budget, provoking an unprecedented lawsuit filed by then-Chief Judge Sol Wachtler. *See, e.g.,* Caher, *Budget for Judiciary Approved Unaltered; $489 Million Increase Passes Without Controversy*, N.Y. L. J., August 6, 2001, at 1. When Governor Pataki took office he found larger financial problems than he had anticipated. Judge Kaye, on her own, reduced the judiciary's budget request, and this gesture, which was much appreciated by the governor, went a long way toward her forging a cooperative working relationship with him. *Id. See also* Caher, *Judiciary Submits Revised Budget; 15-Month Hiring Freeze and Increased Security Reflect a "New Reality"* N. Y L. J., December 13, 2001, at I ("The Kaye Administration has been extraordinarily successful in its budget dealings with the Pataki Administration, and has constantly benefited from the fiscal credibility it has earned with the legislature . . . Since [1994], neither the Governor nor legislature has excised a cent from the judiciary budget. Every Judiciary budget submitted during Governor Pataki's tenure has been passed intact.").

28.   Interview with James Lack, May 9, 2003.

29.   Lippman was seen as an advocate for the jury, not someone with a political agenda. *Supra* n. 28. Marc Bloustein explicitly mentioned the importance of Judge Lippman's lobbying skills. *Supra* n. 16. Lippman was the deputy chief administrator for the courts until 1995 when he was appointed by Governor Pataki to the Court

of Claims, He thereafter became the deputy chief administrative judge, and in 1996 he was appointed the chief administrative judge for New York State.

30. *Supra* n. 28.

31. Shortly after the elimination of all occupational exemptions, a sitting judge was chosen to serve on a jury panel in New York City. *See* Nossiter, Sitting *Judge Is Chosen for Jury Panel*, N.Y. Times, June 12, 1996, at B3. Also newsworthy was then-New York City Mayor Rudolph Giuliani serving as a juror in a personal injury suit in 1999, the first New York City mayor ever to be chosen as a juror while in office. *See* Arena, *It's Rudy—On Duty*, N.Y. Daily News, August 31, 1999, at 5.

32. Sengupta, *New Law Releases Juries in New York from Sequestering*, N.Y. Times, May 31, 2001, at Al.

30 Small-Town Justice, With Trial and Error

WILLIAM GLABERSON

GARY BETTERS THOUGHT HE UNDERSTOOD the law as well as any average American. A school psychologist, he wanted $1,588.60 he said the nearby village of Malone owed him for helping run a summer recreation program. When he brought a small claim in Duane Town Court, he expected that the judge would listen to both sides, then rule.

Like many others who go to court across New York state, he got a crash course in the strange ways of small-town justice.

Although no one showed up to defend the village, Justice William J. Gori started the trial anyway. Although the judge had Mr. Betters testify at length, he neglected to have him swear to tell the truth. And although Justice Gori told Mr. Betters he had another week to submit more evidence, the judge went ahead and decided the case anyway.

Mr. Betters received the news in a letter from the court: his case had been dismissed. No reason was given. "I cannot understand how a defendant can win when they don't even show up," he said in an interview.

The State Commission on Judicial Conduct figured out how. Justice Gori, it seems, had gone to the village offices in Malone before the trial, interviewed the village's chief witness, then informed the village lawyer that he had decided to throw out the case.

Justice Gori told the commission that he had never heard of the elementary legal rule that bars a judge, except in the most extraordinary circumstances, from secret contact with one side of a case. "It's not even explained in my manual," he said.

An unfamiliarity with basic legal principles is remarkably common in what are known as the justice courts, legacies of the Colonial era that survive in more than 1,000 New York towns and villages.

For generations, justices have hailed them as "poor man's courts," where ordinary people can get simple justice with little formality or expense. But there are few more vivid spots to view their shortcomings than here in one of New York's poorest corners: Franklin County, a place of rugged beauty on the Canadian border where only one of the 32 local justices is a lawyer.

The county's justices have repeatedly drawn the attention of state judicial conduct officials, with 15 publicly disciplined since the late 1970's, some twice. Justice Gori's errors pale in comparison with those of some others: One justice freed a rape suspect on bail as a favor to a friend. Another sentenced a welfare recipient to 89 days in jail after she failed to pay a $1.50 cab fare. Franklin County justices have presided drunk, fixed cases and denied lawyers to defendants. One failed to appoint a lawyer for a 19-year-old mentally retarded alcoholic.

Here in Duane, a speck of a town in the center of the county, Justice Gori is in many ways a typical small-town New York justice.

A bricklayer and a former dog trainer with a high school education, he is an approachable man of 59, in jeans hitched up with suspenders. On Thursday nights he ambles down to the volunteer firehouse to hold court, such as it is. His grasp of the law is somewhat shaky. His temper sometimes gets the better of him.

He has no judge's bench, few law books and no court clerk. He is something of an accidental judge, occupying the position for nearly a decade largely because no one else wants it, people here say. Although state officials have reprimanded him twice for fundamental lapses in the conduct of his job, few Duane voters seemed to know or care. "Nobody's ever asked a question about it," Justice Gori said.

He seems well-intentioned enough. Like many justices, he describes his job as public service, and he says he studies the law for several hours every week.

But there is evidence that that may not be enough. When the judicial

conduct commission called Justice Gori to account for his handling of
Mr. Betters's case, his defense was startling, a transcript of the hearing
shows. His own lawyer blamed the state for running the justice courts as
it does: Judges, he said, with so little training—six days of classes, and a
12-hour refresher course once a year—could not possibly know the basic
rules for handling a lawsuit.

The county's district attorney, Derek P. Champagne, says that when
he took office five years ago, he had to drop hundreds of criminal cases
because justices had failed to take any action for so long. Mr. Champagne
says his staff of four full-time prosecutors is too small even to regularly
visit the justice courts, which are separated by great distances.

Franklin County is bigger than Rhode Island. But it has only one
higher court judge, in the county court in Malone. So the part-time
town and village justices—plumbers, meat cutters and school bus drivers—
are often the last word on the law here, with the power to issue search
warrants, conduct trials, put some people in jail and let friends go free.

"The reality is, you basically have to have no qualifications other
than be a voter to put someone in jail, and that's a very alarming situation,"
Mr. Champagne said. "To throw a layperson—some of whom don't have
a high school degree—in that position is just a recipe for disaster."

A Night in Court

"Town of Duane Justice Court is now in session," Justice Gori
announced.

Four bare fluorescent bulbs provided the only light in the roughly
finished meeting room that becomes a court every few weeks. There was
a portable bar against one wall, and a glimpse of the firehouse kitchen,
with its jumble of old soda bottles and coffeepots. The American flag
tacked to the wall had to be pulled back to allow the judge to get at the
thermostat on this icy winter night.

At two pushed-together folding tables sat a nervous teenager, in
court to answer speeding tickets, next to his clench-jawed father. A state
trooper, there as chief witness against the teenager, doubled as the court
security officer.

And behind a battered wooden desk was Justice Gori. Fleshy, with
eyes that water at sentimental moments, he was wearing an open brown
shirt, his T-shirt visible at the neck.

The court computer that he bought with his own money was at
home; it took him two months to figure out how to turn the thing on,

he said. He had no judge's robe. They are too expensive, he said. His judicial salary is $3,750 a year.

"There are certain things that are lacking," he said.

He moved to Duane, population 159, from Saratoga County in his 40's after a divorce, enticed by the chance to hunt with his dogs.

"Maybe it's the solitude," said Justice Gori, who has since remarried. "You get up here at night, when the highway quiets down, you don't hear anything."

Yet people cross paths in Franklin County in unlikely and sometimes volatile ways: Mohawk Indians, the owners of lavish new vacation homes, Adirondack tourists and fishermen, and others who cross the border on less savory business. Drugs and domestic violence seem to be on the rise, and state prisons are big employers.

When Justice Gori moved here about 20 years ago, the prison construction boom offered jobs. After years as a dog trainer, "I picked up my tools and went back to the bricklaying, mason trade," he said.

Like a lot of newcomers to small towns, he wanted to get involved. But he didn't like the sight of blood, so that ruled out volunteer firefighting. He was attracted instead to the court in the weathered firehouse. "Law has always been kind of an interesting thing to me," he said.

That interest, however, does not include a fascination with the technicalities that occupy lawyers. "If you look at the laws, it's all common sense," he said.

Most of his work, since his first election in 1997, has been traffic cases. If there were many serious crimes in Duane, he said, they may have gone unnoticed out in the vast Adirondack nights. "Either we're a nice, quiet town or two people duked it out and one won and one lost, they got up and shook hands and nobody knows about it," he said.

There have been a handful of serious cases, the first phases of some felony prosecutions. Once, state troopers tracked him down on a bricklaying job. They said a local man was growing marijuana, and wanted a warrant to search his property. In the dust and cement, it fell to William Gori, dog trainer and mason, to put aside his tools and measure the rights guaranteed under the Constitution. "I sat down," he said. "Read everything. Looked at all the pictures." The troopers got their warrant.

In the makeshift courtroom on this winter night, he was warmly sympathetic to a woman who had forgotten to put the registration sticker on her windshield. Case dismissed.

But the teenager with the speeding tickets saw the stern Justice Gori. The boy had tickets in a half-dozen Franklin County towns, and his lawyer proposed combining the cases in another court.

No way. "What happens in the town of Duane," Justice Gori declared, "stays in the town of Duane."

That is not always true. The other case that drew the attention of the Commission on Judicial Conduct involved Lucille K. Millett, a Mohawk woman from the reservation that straddles the county's border with Canada. She was outside the Duane court one night in 2004 waiting for her sister, whom she had driven there for a traffic case. Justice Gori summoned Ms. Millett inside, asked for her driver's license and called the state police to run it through their computer.

In an interview, Ms. Millett said she was frightened and embarrassed; no one else was asked for a license. The only sense the sisters could make of it, she said, was that they were the only American Indians in court.

She filed a complaint with the commission, which ruled last year that Justice Gori had no right to demand anything of someone outside his court who faced no charges.

Asked about the case, Justice Gori denied that he harbored any prejudice. He said he thought he was acting within his authority.

"You learn by mistakes," he said. "They say this is improper, I don't do it again."

It is a measure of his isolation that his disciplinary hearings have been among the few times he has had a chance to rub shoulders with the larger legal world. He attends the refresher course each year. But he said the town could not afford to send him to the annual state magistrates' convention, held last year in Niagara Falls, nor could he pay for the trip himself.

Still, he is convinced that he and the other justices across New York are honest people trying to do right. "Economicswise," he added, "you couldn't get the job done any cheaper."

A County at the Edges

The troubles of Mr. Gori and his fellow justices are nothing new. In 1973, the State Commission of Investigation arrived in the Franklin County village of Saranac Lake to examine the work of one justice, a maintenance worker and vacuum-cleaner salesman, whose "inept and mangled handling," it said, had bungled a felony grand larceny case.

What investigators found alarmed them. Money was missing. Records were sloppy. A pile of cash from fines sat in an unlocked drawer. The justice's relationship with the police seemed far too close, and one of his law books was 44 years old.

Astonished, the investigators widened their inquiry to include all the justice courts in the county and then expanded it across New York. Calling for statewide reform, they concluded that "such deficiencies and ineptitude" in the justice courts "simply must not be tolerated."

But little seems to have changed in Franklin County's justice courts since then.

In November 2005, one longtime village justice, Roy H. Kristoffersen, a salesman, resigned after officials began investigating charges, which he denied, that he "rendered favorable dispositions" for the son of the other village justice—in Saranac Lake, the same place that touched off the investigation 33 years ago.

Another justice, Marie A. Cook, a school-bus driver who is still on the town bench in Chateaugay, not only fixed a speeding ticket at the request of a fellow justice, but she was so oblivious to ethical rules, the commission said last fall, that she made an official record of the fix: "Reduced in the interest of Justice Danny LaClair."

Yet another, the town justice who released a rape suspect on bail as a favor to a friend, tried to explain things to the commission: "Maybe you are not familiar with what goes on in the North Country, but we are all more or less friends up there."

Such cases may only hint at the dimensions of the problem in Franklin's courts. A review for this article of rarely seen appeals files in Franklin County Court showed a disturbing trail of legal blunders and judicial ignorance over the last five years.

One justice seemed not to fully understand that criminal charges must be proved beyond a reasonable doubt, wrote the county court judge, Robert G. Main Jr. Another justice skipped over the matter of the constitutional guarantee of a lawyer. Immediately after a woman charged with fraud said she could not afford an attorney, Judge Main said, the village justice took her guilty plea instead of appointing a lawyer.

Such problems are hardly news to many lawyers who make the rounds of Franklin County's justice courts. Some say they avoid the courts because the justices often have trouble following their arguments.

In a place as poor and remote as Franklin County, the failings of modest courts can loom large. Cases too minor to draw much interest from the rest of the legal system—evictions, misdemeanor charges, disputes between neighbors, driving infractions and applications for bail—come with real consequences for small-town residents who may have little money or access to a lawyer.

Alexander Lesyk, the Franklin County public defender for 15 years until 2005, said that while he had some successes for poor clients before local justices, "I don't believe any of them has enough training to handle a trial, to handle constitutional issues, to stand up to and control an attorney on either side when they need to."

But challenging a justice can be bad for business, some lawyers said.

The district attorney, Mr. Champagne, said that when his office hears about justices who stray from the law, it has to be careful. "We're not going to get into a confrontation with a judge we may have to go in front of next week on a very serious preliminary hearing in a murder case," he said.

A Case of Confusion

When Gary Betters got the letter from Justice Gori in March 1999 saying that his claim for back pay had been dismissed, he was very confused. The message was a single paragraph, and garbled at that. Even the date on it was wrong.

But that was only the start of his troubles.

He wrote to Justice Gori, asking for a mistrial. The justice never replied.

Mr. Betters decided to appeal in county court. But he could not persuade any lawyer to take the case; several, he said, told him it would not be in their interest to take on a town justice.

On his own, Mr. Betters filed a complaint with the Commission on Judicial Conduct, and the truth emerged: The commission's investigators discovered that Justice Gori had gone to the Malone village offices before the trial and interviewed the defense's chief witness, the village treasurer, who told him that Mr. Betters was owed nothing.

Justice Gori told the village attorney that he need not show up for the trial because he had already decided to dismiss the case. The attorney was amazed. "A lot of bells and whistles went off," he told the commission.

But when Justice Gori explained himself to the commission in a closed hearing, he said he had never heard of the rule against contacting one side of a case to discuss the evidence. Further, the commission's lawyer argued, a legal motion filed by the village had completely bewildered Justice Gori, even after he made several calls to the state's help line for town justices.

"The whole concept I didn't understand," Justice Gori testified.

It was a damaging admission, but nothing compared with the case made by his own lawyer, John A. Piasecki. He said his client's error-riddled handling of Mr. Betters's suit was an indictment of the system, which put laymen on the bench, gave them little training and left them to interpret the law.

Mr. Piasecki asked whether the state had ever checked Justice Gori's reading comprehension. (It had not.) He even tried to cross-examine the Malone village attorney to show what he argued was the obvious difference between Justice Gori and someone who actually understood the law.

Mr. Piasecki, a Franklin County lawyer himself, urged a "long-overdue correction" for the justice court system, which he said "undermines confidence in the integrity of the judiciary."

The commission was not moved. Justice Gori, it said, had a duty to learn the law. "Town justices wield enormous power in civil and criminal cases," the commission said, "and it is not unreasonable to expect them to know and follow basic statutory procedures."

Yet Justice Gori received the lightest public penalty the commission can issue, an admonition.

As for Mr. Betters, he never found a lawyer to take his appeal. Today, he still feels that his education in Franklin County law cost him a lot more than $1,588.60.

"It broke down my belief in the justice system," he said.

Business as Usual

The judicial career of William Gori began humbly enough.

"Nobody was jumping out of the woodwork wanting this job," said Justice Gori, who raised his hand for the position in 1997 after the sitting justice announced his retirement.

With no opposition, he won the endorsement of the *Republicans* and then the *Democrats* in Duane. The Republican chairwoman, Pamela M. LeMieux, said he impressed party leaders as responsible and "very strict."

In the general election, his only opponent was Gary Anderson, a former accountant who ran as the candidate of what he named the Pine Tree Party. "Nobody wants the job," Mr. Anderson said.

Even the campaign was not especially interesting, Justice Gori recalled. "All I said was: 'I'm Bill Gori. I'm running for town justice and I'm only interested in doing a good job for the town.'" He won, 64 [votes] to 39.

If the process was not a model of meticulous judicial selection, that fact may carry an extra punch in Duane. The town, as it happens, was named for its founders, descendants of the first federal judge in New York.

When President George Washington selected the judge, James Duane, a prominent lawyer, for the post in 1789, he used the nomination to lay out his aspirations for selecting judges in a democracy. The choice of who would sit on a nation's courts was a matter of "the first magnitude," Washington wrote, and the judiciary was "the pillar on which our political fabric must rest."

Today, that fabric is a little frayed in Franklin County.

Thomas Catillaz, a former mayor of Saranac Lake, said that when political parties there find a nominee, "It's usually, 'Thank God somebody's running,'" he said. "And if you're in there, you're in there for 20 years."

When justices are publicly disciplined, that is often the end of the matter. As Justice Gori recalls it, when he received his second admonition last year, the local newspaper in Malone "put it way in the back."

He faced an election after each ruling, but no opponent. Gary Cring, a retired schoolteacher who has lived in Duane for six years, said he had not heard that Justice Gori had been disciplined. Had that been better known, he said, voters might have been less enthusiastic about re-electing him. "People figure he must be doing a good job," Mr. Cring said.

But Mrs. LeMieux, the Republican chairwoman, said it was not the town's job to police its justice. "If he did something that was that serious, I figure the court system wouldn't have allowed him to remain a justice," she said. "If they didn't throw him out, then who are we to judge?"

And so Justice Gori is . . . learning the job as he goes. He does not appear to share his lawyer's disdain for how the justice courts are run.

"I really feel the justice courts are the courts closest to the people," he said, and being a lawyer might interfere with that. "At times, lawyers get hung up in certain things, so that maybe you wouldn't get true justice in certain cases."

But a state police report from 2005 suggested that in Duane, true justice—and empathy for the people—might be works in progress.

It seems that Brandon L. Lucas, a scrawny 19-year-old from the next county, was trying to pay a ticket he had received in Duane for fishing with the wrong kind of bait. Since the firehouse court was empty, as it often is, Mr. Lucas went down the road to Justice Gori's house.

Soon, Mr. Lucas was in the back of a state trooper's car in handcuffs, and in tears. An angry Justice Gori had berated him and called the police, the young man recalled when a reporter tracked him down. He had evidently not seen the sign on the judge's garage: "If you proceed past this point, you are subject to various trespass rules and regulations."

The district attorney decided not to prosecute. And Mr. Lucas made his own decision about wandering into the jurisdiction of Duane Town Court: Don't.

"I'll never go fishing up there again," he said.

PART TEN

STATE AND LOCAL FINANCES

In June of 1978, a financial tremor hit state and local governments in the form of California's Proposition 13 which imposed strict limitations on the ability of that state's local governments to raise revenue *via* the property tax. The 1980s saw a series of smaller quakes and aftershocks that combined to make financing state and local governments arguably the number one problem facing decision makers. During the 1980s and into the early 1990s, several states and cities grappled with budget deficits and financial crises, including Bridgeport, Connecticut, which declared bankruptcy in June 1991.[1] Another round of fiscal stress hit the states right after the 9/11 terrorist attacks, and belt-tightening was once again on the front burner for state legislatures and city councils. It remains to be seen what challenges the 2008 credit crunch will bring. What is for sure is that, once again, as a result of a severe economic downturn, this time, the 2008–09 global financial crisis, state and local finances are under even greater stress.

Such fiscal ups and downs typically plague state and local government finance systems. Scholars characterize them by two basic principles: interdependence and diversity.[2] There is a significant linkage between state and local government finances, and they are strongly influenced by national government fiscal policies and the national economy. On the other hand, an incredible degree of diversity exists across the states and communities relative to the types of revenues on which they rely and the level of fiscal capacity they sustain. Additionally, the ability to weather fiscal storms is tied closely to the elasticity of state and local revenue systems. Revenues (taxes and non-taxes such as permits and user fees) that are more elastic tend to generate higher collection rates during better economic times, and lower collection rates during economic downturns.

In light of these revenue system characteristics, states must constantly utilize innovative approaches to keep the dollars flowing into state coffers. Our first article by Sujit Canagaretna discusses a variety of techniques used in recent years to stem the tide of red ink during economic downturns.

Gambling and lotteries have become common ways for state and local governments to raise non-tax revenues in the last couple of decades, and quite frequently lottery revenues are earmarked for a particular policy area, most often education. In spite of their increased usage, however, lotteries remain highly controversial. In our second article, Bruce Buchanan takes a look at the pros and cons of using lotteries to fund schools, and suggests that they are ". . . proving to be a high-risk gamble."

In their search for alternative forms of revenue, local governments often get quite creative and innovative. For example, Tax Increment Financing (TIF) has been utilized extensively as a way to revitalize blighted urban neighborhoods and stimulate job creation with the hope of generating additional future revenues. Yet, as Richard Dye and David Merriman chronicle in our final article, this strategy is not always successful.

Notes

1. Michael J. Daly, "Watching Bridgeport's Budget Grow," *The Bridgeport Post* 108 (June 23, 1991): A1.
2. Ann O'M. Bowman and Richard C. Kearney, *State and Local Government,* 3rd ed.. (Princeton, NJ: Houghton Mifflin Company, 1996), p. 347.

Questions for Review and Discussion

10.1   What are some methods states have used recently to balance their budgets? Which of these seem best to you? Why?

10.2   What are the pros and cons of state lotteries? What have been their effects on education spending? Should their usage be expanded? Why or why not?

10.3   What is Tax Increment Financing? What have been its effects on local economic development? Do you think it is overused? Why or why not?

31 Budget Balancing Tactics

SUJIT M. CANAGARETNA

THE NATION'S SLUGGISH ECONOMY has triggered the development of innovative budget strategies among state policy-makers.

After a decade between March 1991 and March 2001 of sustained growth, unsurpassed in the nation's economic history, the United States economy continues to feel the lingering effects of the 2001 recession. . . .

States Face Dire Choices

. . . [S]tates continue to confront dire choices. In recent years, states closed a cumulative $200 billion budget gap with a series of actions that ranged from slashing spending to tapping rainy day funds to raising taxes. States had to simultaneously tackle slumping revenues, rising unemployment numbers and exploding health care costs.

. . . In November 2003, 10 states reported that they expected budget shortfalls totaling $2.8 billion during the . . . 2004 fiscal year. That contrasts to November 2002 when 31 states indicated shortfalls totaling $17.5 billion for fiscal year 2003. Notwithstanding these positive developments, the continuing effects of the cyclical downturn and the serious structural problems associated with state tax systems will batter state finances.

Unlike the federal government, practically every state is constitutionally required to balance its budget. Consequently, states adopted some of the more obvious budget-balancing strategies and then began deploying a number of innovative measures to meet their constitutional obligations.

Decoupling from Federal Policies

A number of recent federal fiscal actions have had negative impacts on states. The 2001, 2002 and 2003 federal tax cuts reduced state revenues by an estimated $10 billion. The repeal of the federal estate tax credit in 2001 — to which all state estate taxes were tied — lowered revenues by an estimated $4 billion through September 2004. Finally, the federal bonus depreciation provision . . . cut state revenues by an estimated $14 billion between 2002 and September 2004. While a majority of states (37) have chosen to de-link their tax codes from the federal provisions, a number of others have yet to do so.

Leveraging Technology

States are deploying technology to both enhance efficiencies and save money.

California's Integrated Non-Filer Compliance system (INC) electronically matches data from W-2 forms, 1099s, real property sales, K-1 partnership returns and related records against filed tax returns to identify entities that did not file returns. INC has processed more than 160 million records and generated $182 million since its inception.

Iowa's Tax Gap Compliance Program uses customized software to identify entities that are supposed to file tax returns but did not and entities that filed but did not pay their taxes. This program generated $26 million in tax revenue above baseline collections in three years.

Florida's SUNTAX was designed to allow one-stop registration, cutting-edge accounting for all taxes, and maximization of World

Wide Web and e-filing technology and services. Consequently, the Revenue Department has collected $21 billion in revenue each year, served 1.2 million taxpayers, and processed 6 million transactions. SUNTAX has also generated over $70 million in collections by identifying noncompliance in the telecommunications industry.

Introducing Tax Amnesty Programs

Tax amnesty programs are another popular revenue-enhancing strategy that entices individuals to pay their back taxes. Between 2002 and 2003, 19 states enacted amnesty programs. In Virginia, the 2003 program raised more than $98 million, double the amount expected. Michigan's 2002 program generated $30 million.

Innovative Programs in Transportation

In Minnesota, Gov. Pawlenty released details of a proposal to let solo drivers pay to use the carpool lane along I–394. Socalled HOT lanes—short for High Occupancy Toll—have eased congestion in California and Texas.

Georgia could soon begin accepting proposals for privately financed road and transit projects, according to the state's Transportation Department. Companies could recoup their costs through tolls, transit fare or even long-term road maintenance contracts.

Creative Financing Techniques

Illinois approved a pension financing plan in 2004 that increases the state's general obligations to make payments to five state retirement systems. Otherwise, the pension debt obligations would have been paid from the general fund, costing the state $1.9 billion in 2003 and 2004.

Mississippi will save $7 million to $10 million a year by issuing variable-rate instead of fixed-rate bonds for its Nissan plant.

Kansas authorized its governor to either accelerate property tax payments or delay tax refunds.

South Dakota will now count investment income earned on state cash flow in the year it was earned.

Recouping Costs from the Estates of Deceased Persons

In 1993, Congress ordered states to recover from the estates of deceased persons some of the money spent on nursing home care by Medicaid. While minimal action on this directive was initiated in the past decade, more recently:

Texas drafted rules to recover money from the estates of some deceased Medicaid patients.

In Connecticut, hundreds of low-income elderly and disabled people opted out of the state's prescription drug programs because of the move to recoup expenses from program recipient's estates.

Inventive Measures to Maximize Federal Matching Funds Under Medicaid

States continue efforts to maximize their Federal Medical Assistance Percentage and produce additional revenue. In the area of nursing facilities, one of the more common strategies has been the use of upper payment limits in which local government providers are paid more money than they would otherwise receive, thus generating a greater FMAP. The local providers then return the excess money to the state.

Streamlining Government Services

North Carolina disposed of state-owned surplus real property more efficiently generating $10 million in revenue; consolidated employee death and disability benefit reserve funds saving $55 million; implemented "prior approval" and use of generics in Medicaid prescription drugs for a savings of $97 million; and accelerated the state's debt collection practices for $50 million in additional revenue.

A commission appointed by South Carolina's Gov. Mark Sanford to improve the delivery of state services and generate revenue recently issued its final report. Recommendations contained an estimated savings of $225 million in the first year and more than $300 million annually thereafter.

Prescription Drugs

Lawmakers in Illinois created a statewide, centralized buying club to negotiate the best rates on prescription drugs for seniors and disabled persons. Illinois saves $150 million annually by purchasing these prescription drugs centrally at a volume discount.

Illinois, New Hampshire, Minnesota, Wisconsin, Iowa, Michigan, Vermont and West Virginia continue to press the federal government to permit the importation of lower-priced prescription drugs from Canada. Illinois estimates $91 million in annual savings here.

Although the financial picture in many states remains murky and job growth continues to be tepid, there is room for cautious optimism.

32 Rolling the Dice

BRUCE BUCHANAN

ON MARCH 30, 2006, North Carolina rolled the dice and officially got into the gambling business with a long-awaited and highly controversial state lottery to fund schools.

More than 5,000 convenience stores and other outlets from the Outer Banks to the Smoky Mountains began selling scratch-off lottery tickets to lines of eager patrons. Mike Easley, the state's two-term Democratic governor, made the lottery a cornerstone of his platform and had worked for years to obtain its passage.

Under Easley's plan, 100 percent of net lottery proceeds are earmarked for educational purposes, including class size reduction in the early grades, pre-kindergarten programs, school construction, and college scholarships. And the connection between the lottery and the schools was symbolically apparent that opening day, as State Board of Education Chairman Howard Lee purchased the first $1 ticket.

Like many lottery proponents, Easley, Lee, and others touted the games as a surefire means of significantly boosting revenue for schools. But the results over the past 14 months have been less than spectacular, and revenues for the first year were $75 million less than supporters originally expected.

Despite the hype about lotteries enhancing the coffers of school districts, the benefits often are similar to North Carolina's. Without question, lotteries produce big bucks—nearly $14 billion nationwide in 2004—but school districts that bank on big profits are left scrambling when revenues fail to meet expectations.

Playing the Game

Today, 23 of the 42 states that have lotteries earmark the proceeds for education, as does the District of Columbia. In the remaining states, lottery profits go into the state's general fund.

Michael Griffith, school finance consultant for the Education Commission of the States, says hype often outweighs the actual benefits for schools. In fact, Griffith says, most public schools only receive enough lottery money every year to operate for about one week. Lottery proceeds, for example, represent 5 percent of all public school revenue in New York, for example, and only 2 percent of public school funding in California.

"The truth is that lottery funding as a percentage of overall education funding is still pretty small," Griffith says. "But it's still important."

Research by University of Tennessee professor Rodney Stanley has found that lotteries initially boost school funding. But over time, those increased funding levels almost always vanish. This is due in part to inflation, but also to the ever-changing nature of state budgets.

"A lot of policymakers view them as a windfall of hope," Stanley says. "In the first three to five years, it tends to do fairly well in terms of generating revenue, if the state can keep administrative costs down."

However, that funding soon levels off and even declines, Stanley says. Florida, for example, actually saw per-pupil funding decline, even after implementing a state lottery.

"It depends on the state," says Richard McGowan, an associate professor at Boston College's Carroll School of Management who studies gambling and lotteries. "In many ways, lottery revenue is like revenue that the states received from the tobacco settlement; if the state gets into fiscal trouble, then that revenue is diverted from the original need or capped."

A High-Stakes Gamble

While some states have had lotteries for decades, North Carolina resisted the urge to join the trend. By 2005, it was the only East Coast state without a lottery.

But that didn't mean Tar Heel residents weren't playing the game. In fact, North Carolina's four neighbors—Virginia, Tennessee, Georgia, and South Carolina—all enjoyed brisk lottery sales in border towns, as residents made the short drive for a chance to win big.

Lottery supporters saw this as lost revenue that could be used to fund the state's schools. When Easley took office in 2001, he made the lottery a top priority. The governor wanted to expand education programs, particularly those targeting pre-kindergarten students, but the economy cooled off in the wake of 9/11 and the state's budget situation worsened.

North Carolina's lottery opponents also were far better organized than in other states. An odd coalition of religious conservatives and liberal activists, the opposition believed the lottery would amount to a tax on the poor. Popular former Gov. Jim Martin, a moderate, pro-business Republican, lent his voice to the opponents' cause.

In July 2002, N.C. House Speaker Jim Black pulled a lottery bill from consideration after he and other lottery supporters decided they lacked sufficient votes to pass it. Three years later, however, it passed in the House by two votes and moved to the Senate. There, Lt. Gov. Beverly Perdue—like Easley, a Democrat—broke a 24-24 tie.

The Senate vote only took place after it was learned that two Republican senators who opposed the lottery would not be in attendance that day. Opponents cried dirty politics and sued, but the courts rejected that challenge, clearing the path for state-sponsored gambling.

By law, 35 percent of gross revenues are supposed to go to education. With advertising, administrative costs, and retailers' commissions taking up an additional 15 percent, that leaves about half the total lottery revenue for prizes. Neighboring states earmark a higher percentage for prize money; South Carolina, for example, spends about 59 percent of its lottery income on prizes.

The North Carolina lottery didn't meet the 35 percent requirement in its first year due to start-up costs and slower-than-expected sales. Instead, 27 percent of the first year's take went to the schools.

"The North Carolina lottery was overpromised and oversold," says John Hood, president of the John Locke Foundation, a conservative think tank based in Raleigh.

A Host of Problems

Hood, who has closely monitored school funding and lottery issues for years, says legislators were sold a bill of goods, with education as the carrot. "Lottery advocates felt it necessary to elevate revenue estimates to convince reluctant lawmakers that significant educational investments could be the result," he says.

North Carolina's lottery opponents had a long list of problems and concerns. They believed a lottery disproportionately affects poor people; to date, the highest per-capita lottery spending has come from low-income, heavily minority counties in the state's rural east. They questioned if the lottery would be a reliable source of income. And they wondered if the money would be spent effectively.

To appease those with objections, lottery organizers limited advertising and offered modest purses compared to surrounding states. Hood says that approach backfired, as the North Carolina public gave the lottery a lukewarm reception and continued to play the more lucrative games offered in states such as Virginia and South Carolina.

"What you ended up with was a recipe for revenue shortfall," Hood says.

Even worse, the lottery has been plagued with legal and ethical scandals since the start. Kevin Geddings, an original member of the state commission that oversees the program, resigned after allegations that he hid a business relationship with a lottery vendor. A jury convicted Geddings of five counts of mail fraud based on that deception.

Geddings' woes were only the beginning. Black, one of the lottery's primary proponents, was dogged by allegations that he had accepted bribes while serving as one of the three most powerful leaders in state government. These alleged bribes weren't directly linked to the new lottery, but since Black's fingerprints were all over the effort, it was at the least an unfortunate connection for the games. In February, Black resigned in disgrace and pleaded guilty to a felony charge of accepting illegal gratuities. He will be sentenced this month.

Earlier this year, Easley recommended dropping the percentage of lottery proceeds directed toward education. That money instead would be spent to increase jackpots. The theory is that with higher prizes, more people will play, revenues will increase, and schools will end up with more money, even though the percentage going to education has declined.

However, some critics claim Easley wants to break an important promise in selling the lottery to the public—that proceeds would benefit the public schools.

The Georgia Model

North Carolina and other states wanting to do a lottery right perhaps should take a cue from Georgia. That state's lottery, which started in

1993, is generally regarded as the most effective in the nation for promoting school improvements.

In Georgia, lottery money is earmarked for specific purposes, rather than being poured into a general fund where its ultimate destination might be murky at best. Georgia's lottery money goes to fund HOPE (Helping Outstanding Pupils Educationally) Scholarships.

The HOPE program provides college scholarships, loans, and tuition grants for college students as well as for teachers who seek advanced degrees in areas of critical need, such as math and science. To date, approximately 950,000 students have received HOPE Scholarships over the past 13 years.

Georgia's lottery money also goes to pre-kindergarten programs, school construction, and training teachers to use technology in the classroom. So far, 790,000 students have attended pre-kindergarten paid for by the lottery.

McGowen says other states should consider Georgia's approach when deciding how to spend lottery proceeds. "The lottery shouldn't be used to fund constant needs but should be used to fund building projects and other one-time projects," he says. "In this way the state doesn't become 'addicted' to the lottery."

In addition to specifying how the money will be spent, Georgia's lottery architects also made the program totally self-sufficient and politically independent. A stand-alone nonprofit organization free from oversight of state lawmakers, the program funds all of its own expenses through ticket revenues and does not receive a state allotment from the General Assembly. And because the lottery exists outside the auspices of state lawmakers, they cannot raid the proceeds to pay for anything other than the specific programs funded by the lottery, such as HOPE Scholarships and prekindergarten.

"The whole idea was to create something that wouldn't supplant the general fund—it would be wholly supplemental," says Margaret DeFrancisco, president and CEO of the Georgia Lottery.

That idea came from former Gov. Zell Miller, who ran for office on a pro-lottery platform. Miller grew up in a small town under modest circumstances and was able to attend college because of the G.I. Bill. When he ran for governor, he wanted to start a program that enabled other young people to get that same opportunity at a college education.

Before the HOPE Scholarships, DeFrancisco says, many Georgia natives left the state to attend college and never returned. But since the scholarship program started, a much higher percentage of those students have chosen to stay in Georgia for college and remain in the state after graduation.

The lottery was controversial at first in conservative, religious Georgia, DeFrancisco says. But that controversy has passed, she says, because nearly everyone knows somebody who has directly benefitted from a HOPE Scholarship or lottery-funded pre-kindergarten.

"It's been a remarkable transformation," DeFrancisco says.

The Future of Lotteries

Currently, only eight states—Alabama, Alaska, Arkansas, Hawaii, Mississippi, Nevada, Utah, and Wyoming—do not have lotteries. Among those, Alaska and Wyoming don't need the lottery revenue, as these states have small populations and huge tax revenues coming from natural resources such as oil and coal. Utah is unlikely to get a lottery for religious reasons. And the odds of Nevada getting a state lottery are almost nil, since it would compete with the casino gambling that is the lifeblood of the state's economy.

Griffith says that leaves Arkansas as the state most likely to add an education lottery in the future. Like many other states, Arkansas faces litigation to boost funding for schools in low-income areas, and a lottery is a quick, relatively painless way for a state to come up with extra revenue. Most other Southern states have adopted state lotteries, indicating that whatever moral and religious objections may have once existed in the region to state-sanctioned gambling have diminished.

"Lotteries have become a big deal in the South," says Stanley, the Tennessee State University professor.

Griffith says one major concern for lottery proponents is the lack of future revenue growth potential. By and large, he says, lotteries are maxed out in terms of income—there simply aren't any new games, marketing campaigns, or strategies that can significantly increase the amount of money players spend on tickets.

"States are grasping at ways to improve that," Griffith says. For example, Illinois is considering privatizing its state lottery, which would bring a one-time infusion of money.

Even successful programs such as Georgia's aren't growing at a fast-enough pace to keep up with the rising costs of lottery-funded programs. That's not good news for states where the school-age population is growing, education related expenses are rising, and legal pressure is increasing to fund education programs.

"At some point, we're going to hit that absolute ceiling," DeFrancisco says. "The demand for HOPE Scholarships probably will outstrip the supply and then, the policymakers will have a decision to make."

33 Tax Increment Financing

RICHARD F. DYE

DAVID F. MERRIMAN

TAX INCREMENT FINANCING (TIF) is an alluring tool that allows municipalities to promote economic development by earmarking property tax revenue from increases in assessed values within a designated TIF district. Proponents point to evidence that assessed property value within TIF districts generally grows much faster than in the rest of the municipality and infer that TIF benefits the entire municipality. Our own empirical analysis, using data from Illinois, suggests to the contrary that the non-TIF areas of municipalities that use TIF grow no more rapidly, and perhaps more slowly, than similar municipalities that do not use TIF. An important finding is that TIF has different impacts when land use is considered. For example, commercial TIF districts tend to decrease commercial development in the non-TIF portion of the municipality.

Designating a TIF District

The rules for tax increment financing, and even its name, vary across the 48 states in which the practice is authorized. The designation usually requires a finding that an area is "blighted" or "underdeveloped" and the development would not take place "but for" the public expenditure or subsidy. It is only a bit of an overstatement to characterize the "blight" and "but for" findings as merely *pro forma* exercises, since specialized consultants can produce the needed evidence in almost all cases. In most states, the requirement for these findings does little to restrict the location of TIF districts.

TIF expenditures are often debt financed in anticipation of future tax revenues. The practice dates to California in 1952, where it started as an innovative way of raising local matching funds for federal grants. TIF became increasingly popular in the 1980s and 1990s, when there were declines in subsidies for local economic development from federal grants, state grants, and federal tax subsidies (especially industrial development bonds). In many cases TIF is "the only game in town" for financing local economic development. The basic rules of the game are illustrated in Figure 1. The top panel shows a land area view of a hypothetical municipality. The area on the western border is designated a TIF district and its assessed value is measured. The lower panel of Figure 1 shows the base-year property values in the TIF (B) and the non-TIF (N) areas. At a later point in time, assessed property values have grown to include the increment (I) in the TIF district and growth (G) in the non-TIF area of the municipality.

Tax increment financing carves out the increment (I) and reserves it for the exclusive use of the economic development authority, while

FIGURE 1   TIF and Non-TIF Areas and Value Components

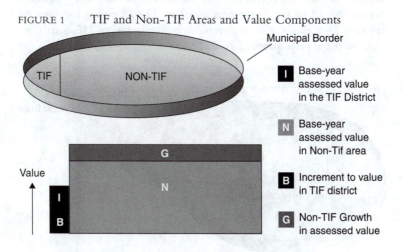

Municipal Border

I — Base-year assessed value in the TIF District

N — Base-year assessed value in Non-Tif area

B — Increment to value in TIF district

G — Non-TIF Growth in assessed value

the base-year assessed value (B) stays in the local government tax base. Thus,

Before-TIF value = before TIF local government tax base = B + N;

After-TIF value = B + N + I + G;

After-TIF tax base available to local governments = B + N + G; and

TIF district authority's tax base = I.

Impacts on Overlapping Governments and Non-TIF Areas

The value increment (I) is the tax base of the TIF district. In most states (like Illinois, but unlike Massachusetts) there are multiple overlapping local governments, e.g., the municipality, school district, community college district, county, township, park district, library district, and other special districts. Figure 2 illustrates this situation with the school district representing all the nonmunicipal governments. To understand the economics and politics of TIF, it is crucial to note that while the municipality makes the TIF adoption decision, the TIF area value is part of the tax base of the school district and other local governments as well. Moreover, the TIF district gets revenues from the increment times the combined tax rate for all local governments together. The following hypothetical tax rates for a group of local governments overlapping a TIF district are close to the average proportions in Illinois.

FIGURE 2   TIF Areas with Overlapping Governments

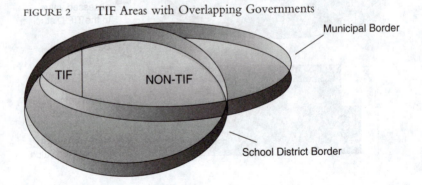

Municipal tax rate	0.15%
School district tax rate	0.60%
Other governments' tax rate	0.25%
Combined tax rate	1.00%

For each 15 cents of its own would-be tax revenues the municipality puts on the line, the school district and other local governments contribute another 85 cents. Thus, there may be an incentive for municipalities to "capture" revenue from growth that would have occurred in the absence of TIF (to collect taxes that would have gone to school districts). Or, municipal decision makers may favor inefficient economic development strategies that do not result in public benefits worth the full cost, since their own cost is only 15 cents on the dollar. TIF proponents would counter that nothing is captured, because the increment to the tax base would not exist "but for" for TIF authority expenditure. That argument, of course, turns on what would have happened to property values in the absence of TIF.

If, as municipalities are often required to assert when they adopt TIF, all of the increment is attributable to the activities of the TIF development authority, then TIF is fair, in that the school district is not giving up any would-be revenues. If, as critics of TIF sometimes assert or assume, none of the increment is attributable to the TIF and all of the new property value growth would have occurred anyway, then the result is just a reallocation of tax revenues by which municipalities win and school districts lose.

The impact of TIF on growth in property values requires a careful reading of the evidence. It is wrong, as those who look only at growth within the TIF district in effect do, to assume to know the answer. Part of the solution is to use appropriate tools to statistically control for other determinants of growth.

It is also necessary to take into account the potential for reverse causality. We want to know the extent to which TIF adoption causes growth. But the causation could go the other way; anticipated growth in property values could lead to TIF adoption if municipalities attempt to capture revenues from overlapping governments. Or there could be reverse causation bias if TIF is adopted in desperation by municipal decision makers in areas where low growth is anticipated. Either way we should ask: Are the municipalities that adopt TIF systematically different from those that do not? If the municipalities are systematically different, we must statistically disentangle the effect of that difference from the effect of the TIF using a technique that corrects for what economists call "sample selection bias."

Impacts on Growth and Property Values

There are two sides to any government budget: revenues and expenditures. As a revenue-side mechanism, TIF is a way of earmarking tax revenues for a particular purpose, in this case local economic development. The effectiveness of economic development expenditures depends on opportunities, incentives, and planning skills that are specific to each local area and each project. By combining data from a large number of TIF and non-TIF municipalities, we can ask; On average and overall, is TIF adoption associated with increased growth in municipal property values? We have addressed this question in two research studies, both of which use statistical controls for the other determinants of growth and for reverse causation due to sample selection bias.

The first study (Dye and Merriman 2000) uses data from 235 Chicago area municipalities and covers preadoption, TIF adoption (or not), and postadoption time periods. We control for the selection bias (reverse causation) problem by first predicting which municipalities adopt TIF and then using that information (a statistic called the inverse Mills ratio) when estimating the effect of TIF adoption on property values in a second stage. Use of selection bias correction was first applied to the study of TIF by John Anderson (1990) and is now standard practice.

Our estimates of the impact of TIF have a number of additional variables controlling for home-rule status, the combined tax rate, population, income per capita, poverty rate, nonresidential share of equalized assessed value (EAV), EAV per square mile, distance to the Chicago loop, and county of location. We found that property values in TIF-adopting municipalities grew at the same rate as or even less rapidly than in nonadopting municipalities. The study design did not get at this directly, but the offset seemed to come from smaller growth in non-TIF area of the municipality (lower G).

Our findings were a surprise to those, especially nonacademics, who naively had inferred TIF caused growth by observing growth within a TIF district (I) without any statistical controls for the other determinants of growth (in I or G). Our findings were quite threatening to those with an interest in TIF, such as local economic development officers who spend the ear-marked funds or TIF consultants who are paid for documenting findings of "blight" or "but for." Our findings were also at odds with an Indiana study that found a positive effect of TIF adoption on housing values (Man and Rosentraub 1998).

Because our findings were controversial, because the effect of TIF was unsettled in the academic literature, and particularly because we wanted to pursue the possibility of a negative cross relationship between growth in the TIF district (I) and growth outside the TIF district (G), we undertook a second study (Dye and Merriman 2003). In addition we wanted to look at whether there are different TIF effects when more municipalities are included and different types of land uses are considered. We used three different data sets: property value data for 246 municipalities in the six-county Chicago area; less complete property value data for 1,242 municipalities in all 102 Illinois counties; and property value data for 247 TIF districts in the six-county Chicago area.

For the six-county sample (similar to our earlier study, but with more years and more municipalities), Table 1 presents the pre- and postadoption growth rates for the TIF-adopting and non-adopting municipalities. These calculations are from raw data, before any statistical controls for other growth determinants or corrections for selection bias. The first row compares EAV growth rates of the TIF-adopting and nonadopting municipalities in the period before any of them adopted TIF. EAV grew slightly faster for municipalities that would later adopt TIF.

The second row shows that in the period after TIF adoptions took

TABLE 1   Mean Annualized Percentage Growth Rates in Municipal EAV for Preadoption and Postadoption Periods by TIF Adoption Status for the New Six-County Sample

Period	Dependent Variable	TIF Status Group	
		TIF Adopters (N = 100)	TIF Adopters (N = 146)
	Growth in		
Preadoption (1980–1984)	Gross EAV = (I + G)/ (B + N)	4.66	4.41
Postadoption (1995–1998)	Gross EAV = (I + G)/ (B + N)	5.20	6.46
Postadoption (1995–1998)	Net EAV = G/N	5.06	

Source: Dye and Merriman (2003).

Note: These are row group means with no statistical controls for either determinants of growth.

place, gross-of-TIF EAV grew less rapidly for TIF adopters. The last row shows that the net-of-TIF EAV growth rate for TIF adopters was even lower, suggesting that growth (I) in the TIF district may come at the expense of property values outside the development area (G). In summary, if we make no statistical adjustment for the effects of other determinants, TIF adopters grew more slowly than nonadopters.

When we use the more recent six-county data in a multivariate regression model with statistical controls for local characteristics and sample selection, we no longer get the earlier provocative result of a significantly negative impact of TIF adoption on growth, but we still find no positive impact of TIF adoption on the growth in citywide property values. Any growth in the TIF district is offset by declines elsewhere.

The second study was designed with particular attention to land use. The property value data is broken into three land use types: residential, commercial, and industrial. Each TIF district also is identified by one of five development purpose types: central business district (CBD), commercial, industrial, housing, and other or mixed purpose. Thus, we can look separately at growth in municipal EAV by type of land use and type of TIF. Unfortunately, the data do not record EAV by land use within TIF districts, so we must settle for the growth in the tax base that is available to local governments. Most of the estimates of effects by land use type are not significantly different than zero. However, commercial and industrial TIF districts both show a significantly negative impact on growth in commercial assessed values outside the district. The second study also extends the analysis to all 102 Illinois counties, which results in a much larger sample of municipalities (see Table 2). The TIF-base EAV (B) is unavailable, so we look at growth in available EAV. The simple means from the larger sample again suggest a negative effect of TIF on growth in property values. When we use t his all-county sample to estimate the impact of TIF in a multivariate regression with statistical controls for other growth determinants and for TIF selection, there is a significantly negative impact of TIF adoption on growth in overall available (non-TIF) property values. This revives the earlier hypothesis that TIF adoption actually reduces property values in the larger community.

When we run separate regressions for available EAV growth by type of land use for the all-county sample, we see more evidence of a zero or negative impact of TIF on property value growth. Again, there is a significant "cannibalization" of commercial EAV outside the TIF district from commercial development within the TIF district.

The TIF district sample of the second study includes 247 TIF districts in 100 different municipalities in the six-county Chicago area. We match

TABLE 2   Mean Annualized Percentage Growth Rates in Municipal EAV for Preadoption and Postadoption Periods by TIF Adoption Status for the 102-County Sample

Period	Dependent Variable	TIF Status Group	
	Growth in	TIF Adopters (N = 205)	TIF Adopters (N = 1037)
Preadoption (1980–1984)	Gross EAV = (I + G)/ (B + N)	3.31	1.86
Postadoption (1995–1998)	Gross EAV = (I + G)/ (B + N)	6.27	7.60
Postadoption (1995–1998)	Net EAV = G/(B + N)	5.19	

Source: Dye and Merriman (2003).
Note: These are raw group means with no statistical controls for either determinants of growth.

TIF base (B) and TIF increment (I) in each year to information for the host municipality. The key results are:

Enormous variation in TIF district size, with an average base of around $11 million.

Enormous variation in TIF district EAV growth rates around an average of 24 percent growth per year.

TIF districts that start with a smaller base tend to have higher rates of growth.

Most of the TIF growth occurs in the first several years, and growth rates decline an average of about 1 percent per year after the initial surge.

Growth rates in the host municipalities are generally much smaller in the TIF district (an average of 3 percent compared to the TIF average of 24 percent).

The estimated relationship between TIF growth and municipality growth is U-shaped; starting from zero, higher growth in the host municipality means lower growth in the TIF district, but the relationship turns positive at a host municipality growth level of about 6 percent.

Conclusion

Tax increment financing is an alluring tool. TIF districts grow much faster than other areas in t heir host municipalities. TIF boosters or naive analysts might point to this as evidence of the success of t ax increment financing, but they would be wrong. Observing high growth in an area targeted for development is unremarkable. The issues we have studies are (1) whether the targeting causes the growth or merely signals that growth is coming; and (2) whether the growth in the targeted area comes at the expensive of other parts of the same municipality. We find evidence that the non-TIF areas of municipalities that use TIF grow no more rapidly, and perhaps more slowly, than similar municipalities that do not use TIF.

Policy makers should use TIF with caution. It is, after all, merely a way of financing economic development and does not change the opportunities for development or the skills of those doing the development planning. Moreover, policy makers should pay careful attention to land use when TIF is being considered. Our evidence shows that commercial TIF districts reduce commercial property value growth in the non-TIF part of the same municipality. This is not terribly surprising, given that much of commercial property is retailing and most retail trade needs to be located close to its customer base. That is, if you subsidize a store in one location there will be less demand to have a store in a nearby location. Industrial land use, in theory, is different. Industrial goods are mostly exported and sold outside the local area, so a local offset would not be expected. Our evidence is generally consistent with this prediction of no offset in industrial property growth in non-TIF areas of the same municipality.

References

Anderson, John E. 1990. Tax increment financing: Municipal adoption and growth. National Tax Journal 43: 155–163.

Dye, Richard F., and David F. Merriman. 2000. The effects of tax increment financing on economic development. Journal of Urban Economics 47: 306–328.

———. 2003. The effect of tax increment financing on land use, in Dick Netzer (ed.), The property tax, land use, and land-use regulation. Cheltenham, UK: Edward Elgar, 37–61.

Dye, Richard F., and Jeffrey O. Sundberg. 1998. A model of tax increment financing adoption incentives. Growth and Change 29: 90–110.

Johnson, Craig L., and Joyce Y. Man (eds.). 2001. Tax increment financing and economic development: Uses, structures and impact. Albany: State University of New York Press.

Man, Joyce Y., and Mar, S. Rosentraub. 1998. Tax increment financing: Municipal adoption and effects on property value growth. Public Finance Review 26: 523–547.

COPYRIGHTS
ACKNOWLEDGMENTS

1. From Francis R. Greene, "Madison's View of Federalism in *The Federalist*," *Publius: The Journal of Federalism* Vol. 24:1, pp. 47–61. Reprinted by permission of Oxford University Press.
2. From "National Center for Interstate Compacts: A New Initiative" by John J. Mountjoy, in *Spectrum: The Journal of State Government*, (Fall, 2004). Copyright © 2004 by The Council of State Governments. Reprinted by permission.
3. From "Trends in Interstate Relations" by Joseph F. Zimmerman, in *Spectrum: The Journal of State Government*, (Fall, 2004). Copyright © 2004 by The Council of State Governments. Reprinted by permission.
4. From "State Constitutional Interpretation" by G. Alan Tarr in *Texas Review of Law & Politics*, Vol. 8, No 2. Reprinted by permission of the author.
5. From Dorothy T. Beasley, "State Bills of Rights: Dead or Alive?," *Intergovernmental Perspective* (Summer, 1989): pp. 13–17. Reprinted by permission.
6. From "Municipal Charters" in *National Civic Review*, Vol. 91, No 1, Spring, 2002. Copyright © 2002 by Wiley Periodicals. Reprinted with permission of John Wiley & Sons, Inc.
7. Excerpt pp. 112–131 from *American Federalism: A View from the States*, 3rd ed. by Daniel J. Elazar. Copyright © 1984 by Harper & Row, Publishers, Inc. Reprinted by permission of Pearson Education, Inc.
8. From Tom W. Rice and Alexander F. Sumberg, "Civic Culture and Govern-

ment Performance in the American States," *Publius: The Journal of Federalism* Vol. 27:1, pp. 99–114. Reprinted by permission of Oxford University Press.

9. From "Mapping the Genome of American Political Subcultures: A Proposed Methodology and Pilot Study" by David Y. Miller, David C. Barker, and Christopher J. Carmen, in *Publius: The Journal of Federalism*, Volume 36, Number 2, pp. 303–315. Copyright © 2005. Reprinted by permission of Oxford University Press.

10. From "Election Systems and Voter Turnout: Experiments in the United States" by Shaun Bowler, David Brockington, and Todd Donovan, in *The Journal of Politics*, Vol. 63, No. 3, August, 2001, pp. 902–915. Copyright © 2001 by Blackwell Publishers. Reprinted by permission of Cambridge University Press.

11. From Robert Brischetto, "Cumulative Voting as an Alternative to Districting: An Exit Survey of Sixteen Texas Communities," *National Civic Review* (Fall/ Winter, 1995). Copyright © 1995 by Wiley Periodicals. Reprinted by permission of John Wiley and Sons, Inc.

12. From "Success for Instant Runoff Voting in San Francisco" by Steven Hill and Robert Richie, in *National Civic Review*, Spring 2005. Copyright © 2005 by Wiley Periodicals. Reprinted with permission of John Wiley & Sons, Inc.

13. From "The Oregon Voting Revolution" by Don Hamilton, in *The American Prospect*, May 2006. Copyright © 2006 by The American Prospect. Reprinted by permission of the publisher.

14. From "The Nuts and Bolts of Public Financing of State Candidate Campaigns" by Craig B. Holman, in *National Civic Review*, Vol. 92, No. 1, Spring 2003. Copyright © 2003 by Wiley Periodicals. Reprinted with permission of John Wiley & Sons, Inc.

15. From "What Color Is Montana" by Walter Kirn, in *The New York Times Magazine*, January 2, 2005. Copyright © by Walter Kirn. Reprinted by permission of the author.

16. From "First Among Thirds" by Greg Sargent, in *The American Prospect*, May 2006. Copyright © 2006 by The American Prospect. Reprinted by permission of the publisher.

17. From "Interest Groups and Journalists in the States" by Christopher A. Cooper, Anthony J. Nownes, and Martin Johnson, in *State Politics Quarterly*, Vol. 7, No. 1 (Spring 2007): pp. 39–53. Copyright © 2007 by the Board of Trustees of the University of Illinois. Reprinted by permission of the University of Illinois Press.

18. From "Perceptions of Power: Interest Groups in Local Politics" by Christopher A. Cooper, Anthony J. Nownes, and Steven Roberts, in *State and Local Government Review*, Vol. 37, No. 3, 2005. Copyright © 2005 by the Carl Vinson Institute of Government, University of Georgia. Reprinted by permission.

19. From "Chief Executive Success in the Legislative Arena" by Margaret Robertson Ferguson, in *State Politics and Policy Quarterly*, Vol. 3, No. 2 (Summer